Baseball's Endangered Species

BASEBALL'S
ENDANGERED
SPECIES

Lee Lowenfish

INSIDE THE
CRAFT OF SCOUTING
BY THOSE WHO LIVED IT

University of Nebraska Press   Lincoln

An earlier version of chapter 6 previously appeared
in *Braves Win! Braves Win! Braves Win! The 1995
World Champion Atlanta Braves*, ed. Bill Nowlin
and Tom Hufford (Phoenix AZ: SABR, 2020).

The University of Nebraska Press is part of a land-
grant institution with campuses and programs on the
past, present, and future homelands of the Pawnee,
Ponca, Otoe-Missouria, Omaha, Dakota, Lakota, Kaw,
Cheyenne, and Arapaho Peoples, as well as those of the
relocated Ho-Chunk, Sac and Fox, and Iowa Peoples.

Library of Congress Cataloging-in-Publication Data
Names: Lowenfish, Lee, 1942– author.
Title: Baseball's endangered species : inside the craft
of scouting by those who lived it / Lee Lowenfish.
Description: Lincoln : University of Nebraska Press,
[2023] | Includes bibliographical references and index.
Identifiers: LCCN 2022044595
ISBN 9781496214812 (hardback)
ISBN 9781496236289 (epub)
ISBN 9781496236296 (pdf)
Subjects: LCSH: Baseball—Scouting—United States—
History. | Baseball scouts—United States—Biography.
Classification: LCC GV880.22 .L68 2023 |
DDC 796.357—dc23/eng/20220923
LC record available at https://lccn.loc.gov/2022044595

Set in Minion Pro by L. Auten.

To every baseball scout who wrote down what players could do, not what they couldn't do.

And to Kevin Kerrane, author of *Dollar Sign on the Muscle*, who has set an almost impossibly high bar in this field.

CONTENTS

ACKNOWLEDGMENTS

I have been a member of SABR (Society for American Baseball Research) since 1976. Its online Baseball Biography Project essays (SABR BioProjects), sometimes also available in published team anthologies, were a wonderful source for me as I looked for clues about baseball scouts who have traditionally avoided using the *I* pronoun. SABR research director Jacob Pomrenke was indefatigable, prompt, and cordial in his responses to my seemingly endless requests. So was Cassidy Lent at the National Baseball Hall of Fame Library in Cooperstown, who always answered my requests promptly and cheerily. A tip of the cap goes to two other Cooperstown mainstays, the retired librarian Jim Gates and John Odell, who has maintained a file of thousands of scouting reports, even though the 2013 exhibit Diamond Mines has not yet attained permanent status. SABR members Mike Hauser, Rod Nelson, Bill Nowlin, Steve Steinberg, and Bob Whalen shared valuable insights at key moments in this project. So did authors David Falkner and Mike Mitchell. A thank you goes to longtime friends Bill E. Collins, who supplied helpful clippings, Johanna Wagner Martin, Edwin Perez, and Jerry Rosenthal. The expert copy-editing of Joseph A. Webb improved this story. I have benefited greatly from discussions with outstanding SABR writers and historians Larry Baldassaro, Robert Garratt, Rick Huhn, Lee Kluck, Dan Levitt, Lyle Spatz, and Dan Taylor. I believe that librarians and archivists are among God's chosen people. Thanks go to Meg Miner at Illinois Wesleyan University and Lorna Kirwan at the Bancroft Library, University of California, Berkeley.

I have belonged to the New York Pro Scouts Association for almost as long as I have been in SABR. I have profited from many conversations with, to name only a few, George Biron, Billy Blitzer, Jim Bretz, John Ceprini, the late Joe DeLucca, Jim Holzer, John Kosciak, Joe McIlvaine, John Morris (former Major League outfielder), Dan Palumbo, Joe Rigoli, Dennis Sheehan, and John Tumminia. I will always treasure John Ceprini's explanation of the difference between his prior job as a New York City detective and his current work as a baseball scout: "When I knock on the door when scouting, I don't move to the side." A special thank you goes to Jay Goldberg for honoring me with the chairman's role for a rousing discussion of scouting at Jay's deeply missed Bergino Baseball Clubhouse in New York's Greenwich Village.

The Mid-Atlantic Scouts Association (MASA), under the leadership of Tom Burns and Rick Matsko, is another group I belong to that is keeping the flame of traditional scouting alive. Conversations with longtime MASA member and honoree Mike Toomey were especially valuable. I will never forget Mike sharing a video he made of Cal Ripken Sr. at a baseball clinic in which he told youngsters, "Baseball is a very simple game. All you need is a bat, a ball, a glove, and a human being." I tip my cap to MASA member Sandy Johnson.

Many thanks go to retired scout Larry D'Amato for his friendship and allowing me to listen in by phone to his online classes on scouting for the Sport Management World Wide (SMWW) group. Many thanks go to the legendary late scout Tom "T-Bone" Giordano for connecting Larry and me. D'Amato's class discussions with John T. Cox Jr., Tony DeMacio, Jed McIntyre, and George Zuraw, to name only a few, provided very helpful insights into the mysteries of scouting and player development.

I also want to acknowledge the important and ongoing work of Roberta Mazur, who since 1984 has been running the Scout of the Year program that every year honors scouts from the eastern, southern, and western regions of the United States. In recent years, an award has been added for international scouting. Kudos also goes to Dennis Gilbert, who, along with Roland Hemond and Dave Yoakum, founded the Professional Baseball Scouts Foundation and for years hosted the can't-miss annual dinner in Los Angeles. During my two visits to the occasion, I have profited from memorable conversations with Bill Clark, the late Jerry Krause, and Gary Nickels. In the latter stages of this book, I enjoyed email and phone insights of Jim Colborn, Murray Cook, Elena Arcaro Didier, Lou DiLullo, Gordon Goldsberry Jr., and Vernona Gomez.

A special thank you goes to Anne Enos, who shared wonderful stories about growing up in a baseball family headed by scout Bill Enos. Her father's meticulous archives added special flavor to my endeavor.

I also give a warm appreciation to my monthly lunch crowd in New York City. We kept the gatherings alive via Zoom during the pandemic, which allowed valuable regulars like Darrell Berger and George Vecsey to still join in. The group started in the 1980s around baseball's first and greatest oral historian, Larry Ritter, and included such talented writers as Bob Creamer, Ray Robinson, and Al Silverman. Their spirit lives on with such talented regulars as Billy Altman, Marty Appel, Richard Goldstein, Steve Jacobson, Dave Kaplan, Ernestine Miller, Jerry Rosenthal, Brian Silverman, and Willie Weinbaum.

Special thanks also go to Mary DeAngelis, who showed me the cribbage board that her New Hampshire cousin Rolfe used to play on with his teammates during the Yankees' dynasty from 1936 to 1943. Baseball is a very difficult game; you will learn in the upcoming pages that relaxation is an important component of winning.

Finally, a warm appreciation goes to Maria Patterson for putting up with the long process this project entailed. Maria, the time for seeing Minor League Baseball games will arrive real soon.

Nothing is like the sound of a bat hitting a ball in a way that has never quite been heard before. Nothing is like the sound of a baseball exploding into a catcher's mitt that has never quite been heard before. The search for new and unique talent has motivated baseball scouts for well over a century. Greg Morhardt, the scout who signed multiple MVP-winner Mike Trout for the Los Angeles Angels of Anaheim, once poetically expressed the essence of the hunt: "I look for dogs who play checkers.... We're looking for the unique."[1] Eyesight and hearing are two of the most precious senses the Creator has given to human beings, and baseball scouts have learned to sharpen these senses. Sure, they have been aided by radar guns and stop watches, but the eyes and ears of the best scouts have been developed to extraordinary lengths by the trial and error of countless trips to watch ballgames all over America and, increasingly, all parts of the world.

Sadly, the first two decades of the twenty-first century have not been kind to traditional baseball scouts. Michael Lewis's best-selling book *Moneyball*, published in 2003, contributed to a wave of more than a hundred scout firings.[2] Lewis came under the spell of Oakland Athletics general manager Billy Beane and his statistically oriented assistants who insisted that their new statistics and interest in "undervalued assets" could replace old-fashioned scouting. When the movie *Moneyball* came out eight years later, another wave of dismissals followed. By the end of the second decade of the twenty-first century, there was no longer a Major League Baseball Scouting Bureau or an

MLB-sponsored scout school. The practice of eyes-ears advance scouting of Major League teams during the season has all but vanished.

The Washington Nationals' surprise triumph over the Houston Astros in the 2019 World Series brought special delight to traditional baseball scouts because Nats general manager Mike Rizzo, himself a former scout and the son of longtime scout Phil Rizzo, surrounded himself with several advance scouts throughout the regular season and playoffs. On the other hand, the Astros, one of the most analytically inclined of the thirty Major League teams, eliminated virtually all of their traditional scouts. This development was as ignominious as the revelation of their high-tech and low-tech sign-stealing operation during the 2017 season.

It remains to be seen whether "eyes and ears" scouts will make a comeback in the foreseeable future. An enormous amount of money and publicity has poured into the so-called advanced-metrics revolution in baseball. A growing number of organizations believe that you can better scout amateur players through high-tech video and other new measuring devices. In their 2019 book, *The MVP Machine: How Baseball's New Nonconformists Are Using Data to Build Better Players*, authors Ben Lindbergh and Travis Sawchik write glowingly of this new development. They take issue with *Moneyball*, claiming it didn't go far enough in its dismissal of traditional scouting and player development. They endorsed what Jerry Dipoto, a former Major League pitcher and currently general manager of the Seattle Mariners, called "better ball." Dipoto boasted, "We're moving at a hyperpace compared to the prehistoric crawl of the saber revolution."[3] Brian Bannister, a pioneer in high-tech photography of the pitching motion and son of former Major League pitcher Floyd Bannister, predicted that his work would change the future of scouting projections. "Maintaining breaking balls is a full-time job now," he said solemnly. The Yankees, the authors reported, now have well over a hundred members in their Player Development department. They were all working toward making players learn new techniques, and if they don't show capacity in this area, they are being weeded out.

It seems likely that the analytic wave is only starting. In his 2019 book, *Scouting and Scoring: How We Know What We Know about Baseball*, Christopher J. Phillips proclaimed, "Amateur scouting is a scientific practice of evaluating bodies."[4] At a time when tensions between owners and players led to a ninety-nine day "defensive lockout" that almost cost a huge chunk of the 2022 season, both sides have found a rare common ground that allows for measuring devices to be placed in players to measure heartbeat, muscle twitch fibers, and other important areas of player physiology.

Baseball always has room for new information and insights. When Branch Rickey was once asked by scout Leon Hamilton how much of baseball he really knew, he replied, "I question whether I know fifty-five percent of baseball."[5] He was eager to learn more about the fascinating and often confounding game. As am I. Like Rickey, I don't belong to an old guard that refuses to reexamine old shibboleths. But I do firmly believe that it is time for a reexamination of the *Moneyball* and better-ball crazes. The pages that follow will present the counterargument that traditional baseball scouting has much value that should not be discarded. There is plenty of wisdom in the old scouting adage "God gave you two ears and two eyes and only one mouth," so it helps to use sight and sound more than one's own voice. Another memorable old scout saying is "Those who can, evaluate; those who can't, measure."

In the pages ahead, you will visit some of the great personages in the history of traditional scouting. You will discover that it is not a requirement to have been an exceptional player or any kind of Major Leaguer but that it does help to have some familiarity playing the game at a high level to sense the climate of intense competition. In an interview with the late P. J. Dragseth for her indispensable book *Eye for Talent: Conversations with Baseball Scouts*, Cincinnati Reds scout Julian Mock said he used to ask prospective scouts five questions:

Do you really love this game?
Are you willing to work harder than you have ever worked in your life?
Are you willing to learn?
Are you able to have fun and laugh at least once every day?
Will you never forget where you came from?[6]

Mock himself never played beyond Auburn University in Alabama, but in a phone interview before he died in 2018, he told me the two questions he posed to any high school player faced with the choice of turning pro or continuing his education: "Are you going to college *to* play ball?" If the answer was yes, Mock advised turning pro immediately. "Are you going to college *and* play ball?" If the answer was yes, Mock advised continuing with schooling.

Older scouts possess such great wisdom that the missed opportunity of younger players and scouts to learn from them is a tragedy. The late Jerry Krause, who made his name as a Chicago Bulls executive in the age of Michael Jordan, loved baseball even more. He told me categorically that he never saw an older scout get worse. Houston Astros manager Dusty Baker has compared veteran scouts to the blues musicians who passed down their tradition over the generations. He laments that so many committed veteran scouts have lost their jobs and thus the opportunity to pass on their knowledge to future generations of players. I have written this book to make sure that their voices from past and present will not be wholly lost. I invite you to savor these tales of a great game seen from the perspective of the diamond detectives who have made their life's work by replenishing baseball with good players and good people.

Baseball's Endangered Species

George Robert "Birdie" Tebbetts was proud to be called a baseball lifer—it was all he ever wanted to be. He was born on November 12, 1912, in Burlington, Vermont, but grew up in Nashua, New Hampshire, where his father, Charles Tebbetts, a clerk for the Swift and Company grocery and meat company, had been transferred. Charles died when Birdie was only three, but Birdie was nurtured by an older brother and many uncles on his mother's side of the family. At an early age, he became mascot and then batboy for the Nashua Millionaires, a top-flight semipro team made up of former pro players and leading collegians. Team owner Francis Parnell Murphy, president of the Thom McAn Shoe Company and later the governor of New Hampshire, became a second father to Birdie, who never lacked for shoes and paternal guidance. One of Birdie's first heroes was Millionaires catcher Clyde Sukeforth, who was on the cusp of his career as a baseball lifer (and the man who introduced Jackie Robinson to Branch Rickey in the first meeting of the two, a couple weeks after the end of World War II). Tebbetts became so adept at mastering Sukeforth's moves behind the plate that he warmed up pitchers before the game. The Millionaires sent out a press release that stated, "Come and see the twelve-year-old catcher!"[1]

At Nashua High School, Tebbetts developed into one of the top catching prospects in the nation while also starring as a football quarterback. The Detroit Tigers won his services when they promised Birdie's widowed mother, Elizabeth Ryan Tebbetts, that he could finish college before he started his pro career. Graduating from Providence College in 1934 with a major in philosophy, he reached the Majors in 1937. He enjoyed a fourteen-year career with the Tigers, Red Sox, and Indians and was selected four times to the American League All-Star team.

He finished his career with exactly one thousand hits and respectable statistics for a catcher: .270 batting average, .341 on-base percentage, .358 slugging average, 38 home runs, 459 runs batted in, 389 walks, and 261 strikeouts. He caught stealing 39 percent of base runners. In 1956 he was voted National League Manager of the Year after leading the Cincinnati Reds to a close third-place finish, the first time they had won over ninety games since their back-to-back pennants in 1939 and 1940. After managerial jobs in Milwaukee and Cleveland, a serious heart condition hastened the end to his Major League managerial career after 1966—he retired with a 781-744 record.

Tebbetts's involvement in baseball was far from over. Always eager to help young players improve their game, he managed the 1967 Marion (Virginia) Mets in the Appalachian League to a second-place finish, ten games above .500. "Being the best means starting at the very bottom," he explained.[2] He devoted the rest of his baseball life to evaluating talent for several organizations, including the Mets, Yankees, Indians, Orioles, and Atlanta Braves. Some sportswriters liked to call him a "super scout," but he wasn't interested in names or titles. If one insisted, he preferred the term *evaluator*. He believed that sizing up a young talent and *projecting* his future was baseball's most challenging and ultimately most rewarding job. He knew that in the best organizations, scouting and player development must be on the same page. Backbiting meant disaster. If scouts groused, "Why are you not developing the tools of my player?" and the player developers shot back, "What did you see in this guy in the first place?" a team could not possibly contend, let alone win a pennant and a championship.

Birdie Tebbetts relished thinking outside the box. When playing, he invented lighter catching gear, an idea that caught on among many of his contemporaries.[3] He encouraged players to adopt nicknames to make them more approachable to fans. (His own "Birdie" came when an aunt thought her bright-eyed, red-haired little nephew's chirping cradle sounds reminded her of a bird.) He believed many players who were not stars might profit from being traded every four years so they would not become too set in their ways. He suggested that front-office baseball people would also be wise to consider shifting jobs every decade. Although a local hero when he played for the 1947–50 Red Sox, he hastened his trade to Cleveland when he told a banquet audience that the team's disappointing 1950 season was because of undisciplined pitchers who behaved like "juvenile delinquents" and "moronic malcontents."[4]

Tebbetts occasionally mused about creating a Hall of Fame for the "Almost Great," and he may have been talking tongue-in-cheek. However, when he started in 1980 to serve on the Baseball Hall of Fame's Veterans Committee, he was very serious when he proposed that scouts become eligible for the Hall. He knew the objections. Scouts were used to serving behind-the-scenes and didn't like to draw attention to themselves. There were many levels of scouting—the area scout, the scouting supervisor, the signing scout, the associate scout—so it might be impossible to separate the scout that first spotted a player from the man that eventually signed him.

Tebbetts wasn't satisfied with the excuses. He insisted that scouts were essential to the well-being and sustained excellence of the game. "Scouts have given so much to baseball," he said. "There isn't anybody in baseball more closely connected to the game. Baseball can't function without the ballplayers, and scouts are the ones who go out and get them."[5] They were willing to pay the price of nomadic travel and disrupted domestic life in their search for prime talent, in the game that was the hardest in sports because failure was a constant companion.

No transcripts are available of what was discussed in the Veterans Committee, but Birdie would occasionally mention to sportswriters some of the people who he felt were worthy of enshrinement. Hugh Alexander was one. Once a speedy outfielder from Oklahoma who regularly ran the hundred-yard dash in under ten seconds, he seemed destined for stardom with the Cleveland Indians until a horrible off-season accident in 1937 cost him his left hand when it was caught in a water pump on an oil rig. In an act of genuine paternalism, Cyril C. "Cy" Slapnicka, Cleveland's virtual one-man scouting staff, began to instruct the twenty-one-year-old in the elements of evaluation. Alexander quickly rewarded Cleveland by wooing pitcher Allie Reynolds away from basketball at Oklahoma A&M. After a few years in Cleveland, Reynolds came into his own as a stalwart starter and reliever for the Yankees' 1949–53 dynasty. Alexander later signed outfielder Dale Mitchell, who played for the 1948 Indians World Series winners and the 1954 pennant winners. When working for the Los Angeles Dodgers, Alexander was instrumental in signing three-quarters of the Dodgers' three-time pennant-winning infield of the 1970s: Steve Garvey, Davey Lopes, and Bill Russell.[6] Alexander also brought his rare evaluative skills to the Phillies and the Cubs.

Another scout whom Tebbetts suggested was Michigan native John Aloysius "Wish" Egan, who was 0-2 for the 1902 Tigers and compiled an 8-26 record with the Cardinals during the next two seasons. He developed into an outstanding scout for Detroit and was the boss of area scout Jean Dubuc, who won 72 of his 85 Major League victories for the Tigers. Dubuc was the scout who signed Birdie for the Tigers. Tebbetts understood that the first connections one makes in the insular and harshly competitive world of pro baseball were often the deepest. He learned that from Egan, who was instrumental in the acquisition of three future Hall of Famers: southpaw Hal Newhouser, whom he observed and tutored from the age of fifteen; pitcher and future United States senator Jim Bunning; and third baseman George Kell, who, on Egan's urging, came to Detroit in a trade with the Philadelphia Athletics. He also signed outfielder Hoot Evers, who later himself became a scout and player developer.[7]

Near the end of his decade of pleading the cause of scouts, Tebbetts gave a remarkable interview to *Boston Herald* writer Michael Globetti. "What a shame that you're not allowed to put in a guy who's been at his job fifty years, who's brought kids in from the mountains, from the jungle, from places nobody's ever heard of," he said. "They are way under publicized but to my way of thinking a scout has to mean more to the game of baseball than anyone else." He added a remarkable detail. "When I was coming up, there was a custom in the major leagues that the first time a player got to the World Series, he paid the way for the scout who signed him to see him play."[8]

Tebbetts never succeeded in getting the Hall of Fame's board of directors to approve his idea, and, in declining health, he left the committee by the end of the 1980s. Like most baseball insiders with a long career in the game,

Tebbetts was always careful about publicly voicing criticism of longtime colleagues, which could offend them. It wasn't until three years after his death in 1999 that portions of the diary Tebbetts kept throughout his career were published as *Birdie: Confessions of a Baseball Nomad*, edited and selected by his cousin James Morrison. The book contained many memorable observations. "While the games go on above ground, the earth is always trembling beneath," he wrote, a reference to the politics that inevitably permeated the baseball business.[9]

He was confident enough about his own evaluating abilities to write down Tebbetts's Golden Rules of Scouting:

You must first "remember who told you" about a certain player.
You must "be open to a change of mind. Ballplayers can improve or decline suddenly and remarkably."
"Your evaluation of a player must be a tightly held secret and is solely owned by your employer."
"Seldom confirm, never deny, always distinguish."[10]

The names of two scouts *always* came up when Tebbetts discussed enshrinement in Cooperstown: Charley Barrett of the St. Louis Cardinals and Paul Krichell of the New York Yankees. Barrett was Branch Rickey's first and most beloved scout who was tirelessly on the road searching for raw talent when the Cardinals made a success of the farm system after World War I. Although Tebbetts spent his Major League playing time in the American League and National Leaguer Barrett died in 1939 as Birdie's career was just beginning, Birdie knew that the Rickey-Barrett method of finding strong arms and swift feet, and developing the other tools by instruction, was a major breakthrough. "Baseball is exactly what Branch Rickey said it was: a race between a man and a ball," as Tebbetts quoted the baseball mastermind.[11]

Tebbetts also argued that no Hall of Fame would be complete without the inclusion of Paul Krichell. From 1921 up to his death in 1957, Krichell's judgment on talent was a major factor in the Yankees winning an astonishing twenty-two pennants and seventeen World Series.

Tebbetts also treasured special personal memories of Krichell, "the first scout who ever showed up [at] my door. . . . Me, a high-school senior in

Nashua, N.H.," he remembered to Michael Globetti. "Can you imagine how unbelievable that must have been? Let me tell you, it was something."[12]

Birdie Tebbetts never tired of saluting "the great fraternity [of] free agent scouts, who get on the road and grind it out, who go from sandlot to sandlot."[13] In part one of this journey with baseball's diamond detectives, I return to the early twentieth century and a chance meeting on a dusty baseball diamond that will change the course of baseball history.

PART 1

THE CARDINALS-YANKEES RIVALRY
THAT DOMINATES BASEBALL, 1919–1964

1

Charley Barrett and the Rise of Branch Rickey's Farm System

One afternoon during the 1904 baseball season, two opponents playing in the low Minors Class C South Texas League met for the first time on a baseball field in Dallas. There might have been a ten-year difference in age between Houston's veteran outfielder Charley Barrett and twenty-two-year-old Dallas rookie catcher Branch Rickey, but both men quickly realized they shared similar views and passions about the game of baseball. They loved speedy players with strong arms, and each was somewhat gifted in those areas. Barrett once stole fifty bases in a Minor League season, and Rickey was fast for a catcher. They shared one grave liability—neither could hit very well. Rickey would go on to enjoy a brief Major League career in parts of three seasons, hitting .239 and slugging .327 in 119 career games for the St. Louis Browns and New York Highlanders (soon called the Yankees). Barrett never rose out of the lower Minors in seven seasons, his batting average never reaching even .200.[1]

They came from different backgrounds. Wesley Branch Rickey was born on December 20, 1881, in rural Scioto County in southern Ohio near Portsmouth. The middle of three brothers, he was raised on a farm in a family that had limited economic means and that took the Methodist religion seriously. By the time he graduated from Ohio Wesleyan University, Rickey loved all kinds of athletics, but he envisioned an ultimate career in law. Thanks to thorough research by Jim Sandoval, baseball enthusiasts have learned that Charles Francis Barrett was born on June 14, 1871, in St. Louis, Missouri, one of at least nine children. His father, a Catholic emigrant from Canada, did not earn much money as a fireman, and Charley dropped out of school at the age fourteen to help his family. One of his jobs was as a night clerk for a messenger service that enabled him to play baseball in the daytime. In 1901, at the late age of thirty, he first entered the Minor Leagues.[2]

Branch Rickey loved Charlie Barrett's succinct description of the essence of the game: "to get on base and get home as fast as possible." They shared a genuine commitment to bringing talented players into the game regardless of their economic standing. The chance to work together building a team did not happen immediately. Barrett retired from professional playing in 1907, the same season that Rickey, catching for the Highlanders against the visiting Washington Senators, entered the record books by allowing thirteen stolen bases—it remains an embarrassing Major League record. Highlanders pitchers were not very good at holding runners on first base, but Rickey was also suffering from a sore arm that he aggravated while demonstrating throwing techniques while coaching the Ohio Wesleyan baseball team. A two-week visit to the spas in Hot Springs, Arkansas, a rejuvenating center that will reappear in this story, did not restore the snap to his throws.[3]

Before the term was invented, Branch Rickey was a multitasker. In addition to coaching football, basketball, and baseball at Ohio Wesleyan, he was taking night school law classes at Ohio State in Columbus. The fervent Methodist teetotaler even found time in 1908 to campaign for local Ohio Prohibition candidates and victorious Republican presidential candidate William Howard Taft. Early in 1909 Rickey's multitasking came to a crashing halt when he was diagnosed with tuberculosis. He needed several months of recuperation at the Trudeau Sanatorium in Saranac Lake, New York. When he was released, his doctor pleaded with him to slow down his working pace. Fat chance of that—in the fall of 1909, Rickey entered the University of Michigan law school. Because baseball remained inexorably in his blood, he applied for and won the job as Michigan baseball coach.

Meanwhile, back in St. Louis, Charley Barrett's pro playing career was over, but he remained a vital presence on the local amateur and semipro scene. He continued to play and coach in local games, keeping tabs on prospective talent, especially in the trolley leagues that attracted players from all over the St. Louis metropolitan area and parts of southern Illinois. He also found a new job as a salesman in a sporting goods store in downtown St. Louis.

One day early in 1909 Barrett walked into the office of St. Louis Browns owner Robert Hedges, trying to interest him in opening an auxiliary ticket office at the store. Barrett thought the timing was right. The Browns were coming off their first-ever winning season in 1908, finishing in fourth place, only seven games behind the pennant-winning Boston Red Sox, while setting an attendance record of over 650,000 fans.

Barrett felt that Hedges would be open to his new marketing idea, especially because Hedges was one of the first owners to add a double deck to his ballpark, a big factor in the record-setting attendance. He pioneered in the creation of Ladies' Day, when women were admitted at a discount if accompanied by a man. He refused to sell alcohol at the ballpark and hired security guards to cut down on fan rowdiness, which helped to keep fans coming back. As Mike Mitchell writes in his thorough *Mr. Rickey's Redbirds*, Hedges was "a baseball visionary, [who] instituted profit-sharing, took out life insurance policies for his players, and experimented with a massive circus-like tent to protect the field during rainstorms."[4]

Hedges listened respectfully to Barrett's proposal, but the idea did not interest him. However, he was impressed by Barrett's enthusiasm and knowledge of the local baseball scene. Hedges's eyes lit up when Barrett told him that in the upcoming season shortstop Art Fletcher from the Southern Illinois mine town of Collinsville should make the Majors with manager John McGraw's New York Giants. (Indeed, Fletcher did, lasting for twelve seasons and capping his career as a Yankees coach from 1929 through 1945.) Hedges listened as Barrett gave him scouting reports on promising, unsigned talent. By the end of the meeting, Charley Barrett was rewarded with something far more important than a ticket office in the sporting goods store. He was now a paid scout for the St. Louis Browns.[5]

In going to work for Robert Hedges, Charley Barrett was joining forces with a man whose career as an owner dated back to 1901. Ban Johnson, the organizer of the new American League, encouraged Hedges to buy the bankrupt Milwaukee franchise and move it to St. Louis. Hedges was a natural choice for the position, a native of rural Missouri and a self-made man who made his fortune in carriage manufacturing. He was wise enough at the dawn of the automobile age to sell his horse-and-buggy company for a good profit.

With the security from a new position as a J. P. Morgan banking associate, Hedges entered baseball as a savvy businessman willing to spend money to make money.[6]

Despite the good 1908 season at the gate, the Browns were still looking up at the Boston Red Sox, Cleveland, and Detroit in the standings. Purchases of excellent defensive shortstop Bobby Wallace and starting pitchers Harry Howell and eccentric but talented southpaw George "Rube" Waddell had not put the Browns over the top—far from it. They fell to seventh in 1909, twenty-eight games under .500 and thirty-five games behind the pennant-winning Detroit Tigers. Starting in 1910 through 1914, the Browns would follow their pre-1908 pattern, regularly competing with the Washington Senators for the worst record in the American League. Washington fans moaned, "First in war, first in peace, and last in the American League," and equally disgruntled St. Louis fans sighed, "First in booze, first in shoes, and last in the American League." Yet Robert Hedges remained confident that building slowly within was the proper method. "It is simply up to the club owners to purchase the raw material, place it properly and pluck it when the proper time comes," he told the *St. Louis Post-Dispatch*.[7]

Hiring Charley Barrett was a first step in that process, and the emerging baseball lifer embarked indefatigably on his new job, realizing that the search for future Major League talent was painstaking and characterized more by failure than success. Meanwhile, Robert Hedges had not forgotten the intense if light-hitting catcher who had played for the 1906 Browns, Branch Rickey; he wanted to bring him on board as his top baseball assistant. They had much in common as teetotalers and hard workers determined to succeed. As coach at the University of Michigan, Rickey brought the innovations of sliding pits, batting cages, and pitching strings. The latter was an ingenious device consisting of two poles with cords attached horizontally and vertically to help hurlers achieve better control.[8]

Rickey's mesmerizing chalk talks to Wolverine players were garnering attention throughout the baseball world. Many of the Detroit Tigers on off-days journeyed the short distance to the Michigan campus in Ann Arbor to listen to his lectures. When Rickey wasn't coaching and studying law, he made time to see amateur games throughout the state of Michigan and adjacent areas, gladly sending tips to Hedges. His ubiquitous presence prompted one sportswriter to dub Rickey the "Mysterious Stranger." While watching games all over the Midwest, the Mysterious Stranger must have bumped into Charley Barrett on his prowl for talent for the Browns. Barrett soon became known as the "King of Weeds," finding diamonds in the rough in the deepest bushes.[9]

Hedges discovered that bringing Branch Rickey into the Browns' fold was not as easy as hiring Charley Barrett. Rickey turned down Hedges's offer to become business manager of a Kansas City Minor League franchise that he was planning to buy. Rickey was glad to provide scouting reports, but after graduating from Michigan in the spring of 1912 with a law degree and three successful seasons as Wolverines coach under his belt, he headed to Boise, Idaho. He planned to start his law career with two Delta Tau Delta college fraternity brothers, and the mountain climate certainly looked more conducive to lasting health for a tuberculosis survivor. Rickey and his partners, however, rounded up very few clients.

In September 1912 Hedges finally made an offer that Rickey could not refuse. For a $7,500 salary ($226,000 in 2022 money)—far more than his virtually bankrupt law partnership was producing—Hedges offered him a job as executive assistant in charge of all baseball activities (the term *general manager* would not be used for another decade). Rickey could still finish a final year of coaching Michigan baseball in 1913 and report to the Browns when the season was over.

Rickey was thrilled with his new situation, not least that finally he would be working closely with Charley Barrett. At the Minor League Rule 5 Draft meetings in late 1912—in which veteran Minor League players not controlled by Major League teams were available—the Rickey-Barrett combination selected thirty players. Ten of them ultimately made the Major Leagues, notably pitcher William Henry "Bill" James, who would go 15-14 with a 2.85 ERA for the 1914 Browns.

When Rickey arrived in St. Louis in the late spring of 1913 with his wife and first child, he realized that a lot of work was needed to get the organization out of its chronic second-division status. He did not expect that near the end of the season he would also be named field manager because the incumbent, hot-tempered George "Firebrand" Stovall, had worn out his welcome. He recently had been suspended for a week for spitting tobacco juice on an umpire and was suspected of secretly recruiting players for the Federal League, the deeply pocketed third-league challenge to the National and American Leagues. Hedges convinced Rickey to add the managerial job to his player acquisition and development duties.

Under Rickey's dual leadership on and off the field, the Browns showed improvement in the standings in 1914, rising to fifth place but still eleven games under .500 and twenty-eight and a half games behind Connie Mack's pennant-winning Philadelphia Athletics. One of the players on the team was fleet outfielder Burt Shotton from rural Brownhelm, Ohio, outside Cleveland, who started his pro career in 1908, a year before Charley Barrett joined the Browns. Nicknamed "Barney," presumably because his speed reminded people of automobile racer Barney Oldfield, Shotton always sang the praises of Rickey's leadership and his willingness to appeal to a player's brain as well as his brawn.[10] Shotton became a lifelong Rickey man, one of his Sunday managers when he took the Sabbath off as a day of rest and his Brooklyn Dodgers manager when Leo Durocher was suspended for the entire 1947 season. Shotton led Brooklyn to pennants in 1947 and 1949, although he lost both World Series to the Yankees.

Rickey's second full season as Browns manager in 1915 was far less successful, as the team fell down to sixth place, twenty-eight games under .500 and thirty-nine and a half games behind the Boston Red Sox in Babe Ruth's first full season as pitcher-outfielder. One momentous acquisition happened for the 1915 Browns when future Hall of Fame first baseman George Sisler arrived after his graduation from the University of Michigan, where he starred as both hitter and pitcher. Sisler's arrival with the Browns was extremely controversial because Pittsburgh Pirates owner Barney Dreyfuss insisted Sisler was his property due to a contract Sisler signed while still in high school in Akron, Ohio. A powerful group of lawyers at Branch Rickey's behest argued that Sisler was not of age when he signed the contract. When baseball's ruling triumvirate, the National Commission (consisting of the two league presidents and Cincinnati Reds owner Garry Herrmann), ruled in favor of the Browns, Dreyfuss was immensely bitter. His discontent with baseball's ruling structure contributed to the rising criticism of the National Commission that reached a tipping point with the discovery in September 1920 of the fixed 1919 World Series. Early in 1921 federal judge Kenesaw Mountain Landis became baseball's sole commissioner.[11]

Rickey and Barrett were delighted to welcome George Sisler to St. Louis, but they would not be around long enough to enjoy firsthand his stellar career. At the end of 1915 Robert Hedges sold the team to local St. Louis ice manufacturer Philip De Catesby Ball. Although the Federal League abandoned its third-league challenge by the end of the 1915 season, Hedges was tired of competing to sign players only to see the bigger-city teams with deeper pockets win out. He grew particularly frustrated with his inability to cement a relationship with the Montgomery, Alabama, franchise in the Southern Association. Though he was able to sign Del Pratt, an outstanding second baseman, Hedges lost too many players to richer owners. Hedges's parting warning about the pernicious effect of big money in baseball had profound influence on Branch Rickey and Charley Barrett. "There are men in both leagues who can buy winners," he warned. "If they allow that ability to run to extremes, the game will suffer greatly. The weak fellows have no chance against men who can bid to the skies for players."[12]

Rickey and Barrett stayed on with the Browns for the 1916 season because Hedges had provided them ironclad contracts, but new owner Philip Ball had no interest in their input. Before Rickey and Barrett left, they brought two young players into the Browns organization, catchers Muddy Ruel and Hank Severeid, both of whom made lasting contributions to the game.

Barrett spotted Herold Dominic "Muddy" Ruel in the St. Louis trolley leagues. The son of a local policeman, Muddy never grew more than five feet nine and 150 pounds, but by high school he was such a well-regarded receiver that he was playing in semipro leagues. Word of his acceptance of money for his athletic talents got around, and he was denied eligibility for his senior year in high school.[13] Barrett and Rickey always felt compassion for players who were victims of unjust rules. Rickey himself couldn't compete in college athletics after his sophomore year at Ohio Wesleyan because he was discovered to have accepted pay for summer semipro baseball to help with his college tuition.

In November 1914 Ruel was signed by the Browns and made the Majors briefly in 1915, his only season with the Browns. He moved on to the Yankees and was catching Carl Mays on the fateful foggy August 1920 day when Cleveland's Ray Chapman was killed by an errant pitch. After some time with the Red Sox, Ruel enjoyed his greatest success with the Washington Senators, catching regularly for the 1924 World Series champions and the 1925 pennant winner. He became a part-time player in his later years, from 1929 through his retirement after the 1934 season. He finished with a career .275 batting average, .365 on-base percentage, and .332 slugging average, the slugging number low because he hit only four home runs.

During his off-seasons, Ruel studied law; in 1927 he was admitted to the United States Supreme Court bar, becoming the first Major Leaguer to reach that pinnacle.[14] He never argued a case before the high court because the appeal of a life in baseball proved too great.

The man who once wryly described the catching gear as "the tools of ignorance" because a catcher gets banged up so mercilessly, Ruel became a pitching coach, a farm director, and an assistant to commissioner Albert Benjamin "Happy" Chandler, who had the unenviable job in early 1945 of replacing the late Kenesaw Mountain Landis. Ruel then became manager of a skidding Browns team in 1947 and part of 1948. He won plaudits from outspoken African American sportswriter Sam Lacy for his considerate treatment of the team's first Black players, Willard Brown and Hank Thompson.[15] (Nothing could help the Browns from their ultimate demise after the 1953 season when they were moved to Baltimore.) Most of all, Muddy Ruel should be remembered as a lyrical exponent of the game. In a memorable 2015 interview with Mark Pelish, his son Dennis Ruel recalled his father describing baseball as "the best mix of skill and fate, human talent and human error, we've been able to conceive." He added, "Baseball is so much like life—there is so much failure."[16]

Henry Laval "Hank" Severeid, the other catcher who Charley Barrett signed for the Browns, was originally signed by the Reds. Born in Story City, Iowa, on June 1, 1891, he arrived in Cincinnati during the 1911 season and became the youngest catcher in the Major Leagues at age twenty. A son of Norwegian immigrants, Severeid saw limited action in his three years with the Reds. Shortly after being sent back to the Minors, Barrett recommended that Rickey sign him for the Browns. From 1915 through 1924, Severeid was the team's regular catcher, noted for his durability and savvy. "As an analyst of the hitters," a contemporary wrote, "there is not a receiver in baseball who can cope [with him]."[17]

In the Browns' finest years of 1921 and 1922 when the team gave the Yankees a run for their money, Severeid played over 130 games each season. Swinging a forty-eight-ounce bat, he hit .324 in 1921 and .321 in 1922 as the team finished a strong third and a close second, respectively. Severeid's last two Major League seasons were also memorable. He backed up Muddy Ruel on the 1925 Washington Senators pennant winners, and in 1926 he finished his career with a flourish, joining the Yankees late in the season and catching all seven games of the World Series. Severeid continued playing in the Minors until the mid-1930s, ultimately settling in Texas. When Severeid finally hung up his spikes, he scouted for the Cubs from 1943 until shortly before his death in 1968. He finished with career numbers of .289 batting average, .342 on-base percentage, and .387 slugging average. In 1941 he was coauthor of *Play Ball! Advice for Young Ballplayers*, written with Charles E. Chapman, a fascinating scout you will meet shortly.

After being dismissed by Phil Ball's Browns, neither Branch Rickey nor Charley Barrett were unemployed for long. Barrett was hired to scout for the Detroit Tigers, and Rickey stayed in town to lead the Cardinals. When local St. Louis business leaders heard that owner Helene Britton was planning to sell the team and it might be moved to another city, they called an urgent meeting to save the franchise. Every person who was asked for advice suggested that Branch Rickey become the team savior. He became president of the Cardinals in early March 1917, only a month before the American entry into World War I. At a luncheon introducing Rickey to faithful Cardinal season ticket holders, the new boss declared, "If I am to be President, I will also be scout."[18]

Rickey inherited Miller Huggins as incumbent field manager. They shared a similarity as possessors of law degrees who preferred the more active life of baseball competition.

Unlike his new boss, Huggins enjoyed a solid thirteen-year career as a Major League second baseman, split almost equally between the Reds and Cardinals. He amassed the respectable career statistics of a .265 batting average, .382 on-base percentage, and .314 slugging average. Also unlike Rickey, Huggins was not drawn to the cerebral analysis of the game. "I believe manager Rickey has a lot of good ideas," he told the *St. Louis Post-Dispatch*. "But I'm not strong for this theory stuff. No ball player can learn how to steal by sliding into sand pits."[19]

Huggins brought the 1917 Cardinals home in third place with an 82-70 record but fifteen games behind John McGraw's pennant-winning Giants. The Cardinals did feature two notable pitchers: Lee Meadows, baseball's first bespectacled pitcher, was 15-9 on the season with a 3.09 ERA. Bill Doak was a twenty-game loser at 16-20, but his ERA was a respectable 3.10. Doak featured a spitball, and when the pitch was outlawed after the 1919 season, he helped to negotiate the grandfather clause that allowed pitchers who moistened the ball to stay in the Major Leagues. Doak also became famous in baseball circles for getting Rawlings sporting goods company to invent a glove with a thumb expanded to equal the first forefinger, an innovation that greatly enhanced fielding.[20]

When the job of managing the Yankees opened up after the 1917 season, Huggins was quickly hired. He undoubtedly would have clashed with Rickey in a long-term relationship, and he certainly was upset that he had not been offered a chance to buy into the new ownership of the Cardinals. Miffed by the departure of Rickey to the National League, American League president Ban Johnson was excited to welcome Huggins to his newer league. Bob Connery, who had signed Lee Meadows and, out of the Texas stockyards, future Hall of Fame second baseman Rogers Hornsby, joined Huggins in New York. One could envision the outlines of the coming Yankees-Cardinals rivalry.[21]

To replace Huggins as manager for 1918, Rickey hired Jack Hendricks from the Minor Leagues, but except for Hornsby, the team did not provide much offense, or pitching and defense, for that matter. It fell to the basement in the war-shortened season, and Branch Rickey was not around to complete the year. As the seemingly endless "war to end all wars" raged overseas, the patriotic Rickey wanted to serve his country even though he was thirty-six years old and the father of four young children. At forty-six, Charley Barrett was too old to engage in combat.

In July 1918 Rickey accepted the invitation of onetime Harvard University football coach Percy Haughton, now advising the United States Army, to join the new Chemical Warfare Corps. He was given the title of major and charged with teaching the soldiers techniques of lightning-quick action using chemical weapons. While sailing to France, he contracted pneumonia—fortunately not the flu that was raging throughout the world.

In his platoon were lieutenants Ty Cobb and Christy Mathewson, two future Hall of Famers with dissimilar temperaments. Cobb was always a bundle of nerves and not very sociable, Rickey remembered in his book *The American Diamond*, while Mathewson was congenial but competitive. He and Rickey often played chess at night, and to the executive's frustration, he never could never win a game against the future Hall of Fame pitcher. George Sisler was en route to join the corps when the truce was signed on November 11, 1918.[22]

Rickey did not make it home in time for Christmas, an event that never started without the presence of Charley Barrett. He did return to St. Louis before the start of the new year. "I wasn't able to get into an actual battle," he told reporters, but he had seen things he would remember for the rest of his life and hoped one day to write about. (Unfortunately, he never did.) He told the St. Louis scribes that when he landed in New York, he refused to discuss baseball issues because he had been away for several months. "Baseball things were strange to me, hence I feared I would say the wrong thing," he said in a moment of restraint he did not always follow in front of the sportswriters.[23]

As Branch Rickey planned for the 1919 season, he was thrilled that Charley Barrett was now on board again as chief scout after his two largely uneventful years with the Tigers. Yet the Cardinals were still one of the poorer teams in baseball. Their main office, a small room in the Railway Exchange Building in downtown St. Louis, was sparsely furnished and not likely to impress a prospective seller of Minor League players. Purchasing players to help build up the roster would require ingenuity.

One day before a scheduled meeting with a Minor League owner, Branch enlisted Charley in a scheme to pilfer some of the heirloom rugs belonging to his wife, Jane, from their home while she was visiting her family in Ohio. Mrs. Rickey's rugs certainly added respectability to the office. After the meeting ended, the conspirators rushed to put the carpets back where they belonged. Whether the Minor League owner fell for Rickey's ruse of solvency and sold the player to the Cardinals is unknown; what is known is that after purchasing future Hall of Fame knuckleballer Jesse Haines from the Kansas City Blues for $10,000 in early 1920, Rickey's Cardinals would never make another big-ticket player purchase. Talent developed in the farm system or from lower-level trade and waiver acquisitions would be the key to the Cardinals' coming success.[24]

Insolvency became a fear of the past when Sam Breadon became principal owner and president of the team. Breadon (pronounced "BRAY-din") had been one of the early investors in the reorganized Cardinals, but by the end of 1919 he bought up enough shares to become majority owner. Born on July 26, 1876, one of eight children of parents of Scottish and Irish lineage, he was raised in the less prosperous, decidedly non-Bohemian part of New York City's Greenwich Village, not far from the Hudson River where he occasionally swam. Because his father died when he was in grade school, he dropped out to go to work. By the turn of the twentieth century, he was earning over $100 a week as a clerk on Wall Street. In 1901 Breadon relocated to St. Louis to join two friends, the Halsey brothers, who were working in a garage in the nascent automobile industry. When the brothers found out that Breadon was planning to start his own enterprise, they fired him. Undeterred, Breadon kept his eye on the prize of an auto business.[25]

Breadon was a hard worker with a knack for making powerful friends. One of them was Marion Lambert, the pharmaceutical entrepreneur who created his fortune in part by marketing Listerine as a remedy for bad breath. Lambert was reportedly so impressed by Breadon's refusal to accept a tip for working on his car that he offered him the opportunity to get in on the ground floor of a new enterprise, the Western Automobile Company. Before long, Breadon owned a Ford car dealership. By the time Branch Rickey came into the Cardinals front office, Breadon branched out into selling luxury Pierce-Arrows.[26]

One of Breadon's first brilliant moves as team president was to sell the land at the Cardinals' decaying old ballpark, once called Robison Field, to the city of St. Louis for $275,000, a tidy sum that provided operating capital. (The local government ultimately built a public school on the grounds.) Breadon didn't mind becoming a tenant of the Browns at Sportsman's Park because the Cardinals finally had money in the bank. When Rickey explained the idea of the farm system to Breadon, he found an enthusiastic listener. The idea of growing the team's own players and watching them develop into Major Leaguers—"ripening into money," in Rickey's felicitous if frank phrase—appealed to Breadon, who, like Rickey, had risen from poverty and was determined to enjoy prosperity.

With the indispensable help of Charley Barrett and a new northeastern scout, Charles "Pop" Kelchner, Rickey planned to build "quality through quantity." He would keep his best players and create a surplus of Minor League players that he could sell. Breadon agreed to a clause in Rickey's contract that provided Rickey with a percentage of every Minor Leaguer's sale price in any year the team made a profit. In later years, Breadon resented the money Rickey was making in addition to earning a regular salary. At the outset of their relationship, however, Breadon was onboard with the plan for the farm system. He financed the first fully controlled Cardinal affiliates in Fort Smith, Arkansas, followed by Houston; Syracuse (its team moved to Rochester in 1928); Danville, Illinois; St. Joseph, Missouri; Topeka, Kansas; Columbus, Ohio; Sacramento; and a bevy of teams in smaller towns that would total thirty-two by the end of the 1930s.

Of course, before the farm system could mass-produce Major League players, they had to be discovered. In 1919 the team couldn't afford a spring-training trip to warm weather sites, so the first tryout camp was held on Francis Field on the campus of Washington University of St. Louis. Hopefuls from all over the Midwest and nearby border states came to the camps. Jim Bottomley was one of the first players to catch the eye of Rickey and Barrett. "I am nineteen years old, and I love to play ball," Bottomley had written the Cardinals from his hometown of Nokomis, located in the coal mining district of southern Illinois. Charley Barrett would keep the touching letter for the rest of his life.[27] The Bottomley family had little money, and Jim's older brother, after serving in World War I, had recently died in a mining accident. Bottomley came to the tryout camp in cardboard shoes with his toes sticking out. But when he approached the baseball in the batter's box, Rickey and Barrett saw the projectable tool of a sweet swing that ultimately brought him to the Hall of Fame.

Bottomley arrived in St. Louis in 1923, the first graduate of Rickey's farm system to make the Majors. In 1924 he set a record for most RBIs in a single game, 12, and he would be a fixture at first base for the pennant winners of 1926, 1928, 1930, and 1931 (although his World Series production was minimal—only 1 home run, 10 RBIs, and a .200 batting average in 90 at bats). He drove in well over a hundred runs from 1924 through 1929, and he rarely missed a game. In a sixteen-year career, Bottomley played in 1,991 games with 2,313 hits, .310 batting average, .369 on-base percentage, .500 slugging average, 219 home runs, and 1,442 RBIs. Befitting the age he played in, when not putting the ball in play was virtually a sin, his walk-strikeout ratio was 664:591. He also contributed one of the more enlightening observations about the pressures of baseball's long season. He suggested that it might be best to win three and lose one, so players could avoid the pressure of streaks, good or bad.[28]

Ray Blades was another player signed from the first tryout camp. Raised in Mount Vernon, Illinois, east of St. Louis, Blades thought his future lay in pitching when he played high school and trolley league ball in St. Louis. Barrett followed his development closely, and he wasn't convinced that the youngster's future was on the mound. Neither was Branch Rickey, who once umpired a game that schoolboy Blades was pitching.[29] When he observed the youngster's blazing speed on the bases, Rickey decided that Blades should be an outfielder. He went on to a ten-year career as a Cardinals outfielder, finishing with career statistics of .301 batting average, .395 on-base percentage, and .460 slugging average. He later became a loyal member of Rickey's baseball family as a St. Louis coach and manager and later as a coach in Brooklyn.

The success of the early tryout camps convinced Rickey and Barrett that the camps must continue and spread to all regions of the country. They always maintained that the farm system was actually the cart that followed the horse of the tryout camp. If a player showed sufficient arm strength and better than average speed, a place would be found for him on a farm club where his progress was carefully monitored. Barrett was so committed to grassroots development that he spent the entire season of 1924 away from St. Louis watching players' progress at the lowest Minor League affiliates while also signing new talent. "Anybody can follow a Class AA team around the circuit and name the star players," he said in a rare comment to a reporter. "The trick is to get out in the 'peanut' leagues and recognize the future stars."[30]

Meanwhile, at the Major League level, the Cardinals were showing flashes of promise, but the National League was still dominated by John McGraw's New York Giants, winners of four pennants in a row from 1921 through 1924. McGraw long coveted Rogers Hornsby, and Giants ownership frequently offered the Cardinals upward of $100,000 for his contract, but Rickey convinced Breadon to hold onto the star because he was such a productive player. He won the Triple Crown in 1922, leading the league in batting, home runs, and runs batted in. His 1924 batting average of .424 is a record likely never to be broken. From 1921 through 1925, Hornsby *averaged* .402, 29 home runs, and 140 RBIS.

Yet the Cardinals were floundering after first division finishes in 1921 and 1922. When advance ticket sales for a home 1925 Memorial Day doubleheader were alarmingly small, Breadon traveled to Pittsburgh to tell Rickey in person that he was being relieved of his managing duties. In naming Hornsby player-manager, Breadon tried to convince the intense Rickey that both he and the organization would be better served if he concentrated on player development. The deposed manager hated to experience defeat on any level and impetuously decided to sell his stock in the team, shares that Hornsby gladly purchased. Breadon's judgment proved correct when the team under Hornsby rallied to a winning record for the rest of the 1925 season and won the 1926 NL pennant and World Series.

Charley Barrett's evaluative hand was felt all over the 1926 world champion Cardinals. In addition to Jim Bottomley and Ray Blades, Flint Rhem, who tied for the league lead with twenty victories, was on the roster. Rhem came from a shipping family in South Carolina that was so prominent that his hometown was named Rhems. His parents were dubious about trusting their son to a business they thought consisted mainly of "cutthroats and roughnecks," but Barrett and Rickey worked their charm on them. He was a "wonderful prospect," Rickey said, if only he would "concentrate his entire effort and thought on the game." According to a SABR BioProject essay by Nancy Snell Griffith, a clause was put in Rhem's 1927 contract that provided a $2,500 bonus if Rhem stopped drinking.[31]

During the 1923 season, Barrett was impressed by the fine-fielding short-stop Tommy Thevenow playing for a Class C Minor League team in Joplin, Missouri. Rickey gave his approval to sign the youngster from Madison, Indiana, a small town in between Louisville and Cincinnati.[32] He emerged as the Cardinals' starting shortstop in 1926, setting a career high of 156 games played, scoring 64 runs, and driving in 63. He capped his only season as a St. Louis regular with a productive World Series, hitting .417 with 10 hits, 5 runs scored, and 4 RBIs, while playing fine defense.

Another indirect Barrett contribution to the championship season was speedy outfielder Clarence Francis "Heinie" Mueller, who he signed out of the St. Louis trolley leagues in Creve Coeur, Missouri. In the middle of the 1926 season, Mueller was traded to the Giants for outfielder Billy Southworth. In only 99 games as a 1926 Cardinal, Southworth hit .317 with 69 RBIs. He later managed the Cardinals to the 1930 World Series, won the 1942 Series over the Yankees, and was the skipper of the 1948 pennant-winning Boston Braves.

After winning the pennant by two games over Cincinnati and four and a half games over the Pittsburgh Pirates, the Cardinals' first world championship was sealed in a dramatic seventh game played at Yankee Stadium in a drizzle that kept the crowd under forty thousand. Veteran pitcher and future Hall of Famer Grover Cleveland Alexander, a midseason acquisition from the Chicago Cubs, pitched two and a third innings of scoreless relief to cement the victory that ended with Babe Ruth trying to steal second base and being thrown out by St. Louis catcher Bob O'Farrell. Ruth said afterward that he didn't think the Yankees could put together three hits to beat Alexander, whose alcohol issues were well-known—but Alexander always denied that he was under the influence that day.

Branch Rickey was a well-known teetotaler whose greatest fear was that an alcoholic would find a partner for his binges. It is not known whether Flint Rhem was one of Alexander's drinking partners, but after Rhem's stellar 1926 season he never achieved consistent success and pitched sparingly in the World Series. He did stay with the Cardinals into the 1932 season and finished his career with a 105-97 record and a 4.20 ERA. He died in Columbia, South Carolina, on July 30, 1969, at the age of sixty-eight.

Another key contributor to the 1926 champions was third baseman Lester Bell from the Pennsylvania state capital in Harrisburg. He enjoyed a career year, putting up impressive offensive numbers of .325 batting average, .383 on-base percentage, .516 slugging average, 17 home runs, and 100 RBIs. He went 7-27 in the World Series with a home run and six RBIs and 4 runs scored. He was not an outstanding defensive player, and during the 1928 season, he was traded to the Boston Braves and wound up having a nine-year Major League career.

Bell was one of the many players signed by the Cardinals' prolific northeastern scout, Charles Schaeffer "Pop" Kelchner, a renowned baseball personage in central Pennsylvania. Kelchner first worked with Charley Barrett and Branch Rickey for Robert Hedges's Browns. Previously, he had provided tips to Connie Mack's Philadelphia Athletics during their heyday in the first years of the twentieth century. His biggest signing was future Hall of Fame pitcher Charles Albert "Chief" Bender, who compiled a 210-127 won-lost record with a career 2.46 ERA. In five World Series, Bender pitched to an even better ERA of 2.44 with a 6-4 record.[33]

Kelchner, born on August 2, 1875, in a farm community in Fleetwood, Pennsylvania, a few miles from the Berks County seat of Reading, never harbored pro aspirations, although his younger brother, Jay, played Minor League Baseball and later scouted. Charles played in high school and for semipro teams in Atlantic City. While attending Lafayette College in Easton, he competed in many sports while becoming proficient in languages—he spoke seven languages total. After graduation, he continued his multitasking as a faculty member at Albright College in Reading, teaching French, German, Latin, and Spanish and coaching baseball, football, and basketball. Students bestowed the nickname "Pop" upon him because they were attracted to his paternal manner. They loved to hear him recite the classics in his very distinctive Pennsylvania Dutch accent.[34]

In 1920 Kelchner took on the job for more than twenty years as the general secretary of the YMCA in the Lebanon Valley area. He started scouting for the Cardinals soon after Branch Rickey arrived in 1917 and continued in that capacity for the Cardinals until his death in 1958. In 1952 Branch Rickey and Connie Mack attended a ceremony in which Albright's baseball stadium was named Kelchner Field. A plaque was installed that read, "Versatile Athlete—Athletic Coach—Teacher of Languages—Loyal Alumnus—Well Known Baseball Scout Nationally—Acclaimed for His Good Sportsmanship and Christian Living—He Played Well in the Game of Life—He Had the Will to Win."[35]

Charles Edward Chapman was the second scout who delivered a key player to the 1926 champions: center fielder Taylor Douthit (pronounced "DOW-thit"). Born in Little Rock, Arkansas, and raised in Oakland, California, Douthit was studying agriculture at the University of California, Berkeley, and playing baseball for the Golden Bears when Chapman, a professor of Latin American history at Berkeley, spotted him. Although Douthit was an All-Star basketball player, he preferred baseball. The Detroit Tigers were interested in signing him, but he was won over when fellow Berkeley man Chapman promised Taylor that he could get his feet wet immediately in St. Louis. After brief Major League appearances in 1924 and 1925, he emerged in 1926 as the Cardinals starting center fielder for the next five seasons. Charles Chapman always insisted that Douthit was a better center fielder than future Hall of Famer Tris Speaker and a competent *batsman*, a term that Branch Rickey also liked to use instead of *hitter*.[36]

In a game with unique individuals at every level, Charles Edward Chapman's story is remarkable. He was born on June 3, 1880, in Franklin, New Hampshire, the son of a druggist who took him to his first baseball game when he was three years old. The youngster never forgot the thrill of a foul ball that whizzed close to him as he was sitting in the stands with his father. After attending prep school, Charles went to Princeton and Tufts and starred on both teams. In 1900 he got the winning hit for Princeton that enabled the team to beat Yale and win the Big Three title. At Tufts, as he put it in one of his two short unpublished memoirs, "I captained the team which mopped up all New England and was undoubtedly one of the best college teams that ever played."[37] During the summers, he played independent league baseball under the name Al Rogers, in case questions of his eligibility to play college baseball were raised. He always opposed the charade of the fake name, believing that any bona fide college student should be allowed to engage in any summer activity of his choice. (He would learn that Branch Rickey strongly agreed with him.)

After graduation from Harvard Law School in 1905, his parents treated him to a trip to the Pacific, where he had a career-altering experience in Japan. A baseball craze had started, and he was enlisted to give a clinic on the game, perhaps the first such event in the nation's history. Unfortunately, while demonstrating throwing techniques, he seriously damaged his shoulder. (In an eerie coincidence, Branch Rickey would shortly suffer a similar injury while instructing players at Ohio Wesleyan.) After his eventful trip, Chapman returned to the States by way of San Francisco, narrowly missing the April 1906 earthquake. He continued to play semipro baseball, but he knew his injury had ended any chance of advancing to the Majors. Not interested in pursuing a law career, he decided on the study of history. Chapman settled in the San Francisco Bay Area and worked his way up from high school teaching to a full professorship at Cal-Berkeley. He became a specialist in Spanish history, ultimately publishing several books and founding the Hispanic Review of History.[38]

Baseball fever still coursed through Charles Chapman's blood. During the 1921 season, he wrote an unsolicited letter to Branch Rickey asking him why no one in baseball was scouting talent on the West Coast. He explained that, having come of age in the 1890s when there was only one Major League, the twelve-team National League, he was distressed to see the league of his youth now usually lose the World Series to the new American League. He insisted the situation would change if only the National League started scouting West Coast talent. Rickey dispatched Charley Barrett to see if the passionate writer was the real deal. After his visit, Barrett wrote back that Chapman had a lot to offer and he was brought on board as a "casual scout," as Chapman described himself in one of his unpublished memoirs.[39]

In addition to signing Taylor Douthit, Chapman brought into the Cardinals fold left fielder Charles "Chick" Hafey, who hailed from the California wine country town of Calistoga. Signed as a pitcher, Hafey caught Branch Rickey's eye with his hitting during spring training, and, like Ray Blades, Hafey was quickly transformed into an everyday player. He became the regular left fielder in 1927 and put up such impressive numbers in the next five seasons that he ultimately landed in the Hall of Fame. His final numbers in a thirteen-year career were .317 batting average, .372 on-base percentage, .526 slugging average, 164 home runs, 833 RBIS, but only 1,466 hits. Rickey always insisted that if Hafey had not suffered from chronic sinusitis, he might have established unbreakable records.

The Cardinals' first world title in 1926, the first for a St. Louis team in forty-one years, led to mass delirium in St. Louis. A special correspondent for the *New York Times* described the celebration: "Flappers and gray-haired men, demure grandmothers and women with babes in arms, college sheiks and men with the marks of human toil upon their all clothes all rubbed shoulders."[40] Grateful St. Louis season-ticket holders held a luncheon in Barrett's honor and presented the self-effacing scout with a diamond-studded wrist watch. Over a hundred people attended, including Sam Breadon, Branch Rickey, and Rickey's assistant, William DeWitt, who started his career as a teenaged peanut vendor at Sportsman's Park and was rising rapidly toward a long career as a baseball executive.[41] In one of his columns, Damon Runyon, the nationally known sportswriter, saluted Rickey and Barrett. He remembered when the Cardinals were so impoverished they had "trouble paying its laundry bills." He applauded the farm system that was now enjoying its first great success. Detractors might brand the idea of developing players inexpensively rung by rung in the farm system as chain-store baseball, but Runyon extolled Rickey and Barrett for winning without paying "fancy prices for ball players."[42]

Barrett and Rickey were well aware that uneasy lies the head that wears the crown. Barrett barely had time to examine his new diamond watch when a crisis arose within the Cardinals organization. Sam Breadon was still furious at an insult hurled at him by Rogers Hornsby during the tense September moments of the 1926 pennant race. The owner had committed the Cardinals to playing an exhibition game against the New Haven Colonials, an Eastern League franchise operated by the young George Weiss (who, as will be explained shortly, would be hired by the Yankees five years later to create a farm system to rival Rickey's). Breadon had also scheduled exhibition games in Syracuse and Buffalo on off days. Hornsby pleaded with Breadon, who unwisely entered the clubhouse after a Cardinals loss, to cancel the Colonials game because the players needed a day off. The owner was adamant about his commitment to Weiss, who had welcomed the Cardinals when they were not a good team, and now his New Haven fans wanted to see a potential champion.

When Hornsby shouted an expletive and told the owner where he could put his exhibition game, Breadon was outraged, and the argument became public knowledge right after the World Series. Always-accommodating Charley Barrett was then distressed and urged the superstar to apologize to his boss, but Hornsby, now a world champion, was in no mood to be cooperative.[43] With his three-year contract just completed—he was the rare star in that period to enjoy a multiyear contract—he asked for another three-year contract, with a hefty increase in salary. The stubborn Texan's intransigence only hardened Breadon's stance; he offered his star only a one-year contract.

Branch Rickey was never in favor of what would soon be the trade. "Hornsby was the hardest player to keep sweet and George Sisler was the easiest player to keep sweet," Rickey later reflected. But for him, Hornsby's talent overrode any personality issues, including his near-addiction to gambling that resulted in significant losses.

Breadon, as owner, decided to trade the star, and shortly before Christmas, the trade of Hornsby to the Giants for second baseman Frank Frisch and thirty-one-year-old journeyman pitcher Jimmy Ring was announced. Rickey had long admired the scrappy switch hitter, who in 1919 came directly to the big leagues from New York's Fordham University. As the Giants were falling short of the pennant in 1925 and 1926, Frisch and McGraw started to feud, so he was available. Cardinals fans, though, went ballistic at Breadon for trading their hero. Many season-ticket packages were canceled, and the owner was hung in effigy. The St. Louis Chamber of Commerce implored baseball commissioner Landis to intervene and cancel the trade.[44]

When Frisch produced a sensational season in 1927, the uproar died down. Breadon said he learned to never again fear fan reactions when making decisions. The Cardinals just missed winning the 1927 pennant, despite Frisch's great year. Jimmy Ring, the throw-in in the Hornsby-Frisch deal, went winless in his one year as a Cardinal. Rickey would always lament that a win or two from the veteran hurler might have made the difference in another close pennant race with the Pirates, this time won by Pittsburgh.[45] (If the Cardinals had won the 1927 pennant, they would have had to play home games in another city because in late September a tornado blew off portions of the upper deck at Sportsman's Park.)

A regular contender now, the Cardinals returned to the World Series in 1928, but the Yankees avenged their 1926 loss with a four-game sweep. St. Louis was still building a near-dynasty with back-to-back pennant winners in 1930 and 1931, and 1931 and 1934 World Series triumphs. Though Charley Barrett never sought public acclaim, his name was becoming known in the wider American culture. Early in the 1932 movie *Fireman, Save My Child*, the first of baseball-loving comedian Joe E. Brown's trilogy of baseball films, Brown's character Smokey Joe Grant is torn between marketing his fire-preventing invention or playing Major League Baseball. He chooses the latter when the screen displays a message: "Will you accept seventy-five hundred dollars from the St. Louis Cardinals [*sic*]. Must have your answer today. Signed Charley Barrett Scout."[46]

The farm system was churning out a host of future regulars. Few paid more dues or won more fan approval than John Leonard Roosevelt "Pepper" Martin who became Branch Rickey's favorite player and one of Charley Barrett's too. Martin, born in Temple, Oklahoma, on Leap Day 1904, February 29, was the youngest of seven children of cotton farmers, Celia Spears and George Washington Martin. When Pepper was six years old, the family moved 120 miles north to Oklahoma City. He didn't finish high school but worked as a newspaper hawker and messenger, an early job path similar to Barrett's. He played baseball on local church and semipro teams. Loving all kinds of competition, Martin also was a halfback for the Hominy Indians, a football team based in Hominy, Oklahoma, featuring many players from the local Osage Native American tribe. In 1923 he played his first organized pro baseball in Guthrie, Oklahoma. When the team disbanded during the next season, Martin headed for a Cardinals tryout camp in Greenville, Texas. He did well enough to receive a 1925 Class D contract from the Cardinals' East Texas League franchise in the same town.[47]

It was in Greenville that Charley Barrett first glimpsed Pepper Martin. "I was attracted right away by his wildness," Barrett reminisced to national baseball writer Harry Grayson.[48] Martin soon began his laborious rise through the increasingly crowded farm system. While playing in Fort Smith, Arkansas, team owner Blake Harper, later Rickey's chief concessionaire in St. Louis, dubbed him "Pepper" (although Rickey and Charley Barrett always addressed him by his given name, something they liked to do with all their players).[49]

Martin was signed primarily as an infielder, but Barrett and Rickey thought his speed might be better suited for the outfield. Although they both loved aggressive players, they thought that his infield play bordered on the reckless. He always played without wearing an athletic supporter, and his throws to first base were frequently accompanied by pebbles from the infield dirt. After riding a shuttle for a couple seasons between the two top Cardinal farm teams in Syracuse and Houston, Martin made his Major League debut in 1928. He appeared in only thirty-eight games, mainly as a pinch runner for the pennant winners. He was back in Houston in 1929 and growing impatient at his lack of progress in the Cardinals system. Yet Martin never let his protracted stay in the Minors affect his performance on the field. The fans loved his aggressive style of play, and, almost always, supporters gave him days to show their appreciation wherever he played.

His breakthrough season came in 1930 as a twenty-six-year-old for the Rochester Red Wings, which had been moved from Syracuse. He hit .363 and amassed 304 total bases. He looked forward to his big chance in 1931 and arrived in spring training after hopping a freight train. When the team hotel clerk saw Martin's disheveled appearance, he told a bellboy, "Count the towels before you leave him."[50] Despite having a good spring training, Martin was back at Rochester when the regular season started. He came close to issuing a play-me-or-trade-me demand for the Majors, but Branch Rickey told him to be patient, that his time was coming soon.

As the trade deadline loomed on June 15, incumbent center fielder Taylor Douthit knew his job was in jeopardy. Scout Charles Chapman's discovery tried his hardest to make a case that he still belonged as a St. Louis regular. Not even a great weekend series at home before the trade deadline could save him. He was dealt to Cincinnati to make room for Martin on the roster. Young Cardinals publicist Gene Karst—who got his job the same way as Charles Chapman got his, by writing an unsolicited letter—never forgot the tears in

Douthit's eyes when he received the bad news about his exile to the tail-end Reds.[51] It turned out that Douthit was suffering from an injured hip, and his career was soon over. He returned to the Bay Area to work in the family insurance and real estate businesses, dying in Fremont, California, on May 28, 1986, at the age of eighty-two.[52]

Once he arrived in St. Louis, Pepper Martin proved he was there to stay by hitting .300 with 7 home runs, 75 RBIs, .351 on-base percentage, .467 slugging average, and 16 stolen bases, as the Cardinals roared to win the 1931 pennant by fourteen games over the Giants. In the World Series against the Philadelphia Athletics, Martin became a national sensation when he set a record with 12 hits along with a batting average of .500 and 5 RBIs. He scored the only two runs in the Cardinals' Game Two 2–0 victory, stretching a single into a double and stealing two bases. Before the third game in Philadelphia, Martin posed with a local policeman writing out a ticket to him for speeding.[53]

Before Game Five in a World Series tied at two games, Cardinals manager Gabby Street moved Martin to the cleanup spot, and he responded with three hits in four at bats with a home run and four RBIs. Although he went hitless in the last two games, he stole a base in the deciding Game Seven and caught the final out in center field. His five stolen bases rattled the concentration of Philadelphia's future Hall of Fame catcher Mickey Cochrane. Denied a third World Series victory in a row, A's owner-manager Connie Mack admitted that his team had no answer for Martin's heroics. His pre-Series comment that Martin was the kind of unpredictable player that could be either a hero or a goat was prophetic. Baseball commissioner Landis was captivated by Martin's spectacular performance. He publicly envied Martin's talents and wished they could change places. Martin said he was fine with that if they could swap salaries. His name now nationally known, a vaudeville company hired Martin to travel the country, telling stories while twirling a lasso. He was being paid a reported $2,500 a week, but Martin abandoned the tour after a few shows, saying he was not an entertainer and preferred being a ballplayer.[54]

Martin was a sparkplug on St. Louis's next World Series champion, the 1934 team that became known to history as the Gashouse Gang (although the term did not become popularized until the following season). New York sportswriter Joe Williams penned a disdainful description of the Cardinals as "slobs who acted like juveniles, used improper English when speaking to people, were never clean-shaven and chewed tobacco and spit all over."[55] The earthy St. Louis players did not mind the criticism. They knew that relaxation from the tense game of baseball was a great elixir.

Pepper Martin on several occasions arrived just before game time because he had been racing his midget automobiles. He had plenty of accomplices for antics that were designed to relax the team and intimidate the opposition. Pitcher Dizzy Dean was one of Pepper's major coconspirators. One late June broiling St. Louis afternoon before a home game against the archrival Giants, Pepper and Dizzy started a fire outside their dugout while wearing thick Indian blankets and whooping and hollering. Anything to rattle the opposition was fair game for these two fun-loving yet fierce competitors.[56]

In 1930 Cardinals associate scout Don Curtis, a prominent grassroots coach in Texas with a passion for discovering pitchers, had signed nineteen-year-old Dean, who was playing on an industrial league team in San Antonio. He was following up on a tip from former Major League catcher Frank "Pancho" Snyder.[57] Much dispute remains about whether Dean's real name was Jay Hanna Dean or Jerome Herman Dean, but there is no doubt that he was born in Lucas, Arkansas, on January 16, 1910. The son of sharecroppers who moved frequently, Dizzy never advanced past the second grade. He and his younger brother Paul, who would join him on the Cardinals, came from such poverty that going into the army at least assured their receiving regular meals and clean clothing.

The six-foot-two, 180-pound Dizzy was such a great talent that he made his Major League debut at the end of the 1930 season, pitching a shutout after the pennant had been clinched. He was not eligible for the World Series and spent 1931 in the Minors, squawking about his low salary and moaning that he had nothing more to prove. In 1932 Dizzy established himself as a big winner for St. Louis, going 18-15 with a 3.30 ERA. The Cardinals, though, fell to seventh place, eighteen games behind the pennant-winning Cubs. In 1933 he improved to 20-18 with a 3.04 ERA, the first of four years in a row he won twenty or more games. Dizzy's duels with the Giants' southpaw Carl Hubbell became a national story, and with Babe Ruth fading from the scene, Dean was more than ready to take up the mantle of baseball's most colorful player.

Carl Hubbell slipped out of the hands of the Detroit Tigers, which never thought he threw hard enough to become a Major Leaguer. Dick Kinsella, John McGraw's main scout, took a break from the 1928 Democratic National Convention in Houston to see a Minor League game and noticed that Hubbell was now throwing a screwball.[58] He made his Major League debut later that season and was on his way to a Hall of Fame career and later a productive career as Giants' farm director. The Cardinals lost the 1933 pennant to the Giants, the eventual World Series winner over the Senators, but they rose to fifth place, only nine games behind the champions.

The 1934 season would become special again for St. Louis, as Dizzy entered the rarified air of thirty-game winners. He went 30-7, and Paul Dean finished 17-9. To fill a hole at third base, Pepper Martin willingly returned to the infield alongside Leo Durocher. Martin turned in another sterling performance in the World Series, hitting .355 with 11 hits, 8 runs scored, and 3 RBIs. The deciding seventh game in Detroit was a huge letdown for the home team. School kids were let out of classes and taken into school auditoriums to listen to the radio broadcast. The game, however, was all St. Louis, with Dizzy pitching a six-hit shutout in an 11–0 romp that was broken open with a six-run third inning. It is most remembered for a seventh inning incident when frustrated Tiger fans threw produce and garbage at Cardinals left fielder Joe Medwick for sliding too hard into third baseman Marv Owen in the previous inning. Martin, Medwick, and center fielder Ernie Orsatti further enraged the crowd by taking the produce and having a catch with it.[59] To restore order, Commissioner Landis ordered Medwick's removal from the game. It deprived him of the chance to tie or break Martin's record of 12 hits in a World Series, a penalty that stuck forever in the craw of the slugger who liked to say that his driving motivation in baseball was collecting "base hits and buckerinos."

Dizzy and Paul Dean won all four games of the 1934 World Series, but the Cardinals did not return to the fall classic until 1942, and by then both pitchers were gone from the Majors. Tensions were growing between Branch Rickey and Sam Breadon. Except for the last week of the 1934 season and the games in the World Series, the Cardinals did not draw well. Breadon was envious of the bigger crowds and the bigger stadium in Detroit. He seriously thought of moving the Cardinals to Detroit, and when the National League threw cold water on the idea, he briefly put the team up for sale. Lewis Haines "Lew" Wentz, an Oklahoma oil man, a bachelor with a philanthropic impulse who was acquainted with the similarly charitable Branch Rickey, came close to buying the team but got cold feet and bowed out. Breadon held on to the team, but his lukewarm attitude toward Rickey turned cold, especially after he retired from the auto industry in 1936 and had more time to enjoy the team and to believe that his high-priced employee was replaceable.[60]

Another factor roiling the Cardinals organization was the decline of Dizzy Dean after he broke his toe on a line drive off the bat of Cleveland's Earl Averill during the 1937 All-Star Game. Dean should have taken more time off to heal, but he was a fierce competitor and returned too soon and hurt his arm. In mid-April 1938, Rickey traded Dizzy to owner Phil Wrigley's Cubs for a serviceable right-hander Curt Davis, two other players, and $185,000 of the chewing gum magnate's cash. Rickey made it clear that Dean was "unsound in arm," but the Cubs wanted the irrepressible star as, at least, a gate attraction.

Dean pitched with great guile for the Cubs, going 7-1 with a 1.75 ERA in thirteen regular season games. He even shut out the Yankees through seven innings in Game Two of the 1938 World Series. Then, the Five O'clock Lightning struck—games started in that era around three in the afternoon so the crucial late innings occurred around five. An eighth-inning rally brought the Yankees to victory, and they were on their way to equal their 1932 World Series sweep of the Chicagoans. Dean retired the next year with a career record of 150-83 and 3.02 ERA and a place in the Hall of Fame in 1953. During his induction speech, he thanked the good Lord for giving him a strong back, a live arm, and a weak mind. Paul Dean, a much more reserved person whose nickname "Dazzy" was a sportswriter's creation, also ended his Major League career in 1939 with a record of 50-34 and a 3.75 ERA.

Meanwhile, injuries also took their toll on Pepper Martin. Though his batting average from 1937 to 1939 was over .300 and his slugging average was over .440, he never again played a hundred games in a season after 1936. He still enjoyed his life to the fullest. During the 1937 season, he organized a Mississippi Mudcat jug band that played before games on the road as well as at home. The lineup was Pepper and pitcher Lon Warneke on guitar, pitchers Bill McGee on fiddle and Bob Weiland on jug, and outfielder Frenchy

Bordagaray on washboard and auto horns. Before he was traded, Dizzy Dean contributed vocals on the "Wabash Cannonball."[61]

Before the home game on June 25, 1939, Cardinals fans, sensing that Martin's career was nearing an end, held a day in his honor. Fans from the farmland showered him with gifts of animals, including two Belgian mares, a heifer, a rooster, a hen, and a sow with seven young. "The infield looked like a county fairgrounds," W. C. Heinz wrote when Pepper remembered the event years later.[62] Charley Barrett made it a point to come off the road to salute his favorite player. He was deeply moved when Martin put his arm around him before the game and thanked him profusely for making his career possible. Like Paul Krichell, Barrett was not used to receiving thanks from players he signed. When Martin repeated his gratitude during the ceremonies on his day, the reticent Barrett replied for the crowd to hear, "You've certainly done your part to make my baseball judgment hold up."[63]

Martin played eighty-six games in 1940, and he could still hit: .316 batting average and .456 slugging average. In 1942 he managed the Cardinals' Sacramento farm club to the Pacific Coast League pennant. Although he never became a formal member of Branch Rickey's baseball family, he was always ready to help out his mentor. He came out of retirement in 1944 to play forty games for the pennant-winning Cardinals but did not play in the World Series that the Cardinals won in six games over their local rival Browns. His final Major League numbers were 1,189 games played, 1,227 hits, .298 batting average, .358 on-base percentage, .443 slugging percentage, 369 walks, 438 strikeouts, 146 stolen bases, and 54 caught stealing. In fifteen games in three World Series, he hit .418 with a .467 on-base percentage, .636 slugging percentage, and 7 stolen bases in 9 attempts.

In 1947 Martin answered a call from Rickey to become field goal kicker for the short-lived Brooklyn Dodgers football team in the All-America Football Conference. In 1949 he managed the Miami Marlins in the Florida State League, but he was suspended for the last few games of the season after trying to choke an umpire who had made a bad call. When Branch Rickey heard about the incident, he admitted, "Pepper does get overzealous at times."[64] Martin made his permanent home in McAlester, Oklahoma, located in the southeastern part of the state, where he built a huge ranch house with an artificial lake that he invited all the area kids to use. In 1961 Martin became recreation director at a local state penitentiary; the job left him plenty of time to engage in all kinds of sports. In the fall of 1964 Pepper Martin was involved in an impromptu baseball game at his ranch. On one play he slid hard as always into second base and got spiked. The wound was not attended to, and it got infected. It never healed, and on March 5, 1965, Pepper Martin passed away at the age of sixty-one.[65]

A mere ten days after celebrating Pepper Martin's career, the world of the Cardinals was shattered by the news that Charley Barrett, sixty-eight, had died at home of a heart attack. In an eerie coincidence, earlier that day, July 4, 1939, at Yankee Stadium, Lou Gehrig gave his memorable farewell speech. Unlike Gehrig, Charley Barrett was not known to be ailing, but the constant travel, lost sleep, and meals taken at all hours must have taken a toll. When Branch Rickey heard the terrible news, he was scouting the Cardinals' top Rochester Red Wings farm team. He rushed home for Barrett's funeral. En route, he sent a telegram to St. Louis newspapers, lauding his late friend's contributions to scouting and developing baseball players.

Rickey was one of the pallbearers at the funeral in St. Louis's Blessed Sacrament Catholic Church along with Sam Breadon; Warren Giles, general manager of the Reds, who got his start in Rickey's farm system; and Bill DeWitt, now the St. Louis Browns president. Breadon said of Barrett, "His word was his bond." Fighting back tears, Rickey said, "He was never a 'yes' man. . . . He was my oldest and closest friend in baseball." He added that Barrett always cared the most for the players at the lowest levels in baseball. Retired Dick Kinsella, the late John McGraw's top scout who would himself die three months later, made the trip from Indiana to pay his respects.[66]

Christmas dinner would never again be the same at the Rickey household because festivities had never started until Charley arrived. In 1946 Branch Rickey Jr., his father's close baseball associate, named his son Branch Barrett Rickey in the scout's honor. (The third-generation baseball Rickey retired before the 2021 season as Pacific Coast League president.) Publicist Gene Karst felt the loss hard. He recalled meeting Charley Barrett for the first time when he started working for the team in 1928. After a round of banter and baseball talk, Barrett looked at Karst, thirty years his junior, and said, "Let's be friends." And so they did for the rest of Barrett's life.[67]

Karst always chuckled at the memory of a dinner sponsored by the St. Louis Holy Name Society that Barrett attended as a guest of honor. The event was designed to support the cause of not "taking the name of the Lord in vain." Barrett was promised beforehand that he would not have to make a speech. When egged on to tell a story about the first player he ever signed, he reluctantly got up and said, "Aw, I can't make no goddam speech." According to Karst, Barrett was never invited again to the dinner.[68]

Charley Barrett never married. He may have been one of the first people that Branch Rickey dubbed "a matrimonial coward," but he was no doubt married to the Cardinals, the baseball organization built up by his dear friend. Like many scouts, Barrett drove a quality car to insure reliability and to impress prospects and their families. In some years he drove a Lincoln Zephyr featuring a license plate with a Redbirds logo that read "Cardinals Scout." The late researcher and bird-dog scout Jim Sandoval estimated that during his career Barrett must have "traveled over 500,000 miles by car, bus, train, airplane, and even a tractor."[69]

The loss of Barrett was felt by players he did not even sign. Southpaw pitcher Hub "Shucks" Pruett, whose greatest claim to fame was his amazing ability to fan Babe Ruth—13 strikeouts in 24 at bats against the Bambino— was one of those players encouraged by Barrett. The pitcher had been raised by an aunt after his father was killed in a horse-and-buggy accident. After seeing him pitch, Barrett told the youngster to drop by the Cardinals' office to discuss signing a contract. When Pruett came by, the Browns were in town, and the Cardinals were on the road, so the pitcher signed with the American Leaguers. After a seven-year career with a 29-48 record, 4.63 ERA, and walking more men than he struck out, Pruett went on to become a prominent gynecologist in the St. Louis area.[70] He was nicknamed "Shucks" by players because he did not use profanity. (When he became a leading gynecologist in St. Louis, Pruett had to endure the joke that for him every day was Ladies Day.)

The news of Barrett's passing deeply moved Charles Chapman, whose career as a casual scout began when Charley sent Rickey his approval. Chapman always kept in mind the importance of makeup and character in evaluating players. He never forgot the story Barrett told him about traveling for days through mountainous country searching for a prospective player. When he finally located him drinking whiskey in a local bar, Barrett left without ever seeing the fellow play.[71]

Charles Chapman was continuing to live an astonishing polymathic life. In addition to his full teaching load at Cal-Berkeley and competing in national bridge competitions with his second wife, he maintained a busy schedule organizing tryout camps for the Reds on the West Coast. Taught well by Barrett and Rickey, he looked for the raw tools that with patient player development could be converted into Major League skills. In 1941 the prestigious Harper & Brothers published Charles Chapman's baseball manual written in collaboration with former big league catcher Hank Severeid, a Charley Barrett signing who you met earlier this chapter.

Entitled *Play Ball! Advice for Young Ballplayers*, the book opened with an introduction by Bill McKechnie, a future Hall of Fame manager who had just led the 1940 Reds to a World Series title. The scout is "the eyes of baseball," McKechnie wrote. "Without him, major league-ball would soon become minor-league ball."[72]

The richly detailed chapters in *Play Ball!* featured colorful titles like "The General of the Ball Game: The Catcher," "The Greyhound of the Gardens: The Center Fielder," and "The 360-Foot Journey: Running the Sacks." The authors took turns breaking up technical discussion with anecdotes from their careers. Severeid, who at the time of his retirement had played in a record number of combined Major and Minor League games, remembered that after the Yankees lost the close 1926 World Series to the Cardinals, Miller Huggins addressed the team. "You gave me all you had," he said, "and when you do that I don't care if you lose ten World Series."[73] Chapman stressed the importance of players getting Minor League experience and not being eager to be rushed to the Majors in their thirst for Major League money. He advised, "Even if one [won't make the Major Leagues], I would recommend trying it for a year or two for the immense advantage to be obtained in human experience and happy memories."

He added a piece of closing, upbeat advice for the players who fell short of their Major League dream: "The game is always looking for those who have the sufficient talents to do the one thousand and one things which do not take place on the diamond itself."[74] Sadly, not long after publication of the book, Chapman suffered a heart attack and died on November 18, 1941, in Oakland, California, at the age of sixty-one.

Despite the passing of Charley Barrett, the vast Cardinals' farm system remained productive, reaching a peak of thirty-two teams and over seven hundred players by the end of the 1930s. Baseball commissioner Kenesaw Mountain Landis was not happy about the extent of the system, "vast as the continent," he railed. Ever since he assumed office as baseball's first sole commissioner in January 1921, he opposed Branch Rickey's control of players. He thought his Cedar Rapids decision on March 23, 1938, giving free agency to more than ninety of Rickey's farmhands, would make a dent in his farm system. Landis fumed that these players were being shuttled from roster to roster in the Cardinals system without being given a chance for advancement. Yet few dominant players were freed in the group, an exception being the teen-aged switch-hitting outfielder Pete Reiser, who was signed by the Brooklyn Dodgers. (If Reiser had played with less abandon, it is commonly believed that he might have become a Hall of Famer, an earlier generation's Mickey Mantle.) Most of the players liberated from Rickey's "chain gang" re-signed with the Cardinals, including George Silvey, who would go to a long career as a St. Louis player developer.[75]

Charley Barrett may have been gone, but his influence on scouting would be immortal not just to players who made the Majors but also to players who became scouts. In 1933 he signed infielder Ross "Rosey" Gilhousen not long after he pitched a no-hitter for Compton Junior College outside of Los Angeles. Gilhousen hurt his arm early in his Minor League career and briefly went into the movie business as a member of the swing crew at RKO-Pathe. He even worked on Gene Autry's first western.[76] The siren call of baseball soon brought Gilhousen back to the game. After scouting for the Pittsburgh Pirates in the 1950s, Rosey's life came full circle when the expansion California Angels, owned by Gene Autry, hired him as one of their first scouts. Scouting director Roland Hemond offered the job. Hemond, a baseball lifer who started his career in the front office of the Boston Braves just before their move to Milwaukee in 1953, loved scouts and player developers. He was tireless in his desire to help those who truly loved the game. Rosey Gilhousen ultimately wound up scouting with the expansion Kansas City Royals, where he was instrumental in the signing of both George Brett and star closer Dan Quisenberry, stories you will hear in upcoming chapters.

The influence of Barrett's northeastern colleague, Pop Kelchner, remained strong in the Cardinals organization. In 1940 Kelchner signed George Kissell from Ithaca College in upstate New York, where his senior thesis was about the development of baseball as a sport. Kissell never made the Majors as a player, but he became a legendary player developer into the early twenty-first century. Branch Rickey marveled, "He looks after details. He is a 'cleaner-upper.' First man out last man in."[77] Though never in the Cardinals organization, Sparky Anderson picked up as much wisdom from Kissell as he could. "He could teach a snake to box," Anderson marveled. Kissell turned down many offers to switch allegiances to another organization, saying, "They will never tear the Redbirds off my shirt."[78]

After the 1950 season, Branch Rickey lost a bitter internal battle for control of the Brooklyn Dodgers to Walter O'Malley. Many Brooklyn scouts and player developers joined Rickey in Pittsburgh, where he became the general manager of the Pirates. Scout Rex Bowen, originally an infielder in the Cardinals system, and Wid Matthews, a former outfielder in the same system, were among them. So was Howie Haak, a former catcher in the Cardinals system who would become a pioneer in Latin American scouting. Knowing reportedly just four words in Spanish, for "throw hard and run fast," Haak would be instrumental in plucking Roberto Clemente from the Brooklyn system in the Rule 5 Draft after the 1954 season when he was not protected after a season with the Dodgers' top farm club in Montreal. Haak also signed pitcher Alvin McBean after a tryout camp in the Virgin Islands that McBean was covering as a photographer. Disappointed at the quality of the campers, McBean answered a dare, tried out, and became the first Major League pitcher from his country.[79]

The Rickey-Barrett influence in scouting and player development would be felt in Brooklyn and Los Angeles even after Rickey departed. Holdover executives Buzzie Bavasi, Al Campanis, and Fresco Thompson were great believers in scouting and player development. *The Dodger Way of Playing*, a three-hundred-page manual that Campanis wrote, concentrated on pitching and defense for more than half of the volume. Peter O'Malley, Walter's son who became president of the team in the early 1970s, treated scouts with special consideration. He quietly took care of widows of scouts after their husbands passed away. Scouts were warmly welcomed on off-season trips to Hawaii, and in 1988 they were part of the contingent that traveled to the Vatican after the Dodgers' surprise triumph over the Oakland Athletics in the World Series. Longtime Dodgers northeastern scout Bob Miske remembered how an aide to manager Tommy Lasorda, as equally ebullient as his boss, started shouting in the holy corridors, "The Dodgers are here! The Dodgers are here!" The enthusiasm was cut short when a papal aide walked by and said sternly, "Shh! This is the Vatican!"[80]

As you shall see during this saga of the diamond detectives, the Rickey-Barrett method lived on deep into the twentieth century and the early twenty-first century. But always standing in the way of its dominance, and an obstacle of any would-be contender, was the formidable Yankees' dynasties. Although Branch Rickey's Cardinals beat the Yankees twice in the World Series in 1926 and 1942, he never won it in his two tries in Brooklyn, 1947 and 1949. He was in Pittsburgh when the Brooklyn Dodgers finally beat the Yankees in 1955. And entitled Yankees fans still argue that the loss was attributable to Mickey Mantle being injured. It was no accident that once George Weiss started presiding over the Yankees' farm system after the 1931 World Series triumph of the Rickey-Barrett Cardinals, the Minor League wheels were grinding in motion to produce the most successful Yankees' dynasty. It is time now to examine now how the Yankees' juggernaut emerged and to look at the indispensable role of another one of Birdie Tebbetts's immortal scouts, Paul Krichell.

2

Paul Krichell and the Rise of the Yankees' Dynasties

Paul Bernard Krichell was perhaps destined to become the indispensable scout in the Yankees' storied history because his New York City roots were deep. Although he was born in Paris, France, on December 19, 1882, he emigrated with his family to the Lower East Side of New York City when he was around five years old. He was the youngest of eight children sired by David Krichell, a cabinetmaker born in western Germany. By the age of eight, Krichell was living in the Bronx not far from the site where Yankee Stadium opened in 1923. In a rare, revealing interview he gave late in his life, he reminisced about "when the Grand Concourse was a dirt road" and how "he fished in the creek that flowed through where second base is."[1]

Krichell never grew taller than five feet seven, but he was a gritty competitor, the kind of stocky catcher for whom baseball always seemed to find a place. College was not a common experience in those days for people from Krichell's background, so when he wasn't picking up money from odd jobs, he made a name for himself on the semipro baseball circuit. In 1905 he was signed by Clark Griffith, the manager of the New York Highlanders, but he was only the batting practice catcher, never playing in any games.[2]

More than most businesses, success in baseball has depended on personal relationships. No connection proved more valuable than Krichell's friendship with Yankees future general manager Edward Grant Barrow. The two men first worked together in 1910 when Barrow was the manager of the Montreal Royals in the International League and Krichell was a catcher. They stayed in touch when Krichell made the Majors the following season as a backup on the St. Louis Browns. His big league career was brief and undistinguished: two seasons, eighty-three games, .222 batting average, .259 slugging average, 0 home runs, 16 RBIs. It was shortened when Tigers star Ty Cobb slid into him while he was blocking the plate. "When you talk about explosion, that was one Cobb must have loaded with TNT," he remembered. Krichell never fully recovered from the knee injury, learning the lesson, "Never stand in front of the plate when Cobb was roaring for home."[3]

Despite his limited playing time with the Browns, Krichell enjoyed being one of the boys. One of his few regrets was that he was denied a chance to be just the third player to catch a ball thrown from the Washington Monument. During one visit of the Browns to the nation's capital, teammate William Henry "Hap" Hogan threw down three dozen baseballs at Krichell, who was crouched at the monument's base. Overwhelmed by the barrage of balls, he failed to catch any, and the Senators' Gabby Street and the White Sox's Billy Sullivan remained the only catchers to successfully pull off this prank.[4]

Krichell continued to play ball in the Minors for a few more seasons. On April 22, 1914, opening day in Baltimore for the International League Orioles, Krichell was catching for Buffalo's Bisons when Babe Ruth made his debut in pro baseball as a pitcher. Before the Babe's first professional at bat, Krichell and starting pitcher George "Slats" McConnell intentionally walked the eighth hitter in the lineup to pitch to the raw rookie batting ninth. McConnell quickly put Ruth in a 0-2 hole, but when he tried to slip a fast ball by Ruth, Krichell remembered, "The kid hauled off and knocked the hands off a clock behind the right field fence."[5] At the plate, Krichell did succeed in getting a single and double off Ruth. Interestingly, playing second base for Buffalo that day was Joe McCarthy, the future manager of the Yankees during their long dynasty from the mid-1930s through the early 1940s.

Krichell, who retired as a player after the 1918 season, coached at New York University in 1919, in addition to tending bar not far from Yankee Stadium. The college job lasted only a year, and with Prohibition looming, bartending hardly seemed secure. So he jumped at the chance to become a Red Sox coach under manager Ed Barrow. In 1918, with Babe Ruth starring on the mound and at the plate, Barrow had won the World Series over the Cubs in his first year leading Boston. In 1919, despite Ruth's leading the league in home runs, slugging, RBIs, and runs scored, the Red Sox fell to sixth place, five games under .500 and twenty and a half games behind the pennant-winning White Sox (soon to reach infamy in the World Series as the Black Sox). After Ruth was sold in January 1920 by owner Harry Frazee to the Yankees, Barrow and Krichell worked for a Red Sox team that crawled up to fifth place but was still nine games under .500 and a whopping twenty-six games behind eventual world champion Cleveland. In Babe Ruth's first year as a Yankee, he responded with a record-breaking 54 home runs—25 more than he belted in his last season in Boston—but the Yankees finished third, three games behind Cleveland and one behind the White Sox.

After the 1920 season, Yankees owner Jacob Ruppert hired Ed Barrow as team business manager—the term *general manager* did not become in vogue until later in the 1920s—to replace Harry Sparrow, who had died during the season. Barrow quickly hired Krichell to take charge of a skeletal scouting staff, the most notable member being Bob Connery, the man who signed Rogers Hornsby and who had come from the Cardinals to New York with manager Miller Huggins. Barrow and Krichell soon clicked as a remarkable front office tandem. From 1921 until his death in June 1957, Krichell was as instrumental to the coming Yankees' success as any of the players, coaches, or managers. One of his ironclad axioms was "If you don't make mistakes, you haven't got the nerve to pick up a ballplayer."[6] He wasn't afraid to speak his mind from his earliest days on his new job. At the Yankees 1921 spring training camp in New Orleans, Krichell ridiculed the current pitching staff as so weak-armed that in his day he "could have handled most of them barehanded."[7]

His appraisal was actually a little harsh and not accurate. The 1921 Yankees received 27 victories from Carl Mays and a combined 33 from Waite Hoyt and Bob Shawkey. Babe Ruth broke his own home run record with 59, as the team won the first of three pennants in a row, each time facing their local rivals, the New York Giants, in the World Series. Pugnacious Giants manager John McGraw scorned the rise of the Yankees, his mere tenant at the Giants' home park, the Polo Grounds. He dismissed Babe Ruth as an overrated slugger and insisted that the National League's Rogers Hornsby was a better all-around hitter than Ruth.

In 1921 and 1922 McGraw won bragging rights by winning the World Series. In 1921 the Giants prevailed five games to three in the last year when the competition was best five-out-of-nine. In 1922 they won four games to none with one tie. In 1923, the season when the Yankees opened majestic Yankee Stadium barely a half mile from the Polo Grounds, McGraw didn't bother to even dress his team in the new ballpark. He chose to get his charges ready for battle in the team's home surroundings.[8] To McGraw's regret, the tide turned in October when the Yankees beat the Giants in six games. McGraw returned to the World Series in 1924, but the Giants lost to the Washington Senators in seven games. He never returned to the Fall Classic, retiring due to illness during the 1932 season. He watched his successor Bill Terry win the 1933 Series over Washington and died in February 1934 at the age of sixty.

Although he never attended college, Paul Krichell would become famous for his college signings. The trail to his most legendary acquisition happened almost by accident on a late April spring afternoon in 1923. Aware that no college baseball games had been scheduled that day in any of the five boroughs of New York City, Krichell noted that Columbia was playing at Rutgers in New Brunswick, New Jersey, about an hour away by train. When he heard the sound of Lou Gehrig's bat launching two home runs against the Scarlet Knights in a 9–4 victory, Krichell experienced the kind of epiphany that scouts dream about. After the game, Krichell traveled back to New York with Columbia baseball coach Andy Coakley, a former Major League pitcher who won 18 games for Connie Mack's pennant-winning 1905 Philadelphia A's and was 58-59 with a 2.35 ERA in a nine-year MLB career. "Gehrig is just another lefty pitcher," Coakley said. He added matter-of-factly that the shy, muscular young athlete played first base and right field when he wasn't pitching.[9]

Krichell made it a point to be in the crowd a few days later when Columbia hosted New York University at South Field on the campus east of West 116th Street and Broadway. Gehrig didn't disappoint; he blasted another mammoth blast that legend says landed close to a college dean walking near the steps of Low Library over 450 feet away. Krichell's mind was made up about signing the slugger. A few days later, Coakley introduced Gehrig to Barrow at the Yankee business offices just south of Central Park. When the executive took one look at Gehrig's tree-trunk legs, he whispered the words to Krichell that many an executive in baseball history would utter about a promising prospect: "Don't let him get away without signing a contract!" Gehrig was ready to turn pro because he knew his working-class parents could use the reported $1,500 bonus money. He was assigned to the Hartford team in the tough Class A Colonial League.

Gehrig was no stranger to Hartford. Two years earlier, he played in the Connecticut state capital under the assumed name of Lou Lewis. It was a bone given to him when Giants coach Art Devlin convinced manager John McGraw to give the youngster a chance against tough competition. McGraw had been unimpressed with Gehrig after he booted some balls at first base during a Polo Grounds tryout, but Devlin knew about Gehrig's mammoth power that had caused a sensation when he blasted home runs out of Wrigley Field in a New York–Chicago high school All-Star Game. Devlin also saw with his own eyes the power display Gehrig put on during his Polo Grounds tryout.[10]

Not used to being away from home, Gehrig didn't perform well at Hartford in 1921. When coach Coakley learned about the Lou Lewis charade, he rushed up to Connecticut and hurriedly brought him back to New York. Coakley knew that Gehrig's college eligibility would be forfeited for accepting money as a pro. (Branch Rickey and numerous other college players, including Coakley himself at Holy Cross and Columbia's other future Hall of Famer, Eddie Collins, had lost eligibility when discovered to have taken money to play.) According to Tara Krieger's thorough essays for SABR's Bio-Project series, Coakley wrote Columbia's rival coaches about the infraction and asked for their understanding. They accepted his idea of a suspension of Gehrig for the 1922 season. During that time, Gehrig's body filled out and he kept sharp training at a local gymnasium in his largely German American Upper East Side Manhattan neighborhood. When it was time for his only Columbia season in 1923, Gehrig erupted with 7 home runs, a .444 batting average (28 for 63), and a superlative .937 slugging average. Pitching in one game, he struck out seventeen Williams College batters, a school record that as of 2022 had been only tied, never broken.[11]

When he returned to Hartford to start his pro career in 1923, homesickness remained a problem, and once again he got off to a slow start. Like all great scouts, Krichell kept close tabs on his player's development. He made a special trip to see Gehrig and relax the anxious player. Krichell's presence undoubtedly helped because Gehrig soon was demonstrating the power tools that already had members of the sporting press dubbing him "the eastern Babe Ruth" and "the greatest college player since George Sisler." Gehrig's final 1923 Hartford numbers lived up to the billing. In sixty-nine games, he hit .304 with 24 home runs, 13 doubles, and 8 triples.

Krichell also took notice of the positive influence on Gehrig of Harry Hesse, his teammate and roommate who always offered an encouraging word and reportedly found blind dates for the shy slugger.[12] A first baseman and outfielder, Harry Hesse would never make the Major Leagues. But Krichell had found a lifelong friend, a baseball lifer who became a highly regarded amateur coach in the New York metropolitan area. During World War II, Krichell hired Hesse as a scout, a position he held for the rest of his life. Among Hesse's later signings for the Yankees were pitcher Roland Sheldon, who won a total of twenty-three games for Yankee pennant-winners in 1961, 1962, and 1964, and outfielder Tom Shopay, who made the Majors as a reserve with the Orioles.[13]

Lou Gehrig made his Major League debut late in 1923; in thirteen games, he was 11-26 at the plate. After an outstanding full season in the Minors in 1924, he returned to the Bronx and in ten games was 6-12. He made the varsity out of spring training in 1925, but with Wally Pipp established at first base, it looked like Gehrig would only be a backup. Fate stepped in when batting-practice pitcher Charlie Caldwell, another Krichell signing, a Princeton graduate, and later Princeton's football coach, beaned Pipp.[14] Gehrig took over first base on May 3, 1925, and would not relinquish the position for the next 2,130 regular-season games. He would become a huge part of seven pennant winners and five world champions.

Owner Ruppert, business manager Barrow, and chief scout Krichell were getting used to winning after three pennants in a row and finally breaking through with the 1923 World Series triumph. Legend has it that Ruppert once said that his ideal game would be for the Yankees to score eight runs in the first inning and then pull slowly ahead. He probably never said that, but baseball historian Steve Steinberg believes that Ruppert grew so nervous during close games that he may have wished for routs most of the time. The Yankees' leaders were not happy when they lost the 1924 pennant to the Senators, finishing in second place three games behind Washington. They felt humiliated when the Yankees plummeted to seventh place in 1925.

A bad omen appeared on the Yankees' circuitous ride north from 1925 spring training. Babe Ruth felt unwell as the train left Florida, and he took a turn for the worse on the leg from Chattanooga to Asheville, North Carolina. It is a measure of Paul Krichell's stature in the organization that he was dispatched by Barrow to accompany the ailing slugger on his way back to New York for medical treatment. The press dubbed Ruth's ailment "the stomach ache felt around the world," its cause probably a combination of the Babe's enormous culinary and sexual appetites. Millions of his fans thought he might be dying. The 1920s may have been called the Golden Age of Sports and the Roaring Twenties, but it was also a time of meteoric rises and falls in popular culture. Silent film comedian Fatty Arbuckle plummeted from fame and fortune after he was charged with manslaughter in the death of a model at a Labor Day party he was hosting in San Francisco. (It didn't matter that he was eventually acquitted and received a rare apology from the jury.) In August 1926, silent movie star Rudolph Valentino died suddenly at the age of thirty-one, and millions of his fans, mainly women, went into mourning.

Unsurprisingly, when word came of the Babe's serious illness, Ruth idolaters feared that the end might be near for the twenty-nine-year-old, hard-living slugger. When his train arrived in New York, thousands jammed Penn Station trying to peek at the ailing hero. To spirit the player away from the crowd and into the safety of a hospital, Krichell and railroad officials concocted a plan to remove bars from car windows in a car at the back of the train so the Babe could be lifted on a stretcher out of sight of his anxious fans. The first stretcher was inadequate, but a second one was found, and he was lifted onto a freight elevator to the street and in an ambulance to the hospital. Ruth was hospitalized for several weeks and didn't return to the lineup until June 1, the day that Lou Gehrig started his consecutive games streak.[15]

Ruth still wound up the 1925 season with 25 home runs. The following year, Ruth, fully recovered, had another spectacular season for the 1926 Yankees, leading the American League with 47 home runs, 153 RBI, 139 runs scored, and 144 walks. The Bronx Bombers were to begin another three-year pennant reign. Although they lost a hard-fought seven-game World Series to the Cardinals, they swept the Pirates in 1927 and avenged their 1926 loss by sweeping the Cardinals in 1928. The Murderer's Row of Ruth and Gehrig, batting third and fourth, was now augmented by a rookie batting fifth. His emergence exemplified another one of Paul Krichell's great rules of scouting: Don't be afraid of taking a chance on a player. If you see a prospect who possesses a great tool even with other weaknesses, don't shy away.

The new addition was second baseman Tony Lazzeri, who was purchased from the Salt Lake City Bees after a sensational 1925 Pacific Coast League season. He compiled astounding numbers even if you consider the season was 197 games played half of the time in the high altitude of Utah: .355 batting average, 60 home runs, 222 RBIs, 202 runs, and 39 stolen bases. Ed Holly, another former Red Sox scout that Barrow brought to the Yankees, was one of the first to alert the team about Lazzeri. When word came that the prospect had recently hit a slump in which he struck out fourteen times in one week, Barrow ordered Krichell to hasten to Utah to file his own report. Remember that this was an age when strikeouts were considered a major embarrassment for a player and detrimental to a team's offense.

Once he evaluated Lazzeri, Krichell was convinced that all Tony needed was to learn the strike zone to become a star in the Major Leagues. The scout was attracted by the gritty makeup of the working-class youngster from San Francisco. Antonio Pezzalo Lazzeri was in his mother Angelina's womb when his parents emigrated from a small town in Tuscany via Genoa in March 1903. Born on December 6, 1903, he was the only child of Agostino and Guilia Lazzeri; his father's occupation, according to Lazzeri's thorough biographer Lawrence Baldassaro, was listed on immigration papers as "peasant."[16] Young Lazzeri showed great athletic promise as both a baseball player and a boxer, but he did not perform well in the classroom and left high school at the age of fifteen. He played local amateur baseball, but the Major Leagues seemed far away. He therefore started training to follow in his father's footsteps as a boilermaker.

His breakthrough season at Salt Lake changed his modest plans. Ed Holly and Paul Krichell were now solidly in his corner. So was Bob Connery, who had become the owner-operator of the St. Paul (Minnesota) Saints in the American Association but still served as an informal adviser to the Yankee brain trust. He, too, forecast stardom for Lazzeri.[17] The Yankees knew that the prospect suffered from epilepsy, a serious neurological disorder characterized by unpredictable seizures. The condition caused the Cubs, who had options on Salt Lake City players, to shy away. The Reds also thought about signing the talented infielder but passed for the same reason. It was the thorough Yankees that sent Holly to examine Lazzeri's medical records in San Francisco. When the scout reported that no other cases of epilepsy were in the Lazzeri family, Barrow and Krichell urged owner Ruppert to buy his contract for $50,000 and two marginal players under Yankees control who never made the Major Leagues. Using the blunt language of a less politically correct time, Krichell later told prominent sportswriter J. G. Taylor Spink, "Tony may have had the fits. But he never had them between two and six, and how many fits did he give A.L. pitchers through the years?"[18]

Converted to second base from shortstop by manager Miller Huggins during 1926 spring training, Lazzeri held down the position for most of the next twelve seasons, playing almost every day. He would be part of six pennant winners and five World Series champions. He finished his career with a .292 batting average, .467 slugging average, 178 home runs, and 1,191 RBIs, numbers that got him elected by the veterans committee to the Hall of Fame in 1991. One of the likely reasons for the delay in Lazzeri's enshrinement was that he never opened up to the press. Getting something out of him was "like mining coal with a nail file," complained one writer.[19] In contrast, he was a very popular teammate, relaxing players in the clubhouse with his antics and pranks. Legend has it he once nailed Babe Ruth's shoes to the floor. Lazzeri's teammates knew the seriousness of his condition, and they always arranged for a support group during road trips in case of a sudden seizure.

It was the same principle of taking a chance on great tools and great makeup despite a possibly significant flaw that led Barrow and Krichell nine years later to encourage West Coast scouts Joe Devine and Bill Essick to keep following Joe DiMaggio. He was burning up the Pacific Coast League in 1934 when he incurred a mysterious off-field knee injury midseason. It considerably cut the upwards of $75,000 asking price of San Francisco Seals owner Charlie

Graham. The official story about DiMaggio's injury was that he slipped getting out of a taxicab while on his way to or from visiting his sister.[20] More skeptical observers surmised that hijinks associated with teenaged carousing might have been the real reason. Whatever the cause, young DiMaggio was out of action for a few weeks, and when he returned prematurely, he collapsed in the dugout and was out for the rest of the 1934 season.

Most teams lost interest in the injured prospect, but not Essick and Devine. Barrow ordered them to accompany DiMaggio on a visit to a Los Angeles orthopedic specialist, who assured them that the injury was not career-threatening. For the cost of what was reportedly $25 for four treatments that broke adhesions in other areas of the prospect's legs, the Yankees got themselves a $25,000 bargain.[21] As the Yankees often did when signing high school players, they agreed to let DiMaggio return to the Seals in 1935. It gave Seals owner Graham another year of DiMaggio's services, enabled Joe to get another year of seasoning, and allowed him to live at home, to the delight of his mother. DiMaggio arrived in the Bronx in 1936 at the start of another Yankees' dynasty, four straight World Series–winning seasons. Before he retired after the 1951 season, DiMaggio would be in center field for seven more pennants and six World Series titles.

In hiring California scouts Bill Essick and Joe Devine, the Yankees brought into the fold two very experienced and accomplished baseball men. William Earl Essick was born on December 18, 1880, in Grand Ridge, Illinois, located about eighty-five miles north of Chicago. The son of a grocer, he was gifted as both a baseball pitcher and a classical pianist. He majored in music at Knox College in Galesburg, Illinois, while starring on the baseball team. He was a good enough musician to play the piano at his graduation.[22] Essick chose baseball as a career, and in his first full Minor League season in 1905, he pitched 466 innings for a poor Portland team and finished with a 13-23 record. He was reportedly nicknamed "Vinegar Bill" because his name was an Americanized version of the German word *Essig*, meaning "vinegar."

While playing in Oregon, he met his future wife Eula Bennett, who was an opera singer. In 1906 he was purchased by the Cincinnati Reds, but he only pitched 61 innings in his brief two-year Major League career. He finished with a 2-4 record and a somewhat impressive 2.95 ERA, though he gave up

62 hits, walked 24, and fanned one less. He soon realized that his future lay in coaching and managing. He developed an important friendship with Reds owner Garry Herrmann, who, as a member of baseball's ruling triumvirate, the National Commission, provided Essick with many contacts within the game. In return, Essick tipped off Herrmann about promising Minor League players, including future Hall of Fame Cincinnati outfielder Edd Roush.[23]

From 1919 to 1922, Essick managed the Los Angeles–area Vernon Tigers of the Pacific Coast League to four straight pennants. Betting scandals swirled around the PCL in addition to the Major Leagues, but he kept the Tigers on top. Early on, he developed a good business relationship with the Yankees. In 1919 he engineered a deal that sent outfielder Bob Meusel to New York for four players and a reported $50,000 in cash. Starting in 1923, however, Essick's team fell out of contention. After a particularly bad 1925 season, he sensed that his ride was coming to an end. Knowing that the Yankees were upset at their fall to seventh place in the same season, he arranged a meeting with Ed Barrow. He was quickly hired to start scouting in 1926 and remained a vital Yankee scout until shortly before his death in 1951.

Essick's first scouting recommendations were not overwhelming successes. In 1927 the Yankees purchased shortstop Lyn Lary and second baseman Jimmie Reese from Charlie Graham's San Francisco Seals for the whopping price of $125,000, most of it for the highly touted Lary, who never established himself in New York. Lary did play for twelve years in the Major Leagues, collecting 1,239 hits with a .269 batting average, .369 on-base percentage, and .372 slugging average, but he was only a Yankees regular in the non-pennant-winning seasons of 1930 and 1931.

Jimmie Reese, born James Herman Solomon in New York City in 1901, collected only 742 at bats in a short three-year career, but he became a baseball lifer. His coaching and scouting career lasted into his nineties. Reese—who adopted his mother's maiden name—became one of the most adept fungo hitters in baseball history. He used a special thin bat, flat on one side, that could hit not only grounders but line drives at fielders. When with the Yankees, he roomed with and often traveled with Babe Ruth. As a California Angels coach in his later years, Reese made such an impact on Nolan Ryan that the pitcher named his second son Reese Ryan. One of the truly beloved people in baseball, Reese exuded optimism in the difficult game of baseball where someone must lose every day. He preached and practiced the gospel of hard work, always ending with the mantra "You never know, the best of your life [may be] five minutes ahead in this game."[24]

In 1929 Essick struck pay dirt with the signing of high school southpaw Vernon Louis "Lefty" Gomez. Gomez hailed from the aptly named Northern California ranching town of Rodeo that was home to many cowboys. Rodeo was only thirty miles from San Francisco, but the Golden Gate Bridge had not yet been built. Gomez's part of the country was so remote, his daughter Vernona Gomez—author of an indispensable biography of her father, *Lefty: An American Odyssey*—wrote in a March 2021 email that the young pitcher only knew about the Yankees from reading issues of the *New York Times* that speeding trains dropped off on the railroad platform on their way to Oakland.[25]

Scouting Gomez and others in the area required the determination of an able and passionate scout like Bill Essick. When Essick saw the youngster pitch in a local semipro game, his eyes lit up. He was only carrying 125 pounds on his six-foot-one body, but the scout projected accurately that Gomez would grow into his body. He finished his thirteen-year career with the Yankees with a 189-102 record and was undefeated in six World Series decisions with a 2.86 ERA, better than his regular-season 3.34 ERA. He was elected to the Hall of Fame in 1972.

Gomez's sense of humor loosened up his teammates, and, unlike Tony Lazzeri, he was very popular with the press and public. In one of his first World Series appearances, he asked the umpire for time so he could follow the flight of an airplane over Yankee Stadium. Gomez was genuinely interested in flying and ultimately became a licensed pilot. He possessed a genuine wit that sportswriters ate up. "I was never nervous when I had the ball," he said, "but when I threw it I was scared to death." His needle was gentle enough that he could even get away with tweaking Paul Krichell when the scout made a rare appearance at the ballpark. Gomez cracked that the scout was really over seven feet tall but his bowed legs made him look closer to five feet.[26]

In 1930 Bill Essick signed another Yankee fixture of the future, shortstop Frank Crosetti. Born in San Francisco on October 4, 1910, the younger son of an immigrant fisherman from Genoa, Italy, Crosetti—like Tony Lazzeri—was not interested in formal schooling. He dropped out at age sixteen and started to make a name for himself on the local semipro scene. When Essick spotted him playing for the San Francisco Seals, he saw him as a superior talent on both sides of the ball. He hit over .300 in both 1930 and 1931, and Essick convinced the Yankees to pay more than $30,000 for his contract. As with Joe DiMaggio's signing a few years ahead, Essick recommended that Crosetti play another season with the Seals to get another year's experience under his belt. He never developed into the hitter that Essick expected, finishing his seventeen-year, 1,682-game career with a .245 batting average and .354 slugging average, but his defense and leadership were a big part of the Yankees' success. As a player, he cashed six World Series–winner checks in seven tries and added ten more as a third base coach.[27]

The year 1931 would be very significant in the history of the Yankees, but not for anything that happened on the field. The Bronx Bombers missed the World Series for the third straight year because of Connie Mack's Philadelphia Athletics' juggernaut led by Robert "Lefty" Grove on the mound, Al Simmons in the outfield, and Mickey Cochrane behind the plate. The first notable event in Yankee off-the-field history was the hiring of Joseph Vincent McCarthy as manager. Miller Huggins had died late in the 1929 season, and former Yankees pitcher Bob Shawkey's 86-76 record as manager in 1930 was eighteen games behind the Athletics. McCarthy was available because he was fired by the Cubs during the 1930 season even though he led them to the World Series in 1929. In another example of Paul Krichell's behind-the-scenes stature, he was told by Barrow to alert McCarthy that Jacob Ruppert wanted to interview him after the 1930 World Series.[28]

The second important hiring came after the 1931 World Series when George Weiss came aboard as the first Yankees farm director. Ed Barrow was skeptical about the farm system idea, but owner Ruppert was all in. Ruppert directed Weiss to beat Branch Rickey's Cardinals at their own game by developing a trimmer but more effective player development program.

Around the same time, the Yankees hired Joe Devine as a West Coast scouting supervisor to work with Bill Essick. With the move, the Yankees nabbed a first-rate scout and player developer who already signed four future Hall of Famers for the Pirates.

Joseph Vincent Devine, born in Oakland, California, on March 3, 1892, took to the game at an early age. Like many scouts, he quickly became active as a player and coach on the East Bay amateur baseball scene, but he was a rarity in that he actually played very little pro baseball. Although invited to Red Sox spring training in 1917, he went to work in a Seattle shipyard when the United States entered World War I. He was soon asked to manage the workplace team.[29] After the war, Devine found many opportunities to manage Minor League teams in the Pacific Northwest and western Canada. Pirates owner Barney Dreyfuss, whose team regularly contended for National League honors with the Giants and Cubs, took notice and hired him as a scout after the 1924 season. Almost immediately, Devine delivered a bonanza to Pittsburgh when he signed three future Hall of Famers from the San Francisco sandlots: brothers and outfielders Paul and Lloyd Waner and shortstop Joe Cronin.

The Waners were raised in the small town of Harrah, outside Oklahoma City, by a well-to-do farmer who was not enamored with baseball as a profession. He wanted his sons to get an education. Paul was attending nearby Ada State Teachers' College, with thoughts of ultimately going to Harvard Law School, when a San Francisco Seals scout liked what he saw in Waner as a pitcher and convinced him to turn pro.[30] When Waner suffered an arm injury from overuse in one Seals game, he thought his career might be over. Yet he stayed around shagging flies for Major Leaguers who were working out prior to the regular season. When given a chance to take batting practice, Waner's performance lit up scouts' eyes, including those of Joe Devine, who convinced the Pirates that he was worth the Seals' reported $100,000 price tag. Paul Waner weighed only 125 pounds as a nineteen-year-old prospect and never added more than twenty-five pounds to his five-foot-nine frame, but Devine accurately projected that his sweet level left-handed swing would play well in the Majors.

Although the Pirates were swept by the Yankees in the World Series, in 1927 the Waners were a key part of Pittsburgh's successful National League championship season. Despite the crushing loss, Paul and Lloyd were given a parade back home in Oklahoma. Reminiscing to Lawrence Ritter for an expanded edition of his classic oral history, *The Glory of Their Times*, Waner explained the reason for Harrah's celebration for a losing team. There had been a bet in town that the Waners would outhit Ruth and Gehrig in the World Series, and the brothers won, .367 to .357.[31]

Giants manager John McGraw did not believe in the farm system and hired only a few scouts without introducing a real scouting system. Yet Paul Waner's success against the Giants infuriated him. "That little punk don't even know how to put on a uniform but he's removed three of my pitchers with line drives this week," McGraw groused after one loss to Pittsburgh.[32] He added that his scouts might not have signed Christy Mathewson if they saw him. Paul Waner went on to collect 3,152 hits, only the eighth player at the time to reach that elite status of 3,000 hits, and retired with a career .333 batting average, .404 on-base percentage, and .473 slugging average. Younger brother Lloyd collected 2,459 hits, with a .316 career batting average and .394 slugging average. Paul Waner, after retirement as a player, became a highly regarded batting coach and occasional scout. He also operated a batting cage in the Pittsburgh area. Pirates shortstop Dick Groat, who won the 1960 National League batting championship and MVP in their World Series–winning season, always praised Waner for providing good hitting tips.[33]

From the moment Joe Devine laid eyes on Joe Cronin on San Francisco–area playing fields, he saw a player who lived for baseball and would do anything to reach and excel in the Major Leagues. Devine outbid the Seals for the shortstop and brought him into the Pittsburgh fold, along with another infielder, Ed Montague, who never made the Majors. But as a scout for the Giants, Montague was part of the group recommending the signing of Willie Mays.[34] (Montague's son, Ed Jr., became a longtime National League umpire.) Joe Cronin played only briefly with the Pirates but reached stardom in the early 1930s with the Senators, where his father-in-law, Washington owner Clark Griffith, traded him to the Red Sox because Griffith faced cash shortages during the Great Depression. Cronin went on to become general manager of the Red Sox and later president of the American League.[35] Before Devine left the Pirates, he delivered a fourth future Hall of Famer to Pittsburgh, outfielder Joseph Floyd "Arky" Vaughan, who arrived in the Majors as a twenty-year-old in 1932. He enjoyed a fourteen-year career, mainly with the Pirates, with 2,103 hits, a .318 batting average, .453 slugging average, and an almost unfathomably efficient walk-strikeout ratio of 937:276.

Joe Devine was available to the Yankees for the same reason as Bill Essick had been a few years earlier. Devine was managing the San Francisco Mission Reds in the Pacific Coast League, but the team went into a tailspin, and the owners, growing impatient, looked for a scapegoat. Devine jumped at the chance of working under Paul Krichell. Devine carefully followed Joe DiMaggio's Minor League development, as noted, and he worked well with Krichell. The Yankees were on the verge of their greatest dynasty to date. It did not start immediately. In his second year managing in New York, Joe McCarthy did lead the Yankees to a 1932 World Series sweep over the Cubs, but the Senators won the pennant in 1933. The Tigers, led by player-manager Mickey Cochrane, who had been sold by Connie Mack because he couldn't afford to pay him, won back-to-back pennants in 1934 and 1935 and the 1935 World Series over the Cubs.

It was no coincidence that the Yankees started a streak of four straight championships when Joe DiMaggio arrived in the Bronx in 1936. Nor was it an accident that they stayed on top, because Barrow and Krichell understood the truth of Branch Rickey's axiom: "It is better to trade a player one year too early than one year too late." Sensing that Tony Lazzeri was beginning to decline, Bill Essick zeroed in on Joe Gordon, whose career he was following as a sensational high school player. Born in Los Angeles, Gordon moved with his family to Portland, Oregon. Like so many notable scouts, Essick actively promoted youth baseball leagues and always put in a good word for the Yankees. He kept tabs on Joe Gordon as he enrolled at the University of Oregon, where he starred again. Essick wooed Gordon away from college by assuring him that his time in the Minors would be short. After playing for the Yankees' top farm team, the Newark Bears, in 1937 (which posted a 109-43 record with a .717 winning percentage, third best in Minor League history), Gordon replaced the released Lazzeri as a durable regular in 1938.[36]

Gordon played for eleven seasons, and his career numbers didn't jump off the page: .268 batting average, .357 on-base percentage, .446 slugging average. But his power numbers for a second baseman in his time, 253 home runs and 975 RBIs, were solid, and he was an excellent defender who played in six World Series, winning four as a Yankee and one as a member of the 1948 Cleveland Indians. He was traded to Cleveland before the 1947 season for pitcher Allie Reynolds, who developed into an indispensable Yankee arm as both starter and reliever. Gordon was posthumously elected to the Hall of Fame in 1992.

Not long after Gordon's signing, Essick took on additional responsibilities scouting in the region of his birth, the Midwest. He became a familiar presence at high school and American Legion games. A local sportswriter described him as "a symphony in brown" wearing a brown suit and brown shoes and straw hat.[37] In 1938 Essick traveled to Lawrence, Kansas, to convince high school graduate Ralph Houk to forgo college play at the local University of Kansas. After rising to the rank of major during World War II, the only Major Leaguer to attain that status, Houk became a backup catcher to Yogi Berra on the post–World War II Yankees. He parlayed an eight-year career with only 158 at bats and a .272 batting average and .322 slugging average into the Yankees managership after Casey Stengel's forced retirement. After four straight World Series appearances from 1961 through 1964, with two championships in his first two tries, Houk became Yankees general manager and later managed the Tigers and the Red Sox.

Meanwhile, up in Northern California, Joe Devine's local youth team, the Kanely Yankees, were becoming a fertile ground for future Yankees talent. Devine made sure that the Yankees supplied plenty of hand-me-down pinstripe uniforms that, of course, made a great impression on the eager hopefuls. The story of the signing of a sensational San Francisco high school infielder, Robert William "Bobby" Brown, is a classic example of the powerful attraction of the Yankee brand. Many teams were eager to sign Brown, and Reds scout Charles Chapman even invited him to Cincinnati for a workout and then a road trip with the team. But Brown had his heart set on signing with the Yankees. After service in World War II, the left-handed-hitting third baseman became a key part of four World Series champions, 1947 and 1949–51. His .439 batting average and .707 slugging average in seventeen postseason games ranks high in baseball annals. In 1952 he served in the Korean War and then in 1954 retired at the age of thirty-one to pursue his medical career; later, he became a noted Dallas, Texas, cardiologist and president of the American League. He died at the age of ninety-six in 2021.[38]

In addition to Bobby Brown, Devine's Kanely Yankees turned out a remarkable number of other Major Leaguers who shone after World War II, among them future Yankees second basemen Jerry Coleman and Billy Martin, third baseman Andy Carey, versatile middle infielder Gil McDougald, and backup catcher Charlie Silvera, who later enjoyed a long career as a Chicago Cubs scout. A bevy of other Devine signings went on to fine Major League careers with teams other than the Yankees. Among them were outfielder Jackie Jensen with the Senators and Red Sox, catcher Gus Triandos with the Orioles, and pitcher Milo Candini with the Senators and Phillies. Probably Devine's favorite among the group that had Major League success other than with the Yankees was southpaw Bill Wight.

Devine saw great promise in the young left-hander from Rio Vista, sixty miles inland from San Francisco. He attended McClymonds High in Oakland (where, after World War II, such future stars as Frank Robinson and Vada Pinson and basketball's Bill Russell would play for coach George Powles, who later became a bird-dog scout for the Reds). Devine wooed Wight away from playing for the University of California, Berkeley, and nurtured his way through the Yankees' farm system. World War II interrupted Wight's advancement, but he served stateside at Oakland's St. Mary's College naval base, where he shone on a team he co-managed, with future Hall of Famer Charlie Gehringer, that featured star shortstop Bill Rigney, later New York Giants utility infielder and San Francisco Giants manager. Wight developed an exceptional pickoff move to first base that awed baseball people on every level.[39]

Unfortunately, Bill Wight never mastered the essential art of control. His wildness led the Yankees to trade him to the White Sox on the eve of 1948 spring training. Chicago trained in Arizona, but Wight had already started driving from his California home to the Yankees camp in Saint Petersburg, Florida. The *Chicago Tribune* tried to alert the pitcher with the headline "Note to Bill Wight: Get in Reverse and Head to California." The SOS didn't reach the pitcher, and only when Wight pulled into Clearwater twenty miles from Saint Petersburg did he receive the news that he would have to head back west to Arizona.[40]

Wight wound up a twelve-year career for eight Major League teams with a lifetime record of 77-99, 3.95 ERA, and an unimpressive 714:574 walk-strikeout ratio. Yet Joe Devine thought so much of his baseball intelligence that not long after he was traded, he nominated him to become president of the Yankee Alumni Association. Devine created the group, whose previous president was Charlie Silvera. "Once a Yankee, Always a Yankee," Devine explained about his decision to tap Bill Wight. At a January 1951 San Francisco banquet, Wight voiced his deep appreciation for Devine's counsel the year he was traded. "In June I was despondent, in July my wife was telling me how to pitch, by August I was listening to her," Wight said.[41] (Bill Wight became an outstanding scout for the expansion Houston Colt .45s, signing Joe Morgan for Houston and later Dusty Baker and several others for the Atlanta Braves, the stories of which will appear later in this saga.)

Tragically, Joe Devine would not live to enjoy another banquet. In late August 1951 while on a scouting trip in Idaho, he turned around from the driver's seat of his car to adjust the back seat. He broke his arm, and, before long, an infection set in when pieces of the bone got into his bloodstream. He was flown in Yankees co-owner Del Webb's private plane to a hospital in San Francisco. He rallied for a while and felt good enough to go home. Like any baseball lifer, he missed scouting at a ballpark, so he headed to a San Francisco Seals game but fell ill again at the park. He died on September 30, 1951, at the age of fifty-six.[42]

Even before the Yankees solidified their scouting stronghold on the Pacific Coast, the team was making inroads in the South. In 1927 Johnny Nee came aboard. Born in Thayer, Missouri on January 15, 1890, Nee never reached the Majors as a player, but by the 1920s he was already a player-manager in the Minors. In his first weeks on the job with the Yankees, he recommended Bill Dickey, a strapping six-foot-one, 175-pound catcher for the Jackson Generals in the Class A Southern League. "I will quit scouting if this boy doesn't make good," Nee wrote Paul Krichell with the kind of firmness and confidence that the scout loved.[43] By 1928 Dickey was in Yankee pinstripes, and starting in 1929 he caught more than a hundred games for thirteen straight seasons.

The earlier Yankee champions did not feature a dominant catcher, but Dickey would change that in a hurry. He wound up his seventeen-year career with a .313 batting average, .382 on-base percentage, .486 slugging average, 202 home runs, and 1,289 RBIs, and in 6,300 career at bats, he struck out only 289 times. Bob Feller declared that if Dickey caught for Cleveland, he would win forty-five games a year.[44] After briefly serving as a Yankees manager in 1946 when Joe McCarthy resigned, Dickey served as a Yankee coach for about a decade after his retirement and was widely credited for turning Yogi Berra into an excellent receiver. He was swiftly elected into the Hall of Fame in 1954. Though not an actor, Dickey appeared as himself in two Hollywood films of the 1940s: *Pride of the Yankees* and *The Stratton Story*.

A great example of what would today be called the power of the Yankee *brand* can be seen in Johnny Nee's spring 1932 signing of right-handed pitcher Ferdinand Spurgeon "Spud" Chandler. Born in Commerce, Georgia, on September 12, 1909, Chandler grew up in Franklin County, the same area that produced Ty Cobb. Chandler's fierce competitiveness on the playing field evoked memories of Cobb, and he didn't discourage the comparison. The Giants and Cubs were interested in signing him after high school, but he chose to enroll at the University of Georgia, where he pitched and was a triple threat in football as quarterback, runner, and kicker.

In November 1931 Chandler led the Bulldogs to a 7–6 win over New York University at Yankee Stadium. After the game, he walked to the mound and started throwing footballs through the uprights. He told the press that he wanted to get a sense of how it would feel when one day he would be throwing baseballs from the same mound. The Cubs still wanted him, but when Nee made a competitive offer, Chandler signed with the team of his dreams.[45]

Football injuries came back to haunt Chandler. He developed chronic elbow pain, and his rise through the Minor Leagues was not swift. He made the Majors early in the 1937 season, but it was hard to break into a rotation led by Lefty Gomez, Red Ruffing, and Monte Pearson. He collected three World Series checks from 1937 through 1939 without seeing any Series action. From 1940 through 1943, he became a reliable starter, improving his earned run average each year. In the wartime season of 1943, his 20-4 record and 1.64 ERA was the best combination by any pitcher since Walter Johnson.[46]

Chandler won the 1943 American League MVP in what was admittedly a weakened wartime season. Stateside military service occupied Chandler for the next two years, but he returned in 1946 to win twenty games at the age of thirty-nine. He went 9-5 with the world champion 1947 Yankees but retired before the start of the 1948 season. His 109-43 career record and .717 winning percentage are the best in Major League history for anyone with over a hundred wins.

In an interesting twist of baseball fate, Chandler started scouting in the South for the Yankees shortly after Johnny Nee left the organization to join the Phillies. Nee was hired by Robert Ruliph Carpenter Jr., the team's wealthy new owner who had purchased the franchise after Commissioner Landis, in one of his last acts before his death in late November 1944, banned prior owner William Cox for his betting and gambling activities. An heir to the DuPont Chemical Company fortune, Carpenter was beginning to throw money around in an effort to revive the moribund franchise. He bestowed a reported $65,000 bonus upon southpaw Curt Simmons and $25,000 to future Hall of Fame hurler Robin Roberts. The expenditures helped the Phillies win the 1950 pennant, but the Yankees swept them in a closely contested World Series, the first three games decided by one run, with Game Two going into extra innings before Joe DiMaggio hit the tiebreaking home run. The Phillies then fell out of contention for more than a decade; undaunted as scouts must be and always looking toward the future, however, Johnny Nee scouted for the Phillies until his death in 1957. He once voiced a trenchant scouting axiom: "May all your mistakes reach Triple-A."[47]

Spud Chandler's scouting career with the Yankees was short. By the early 1950s he joined the Cleveland organization as both scout and Minor League manager. He also became part of an informal group of four regional southern scouts who would compare notes on prospects. The others were Cincinnati's Paul Florence, the Senators' and Twins' Ellis Clary, and Chandler's onetime Yankees teammate Atley Donald.[48] Ellis Clary and Chandler shared a special bond as good old boys from Georgia. Clary hailed from Valdosta, a huge football hotbed. "They wouldn't know a baseball player from a crate of pineapples," he told me in my only encounter with him. Clary's sense of humor was so infectious that fellow scout Leon Hamilton said that he thought Ellis could even make a dog laugh. When late in his scouting career Clary suffered a heart attack on the road, he ordered Chandler to write down the mileage on the ambulance so he could report it on his expense account.[49]

Though no longer scouting for the Yankees, Spud Chandler did help his former team in the late 1950s. While serving as the Kansas City Athletics' pitching coach, he smoothed out the delivery of Ralph Terry before he was traded to the Yankees to become part of the starting rotation that played in five consecutive World Series from 1960 through 1964. Chandler finished his scouting career with the Atlanta Braves and then retired to his Georgia home where he lived until his death in 1992.[50]

Richard Atley Donald was a less flamboyant personality than Spud Chandler, but his transition from Major League pitcher to a Yankees southeastern-area scout was more fruitful. Donald's family roots were in Sumter, South Carolina, but not long after the Civil War, they moved by covered wagon to Morton, Mississippi, where he was born on August 19, 1910. When he was eighteen months old, the family, traveling most of the way by barge down the Mississippi River, relocated to Downsville, Louisiana, north of New Orleans. Young Atley developed an early liking to baseball.

He threw very hard, but Johnny Nee and most scouts were not convinced that he could ever learn to control and command his pitches. Donald went on to pitch college ball at Louisiana Tech, but his coach's enthusiastic letter to the Yankees went unanswered. Johnny Nee may not have liked Donald's stuff, but he liked his makeup. He suggested that Donald travel to the 1934 Yankees spring training camp in Saint Petersburg, Florida, and ask manager Joe McCarthy for a chance to throw batting practice. Excited by the idea, Donald hitchhiked to Saint Petersburg, where McCarthy let him pitch to Ruth, Gehrig, and Lazzeri. The skipper was impressed, comparing him to Lon Warneke of the Cubs. To add to Donald's delight, Ruth and Gehrig invited him to join them in a game of pepper, the onetime essential training exercise in which players stood in a circle with gloves poised, fielding bunts and sharper hits from a batter and then rotated to have their own turn at bat.[51]

Donald quickly signed a contract and was sent to Class C Wheeling, West Virginia, in the Piedmont League and started his climb up the loaded Yankee system. He was a big winner for the outstanding 1937 Newark Bears, but the

Yankees depth of talent kept him on the farm for another season. He arrived to stay in the Majors in 1939. In an eight-year career, not interrupted by military service because of vision problems, he wound up with an impressive 65-33 record. One day in 1939 his fastball hit the upper 90s, and then the hypercompetitive Bob Feller was clocked at nearly 100 mph on one of his throws. Feller was on his way to a Hall of Fame career. Atley Donald never fully mastered the strike zone, finishing his career with 369 walks and 369 strikeouts.

After retiring, Donald almost immediately started on a Yankees scouting career. His first notable signing was catcher Clint Courtney, whom he inked in 1949 at the Courtney family's sweet potato farm in Coushatta, Louisiana.[52] Courtney, baseball's first bespectacled receiver, played only one game for the Yankees late in 1951 before being traded to the Browns at the start of an eleven-year career as a player for second division American League teams. He went on to become a highly regarded coach in the Braves organization. Donald later signed catcher Jake Gibbs out of the University of Mississippi, where he had starred at quarterback, and outfielder–first baseman Ron Blomberg, who in 1973 became the first designated hitter in Major League Baseball.

Donald's most significant signing was the hard-throwing, slender southpaw Ron Guidry, a fellow Louisianan from Lafayette, Louisiana. He had followed Guidry's career from high school to the University of Southwestern Louisiana. Many scouts were on Guidry's trail, but Donald was the only one who knew that Guidry had not enrolled for the spring term at USL, making him eligible for the June 1971 draft. The Yankees chose him in the third round, the sixty-seventh pick in the nation. Donald hustled over to the Guidry family household to bring the southpaw into the fold.

After an evening meal with the family, the future "Louisiana Lightning" signed a contract. He needed five years of Minor League apprenticeship but wound up enjoying a fourteen-year career, finishing with an outstanding 170-91 record despite never growing more than five feet eleven and 162 pounds. For reasons never explained to him, Donald was not rehired as a scout for 1979 and lived out his years in Louisiana, passing away in 1992.[53]

As the Yankees' expanded regional scouting operation kept bearing fruit, Paul Krichell was keeping his focus on the college scene in the Northeast. He first scouted lanky right-hander Johnny Murphy at Fordham Prep in the Bronx. When he continued to shine at adjacent Fordham University, Krichell signed Murphy and oversaw his Minor League development. Murphy arrived to stay as a Yankee in 1934 and pitched for over eleven seasons with the Bronx Bombers, winning 73 of his 93 victories out of the bullpen. In the 1920s Firpo Marberry of the Washington Senators was probably baseball's first closer, but Johnny Murphy became prominent in that role from 1935 through 1943. During one spring training, irrepressible Lefty Gomez was asked how many victories he expected during the season. He answered, "Ask Murphy."[54]

Murphy's off-the-field career was noteworthy. In 1944 and 1945 he engaged in secret work on the atomic energy project in Oak Ridge, Tennessee.[55] In 1946 he played an important role as the American League player representative on baseball's first pension committee. After his retirement as player, he worked until the early 1960s in the Red Sox scouting and player development department, rising to farm director. Before their debut season in 1962, the Mets named him their first scouting director. He was general manager when the 1969 team became the first expansion franchise to win a World Series. It is not an exaggeration to say that if Murphy had not died of a heart attack in January 1970, the history of that inconsistent franchise might have been very different. He was committed to building a winning team with strong starting pitching. (When the pitching mound was lowered from sixteen to twelve inches after the 1968 season to aid the hitters who were enduring record-low batting averages, Murphy insisted that if they lower the mound to the ground, good pitching would still stop good hitting.)

Paul Krichell enjoyed considerable assistance from a fellow Yankees northeastern scout, Henry Eugene "Gene" McCann, who joined the Yankees' East Coast scouting staff in 1927. Born in Baltimore on June 13, 1875, McCann pitched for Brooklyn in the early twentieth century before a sore arm ended his career. He followed the path of many who stayed in the game—managing in the Minors and doubling as a scout, finally working full time for the Reds in 1919 and 1920. (Cincinnati's 1919 World Series triumph was obviously tainted by the Black Sox, but many believe that the Reds would have triumphed even if all the White Sox were playing to win.)

McCann built a solid connection with Dartmouth College baseball coach Jeff Tesreau to help the Yankees land another key component in their coming dynasty, infielder Robert Abial "Red" Rolfe. Born on October 17, 1908, in Penacook, New Hampshire, he was the middle child between two sisters. His father, Herbert, ran a lumber mill in town. The family traced its lineage to England in the seventeenth century; Rolfe joked that his ancestors didn't come over on the Mayflower but probably the next boat.[56] After starring in all three major sports at Penacook High School, he continued his fine play as the Big Green's shortstop. He profited from the coaching of Tesreau, who won 119 games for John McGraw's Giants.

After some Minor League apprenticeship, Rolfe arrived in the Bronx to stay in 1935. Shifted to third base by manager Joe McCarthy, he became a steady everyday presence at the hot corner in a ten-year career highlighted by five world championship teams, 1936–39 and 1941. Batting second in the powerful Yankee lineup, he scored a hundred runs or more seven consecutive seasons and wound up with career numbers of .289 batting average, .360 on-base percentage, .413 slugging average, 67 home runs, 497 RBIs, 526 walks, and 335 strikeouts.

The Yankees beat out Connie Mack's A's for Rolfe's services. Permanently consigned to second division status after his three straight World Series appearances from 1929 through 1931, Mack said enviously that if he had nine Red Rolfes on his team he could go fishing and not come back until it was time for the Series. Rolfe was blessed with an ideal temperament for a baseball player, never getting too high or too low. Some baseball observers praised him for contributing to a relaxed Yankees clubhouse by teaching the game of cribbage to his teammates. After Rolfe retired, he briefly coached for the Yankees in 1946 and then became farm director of the Tigers. He rebuilt the system from two to twelve teams and managed from 1949 through part of 1952. His 1950 team finished only three games behind the Yankees. But the Bengals couldn't sustain success in the two following seasons, and he left pro baseball. He concluded his sports career as the athletic director at his alma mater, Dartmouth. He died on July 8, 1969, from complications of an almost lifelong battle with chronic ulcerative colitis.[57]

In addition to his help in the Red Rolfe signing, McCann delivered two other college men and prominent contributors to Yankees' dynasties. In 1937 twenty-year-old left fielder Charlie Keller was signed off the University of Maryland campus in College Park. Keller was a great all-around athlete with an enormous passion to win and a formidable work ethic that placed him high on the Yankees' wish list. He was the oldest son in a family of farmers living in Middletown, Maryland, near Frederick. When he was growing up, Keller rose before dawn to milk cows and perform other farm chores. His exploits on the playing fields became well known in the area, and McCann followed him closely as he went on to the university in College Park, with McCann likely promising to pay Keller's tuition. Terrapins baseball coach Morgan Shipley compared Charlie's power to National League home run champion Hack Wilson, whom the coach had managed in the Minor Leagues. Keller didn't develop a big head because of his athletic success; he actually dug ditches on the land that became the arts and sciences building on the Maryland campus.[58]

Krichell journeyed down to the family farm for the closing, sealing the deal by placing the contract against the wall of a barn for the future star to sign it.[59] After two years at the Yankees' loaded Newark farm team, he arrived in the Bronx to stay in 1939. Because of injuries, Keller only enjoyed six seasons in which he played more than a hundred games. He still wound up with career numbers of .286 batting average, .410 on-base percentage, a very impressive .518 slugging average, and 189 home runs and 760 RBIs. He was nicknamed "King Kong" for his impressive build and long-ball prowess, but it was a label he detested. He went into the horse breeding business in his hometown after retirement. His young brother, Hal Keller, fourteen years his junior, never saw him play, but he was inspired by his career and became a prominent scout for the Washington Senators, Texas Rangers, and Seattle Mariners.

In 1941 McCann made a second significant signing, right-hander Vic Raschi from Springfield, Massachusetts. When Vic was just a high school freshman, McCann made an arrangement with the pitcher's carpenter-father, Massimino Raschi. Once again, he indicated that the Yankees would pay for Vic's college tuition if the family assured the team that they could have first crack at signing him once he felt ready to turn pro. McCann arranged for the prospect to enroll at Manhattan College (located, incidentally, in the

Bronx), but somehow the paperwork never was completed. So Raschi started at William and Mary College in Williamsburg, Virginia, in the fall of 1938 and decided to sign after the 1941 college season. He went on to become one of the three aces of the Yankees' five straight World Series champions from 1949 to 1953. Unfortunately, Gene McCann did not live to see Vic Raschi's rise to stardom, as he died in late April 1943 at the age of sixty-seven.[60]

McCann did live to see the flourishing of the Yankees' farm system under the competent administrative hand of George Weiss, which had grown to ten teams on the eve of World War II. McCann was intimately involved with the teams in the East, making sure that his signings were being taught to play the right way. The system was obviously not as huge as Rickey's St. Louis Cardinals behemoth that totaled thirty-two teams by the end of the 1930s, but it was more efficient and successful. Many observers considered the Yankees' two top teams in Newark, New Jersey, in the International League and Kansas City in the American Association better than the tail-end teams in either Major League. In a classic 1937 Little World Series between the Yankees' Newark Bears International League winners and the Cardinals' Columbus Redbirds American Association champions, the Bears roared from a three-games-to-none deficit to win the next four games and the title of the best Minor League team (at least in the eastern half of the United States).

In the summer of 1936 Weiss took another page out of the Rickey book by scheduling the Yankees' first tryout camp, with Krichell on hand to supervise it, at Yankee Stadium while the team was on the road. One player that immediately caught Krichell's eye was Phil Rizzuto, a five-foot-six, 150-pound shortstop from Brooklyn, New York. Spurned as too little by the Dodgers and the Giants, Krichell's eyes lit up when he saw Rizzuto's "quick hands, Double Play hands!" on ground balls and his quick release on throws from shortstop to first base.[61] Rizzuto required several years of seasoning in the Minor Leagues, where the Yankees' system made sure a veteran double play partner at second base could help him defensively. Starting in 1941 the Yankees found their successor to Frank Crosetti at shortstop for the next fourteen years that included seven World Series victories in nine tries and a 1985 Hall of Fame induction.

Another future Hall of Famer came out of post–World War II tryout camps. In 1946 Krichell noticed a slender five-foot-ten Eddie Ford trying to capture his attention as a first baseman. When Ford was not one of the players selected to come back for a second day of workouts, Krichell consoled the youngster. If nothing else, he hoped that he could make a Yankee fan out of a disappointed player. He told Ford that he showed promise as a pitcher and he should stick with that position. The following year, he came back to the tryout camp with a curveball that Krichell remembered as "a sweet, old-fashioned hook you could hang your hat on."[62] Now known as Whitey Ford, a name that his Binghamton manager Lefty Gomez bestowed upon him, Ford arrived in the Majors in the middle of the 1950 season. He contributed nine wins and a World Series–clinching victory. He went on to a sixteen-year Hall of Fame career as the winningest pitcher in Yankee history, 236 wins and only 106 losses.

Krichell did not usually scout high school games, but he made an exception in the case of a heralded young pitcher from Naugatuck, Connecticut, Frank "Spec" Shea. Like many top prospects, Shea doubled as a shortstop and outfielder on days he wasn't pitching. It seemed, however, every time Krichell made a trip, Shea wasn't pitching or there was a rainout. He kept trying, and one day he was caught speeding on his way to a game. When the police officer found out who he was, he not only waived the ticket but also escorted him to the game.[63]

Krichell liked what he saw in Shea's arsenal, and he became easy to sign because his father, a former prospect himself that chose marriage and a family over baseball, raised young Frank as a Yankees fan. In the days when fans could run out on the Yankee Stadium field after games, Frank Shea, like Spud Chandler before him, would go out to the mound to imitate his future tosses. Three years of military service in World War II, including being part of the Normandy D-Day invasion, delayed Shea's career. As a twenty-seven-year-old rookie in 1947, Shea won fourteen games for the world champion Yankees, including two in the World Series triumph over the Dodgers. He also became the first rookie to win the All-Star Game.

Shea couldn't crack the top three in the rotation, of Allie Reynolds, Vic Raschi, and Eddie Lopat and was traded early in the 1952 season with Jackie Jensen, one of Joe Devine's prizes, to the Washington Senators for outfielder and first baseman Irv Noren. Shea ended his career with a 56-46 record and

3.96 ERA. He remained in his hometown of Naugatuck, an affable member of his community. In the early 1980s Robert Redford called upon Shea for coaching to make his baseball skills believable for the movie version of Bernard Malamud's novel *The Natural*.[64]

The Yankees' scouting and player development organization had kept working smoothly despite the death of owner Jacob Ruppert on January 13, 1939. After losing the 1940 pennant to the Tigers, the Yankees won the 1941 World Series over the Dodgers and avenged a Series loss to the Cardinals in 1942 with a victory in 1943. Then came another brief lull in the team's astounding run of championship success. The Yankees fell to third place in 1944, the only season in which two St. Louis teams squared off in the World Series, the Cardinals beating the Browns in six games. The Tigers won the pennant and World Series in 1945, with the Yankees falling to fourth place.

In January 1945 ownership of the team changed hands as the estate of Jacob Ruppert sold out to a consortium led by Daniel Reid Topping, heir to a tin and copper mining fortune, and Del G. Webb, a western construction magnate and former Minor League pitcher. Larry MacPhail, the flamboyant former general manager of the Reds and Dodgers, was named president, with a slice of ownership as well. One couldn't have imagined a greater contrast to the staid Yankee leadership under Ed Barrow, George Weiss, and manager Joe McCarthy than Larry MacPhail, of whom his Brooklyn manager Leo Durocher once said, "There is that thin line between genius and insanity, and in Larry's case it was sometimes so thin that you could see him drifting back and forth."[65]

The new team president was a passionate showman who, while serving in the American army during World War I, tried to kidnap the defeated Kaiser Wilhelm of Germany and bring him to trial. (All MacPhail got for his efforts was a stern reprimand and the Kaiser's imperial ashtray that became a family keepsake.) He entered the business world upon returning home but kept alive his love affair with sports by refereeing college football games, insisting that he invented the hand signals for penalties to inform fans.[66] At the height of the Great Depression, MacPhail got into baseball by turning the Columbus, Ohio, Redbirds into a profitable organization within Branch

Rickey's farm system. In 1935 he became Cincinnati's general manager and introduced night baseball lights to the Majors, an innovation he brought to Brooklyn as the Dodgers' top executive in 1938. He brought Red Barber from Cincinnati to announce Dodger games on the radio, breaking the ban against such broadcasts that the three New York teams had enforced. In 1941 Brooklyn won the borough's first pennant in twenty-one years, but they lost a dramatic five-game World Series to the Yankees. The crucial fourth game four turned on a two-out ninth inning missed third strike by Brooklyn catcher Mickey Owen that led to a game-winning rally sparked by Gene McCann's prize signing, Charlie Keller.

After a close second place finish to the Cardinals in 1942, MacPhail resigned to rejoin the military as a colonel in the acquisitions department in Washington, where he met Dan Topping and the idea of Yankee ownership began to percolate. No doubt, MacPhail's promotional style brought fans to the ballpark—he sponsored fashion shows before games, hired bands to liven up pregame activities, and established the first Stadium Club for well-heeled customers to gather far from the crowd of poorer people. His policies worked at the box office, with the Yankees drawing in 1946 a record of over 2.2 million fans, but the Yankees still finished third.

MacPhail's flamboyant style was too much for Edward Barrow, who retired after the 1945 season. Joe McCarthy, fighting chronic illness exacerbated by alcohol issues, resigned in May 1946, replaced first by Bill Dickey and then Johnny Neun. (McCarthy would soon resurface as Red Sox manager, leading the team to the 1948 pennant.) Although Bucky Harris, the onetime boy manager of the 1924 World Series–winning Washington Senators, won the 1947 pennant and the World Series, it was a tumultuous season. At a victory party after beating Jackie Robinson and the Brooklyn Dodgers in seven games, an inebriated MacPhail fired George Weiss only to announce when sobered up the next morning that he was retiring from baseball. (His son Lee MacPhail stayed on working in the scouting department.) Topping and Webb immediately rehired Weiss.

After a disappointing third place finish in 1948 to Joe McCarthy's Red Sox, the owners decided to replace Bucky Harris with another manager. It was time for Paul Krichell's last great evaluative gift to the Yankee organization.

George Weiss asked him to make a trip to Oakland to see if Casey Stengel was interested in managing the Yankees. Krichell had played against Casey in the Minor Leagues, and both he and Weiss considered Stengel a very able baseball man. Most of the press and the fans, however, were very skeptical because Stengel's previous Major League managerial jobs with the Brooklyn Dodgers and the Boston Braves had not been successful. In nine seasons, his teams never got out of the second division; they lost 160 games more than they won, and sportswriters, especially in Boston, regularly lampooned him.

Yet Krichell believed that Stengel was the right man for the job. Like all good scouts, he did not waver in his opinion. He was prescient, as Casey would outdo his predecessors in the Yankees' managerial chair, winning a still-unprecedented five consecutive World Series from 1949 through 1953, and two more in 1956 and 1958, along with four American League pennants before his forced retirement at the age of seventy after the 1960 season.

For his part, Stengel knew that he was coming into an organization blessed with top-drawer scouts. Tom Greenwade was one of the newer ones in the fold, having been plucked by Larry MacPhail from Branch Rickey's Brooklyn Dodgers in December 1945, just two months after Jackie Robinson's signing had been made official. Greenwade secretly scouted shortstop Robinson for the Dodgers during Robinson's brief 1945 season with the Kansas City Monarchs of the Negro Leagues. He filed a report saying that he was a great athlete and competitor but didn't have the arm and footwork for shortstop. Two years earlier, Greenwade had been sent by Rickey on another secret mission to Mexico to evaluate another possible racial pioneer, infielder Silvio García. Nothing came of that plan because Garcia was drafted into the army of his native Cuba. It also didn't help his prospects that the fiery player, when asked how he would react to a racial taunt, replied he would punch out the offender.[67]

Like Kansas City–born Casey Stengel, Tom Greenwade was a Missouri native but hailed from the rural southwestern section, the small town of Willard, where he was born on August 21, 1904. Greenwade pitched in the Minors for a few years in the 1920s, but, unsatisfied with his progress, he switched to independent leagues and even a stint with House of David teams. A bout with rheumatic fever kept him out of competition for a couple of years. When the Great Depression hit, he worked for the Internal Revenue Service, but in 1937 he joined the scouting staff of the St. Louis Browns. In 1940 Larry MacPhail wooed him to Brooklyn, where he was involved in the signing of pitchers Rex Barney and Cal McLish and future Hall of Famers Gil Hodges and Pee Wee Reese, who was playing for Louisville in the Red Sox organization.[68]

Scouting for the Yankees, Greenwade recommended Hank Bauer, Elston Howard, Bobby Murcer, Ralph Terry, and Bill Virdon (who was traded to the Cardinals in the deal that brought Enos Slaughter to the Bronx before the start of the 1954 season). Like all great scouts, Greenwade realized that makeup, the ability to rise to the occasion in stressful situations, was a vital key to success on the Major League level. Nobody could match Henry Louis "Hank" Bauer in that regard. Bauer was the youngest of nine children, born in East St. Louis, Illinois, on July 31, 1922, into an Austro-Hungarian working-class family. His oldest brother, Herman, was considered the best athlete, but he was killed in action in France in 1944. Neighbors remembered Hank as someone who always was running around with a bloody nose. He grew up idolizing local hero Enos Slaughter, who believed, "It's no fun playing if you don't make somebody else unhappy."[69] Los Angeles sportswriter Jim Murray later memorably described Bauer's face as "looking like a clenched fist."

Bauer fought with distinction in the Pacific during World War II. Surviving multiple bouts of malaria, he was awarded two Bronze Stars and two Purple Hearts for his service on Guam and Okinawa. In 1946 he was signed by Greenwade with the assistance of his associate Danny Menendez (later an expansion Montreal Expos scouting director). Arriving in the Majors in 1949, Bauer became a key part of the Yankees corner outfield lineup for the next ten years until his departure to Kansas City in the trade for Roger Maris. He and Yogi Berra were the only two players ever to win nine World Series. After his playing career, Bauer managed the Baltimore Orioles to the 1966 world championship and later had less success as skipper of the Kansas City and Oakland A's. He spent his retirement doing a little scouting and playing golf until he gave it up in 1978. "The only time I ever hit to right field was on a golf course," he said.[70] He died in 2007 at the age of eighty-four.

Of course, Tom Greenwade became best known for signing Commerce, Oklahoma, high school shortstop Mickey Mantle. It was another case of the Yankees doing due diligence on a prospect with a serious ailment. Mantle suffered polio as a youngster, and there were questions about his durability. No doubt, the youngster possessed amazing tools: a switch hitter with blinding speed on the bases and a quick bat from both sides of the plate. There wasn't much competition for his services. Greenwade felt confident enough that he had established an inside track with Mantle's father, Mutt, that he encouraged father and son to skip graduation services in 1949 and play in a top-flight game a few miles away in Coffeyville, Kansas. Mickey did very well in the game, hitting a home run left- and right-handed, perhaps the first time Greenwade had seen him bat from the right side.

After the game, he told the Mantles that Mickey was not a very good shortstop but he would take a chance on him as a hitter. He was offered $400 to play for the Yankees farm club in Independence, Missouri, along with a $1,100 signing bonus. The hoopla in the New York press for Joe DiMaggio's eventual replacement began quickly, but Mantle struggled in his first weeks as a Yankee in 1951. Being assigned uniform number 6, to follow Ruth's number 3, Gehrig's number 4, and DiMaggio's number 5, added too much pressure, and the Yankees sent him down to Kansas City for more seasoning. According to Tom Greenwade's son Bunch, Mickey actually called the scout before he told his father the bad news.[71]

Despondent at his demotion, Mickey thought about quitting the sport, but Mutt Mantle threatened to bring him back to Commerce to work in the coal mines. He soon recovered his stroke in the Minors and returned in time to help the Yankees win the 1951 World Series, the final out recorded by a diving catch in right field by Hank Bauer. With Joe DiMaggio's retirement after the season, Mantle patrolled center field for most of the next seventeen seasons on his way to the Hall of Fame.

In addition to finding great talent for the Yankees, Greenwade recommended a notable scout, Lou Maguolo, to his new employer. The endorsement of Maguolo was Greenwade's gratitude to a man who put in a good word for him when Greenwade started his scouting career with the Browns in 1937. Louis Dewey Maguolo, born in the southern Illinois town of Edwardsville on June 8, 1899, was the fourth of five children of Ferdinand Maguolo, a master carpenter who migrated to the Midwest from Venice, Italy. When Louis was two years old, the family moved to St. Louis, where Ferdinand set up a furniture store near his house in a tough Irish neighborhood known as Butchertown. Ferdinand did not approve of his son's passion for baseball. The eldest child in the family, George Maguolo, fulfilled his father's dream of success and respectability in the New World by becoming a renowned architect. He built 20 Exchange Place, one of the notable office buildings in the New York's Wall Street financial district, and the firm of Maguolo and Quick became nationally known. During World War II, Maguolo invented a device for the delivery of bombs to airplanes, which was of great use during the D-Day operations.[72]

Lou Maguolo did attend the prestigious Washington University in St. Louis and captained the baseball team in his senior year. Yet like so many future baseball lifers, he was possessed by the burning desire to play and teach the game. Despite his diminutive size of five feet five and 135 pounds, he developed into an excellent center fielder. During summers, he once played under an assumed name on a team supervised by Branch Rickey and Charley Barrett.[73] When he realized that he lacked Major League talent, he tried working as a civil engineer in Wisconsin. But he couldn't stay away from the ball field. In 1926 he returned to St. Louis to teach physical education and history at McKinley High School while, of course, also coaching the baseball team.

His teams were very successful, winning numerous titles, and his advice was eagerly sought by pro baseball people. After years as a bird dog for the Browns, in 1936 the team named him a full-time scout. Maguolo brought several players into the organization who contributed to the Browns' one American League pennant in 1944. He also signed slugger Roy Sievers, whose greatest success would come with the 1950s Washington Senators.[74]

After the end of World War II, the Browns fell back into their losing ways and entered the death throes that ultimately led to their transfer to Baltimore. Aided by Tom Greenwade's recommendation, Maguolo joined the Yankees in 1948 and would remain with them for the rest of his career. He did not wait long to deliver a prize to his new employer. In 1950 he signed shortstop Bill "Moose" Skowron on the campus of Purdue University after Bill led the Big Ten in hitting—and Skowron also pitched. He was also a versatile football player, playing halfback, punting, and place-kicking. By 1954 Skowron reached Yankee Stadium, established now as a slugging first baseman with surprisingly soft hands in the field. He was an All-Star in consecutive seasons from 1957 to 1961 and in thirty-nine World Series games hit 8 home runs and drove in 29. The last four came for the 1963 Los Angeles Dodgers in their sweep of the Yankees. In another example of the mystique of the Yankee brand, Skowron admitted later that "it killed him to beat them" because once a Yankee, always a Yankee.[75]

Another key Maguolo signing came in 1953 when seventeen-year-old Tony Kubek, a shortstop from Milwaukee, Wisconsin, was inked. In a January 2021 phone interview, Kubek reminisced about his tryout at Comiskey Park before the Yankees started a weekend series against the White Sox: "There was no one in the ballpark except Casey Stengel, [pitching coach] Jim Turner, coach Bill Dickey, Maguolo, and another scout, Fred Hasselman. They were all sitting behind home plate."[76] After displaying his wares in a batting practice session, Kubek took ground balls at shortstop and then shagged flies in the outfield off the bat of second baseman Jerry Coleman, who the previous day had returned to the team after serving in the Korean War, as Kubek remembered. After the tryout, Kubek and his father were invited to watch the series against the White Sox. The senior Kubek had been a Minor League shortstop for the Milwaukee Brewers, but because of family responsibilities during the Great Depression, he gave up his Major League dream. By the end of the weekend, Kubek's father signed a contract for his son. He had been won over by his son's eagerness to play and Maguolo's pitch that Tony Jr. could soon replace Phil Rizzuto as shortstop.[77]

Kubek reported to spring training in 1954 and was assigned to the Owensboro Oilers in Kentucky, in the Class C Kentucky-Illinois-Tennessee League. Like so many of the great scouts, Maguolo did not forget the players he signed. He kept tabs on Kubek's development and was delighted when the teenager got off to a good start at Owensboro. In the middle of the season, Tony received a big package in the mail. It was a handmade wooden lamp with the likeness of a glove palm up in the center. On the side was the barrel of a Hillerich & Bradsby Louisville Slugger held by a player. It was a gift from the scout who came from a family of woodworkers, all of whom knew their craft. (Maguolo was very generous with his crafts. Before one Philadelphia A's home game in 1941, he presented Connie Mack with an intricate sculpture in three parts to honor his long contribution to the game.)[78] Tony Kubek went on to enjoy a solid nine-year career with the Yankees, participating in five World Series as both a shortstop and an outfielder and later became a Hall of Fame broadcaster.

Fred Hasselman, who joined Maguolo for the Kubek tryout, was another key part of the Yankee midwestern scouting system. Weighing in at over three hundred pounds, he could have been called Mutt to Maguolo's Jeff. Hasselman operated one of the most thorough Chicago amateur baseball programs and was always providing advice and encouragement to prospects and would-be scouts. Hasselman and Maguolo worked together on the signing of outfielder and first baseman Norm Siebern, who later would be one of the three players sent to the Kansas City A's when the Yankees acquired Roger Maris. (More on that story is coming up in the chapter on Art Stewart.) Infielder Jerry Lumpe and outfielder and future Hall of Fame manager Whitey Herzog were the other two Yankee farmhands in the deal, all signed by Maguolo.

Hasselman also mentored teenaged Jerry Krause, who later earned fame as a key builder of the Chicago Bulls basketball dynasty. Krause never forgot the thrill of being asked by Hasselman for tips on local Chicago amateurs. He became famous for his work with the Bulls and sparring with the huge egos of superstar Michael Jordan and coach Phil Jackson, but Krause never abandoned his love affair with baseball. "I've never met an older scout that didn't get better at his job," Krause told me in a 2010 interview.[79] When he left the Bulls, Krause spent his last years scouting for the Yankees, White Sox, and Mets.

As Casey Stengel continued to maintain Yankees dominance on the Major League field and share his hard-earned wisdom at the team's innovative pre–spring training camps for prospects, Yankees' scouting in the South continued to bring in new blood. Second baseman Bobby Richardson, who in 1959 became Tony Kubek's double play partner in the Bronx, recalled in an October 2020 phone conversation that Spud Chandler scouted him when he was only fourteen. Chandler left the organization shortly thereafter, but new scout Bill Harris, who previously worked for the Giants, signed Richardson shortly after his graduation from high school in Sumter, South Carolina.[80]

During the long glory years of the Yankees, Paul Krichell rarely talked to the press. Shortly before World War II, he did once explain his philosophy. "Scouts should be honest and have initiative. Above all, scouts should be one hundred percent organizational men," he insisted. "Credit for any player reaching the major leagues should be given to the team's entire scouting system."[81]

In his twilight years in the 1950s, Paul Krichell did open up a little. "What's it take to be a concert pianist? It takes something you don't know you got," he said. With characteristic bluntness, he continued, "Any dope can see size, power, speed, and coordination. Desire and poise under fire are something else." He went on to say that it takes "guts in scouting . . . to turn down a prospect that other teams are busting to land." He took pride in choosing players like Tony Lazzeri and Joe DiMaggio. They might have something physically wrong, but scouting intuition said the player would overcome the liability.[82]

Like most scouts, Krichell occasionally mused about the ones that got away. In the mid-1920s, while scouting in Maryland, he missed out on signing future Hall of Famers Jimmy Foxx and Mickey Cochrane. He seemed to have a shot at local boy Foxx, he told sportswriter W. C. Heinz, and was intrigued by a collegian called Mickey King. He lamented being sabotaged when Ed Barrow telegraphed him that he must immediately track down an AWOL Minor Leaguer who had bolted the Saint Paul, Minnesota, farm club with whom the Yankees had a working agreement. The home office counted on Krichell to use his considerable powers of persuasion to bring the player back into the fold to make sure the Yankees hadn't lost the money invested in him. As a result, they lost the services of two future Hall of Famers, Jimmy Foxx and "Mickey King" who turned out to be catcher Mickey Cochrane.[83]

In one particularly wistful moment, Krichell looked at his office walls plastered with nearly two hundred photos of players he signed. "Sometimes I think I'm living in a house haunted with the ghosts of these men," he lamented. Memories of the departed Joe Devine and Bill Essick might well have come to mind. In the old days, he went on, the Yankees were subject to a lot of chicanery from other teams who "tried every means—all of 'em foul—to deal us out. They still do. But in those days there was a sport and spirit to it." Today, Krichell bemoaned, "it was all salesmen and hucksters building up young players. Wanderin' minstrels." He sighed wearily, "Maybe I've become like that old man and his fish."[84] He was referring, of course, to Ernest Hemingway's novella *The Old Man and the Sea* which came out as an entire *Life* magazine issue in 1953. In one poignant moment, an old Cuban fisherman elegized about Joe DiMaggio.

In a 1954 interview Krichell gave to J. G. Taylor Spink, editor and publisher of the influential *Sporting News*, he declared he saw nothing good coming out of the big bonus signings of unproven young players. For the most part, the Yankees had stayed out of competition that the Tigers had started by giving outfielder Dick Wakefield more than $50,000 in 1942. It really heated up when Phillies owner Bob Carpenter shelled out big bucks for Curt Simmons and Robin Roberts. In 1948 Louis Perini, one of three owners of the Boston Braves known as the "Three Shovels" for their contracting businesses, paid a reported $85,000 for high school southpaw Johnny Antonelli (who did eventually have a fine Major League career with the New York and San Francisco Giants).

Starting in 1953 and lasting through the 1957 season, Major League Baseball passed a rule that required every player that received a bonus of more than $4,000 to remain on the Major League twenty-five-man roster for two full seasons. Because roster spots were precious and Casey Stengel platooned regularly, the Yankees continued to abstain from bonus spending until 1954, when they decided to sign first baseman Frank Leja after his high school graduation in Holyoke, Massachusetts. He played in only twelve games in 1954, mainly as a defensive replacement, going 1 for 5 at the plate. He played even less in 1955, just seven games going 0 for 2.

It was not a happy experience for Leja, who felt ostracized by many Yankee veterans who resented that he received a bonus greater than even star players were earning in salary. Press reports listed his bonus as $40,000 or more, but Leja years later told author Dennis Snelling that he received no more than $25,000. Leja added that in the entire Yankee organization, Paul Krichell was "the only guy who would talk to him." When the Major League minimum salary was raised a thousand dollars before the start of the 1955 season, Leja asked for an adjustment on his contract. The surprised Yankees told him to see baseball commissioner Ford Frick, who asked the bonus baby if he did not already have enough money.[85] After the 1955 season, Leja was sent to the Minor Leagues, where he played in several organizations before getting 16 at bats without a hit for the 1962 California Angels. He retired shortly after and returned to Massachusetts, where he worked in the fishing business and helped in coaching amateur baseball. He died on May 3, 1991.

Before the start of 1955 spring training, the Yankees introduced to the press another bonus boy, eighteen-year-old shortstop Thomas Edward "Tom" Carroll. He was a local boy from Queens attending Notre Dame University, but the lure of joining the pinstripes proved irresistible. He was quickly labeled as Phil Rizzuto's future replacement, and the Scooter even attended the press conference. Although, as seen, Paul Krichell was not shy about decrying the bonus craze as wasteful, he played good soldier. "I have signed the shortest and the tallest," he quipped.[86] Rizzuto was not much more than five feet five, and Carroll stood six feet three. Tom Carroll would be Paul Krichell's last signing.

Carroll said that the Cubs, Red Sox, and Tigers offered more money than the Yankees' reported $50,000, but he was delighted with his choice.[87] Yet he would play just a little more than Frank Leja in the next two seasons, fourteen games in 1955, going 2-6, and thirty-six games in 1956, going 6-17. Then he was sent to the Minors. After the 1958 season, he was traded to the Yankees' favorite trading partner, the Kansas City Athletics, where he went 1-7 in fourteen games in 1959. He never returned to the Majors. Carroll's postplaying career was more interesting. He worked for twenty-seven years for the Central Intelligence Agency (CIA) and later was a corporate consultant in Latin America. He died in late September 2021 at the age of eighty-five.[88]

The Yankee dynasty still kept rolling because Tony Kubek emerged as Rizzuto's replacement by 1957, as the retired shortstop entered the broadcasting booth. After losing to the Brooklyn Dodgers in 1955, the Yankees ran off three more American League pennants in a row. In 1958 they avenged their 1957 loss to the Milwaukee Braves, coming back from a 3-1 deficit. After losing to the White Sox in 1959, they started another streak of five World Series appearances in a row.

Paul Krichell would not be around to enjoy the continued success on the Major League level. In 1955 he suffered a severe attack of ileitis, the same serious intestinal condition that afflicted President Eisenhower. He lost sixty pounds in six months and had to miss spring training for the first time, before stabilizing for a little while. Then his wife began to fail, and she died on April 11, 1957. Less than two months later, Paul Krichell passed away on June 4 1957, at the age of seventy-four. He was eulogized in a private ceremony presided over by Yankees broadcaster Red Barber and laid to rest in a cemetery in Valhalla, New York, not far from the headstone of Lou Gehrig.[89]

Krichell's passing, coupled with the deaths in 1951, six weeks apart, of Joe Devine and Bill Essick, left gaping holes in the Yankees' diamond detective staff. The team had never made any concerted effort to sign stars from the Negro Leagues. George Weiss bluntly remarked that Yankees fans did not want to sit in the same ballpark with people of a different color. Elston Howard, a graduate of a segregated high school in St. Louis whom Tom Greenwade signed in 1951 from the roster of the Kansas City Monarchs, was the exception. The versatile Howard preferred playing outfield, but from 1958 through 1966 he basically replaced Yogi Berra as catcher. The Yankees signed and developed colorful first baseman Vic Power, but decided he was too colorful on and off the field and traded him to Kansas City after the 1953 season.

In 1949 the Yankees did sign Monarchs outfielder Bob Thurman and assigned him to their top Newark Bears farm team, but later that season he was traded to the Cubs organization. After playing on a legendary Puerto Rican winter league team with Willie Mays and Roberto Clemente in the winter of 1954–55, Thurman wound up with the Reds as a pinch-hitter deluxe from 1955 through 1958. He was over forty years old at the end of his Major League career, but he had lied about his age in order to be signed. He later became a scout for the Twins and Royals and spent his last years with the Major League Baseball Scouting Bureau that was established before the 1975 season.[90]

Despite the loss of Krichell, the Yankees continued to win many World Series. They were not as dominant as Casey Stengel's still-unprecedented five consecutive championships from 1949 to 1953, but after the New York Giants' sweep of 111-win Cleveland in 1954, the Bronx Bombers appeared in the next four fall classics. They avenged the 1955 loss to the Brooklyn Dodgers in 1956, and did the same to the Milwaukee Braves in 1958. Former Yankees farmhand Lew Burdette won three games for Milwaukee in 1957, including a Game Seven shutout. After losing the 1959 pennant to the White Sox, whose manager Al Lopez had led Cleveland in 1954, the Yankees played in the World Series from 1960 through 1964. Significantly, their only victories were back-to-back titles in 1961 over the Reds in five games and in 1962 over the Giants in seven games. Willie McCovey's last-out line drive into the glove of second baseman Bobby Richardson, scout Bill Harris's signing, was one of the most memorable moments in World Series history.

The Yankees made significant changes to their hierarchy after Bill Mazeroski's dramatic bottom-of-the-ninth home run brought the Pirates to victory in the 1960 World Series. Ralph Houk, Bill Essick's signing, became the manager in 1961. Owners Dan Topping and Del Webb feared that another team might hire Houk, who had been a big success managing the Denver Bears, the farm team that replaced the Kansas City Blues when the Athletics arrived from Philadelphia in 1955. Roy Hamey, a journeyman executive who previously held high positions with the Phillies and Pirates, replaced George Weiss. Yankees owners cited the age of their former employees. Stengel said caustically, "I'll never make the mistake of being seventy again."

After their back-to-back victories in the 1961 and 1962 World Series, the Yankees were swept by the Los Angeles Dodgers, who were led by the arms of Sandy Koufax and Don Drysdale. It was the first time the haughty Bronx Bombers ever suffered such an embarrassment. In 1964, under new manager Yogi Berra with Ralph Houk replacing Roy Hamey in the general manager's chair, the Yankees needed the heroics of rookie pitcher Mel Stottlemyre to make the Series. Called up in August from Richmond in the International League, he went 9-3 to help the team win the pennant. His 9 victories brought back memories of Whitey Ford's same number in 1950 in his rookie year. Coincidentally, Stottlemyre replaced the disabled Ford, who was suffering with hip arthritis and entering the twilight of his career. Veteran scout Eddie Taylor, who briefly played third and short for the Boston Braves in 1926, signed Stottlemyre in 1961 as a nineteen-year-old on the campus of Yakima Valley Community College in Washington. Taylor accurately projected that Mel's ability to throw his sinker low in the strike zone would compensate for his lack of velocity.[91]

Stottlemyre went on to have an outstanding World Series against the Cardinals, holding his own in three matchups with future Hall of Famer Bob Gibson. In Game Two, he beat Gibson, 8–3, and received a no-decision, allowing just 1 run in a seven-inning effort in Game Five. Pitching on two days' rest in the deciding seventh game, Mel kept things close until the fourth inning when an injury lessened his effectiveness, and Gibson completed the victory. Stottlemyre would never pitch in the postseason again, but he was a consistent starter throughout his eleven-year career, finishing with a 164-139 record and 2.97 ERA. He became an outstanding pitching coach for both the Mets and the Yankees, and two of his sons, Todd and Mel Jr., followed in his footsteps as Major League pitchers and pitching coaches.

Immediately after the Series, in one of the more bizarre post-Series moments in baseball history, Yankees manager Yogi Berra was dismissed and replaced by the winning Cardinals manager Johnny Keane. The change backfired. In 1965 the Yankees finished eight games under .500 in fourth place, twenty-five games behind the pennant-winning Minnesota Twins, whose core of star players led by slugger Harmon Killebrew were home grown by the scouts and player developers of the Washington Senators (although they did lose a stirring seven-game World Series to the Los Angeles Dodgers and Sandy Koufax). The bottom fell out for the Yankees in 1966 when they plunged to the basement, nineteen games under .500 and twenty-six games behind the eventual world champion Baltimore Orioles, a team that had risen from the moribund shell of the St. Louis Browns.

It was not an auspicious start for the Yankees' new owners, the Columbia Broadcasting System that had finalized a deal with owners Topping and Webb late in the 1964 season. For team president, the network hired Michael Burke, a former World War II intelligence officer who had been working for CBS as a corporate acquisitions executive. The Ringling Brothers circus had been one of Burke's purchases for CBS, but he quickly found out that the entertainment value of the storied baseball franchise was sinking.[92] He oversaw a bare farm system that stopped producing star Major Leaguers like Kubek, who retired after 1965, and Richardson, who ended his career after 1966. The aging of Mickey Mantle, who retired after the 1968 season, and the 1965 trade of Roger Maris to the Cardinals, for journeyman third baseman Charlie Smith, added to the woes in the Bronx. By 1966 a team traditionally proud of its predominantly home-grown talent could boast only five farm system products on its Major League roster.[93]

Jim Russo, in his 1992 memoir, *Super Scout: Thirty-Five Years of Major League Scouting*, wrote that he saw the handwriting on the wall when the Yankees were not big players in the bidding for two great high school pitching prospects and future Baltimore twenty-game winners, southpaw Dave McNally from Billings, Montana, signed in 1960, and future Hall of Famer Jim Palmer from Scottsdale, Arizona, signed in 1963 despite a knee injury incurred in an automobile accident.[94] Baltimore's commitment to Palmer was reminiscent of the Yankees' commitment thirty years earlier to Joe DiMaggio when they were convinced his knee injury was minor.

Both pitchers rose quickly in the Orioles system. McNally arrived in the Majors to stay in 1963 and finished his career with 184-119 record, all with the Orioles, except for a partial final year in 1975, when he was 3-6 with the expansion Montreal Expos. (His name became more famous for his being part of the Andy Messersmith–McNally grievance that by the end of 1976 opened the door to baseball free agency.) Palmer arrived even more quickly, winning five games in 1965 on his way to a Hall of Fame career and a 268-152 record with 2.86 ERA, all with the Orioles. Each pitcher won one of the four games in the Orioles' surprise sweep of the LA Dodgers in 1966. They were key contributors to Baltimore's mini-dynasty of three pennants in a row from 1969 through 1971, although the Orioles won only the 1970 World Series over the Reds. With Mike Cuellar and Pat Dobson, McNally and Palmer were part of Baltimore's four 20-game winners in 1971.

Not surprisingly, Baltimore's success was built on a strong scouting and player development system. Some members were holdovers from the St. Louis Browns, including Jim Russo, brother of prominent St. Louis sportswriter Neal Russo, who had been hired in 1951. By the 1960s Russo was the Orioles' Midwest scouting supervisor, overseeing more than a dozen associates. He also advised on trades within the American League. Former Major League pitcher Bill Werle advised on National League trades, including the blockbuster that brought future Hall of Fame outfielder Frank Robinson to Baltimore in 1966.[95] Former Major League infielder Dee Phillips became the Orioles' man in Texas, signing outfielder Don Baylor and infielder David Allen "Davey" Johnson, who later became manager of the 1986 World Series–winning Mets and several other teams.[96] Al Kubski, a former Minor League infielder originally from the Baltimore area, relocated to California and brought into the Orioles' nest versatile middle infielder Bobby Grich.

In between the Orioles World Series appearances, the 1967–68 Tigers won back-to-back pennants for the first time since 1934 and 1935. Under general manager Jim Campbell and scouting director Hoot Evers, a former Tigers outfielder, the team focused heavily on signing local talent and patiently developing them in the Minors. Catcher Bill Freehan, who had starred in both baseball and football at the University of Michigan, signed after his junior year in 1961 to a bonus in excess of a $100,000. He established himself as a regular in 1963 and won five Gold Gloves in a row from 1965 through 1969. Also in 1961, slugging outfielder Willie Horton, one of fourteen children, was signed after graduation from Detroit's Northwestern High School. A year earlier, he and Freehan had played on the same team in a national sandlot tournament in Altoona, Pennsylvania.[97]

More local flavor came from outfielder Jim Northrup, an all-around athlete who was signed off the campus of small Alma College in Alma, Michigan. Center fielder Mickey Stanley was signed after high school in Grand Rapids by Paul Sullivan, who was both an area scout and his high school coach. Sullivan earlier mentored future Hall of Fame southpaw Jim Kaat and later two-time World Series champion Kirk Gibson.[98] In a huge gamble, Tigers manager Mayo Smith, who had spent years in the Yankees' player development department before managing the Phillies, moved Stanley to shortstop for the 1968 World Series against the Cardinals. The move enabled Al Kaline, the future Hall of Fame right fielder, to return to the lineup after a serious leg injury. Behind three excellent games by Mickey Lolich, the Tigers dethroned the Cardinals in seven games.

That the Yankees' decline from 1965 through 1975 occurred when the Major Leagues expanded and the free agent amateur draft was introduced was not coincidental. Building a new organization from the bottom up was enticing for many executives and scouts. In the next section of this book, I will look at the story of two expansion franchises, the New York Mets and the Kansas City Royals, largely through the eyes of two scouts, Red Murff and Art Stewart.

PART 2   TALES FROM BASEBALL EXPANSION ERA

3

Red Murff Joins the Scouting
Brotherhood with Mets and Expos

John Robert "Red" Murff, born in the central Texas town of Burlington on April 1, 1921, was the fifth of nine children of Louis Ellison Murff and Ollie Lieu Bell Murff. No high school baseball was in nearby Rosebud where Red grew up, and he made little impression on scouts scouring the local amateur leagues. He did not shine in serious competition until he joined the Army Air Corps after the bombing of Pearl Harbor on December 7, 1941. After spending his first months training on the campus of Gettysburg College in central Pennsylvania, he then was stationed at Maxwell Field in Montgomery, Alabama, for most of the war. Willing to play any position as well as pitch for the baseball team, Murff hit .466 and held his own against such future Major League hurlers as the Red Sox's southpaw Mel Parnell and the Cardinals' Royce Lint. He later admitted, "I didn't know I had talent until I got into the service."[1]

After the war, Murff worked as a district manager and chemical plant supervisor for oil companies in Texas City, thirty-five miles southeast of Houston. Despite his advancing age, the husky six-foot-three 195-pounder began to attract notice for his play on company and area semipro teams. Never getting enough of the diamond sport, Murff also caught for area softball teams. In 1950, at the advanced age of twenty-nine, Murff accepted a contract from the Baton Rouge Red Sticks in the Class C Evangeline League. He was named the league's Rookie of the Year after compiling a 17-4 record with a 2.96 ERA; he also batted .331 with 65 RBIs. Earning a promotion in 1951 to Texas City in the Class B Gulf Coast League, Murff concentrated on pitching and was 17-4.[2]

The late bloomer finally in 1952 was able to earn enough money to give up his day job. He won twenty-three games for the Tyler City East Texans in another B league, the Big State League, and hurled a no-hitter. He cherished the opportunity to compete with returning World War II veterans, many of whom had served on the front lines. As he remembered in his insightful 1996 book written with Mike Capps, *The Scout: Searching for the Best in Baseball*, "One of my friends who had fought on Guadalcanal told me that thoughts of making an important play in a big game, the thought of getting a hold of one and knocking it out of the park, kept him going through some bitterly tough, cruel battles."[3]

In 1953 he was promoted to the Dallas Eagles in the AA Texas League, where he remained for the next three seasons. He won twenty games twice, but his age obviously was a handicap. The Milwaukee Braves were interested in purchasing Murff's contract, but an agreement couldn't be reached between Dallas owner Dick Burnett and Braves scout Earl Halstead. The story goes that Burnett and Halstead finally agreed to play a gin rummy game with the winner getting to sign Murff. Halstead won, and the asking price for the pitcher dropped to around $40,000 and three players. Technically, since the Eagles had a working agreement with the Giants, the New York team agreed to transfer his contract to Milwaukee.[4] One of Murff's Dallas teammates was first baseman-outfielder Bill White, on his way to the Majors with the New York (and later San Francisco) Giants, Cardinals, and Phillies. In a November 2020 phone interview, the retired broadcaster and former president of the National League remembered Murff as a helpful teammate and one of the first to specialize in throwing the slider.[5]

When he was introduced on 1956 opening day in Milwaukee's County Stadium, it was the first Major League game that Red Murff ever attended. At the age of thirty-five, Murff was one of the oldest rookies in Major League history. Relieving starter Lew Burdette in the seventh inning with runners on first and third and one out, Murff completed a 6–0 shutout over the Chicago Cubs. He started the third game of the season at St. Louis, but in the third inning he ruptured a disc in his back and he could not continue.[6]

Leg and more back injuries started to plague the veteran rookie at a time in baseball when rehabilitation procedures were inadequate if not downright primitive. Murff did not start another game for the 1956 Braves and only one in 1957 before he was sent back to the Minors. His final career numbers were 2-2, 4.65 ERA, 50 innings pitched, 56 hits, 18 walks, and 31 strikeouts. He could at least be proud that during his brief Major League career, thirty-one of his strikeout victims were five future Hall of Famers: Ernie Banks, Roberto Clemente, Willie Mays, Frank Robinson, and Jackie Robinson. Although he missed the Braves' 1957 World Series triumph over the Yankees, he was rewarded with a World Series ring.[7]

Murff continued to pitch in the Minors for three more seasons and also played and managed in the Puerto Rican winter league. In 1960 he served as player-manager for the Jacksonville Braves, Milwaukee's Class A affiliate in the South Atlantic League. One of his players was a struggling young pitcher named Phil Niekro, who came to realize that he didn't throw hard enough to make the Majors. He started to work on a knuckleball, an experiment his manager encouraged. When inducted into the Hall of Fame in 1997, Niekro paid homage to Murff's encouragement without which he never would have reached baseball's pinnacle.

After the 1960 season, Red Murff, now thirty-nine, finally hung up his spikes. He posted a career Minor League record of 146-95 and 2.94 ERA. The late bloomer knew that he must find a way to stay in the game in some capacity. In the winter after the 1957 season, Murff first picked up the scouting bug when Milwaukee scout Ted McGrew asked him to organize tryout camps in the Dominican Republic. He was honored to be tapped by McGrew, a former Major League umpire who became a legendary scout. While working for the Brooklyn Dodgers, McGrew recommended a trade for a Red Sox Minor League shortstop, the future Hall of Famer Pee Wee Reese. A quarter century later, while scouting for the Los Angeles Dodgers, he urged a trade for Washington Senators pitcher Claude Osteen. In exchange for slugger Frank Howard, Osteen became a valuable Dodger third starter to complement Sandy Koufax and Don Drysdale on Los Angeles's 1965 and 1966 pennant-winning teams; he finished an eighteen-year career with six teams and a 196-195 record and a 3.30 ERA.[8]

When the Major Leagues voted in the summer of 1960 to expand to ten teams each, it meant not only many more jobs for Major League players but also more work for scouts and coaches. Gabe Paul, an experienced baseball man and most recently the general manager of the Cincinnati Reds, was now the general manager of the Colt .45s expansion franchise. He had been impressed by Murff's work in Jacksonville, especially liking his empathy for players in a game where someone must lose every day. Paul also noticed that unlike most managers and coaches who cared only about the outcomes of games, Murff seemed interested in projecting players' future. In 1961 Paul hired him to scout Texas and Oklahoma for the new franchise that would debut the following season. Murff was on his way to join a profession he would memorably describe in *The Scout* as "an underground brotherhood without the secret handshakes."[9]

One of Murff's first recommendations was Jerry Grote, a high school short-stop from San Antonio, Texas. Murff acted on a tip from Del Baker, a former Major League catcher, coach, and manager, who was an informal adviser to Grote's high school team. Both talent scouts agreed that Grote possessed strong yet soft hands and exuded grit and passion for the game.[10] The best athletes in high school usually played shortstop and pitched, and Grote certainly fit the profile, throwing two no-hitters. Murff, however, projected him as a catcher. He had "the classic look of a catcher," Murff recalled. "Stocky body, great arm, fiery temper, and he always knew where the ball was."[11] The amateur free agent draft was still a few years away, so there was competition for Grote's services from the Orioles and Dodgers. Murff prevailed, convincing his Houston superiors that Grote was an outstanding defensive catcher, and projected that the nineteen-year-old would become an adequate big league hitter capable of delivering at clutch times.

When Gabe Paul left the Colt .45s to become the Indians' general manager, Murff's position in Houston grew shaky. He didn't always see eye-to-eye with new Houston GM Talbot "Tal" Smith. When his old friend Wid Matthews, the Mets scouting director who came out of Branch Rickey's scouting tree, offered him a position with the National League's other expansion team, Murff seized the opportunity.[12] The Mets had just completed a horrendous 40-120 debut season but drew almost a million fans to the rickety Polo Grounds, the former home of the New York Giants that would soon be demolished. In 1964, when the new Shea Stadium was opened in Queens, the Mets started to outdraw the Yankees despite the Bronx Bombers being at the end of another dynasty of five consecutive pennants. New York fans obviously craved a replacement for the Dodgers and Giants more than they cared to support a team whose constant winning, some wags cracked, was like rooting for General Motors or U.S. Steel.

When the Astros released Grote during the 1965 Minor League season, Murff convinced the Mets to sign him. He arrived in New York the following season and was a key part of the 1969 and 1973 pennant winners. Later, he was a reserve catcher on the back-to-back 1977–78 Los Angeles Dodgers National League champions (who lost the World Series to the Yankees each year). Grote never had much to say to the press, and his silence was often interpreted as surliness. But he clearly was a first-division player, the perceptive, evaluative term from the days of two eight-team Major Leagues. Grote's value to a team far exceeded a career offensive stat line of .252 batting average, .318 on-base percentage, .326 slugging average, 39 home runs, and 404 RBIs. Base runners feared his throwing arm so much that there were fewer stolen base attempts against him than virtually any other catcher in the National League.

In addition to recommending Grote, Murff landed another key member of the Mets' future champions, southpaw Jerry Koosman. During the 1964 season, Koosman was in the army, pitching and playing outfield for the Fort Bliss team in El Paso. Mets farm director Joe McDonald was told by a Mets' usher, John Lucchese, that his son was catching Koosman at Fort Bliss and he deserved a look. When Murff hustled over to see the southpaw in action, his initial appraisal was that the young lefty possessed an easy delivery and a lively fast ball, but he was definitely overweight. After an initial chat, Murff learned that Koosman rarely played against tough competition. He grew up in the small town of Appleton, Minnesota, and joined the army after a dispute with his junior college coach. A firm exponent of tough love, Murff told the young man he had a future in pro baseball if got himself into better shape.[13]

There was still a free market for a pitcher who wouldn't turn twenty-two until December. Koosman's father hoped the local Minnesota Twins would sign his son, but Murff won out. Delighted that a slimmer Koosman pitched well in tough competition at a regional army tournament, he gave the southpaw a $1,100 bonus, four hundred dollars less than a figure he originally suggested at their first encounter. Koosman joked later that if the price kept falling, he might have wound up paying the Mets to play.[14]

Koosman won nineteen games as a 1968 Mets rookie, and he became part of a huge one-two punch with future Hall of Famer Tom Seaver on the 1969 Mets championship team. They reprised that role in their less spectacular 1973 pennant year when 82-79 was good enough to win the NL East—the Mets ultimately lost a hard-fought seven-game World Series to the Oakland Athletics. In a nineteen-year career, Koosman won 222 games and struck out 2,556 while issuing only 1,198 walks. It was a measure of his enduring value that when the Mets traded him to the Twins after the 1979 season, they received Minor League southpaw Jesse Orosco in return. Orosco wound up pitching for nineteen seasons, starred as the closer on the 1986 world champions, and retired with 140 career saves.

The story of how Tom Seaver became a Met was more convoluted. He was picked by the Dodgers in the eighth round in the first draft in 1965, but he elected to keep pitching at the University of Southern California for highly successful coach Rod Dedeaux. Since he was over twenty-one, he was eligible again in the January 1966 draft, and the Atlanta Braves made him the twentieth overall pick. West Coast scout Johnny Moore, who in 1949 signed future Hall of Fame third baseman Eddie Mathews, was elated and so was Braves general manager John McHale. However, Dedeaux protested the pick because the Trojans' season had already begun. His complaint was technically accurate but questionable because the Trojans had played only two exhibition games against military teams and Seaver had not pitched in either one. Moore probably did not know about the exhibition games on the schedule, but in the new era of draft regulations, college coaches were looking for any MLB slipups to keep their players in the fold.

Despite Dedeaux's wishes that his ace return to the Trojans, the NCAA declared Seaver ineligible because of his contact with the Braves. Recently elected baseball commissioner William Eckert voided the Braves' pick and prohibited them from contact with Seaver for three years. Seaver was now stuck in limbo between college and the pros, and his father, Charles, a prominent Fresno, California, executive in the raisin business, threatened a lawsuit against MLB. Eckert and his assistant Lee MacPhail proposed a drawing for any teams interested in signing Seaver. The Mets' West Coast scout Nelson Burbrink, later their director of player development, urged the team to enter the lottery, joining Philadelphia and Cleveland. Shortly before the start of the 1966 regular season, Lee MacPhail picked the name of the Mets out of a hat. It would be an epochal moment in the young history of the New York Metropolitans baseball club.[15]

Like most scouts, Red Murff pooh-poohed the idea of the draft because it would curb his competitive ability to woo and even hide prospects. However, he understood that to stay in the baseball scouting business, he would have to adjust. His signing of Ken Boswell showed his resiliency. Boswell was a promising left-handed-hitting infielder from Travis High School in Austin, Texas. Like Jerry Grote, Boswell was playing shortstop when Murff first scouted him. He loved the youngster's determination that no ball would ever get by him, but he projected him as a pro second baseman. Although Boswell was going to Sam Houston State College, he was not happy in school and preparing to drop out. When Murff saw Boswell's eagerness to start a pro career, he urged the youngster to write the commissioner's office asking to be entered into the draft. High school graduates, college players after their junior year, all players over the age of twenty-one, and community college players after their first year of schooling were all eligible.

It took time for Eckert's office to reply, but a positive letter came just before the draft.[16] The six-foot-one 170 pounder was picked by the Mets in the fourth round, and he became the most prominent part of a second base platoon on the Mets 1969 and 1973 pennant winners. The unexpected power output of his second base cohort Al Weis in the 1969 World Series has played its part in obscuring Boswell's place in Mets history. He also had his detractors in the organization, such as Whitey Herzog, the Mets' player development director, who believed that the second baseman had to be prodded to get the most out of his ability.[17] Boswell never received more than 400 official at bats in any of his eleven Major League seasons, all but three with the Mets, but he played in 930 games and finished with career numbers of .248 batting average, .313 on-base percentage, .337 slugging average, 31 home runs, 244 RBIS, 240 walks, and 239 strikeouts.

Red Murff was fast becoming a southwestern area scouting legend, covering Texas, Louisiana, Oklahoma, and New Mexico. He hit the highways and back roads in his Oldsmobile 88, taking full advantage of his vast network of bird-dog scouts and high school and college coaches. It was said that he knew on a first-name basis coaches in one hundred Texas counties. He cut quite a figure stepping out of his luxury car, wearing a spotless dress shirt and tie and freshly pressed trousers, his bald head shining in the sunlight. It was hard for prospects and parents not to be impressed.[18]

Without a doubt, the greatest laurel in Murff's scouting career came from his advocacy for Nolan Ryan, who became the Mets' tenth round selection, the 295th player chosen in the first draft in 1965. (There is some dispute about the round Ryan was drafted in because not every team made a choice in each round and some teams took more players than others because they needed to stock more farm teams.)[19]

Branch Rickey loved to say that "luck is the residue of design," so it must have been destiny one spring afternoon in 1964 that led Red Murff to visit a friend at a game at Clear Creek High School after Murff scouted a tournament in Galveston. On the mound for rival Alvin Texas High School was junior Lynn Nolan Ryan, a gangly, chicken-chested, six-foot-two 140-pounder. His coach, Jim Watson, didn't even think he was the best pitcher on the team, but Murff obviously was going to make up his own mind. Once he heard the *whoosh* of Ryan's fastball exploding into the catcher's glove, he knew he was witness to one of those rare epiphanies in scouting. "You don't have to see it but one time to know it's there," he would say many times thereafter.[20]

Murff immediately pulled coach Watson aside and told him not to send the scores of any Alvin High games to the newspapers. He didn't want the press to build up Ryan's abilities to alert other scouts. He made sure his associate scout Robert "Red" Gaskill saw every one of the raw prospect's games. Fearing ignorant high school coaches might ruin his newly discovered treasure, Murff became essentially Ryan's private coach. The scout later told Tyler, Texas, sportswriter Phil Hicks, "Back then, the baseball coach was a football coach whose defense didn't play well in the fall or an assistant football coach who was in the doghouse because the team didn't tackle well."[21]

Murff grew even more enthusiastic about Ryan's future when he started to get to know his family. Nolan, the youngest of six children, was born in Refugio, Texas, on January 3, 1947, but the family moved to Alvin, outside Houston, when he was an infant. Martha Lee Hancock, Nolan's mother, was reportedly descended from the Declaration of Independence signer John Hancock. Murff established a quick bond with Nolan's father when he found out that, like himself earlier in life, Robert Ryan worked in the oil industry as the supervisor of an oil processing plant. Nolan's dad also worked as a distributor of the local *Houston Post* newspaper. Murff was thrilled to learn that since Nolan was eight years old, he spent predawn hours with his father throwing copies of the morning paper to doorsteps all over town. There was no doubt about the youngster's work ethic and strength of his arm. By the time he was in junior high, Ryan could throw a football virtually the length of the field.[22]

Murff started sending enthusiastic scouting reports to the Mets front office. "Skinny right-handed junior. Has the best arm I've ever seen. Could be a real power pitcher one day," read one.[23] "Has the potential to be a high-performance starting pitcher on a major league staff. A smiling, friendly faced kid. Wide shoulders, long arms, and strong hands. Good hands," read another.[24] The Mets sent scouting director Vaughn "Bing" Devine, later a Mets and Cardinals general manager, to see what Murff was raving about. As often happens in the capricious world of baseball performance, Devine was not impressed by his first glimpse of Ryan. The youngster was knocked out in the third inning, and Devine wondered why he made the trip.

Murff stuck by his evaluation. He insisted that sixteen-year-old Nolan Ryan threw harder than two hard-throwing right-handers he had watched the night before, Cincinnati's Jim Maloney and Houston's Dick "Turk" Farrell. Anyone is entitled to a bad day, Murff insisted. It turned out that Ryan had not been expected to pitch because he had thrown an extensive side session the previous day. Not only that, but Coach Watson, unhappy with his team's concentration level, forced them into punitive running drills. Devine was still skeptical about Ryan and sent Murff on a scouting trip to judge other pitchers for the upcoming draft. Murff's reports came back with a firm assessment: "Have not seen anyone throw harder than Ryan."[25]

When June 5, 1965, dawned at the Commodore Hotel near Grand Central Station in New York City, all of baseball understood that a new era was beginning with the introduction of the free agent amateur draft. The Mets had lost 109 games in 1964, and the Kansas City Athletics "only" 105, but the A's received the first draft pick. They selected Arizona State outfielder Rick Monday, who would go on to a solid career with the A's, Dodgers, and Cubs—nineteen seasons, 1,619 hits, .264 batting average, .362 on-base percentage, .443 slugging average, 241 home runs, and 775 RBIs. Monday is also remembered for two special moments. At the plate, he homered off Steve Rogers in the top of the ninth inning of the final 1981 National League Championship Series game between the Dodgers and Montreal Expos to propel Los Angeles into the World Series against the Yankees where they avenged their recent losses by winning in six games. Playing in the outfield during the 1976 season, Monday snatched an American flag from father-and-son protestors before they could set it on fire.

The Mets were next on the clock, and Red Murff knew that Nolan Ryan was not high on his organization's list. In fact, his regular reports on other prospects—"doesn't throw as hard as Nolan Ryan"—had become a Mets in-house joke. So it was no surprise when the Mets used the second pick in the nation on Les Rohr from Billings, Montana, a strapping six-foot-five, 205-pound left-hander. Injury shortened his career and he finished with a 2-3 record and 3.70 ERA in only six games. In the second round, the Mets picked a high school catcher who never signed. In the third round, they chose Louisiana State University shortstop Joe Mouck, who never made the Majors. Murff was at least happy that the Mets picked Ken Boswell in the fourth round.

The draft dragged on and on, and the Mets and their nineteen rivals kept ignoring Nolan Ryan. As Murff fretted, the Mets picked several pitchers, a catcher and two outfielders, all of whom never made the Majors. In the ninth round, they chose Jim McAndrew from the University of Iowa, who was a valuable fourth starter in 1969 and won 36 games for the Mets in an injury-shortened career. Then in the tenth round, as Murff let out a deep sigh of relief, Lynn Nolan Ryan became Mets property.[26]

When it came time to discuss contract terms with Robert Ryan, Murff realized that he would be upset by how low his son had fallen in the draft. The scout explained that no one can ever truly guarantee beforehand a draft position. Since both father and son wanted Nolan to start his career as soon as possible, it did not take long for Mr. Ryan to agree to a reported $30,000 package with a $7,500 bonus once Nolan made the Major Leagues. Given the six-foot-four, 240-pound size of the senior Ryan, Murff was confident that his slender son would soon grow into his body. The scout kept in touch with Ryan as he worked his way up the Minor League ladder. He always tried to live by his adage: "I may change teams, you may change teams, but I will *always* be the scout who signed you, and always will be available for you" (italics in original).[27]

Ryan's powerful arm and wildness led to dramatic moments from his earliest days in the Minors. While pitching for the Marion Mets in the Western Carolina League against the Lexington (North Carolina) Giants, the eighteen-year-old hurler had a no-hitter going into the bottom of the ninth inning. Then he walked the bases loaded, and nineteen-year-old Bobby Bonds, a future star before he became known as Barry Bonds's father, broke up the no-hitter by hitting a game-winning grand slam.[28]

Ryan wound up needing three years of seasoning in the Minors, striking out 441 in 291 innings. His innings were relatively low because he fulfilled military obligations during the height of the Vietnam War. When he came up to the Mets for the 1968 season, much was expected of him. The May 31, 1968, issue of *Life* magazine pictured him soaking his hand in pickle brine to reduce the pain and swelling from blisters on his fingers.[29] He finished his rookie season with a 6-9 record and 3.09 ERA for a team that finished ninth but improved to sixteen games under .500. He struck out 130 batters in 134 innings, but his seventy-five walks were alarming.

In the 1969 championship year, Ryan enjoyed his only winning season as a Met, with a 6-3 record and 3.53 ERA. He struck out 92 batters in 89 innings but still issued 53 walks. His innings total was low because of continuing military obligations. He enjoyed his greatest Mets highlight when he pitched the last seven innings of the tie-breaking third game of the World Series and got the win against the heavily favored Baltimore Orioles. The Mets went on to win the next two games and the world championship.

His last two seasons in New York were disappointing. In 1970 he was 7-11 with a 3.42 ERA, with 97 walks and 125 strikeouts in 131 innings. In 1971 his record was 10-14, with his ERA ballooning to 3.97. In 152 innings, he gave up 125 hits and the alarming number of 116 walks with only 137 strikeouts. The memory of the Mets "miracle" of 1969 was fading fast, and Ryan was disillusioned about the progress of his career. He may have even thought about retiring if he wasn't traded. On December 10, 1971, Nolan Ryan received his biggest break since Red Murff became his informal coach and greatest advocate. A trade to the California Angels was announced during the baseball winter meetings. In exchange for shortstop turned third baseman Jim Fregosi, the Angels received Ryan, outfielder Leroy Stanton, Minor League pitcher Don Rose, and Minor League catcher Frank Estrada.

Many followers of the Mets were shocked at the news because Ryan was still only twenty-four years old and not yet in the prime of his career. But Mets general manager Bob Scheffing and manager Gil Hodges defended the trade, thinking that Fregosi would bounce back from an injury-plagued season marred by a serious foot injury. They also thought that Ryan had been given more than enough chances to learn control and command. It turned out that Jim Fregosi was on the downside of his career and was traded just a year later to the Texas Rangers. (He later became a Major League manager for the Angels, White Sox, Phillies, and Blue Jays.) Leroy Stanton had five fairly productive years with the Angels, twice driving in more than 80 runs; in his next-to-last Major League season with the new expansion Seattle Mariners, he drove in a career-high 90 runs. The other two players traded by the Mets in the Ryan-Fregosi deal had very brief Major League careers.

Freed from the pressures of the Big City, Ryan became an ace and work-horse on a pitching staff that needed his durability. Except for southpaw Frank Tanana, the Angels lacked consistent arms. ("Tanana and Ryan / Then Start Cryin'" was one wit's updating of the 1948 Boston Braves lament "Spahn and Sain / Then Pray for Rain.") Pitching coach Tom Morgan, the former Yankees hurler originally signed by Bill Essick, fine-tuned Ryan's delivery and taught him a better grip for his curveball.[30] In 1973 Ryan struck out 383 American

League batters, breaking Sandy Koufax's record for most strikeouts in a single season. It was a special honor for Ryan because the southpaw had been his idol. When Ryan had the curve working, Dave Duncan, an opposing catcher who later became Tony LaRussa's longtime pitching coach, said, "Ryan doesn't just get you out. He embarrasses you."[31]

In 1980 Nolan Ryan took advantage of free agency to move to the Houston Astros and later joined the Texas Rangers. He became a physical fitness fanatic and pitched into his forties, hurling his seventh no-hitter in 1991 when he was forty-four. In August 1993, the last season of his twenty-seven-year Major League career, Ryan famously stood his ground when the younger White Sox third baseman Robin Ventura stormed to the mound after being hit by a Ryan pitch. Immortalized on YouTube and other social media sites is Ryan's placing Ventura in a headlock and pummeling him. When Ryan was inducted into the Hall of Fame in 1999, he gave heartfelt thanks to Red Murff who "wasn't discouraged by my build and the way I threw the baseball." His final stat line read 324-292, 3.19 ERA, 222 complete games, 61 shutouts, 2,795 walks, and 5,714 strikeouts.

A fascinating exploration into alternate history is to ask whether Nolan Ryan's career in New York might have blossomed if Red Murff remained in the Mets organization. Although Murff always said that neither he nor any scout could have known how dominant a pitcher the teenaged Ryan would become, he likely would have raised his voice in opposition. So would have someone with more organizational power like Mets general manager Johnny Murphy. Murphy, the Yankees closer during their mid-1930s through early 1940s dynasty, deeply believed that good pitching would stop good hitting. A sign of how dominant Mets pitching had become was that the 1969 world champions scored only fifteen more runs than the hapless 1962 team that lost 120 games. But in January 1970, just weeks after the Mets' surprise World Series triumph, Murphy died of a heart attack at the age of sixty.

Although speculating about alternate history is indeed fascinating, in real time Red Murff wasn't even around to celebrate the 1969 triumph. He left the Mets late in the 1968 season. He later explained that he was miffed that the Mets had failed to sign its fourth-round draft pick, Corpus Christi, Texas, high school pitcher Burt Hooton. Murff was very bullish about the six-foot-one 210-pounder who was showing signs at a young age that he was mastering a knuckle-curve that flummoxed batters expecting higher velocity from someone his size. When the Mets refused to meet the demands of Burt's father, who wanted the team to pay for some of Burt's college education, Hooton enrolled at the University of Texas.[32] Three years later, the Cubs drafted and signed Hooton, who went on to a productive career mainly with the Dodgers, winning 151 games. "If they didn't want to sign someone like Hooton, they didn't need me," the proud scout later explained.[33]

Red Murff wasn't unemployed for long. An offer to start from the ground up with a third expansion team, the Montreal Expos, proved too good to turn down. The Expos and the San Diego Padres were slated to start play in April 1969 in the National League, while the Kansas City Royals and Seattle Pilots were the newcomers in the American League. Fortunately, the Major Leagues were working in tandem, unlike during the first expansion when the American League, upset that the senior circuit obtained prime markets in New York and Houston, jumped the gun in 1961 and hastily started play with the California Angels in Anaheim and the second Washington Senators franchise in the nation's capital, as the original Senators had moved to Minneapolis–St. Paul. Fear of the United States Congress's reexamination of baseball's antitrust exemption prompted the hasty decision to add a replacement team in the nation's capital.

It was a dramatic move for the National League owners to admit into its exclusive club Montreal, a bilingual city in a foreign country. Oft-reelected Montreal mayor Jean Drapeau, a charismatic salesman, made a convincing presentation to the owners at the 1967 Winter Meetings that a new stadium with a retractable roof would be built within two years. Of course, construction took far longer, and it did not open for baseball until after the 1976 Montreal Olympics. Montreal had a long history of support for Minor League Baseball, dating back to 1897 and truly flourishing after World War II, when the Montreal Royals featured such future Hall of Famers as Jackie Robinson, Duke Snider, and Don Drysdale.

Red Murff was joining an organization that looked strong from the top down. Expos owner Charles Bronfman was one of the heirs to the Seagram liquor fortune founded in western Canada by his grandfather Samuel. It made Charles one of the richest men in North America, but early on in his life he decided that he wasn't going to be an idle member of the plutocratic class. As he recounted in his engaging 2016 memoir, *Distilled*, he left Montreal's prestigious McGill University after only one year to work at expanding his father's business. With regard to the Expos, he expected several business partners, but when they all backed out, he manfully accepted the role as full owner.[34]

National League officials selected John McHale as the team's first president, and Bronfman was happy to defer to his judgment. "What did I know about the nuances of baseball?" the owner remembered in an expression of humility not often associated with baseball owners.[35] McHale came to the job after working as assistant to baseball commissioner William Eckert (who succeeded Ford Frick in 1966 but resigned after only three seasons on the job, replaced by former National League lawyer Bowie Kuhn). McHale was a former Notre Dame football player who was signed by Tigers' scout Wish Egan after his sophomore year in 1940. McHale's Major League career was inconsequential—64 games, 114 at bats, .193 batting average, .258 on-base percentage, .281 slugging average, 3 home runs, and 12 RBIs. He could say that he was a rare individual who played both college football—for Notre Dame against Army in 1940—and Major League Baseball—for the Tigers against the Yankees in 1947—at Yankee Stadium.[36] After his brief Major League playing career ended with one at bat in 1948, McHale immediately went to work in the Detroit farm system, rising to farm director in 1954 and general manager in 1957 and 1958. In 1959 he became Milwaukee Braves general manager and traveled with them to Atlanta in 1966 before going to work in the commissioner's office.

For Expos general manager, McHale named longtime Braves Minor League coach Jim Fanning. Fanning had been a backup catcher for the Cubs from 1954 to 1957 who played only sixty-four games in his career, but he was a respected baseball lifer who worked for the Expos for the rest of his career. McHale's choice for the team's first scouting director was Melvin Croydon "Mel" Didier (pronounced "DID-ee-yay"). A lifelong Louisianan, Didier was very familiar with the work of Red Murff in east Texas, and he quickly hired the slightly older man as an area scout. It was nice to have Murff on his side instead of as a fierce rival.

Mel Didier, the second youngest of six sons, was named for Mel Ott, New York Giants Hall of Fame slugger who had played ball with Mel's dad, Robert Irby Didier Sr. Ott had been signed as a sixteen-year-old by Dick Kinsella, John McGraw's primary scout, and came to New York immediately without a stop in the Minor Leagues. A few years earlier a Yankees scout was interested in signing Irby (pronounced "OY-bee"), but his father, who ran a general store and spoke no English, confronted the scout with a shotgun. With Irby translating, the elder Didier roared, "If you ever try to take my boy away for that foolishness, I'll kill you.... He's going to work."[37] Irby became a Louisiana state bank examiner but never lost his love of sports, a passion he passed down to all his children.

When Mel Didier was eleven, the family moved to Baton Rouge, where, like so many future scouts in this story, he became a whirlwind of athletic activity, playing all kinds of sports and organizing local baseball teams with his youngest brother, Gerald. When the United States entered World War II, two of Mel's older brothers were captured in action in Europe. Every Sunday, Mel's mother, Edith Pilcher Didier, took him to church to pray for the safety of her captured sons. Fortunately, the two sons both survived their ordeal, one of them managing to escape from prison.[38] With two of her sons in military service, Edith insisted that Mel stay near home for college. He went on to star in both baseball and football at LSU and then signed with the Detroit Tigers in 1947. Unfortunately, shoulder injuries ruined his pitching career. He retired after the 1949 season with disappointing Minor League numbers of 11-15, 6.33 ERA, 234 hits allowed in 202 innings, and a walk-strikeout ratio of 115-77. Not wanting to lose his fine baseball mind and heart, John McHale quickly hired Mel as a scout.[39]

For the next two decades, Didier went back and forth between scouting for the pros—first with Detroit and then following McHale to the Braves—and coaching football on the elementary, high school, and college freshman level. Didier befriended Paul "Bear" Bryant when he coached at Texas A&M in the 1950s. He picked up ideas about using tackling dummies to teach catchers how to block home plate and middle infielders how to avoid sliding base runners and still turn double plays.[40] Didier's 1967 and 1968 LSU freshmen went undefeated, and it was rumored he might replace varsity coach John

McClendon. But doctors warned the intense workaholic that the pressure of Division I football would be too great on his heart. He never lost his love for baseball, and he eagerly accepted the offer to join in the adventure of a new franchise.

Didier was glad that Red Murff was now on his side as a fellow talent hunter as the Expos franchise began its climb towards respectability and contention. No one expected miracles in the first year of an expansion team, and under Gene Mauch, who previously managed the Phillies, they lost 110 games. They did have an emerging star in first baseman and outfielder Rusty Staub, who Murff and Didier knew well because he hailed from New Orleans. There were some special highlights early in the first season. The Expos made their debut at Shea Stadium, no one dreaming that a few months later the field would be the site for the home team's world title. It was a wild game in which Tom Seaver didn't have his best stuff and got knocked out early. It went back and forth until the Expos won, 11–10.

Barely a week later, on April 17, 1969, at Philadelphia's Connie Mack Stadium, Expos right-hander Bill Stoneman pitched a no-hitter, by far the earliest milestone for an expansion team. A sign of the genuinely compassionate nature of the new Montreal organization was a ceremony it organized at home plate when Stoneman and the team returned from the road trip. The organization presented the pitcher with a Renault automobile, out of which stepped Stoneman's parents, flown in from California, and his brother who had just returned from Vietnam.[41] (After his retirement as a player, Stoneman became an Expos general manager and later served in the same role with the Angels.)

John Bateman, one of Red Murff's first signings for his Expos, caught Stoneman's masterpiece. In 1963, as a member of the expansion Houston Colt .45s, he was behind the plate when former Milwaukee Brave Don Nottebart threw his no-hitter, so Bateman became the first expansion catcher to be part of two special pitching gems. As his knowledge of the Colt .45s organization enabled Murff to recommend Jerry Grote to the Mets, so did his memory of John Bateman pay off. With shades of Jim Bottomley writing to the Cardinals before the first St. Louis tryout camp in 1919, Bateman had written to Colt .45s' officials, describing himself as six feet tall, 243 pounds "and ready to play baseball."[42] As with Jerry Koosman a few years earlier, Murff was not pleased with the girth of the corpulent catcher. He told him to lose weight, and Bateman took the criticism to heart and shed twenty-five pounds. Murff thought Bateman had been the best player at the Colt .45s' camp, and he quickly signed without any haggling on a bonus.

Born on July 21, 1940, at the Fort Sill army base in Lawton, Oklahoma, where his father was stationed, John Alvin Bateman grew up as an active but undisciplined youth, as his parents separated when he was young. In his teenage years he went to live with his father, now an army sergeant, but he couldn't wait to get away from home and start his pro career. He won raves from Houston's top executive Paul Richards for a throwing arm, drawing comparisons to Cubs Hall of Famer Gabby Hartnett.[43] (One always wonders how wise it is to heap such lofty praise upon a young player.)

Bateman reached the Majors in 1963 and became Houston's primary catcher. In 404 at bats, he hit only .210, slugged .334, and suffered through a rather embarrassing ratio of 13 walks to 103 strikeouts. He was back in the Minors for most of the next two seasons, rooming some of the time with Jerry Grote. Ultimately, they decided to find other roommates because neither one was hitting. Grote was gone to the Mets after the 1965 season, and in 1966 Bateman had his most productive season in Houston with a .279 batting average, 20 home runs, 74 RBIs, and a more respectable 39:70 walk-strikeout ratio. Unfortunately, the catcher could not sustain his success and he was made available in the October 1968 expansion draft. In his four full seasons in Montreal, Bateman never established himself as a consistent offensive player and his walk-strikeout ratio deteriorated. Injuries also hampered his career. Barry Foote replaced him by 1974, and future Hall of Famer Gary Carter was waiting in the wings, becoming the regular in 1977.

John Bateman did become a colorful fan favorite, sometimes too colorful. After the 1970 season, he created a sensation when he was shown on television participating with Quebec police in a raid on a paramilitary cell.[44] It was a time of social disturbance caused by the separatist Quebecois movement. After his retirement, he returned to Texas, where he died in 1996.

The 1969 amateur draft was the first that Red Murff worked on for the Expos, and his influence was quickly demonstrated by the team's first-round choice, left-hander Balor Moore from Deer Park, Texas, located about twenty miles outside of Houston. Murff had been following the prospect since the seventh grade and was enthralled by an arm he thought as promising as Nolan Ryan's had been. Like Ryan, Moore could already throw a football almost the length of the field. Balor's family was supportive of their son's baseball passion and moved closer to Houston so he could face better competition. The Moore family did not understand the baseball business, and when Murff told them that he was the Expos' number one draft choice, they thought they would have to pay the team for the privilege.

Unfortunately, Balor never developed in Montreal. He was brought up in May 1970, making him at twenty the youngest Expos' pitcher. He later pitched for the Angels and for the Blue Jays in their first three years as an expansion team and retired with a 26-48 record and 4.51 ERA. He became successful in business, and in a 2016 interview with a Toronto blog, he fondly remembered his baseball career, but he wished he could have relaxed more and allowed his God-given talent to take over. "I tried too hard because I was always afraid of losing it," he said.[45] The 1969 draft did produce two future Major Leaguers who, while not stars, had fairly long careers. Terry Humphrey, a catcher and first baseman from a Los Angeles community college who was picked in the thirty-ninth round, played for seven full seasons. Outfielder Tony Scott, a high schooler from Cincinnati, was chosen in the sixty-ninth round and managed to last for eleven seasons in the Majors.

The 1970 draft was more productive. The aforementioned Barry Foote was the number one pick from Smithfield, North Carolina. Phil Garner, a second baseman from the University of Tennessee, was picked in the eighth round; he made the Major Leagues in 1973 and wound up winning World Series rings for Oakland and Pittsburgh and then became a Major League manager. More late-round magic was conjured up by Didier's staff again when San Francisco high school outfielder Jerry White was picked in the fourteenth round—he would have an eleven-year career. In the eighteenth round, pitcher Dale Murray was chosen from Blinn Junior College in Texas. Murray's career would be defined by who he was traded for: after the 1976 season, the Expos got Tony Perez from Cincinnati's Big Red Machine champions for him and Woodie Fryman, and Murray was traded by the expansion Blue Jays to the Yankees in a multiplayer deal in which Toronto received slugging first baseman Fred McGriff, who was still a Minor Leaguer.

Before the 1971 draft, Mel Didier took on additional duties as player development director as well as scouting chief. In his first draft as scouting director in 1971, he selected a Huntsville, Alabama, high schooler, Condredge Holloway, who played shortstop and quarterback. However, he couldn't talk Holloway and his mother out of an athletic scholarship to play both sports for the University of Tennessee. The time had not yet come for the NCAA to allow an athlete to play professionally in one sport while keeping college eligibility in another sport. Holloway went on to an excellent career on the Tennessee Volunteers football field and later starred in Canadian football, but he always felt some wistfulness about not pursuing a baseball career.[46] Red Murff shared Didier's disappointment that Holloway never tried pro baseball.

The 1971 draft was not totally barren. The Expos chose future ace Steve Rogers from the University of Tulsa as the fourth pick in a delayed June secondary draft. In 1967 Tom Greenwade urged the Yankees to draft high schooler Rogers in the sixtieth round, but he was not ready for the pros.[47]

The Expos did have a successful 1972 draft by picking two California high schoolers, Ellis Valentine in the second round and Gary Carter in the third. Both youngsters were signed by California-area scout Bob Zuk, who seemingly made a specialty of discovering good hitters. While working for the Pirates, Zuk signed Willie Stargell from the baseball-rich area of Oakland, California.[48] When Gary Carter reported to instructional league in late 1972, Didier handed him a catcher's glove. Carter was almost shocked because he had always been an infielder and outfielder and never thought of catching. Didier was insistent, sensing that the earnest, hard-working fellow possessed the skills and leadership to be an excellent receiver. He wound up with a nineteen-year Major League career, the first eleven with the Expos. He won his only World Series ring with the 1986 Mets and retired with impressive offensive numbers for a catcher: .262 batting average, .335 on-base percentage, .439 slugging average, 324 home runs, and 1,225 RBIs. In an age when strikeouts were no longer a blot on the character of a player, he put up an admirable 848:997 walk-strikeout ratio. He was voted into the Hall of Fame in 2003 before his untimely death of brain cancer at the age of fifty-seven in 2012.

As often happens in the unpredictable world of the amateur draft, Ellis Valentine, a higher pick than Carter, faded after he hit more than 20 home runs from 1977 to 1979 in Montreal. He was traded to the Mets in 1981 and never recaptured his form, playing in less than a thousand Major League games in a ten-year career. There was no doubt that God gifted Valentine with the superior tools of a strong throwing arm and a sweet, power-loaded swing. However, he became a poster boy for the dangers of partying too much and forgetting to work daily at his improving his craft.[49]

The 1973 draft provided mixed results. The number one pick, outfielder Gary Roenicke, came from an athletic family and was signed after high school in Covina, California. He only played twenty-nine games for Montreal in 1976 before he was traded to the Orioles and became a successful platoon left fielder for Baltimore's contending teams of the late 1970s and early 1980s. The twenty-third-round pick, Dalton, Massachusetts, high school pitcher Jeff Reardon, did not sign and six years later made the Major Leagues with the New York Mets. In 1981 he was traded to Montreal for Ellis Valentine and enjoyed six successful years as a closer for the Expos, leading the National League in saves in 1984. The prize of the 1973 draft turned out to be Warren Cromartie, the team's first pick in the June secondary draft. The Miami Dade North College outfielder became a regular left fielder from 1977 through 1983 and part of the core of the Expos contending teams.

Everyone associated with an expansion team in a foreign country knew that success was not going to come easily. Mel Didier was ready to do anything to help that cause. In February 1974 he was asked by owner Charles Bronfman and team president John McHale to undertake a secret mission to Cuba to see if Fidel Castro's government would be receptive to allowing some of their renowned amateur players to become part of the Expos organization. Unlike the United States with its trade embargo against Cuba, Canada enjoyed normal relations with the island nation ninety miles from the coast of Florida. Didier presided over a series of baseball clinics with Cuban coaches, who listened raptly to his every word. Red Smith, an Expos area scout in Florida with good connections in the Caribbean, told Didier to stress the "revolutionary" nature of Mel's program of using football tackling dummies to instruct catchers on blocking the plate and second basemen in turning the double play.

The idea of an actual working agreement between the Expos and Cuban baseball proved impracticable. Castro and his government were fearful of defections, and when Commissioner Bowie Kuhn found out about Didier's journey, he threatened to suspend him for two years if he ever again undertook such an unauthorized mission. Didier had quite an adventure returning home to North America. He had come to Cuba via Mexico City, but a return flight was not available. Ultimately, Castro himself arranged for Didier to find a seat on a plane heading to Moscow with a stopover in Madrid from where Didier enplaned back to the United States in time for spring training.[50]

The 1974 draft for Montreal was not very fruitful, but it had an interesting aspect because the Expos picked shortstop Hubie Brooks in the nineteenth round, from a high school near Los Angeles. He did not sign but went on to Arizona State University, where the Mets drafted him four years later. Brooks would come to Montreal in 1984 as the key return in the Mets' trade for Gary Carter. Better fortune came to the Expos in the eleventh round of the 1975 draft when center fielder Andre Dawson from Florida A&M University in Jacksonville was chosen.

As has happened with many scouts, Didier was looking at a player on the team opposing Dawson's A&M Rattlers when he noted the bat speed of the Miami-born center fielder that reminded him of Hank Aaron. He also liked the hustle that Dawson showed on every play.

When Didier found out that Dawson was a sophomore eligible for the draft because a football knee injury cost him a year, his eyes lit up. He found out that other scouts were not aware of Dawson's eligibility or his potential. On draft day, Didier bided his time and didn't pick Dawson until the eleventh round. The delay drove Expos scout Bobby Mattick apoplectic as he feared another team would swoop in and pick Dawson. But after nearly 250 players had been chosen, Andre Fernando Dawson became a member of the Expos organization.[51]

Dawson did not need much Minor League seasoning. He became a Montreal regular in 1977, the same year that the new Olympic Stadium was converted into a baseball park. Although Dawson's knees took a tremendous pounding from the stadium Astroturf, he became a feared hitter, excellent outfielder, and quiet team leader. He was part of a core group of Montreal players that in 1978 won ninety-one games, the first season in their history that they finished over .500. They contended through the 1981 season, the year they fell one inning short of the World Series when the Dodgers' Rick Monday homered in the top of the ninth off Steve Rogers to break a 1–1 tie and lead Los Angeles into the Series, where they beat the Yankees.

Also in 1975 Red Murff was voted Scout of the Year by members of the Montreal baseball community. Although he found no new Ryan or Koosman, he was revered for his work as a devoted advocate for the game. Murff was excited about a second chance program that Didier established when he became scouting director. Players ages eighteen to twenty-five that had not been drafted or had been cut by organizations were invited to a tryout camp in Homestead, Florida. Didier estimated that three future Minor Leaguers and one Major Leaguer that sipped the proverbial cup of coffee came out of the program.[52] Back home in Texas, Murff started coaching baseball in 1972 at the University of Mary Hardin–Baylor, a Christian university located in Belton near where he lived. He started an innovative program of his own in which released professional ballplayers and discharged military veterans could enroll at the college, engage in top-flight competition, and have a chance to get rediscovered by pro baseball.[53]

Sadly, for all of the hopeful signs in the Expos organization, 1975 turned out to be a year of regression on the Major League level. The team slumped to twelve games under .500, and after the season Gene Mauch was gone as manager. As proof that not every decision made out of the box was a good one, his replacement Karl Kuehl turned out to be a poor choice. He was a highly respected teacher and player developer who had worked closely with Mel Didier in spring training when brought over from the Milwaukee Brewers staff in the early 1970s. Kuehl loved one of Didier's adages: "Baseball fields are not made to walk on; they're made to run on."[54] But his only prior managerial experience was as a twenty-one-year old player-manager for Salem, Oregon, in the Class B Northwest League.[55] The Expos staggered to a 42-85 record before Kuehl was replaced by Charlie Fox, a more experienced scout and player developer, but he finished the season not much better, going 12-22. It was the Expos' worst year since they lost 110 games in their first season. (Kuehl did bounce back nicely, joining the Twins as a coach for the next six seasons. From 1983 through 1995, Kuehl was a key piece of Oakland's player development program that built the Athletics' three pennant winners in a row from 1988 through 1990. He also became renowned among players and coaches for his authorship with self-taught sports psychologist Harvey Dorfman of the seminal 1989 book *The Mental Game of Baseball*.)

After the 1975 season Mel Didier left the Expos when the Los Angeles Dodgers made him an offer that he could not refuse. He always wanted to work with Al Campanis, who had become the all-but-official general manager of the Dodgers when Fresco Thompson died in 1968. "He was the smartest baseball man I've ever been around," Didier remembered in *Podnuh Let Me Tell You a Story*. "Arrogant, at times, a know-it-all, at times, but deep down, he had a great heart."[56] They both believed that scouting and player development must go hand in hand. Didier's first stint with the Dodgers only lasted a year because owner Walter O'Malley wanted him to help entertainer Danny Kaye in his first years as expansion Seattle Mariners owner. When Kaye discovered that his wealthy partners were not interested in building a competitive organization, he left baseball. Mel Didier spent the last thirty years of his baseball life serving a variety of teams. He looked back warmly at his six years with the Expos, holding dear memories of "kids riding their bicycles with little Montreal caps with their radios on listening to games."[57] His last job was working for Canada's other team, the Toronto Blue Jays, until shortly before his death on September 10, 2017, at the age of ninety-one.

Mel Didier lives on in the forty-seven-minute 2014 video *Scout's Honor*, which SHMD Productions released in 2014 on DVD and in his 1972 instructional book *Power Baseball: Dynamic Techniques of Winning*, which Didier wrote with Gerry Arbic. The book stands very well alongside the Charles Chapman and Hank Severeid volume of thirty years earlier, *Play Ball!* Didier and Arbic's rules on practice methods are evergreen. "Say it once; *do* it a thousand times," the authors advised. "Do not prolong it or fool around; be all business. Boys like orderliness." They asserted that "daring, aggression, and study are necessary for base running." Those traits can be applied to hitting, too, because "good hitters never learned to hit with the bat on their shoulder."[58]

Red Murff soldiered on as an Expos scout through the 1985 season. His last major input came with the signing of Rice University left-hander Norm

Charlton as the Expos' 1984 number one draft choice. Charlton was a free-spirited man who triple-majored at the university in Houston in political science, religion, and physical education. He once quipped, "If I can't argue you out of it, or preach you out of it, I will beat it out of you." He did not develop quickly enough for the front office, and after two years pitching for West Palm Beach in the Class A Florida State League, he was traded to the Reds, where he earned his greatest fame as part of the 1990 world champion Reds' "Nasty Boys" bullpen with Rob Dibble and Randy Myers.

In 1986 Murff went to work for the Atlanta Braves; he soon recommended local Houston product Mike Stanton, a left-handed pitcher who was picked in the thirteenth round of the 1987 draft out of Alvin Community College. A football injury killed Stanton's gridiron dreams, and he was convinced to turn pro and turn down a University of Arkansas athletic scholarship.[59] Stanton's connection to Nolan Ryan's hometown of Alvin must have sent a shiver of recognition through Murff. Stanton became a valuable reliever for the first wave of Braves' playoff teams in the early 1990s and then aided the most recent Yankee dynasty from 1998 to 2001.

In the months before the 1990 draft, Murff lobbied hard for the Braves to choose Todd Van Poppel as their number one draft pick in the nation. Once again, he compared a hard-throwing Texas right-hander to Nolan Ryan. The youngster's family hired top agent Scott Boras, who claimed that Van Poppel wanted to accept a scholarship offer from the University of Texas. They never met with the Braves, and Van Poppel wound up signing with the Oakland Athletics after that team drafted him. Braves' evaluators always felt that Boras and the A's might have made a secret deal; nevertheless, Van Poppel never fulfilled his promise. His career numbers were a paltry 40-52, with a 5.58 ERA. The "consolation prize" for the Braves turned out to be future Hall of Fame third baseman Chipper Jones (about whom you will learn more in an upcoming chapter on scout Paul Snyder).

In 1996 Murff published *The Scout: Searching for the Best in Baseball*, with the help of Dallas television personality Mike Capps, who twenty years earlier had been signed by Murff to a Minor League contract. His cousin Billy Capps was a longtime Cubs scout, so Mike brought to the collaboration an intimate understanding of the difficulties of becoming a Major League player. Like the work of earlier literarily inclined scouts Charles Chapman and Hank Severeid, Murff's *The Scout* is filled with trenchant observations. In the days before the draft, "we literally baby-sat our players," he wrote. Although it helps genetically to have a father who played the game, Murff warned, "You cannot make your son want to play. He has to want it and want it badly." True to his reputation as an opinionated man, he said, "Baseball, like any other business, simply doesn't improve by being manned by a preponderance of yes-men."

He concluded *The Scout* with the optimism of a baseball lifer: "Baseball has never stopped being a game for the average Joe," he wrote. He added that he was just "a regular good old boy who used to take a punch in the nose to get someone to play catch with him and who later searched the world for thirty-three years to find others who can do five things really, really well."[60] The five dearly desired things were, of course, running, throwing, fielding, hitting, and hitting with power. John "Red" Murff died in Tyler, Texas, on November 28, 2008, at the age of eighty-seven.

After Red Murff and Mel Didier left the team, the Montreal Expos had one more great run of contention. If the Players Association had not called a strike in mid-August 1994, the Expos likely would have made the playoffs, and quite possibly the World Series, for the first time. They had the best record in baseball, 74-40, but a month later as the strike continued, the owners canceled the World Series. The Expos had been largely built through the draft, except for future Hall of Fame right fielder Larry Walker, who had been signed in 1984 by an area scout Bob Rogers after performing in a summer tournament in western Canada. A native of British Columbia, Walker was primarily a hockey player until he chose baseball and by 1989 became an Expos regular.

The arrival of Gary Hughes as scouting director in 1986 intensified the emphasis on signing athletes with high ceilings. Delino DeShields, the 1987 first-round draft pick, was convinced by Hughes to turn down a basketball scholarship to Villanova, where he could have been the starting point guard. Marquis Grissom, 1988's third-round pick, was on a football scholarship at Florida A&M, Andre Dawson's alma mater, when Hughes sold him on a baseball career.

Gary Hughes loved all-around athletes. When scouting for George Stein-brenner's Yankees in the early 1980s, Hughes had been pressured by "the Boss" to use a second-round pick on John Elway, Stanford's All-American quarter-back. Hughes thought that the second round was too high for a player who likely would choose football, but obviously he did not own the team. Elway did play a year for the Yankees' Oneonta, New York, short-season Class A farm club in the New York–Penn League and led the team in every offensive category, before choosing NFL football with the Denver Broncos. When Hughes joined the expansion Florida Marlins before their first season in 1992, he drafted John Lynch, another outstanding Stanford football player. Lynch pitched in the Minors for two mediocre seasons before choosing football and went on to a Hall of Fame career as a defensive back. Hughes always liked to say that he drafted two Hall of Famers, except they were in another sport.

The strike finally ended in late March 1995, and before a shortened 144-game season resumed in late April 1995, most of the Expos' stars from the powerful 1994 team were traded—Walker to the Colorado Rockies, Gris-som to the Atlanta Braves, and reliever John Wetteland to the Yankees. Montreal would never really contend again, and after the 2004 season, the franchise was moved down the Eastern Seaboard, where it became the Washington Nationals.

The Toronto Blue Jays now had Canada all to themselves. Established in 1977, they made their first American League Championship Series in 1985 and became the first Canadian team to win the World Series in 1992 and then repeated in 1993. Under the stable ownership of the Labatt Brewing Company that hired competent business executives Paul Beeston and Peter Hardy, Toronto's rise to the top echelon in baseball happened quickly. It really took off after the 1981 season, when Bobby Cox arrived from Atlanta to become field manager.

Cox worked well alongside gifted General Manager Pat Gillick. Gillick was a former USC pitcher who toiled in the Baltimore Orioles farm system for four seasons before he realized he would never reach the Majors. He started out his evaluating career with Houston, moved on to the Yankees, and then welcomed the challenge of starting with an expansion team. Gillick worked at first under General Manager Peter Bavasi, one of the baseball executive sons of Buzzie Bavasi, and then became the top man after the 1978 season. One of his early moves as general manager was to bestow upon both Bobby Mattick and Al LaMacchia the title of vice president in charge of scouting, the highest position scouts ever received. As Stephen Brunt wrote in his valuable 1997 book *Diamond Dreams: 20 Years of Blue Jays Baseball*, "It wasn't just the savvy, but the continuity; for two decades, the three men worked as one."[61]

Mattick was the classic baseball lifer, whose father Wally, nicknamed Chick, had been an outfielder who played sparingly for the Cubs and Cardinals in the 1910s. Bobby was the starting shortstop for the 1940 Cubs, but he lost his job the next season to another future scout, Lenny Merullo. After World War II, Mattick became a leading youth coach in the San Francisco Bay Area. In the 1950s he funneled great talent to the Cincinnati Reds, including future Hall of Famer Frank Robinson, Curt Flood, Tommy Harper, and Vada Pinson. He scouted for several teams, including the Expos from 1972 through 1975, before coming to Toronto. In 1980, at the age of sixty-five, Mattick was hired as the second manager of the Blue Jays. He had never managed before, and like Karl Kuehl in Montreal, he was miscast in that role during his two losing seasons at the helm. He was delighted when Gillick returned him to his first loves of scouting and player development.

Al LaMacchia, a native of San Antonio, Texas, was another baseball lifer. Signed by Lou Maguolo of the St. Louis Browns, he drifted to the Pirates organization briefly, and then Maguolo arranged for his return to the Browns. LaMacchia pitched in sixteen games for St. Louis in the war years of 1943 and 1945 and finished with a 2-2 record and a 6.46 ERA. He knew that his future lay in coaching and scouting. After starting on his new craft with the Phillies in the late 1950s, he worked for the Milwaukee and Atlanta Braves from 1961 through 1975, where one of the key players he advocated for was future MVP Dale Murphy. Gillick would later comment that if he wanted advice about a number-one draft choice, he usually relied on Mattick, but LaMacchia was a wizard in finding the later-round gems.[62]

Gillick's first three drafts as general manager did not turn up any future core pieces, but the 1982 draft provided a decent haul. The Blue Jays' picks in the second and third rounds, southpaws David Wells from Point Loma High School in San Diego and Jimmy Key from Clemson University, enjoyed highly successful careers. The sixth-round pick, Pat Borders from Lake Wales High School in Florida, needed several years of Minor League training and a conversion from third base to catcher, but he wound up behind the plate for Toronto's World Series winners.

Gillick subscribed to the theory of many rivers for developing a championship team. With the help of his hard-working scouting staff, he utilized the Rule 5 Draft of Minor Leaguers with six years of previous experience to come up with such key players as outfielder and DH George Bell, third baseman Kelly Gruber, and first baseman Willie Upshaw.

An early Blue Jays' hire was Epinanio "Epy" Guerrero, a Dominican Republic scout whom Gillick first met in Houston. Epy, whose older brother Mario was a Major League infielder for eight seasons, became a great asset to the Blue Jays. His dragnet reached deep into that baseball-loving country. He founded one of his country's first baseball academies and brought in players like shortstop Tony Fernández and fellow infielder Dámaso García on the basis of their raw athletic tools and willingness to learn. (Sadly, both Fernández, 57, and García, 63, died in 2020.) Five of Epy's sons have been hired in some scouting or coaching capacity by Major League organizations.[63]

Pat Gillick left the Blue Jays to join the Seattle Mariners in 1999 and was there when the team won 116 games in 2001 only to lose to the Yankees in the ALCS. He moved on to the Phillies, where he presided over the 2008 world champion and 2009 runner-up to the Yankees. When he was elected to the Hall of Fame in 2011, he asked two of his scouts, Bob Engle and Don Welke, to take bows. Originally from Pop Kelchner country in Lebanon Valley, Pennsylvania, Engle belonged to the first group hired by the expansion franchise. He called his twenty-four years in Toronto "baseball utopia for people who were involved in scouting and player development."[64] Engle supervised the drafting of four Cy Young Award winners: Chris Carpenter, Roy Halladay, and Pat Hentgen for the Blue Jays and Félix Hernández for the Mariners.

Don Welke was raised in northern Illinois and liked to joke, "I went to Harvard"—the high school in his hometown of Harvard, Illinois. He played several sports at Carthage College, located on the border of Illinois and Wisconsin, but never played any pro ball. Among his first scouting jobs was as an instructor at the Royals Academy in Sarasota, a learning experience that he treasured. Like Bob Engle, he joined the Blue Jays early on and ultimately became one of Gillick's special assistants. He was a passionate advocate for southpaw pitcher Jim Abbott, whom the Blue Jays drafted in the thirty-sixth round in 1985. Abbott had his heart set on going to the University of Michigan, and ultimately the pitcher who made the Major Leagues with no right arm was drafted by the California Angels. Welke was always looking for athletes who made the game look easy when, of course, it never is. As a player developer, he was instrumental in convincing Dave Stieb, the Blue Jays' first ace, that his future lay on the mound and not as an everyday third baseman.[65]

It is too bad that a rivalry between Canada's two big eastern metropolises, Montreal and Toronto, never came to consistent fruition. It was a lovely gesture of appreciation when the Blue Jays invited Charles Bronfman to throw out the first ball before their first World Series game in 1992.

Next, I want you to meet Art Stewart, a devoted Yankees fan from Chicago who became a scout for his favorite team. Then the capriciousness of baseball life, like an unpredictable knuckleball, brought him to the Kansas City Royals.

4

Art Stewart and the Rise of the Kansas City Royals Expansion Franchise

If Art Stewart had his way, he might have worked forever for the New York Yankees. Although he was raised on the north side of Chicago not far from Wrigley Field, he was born on February 6, 1927, the same birthday as Babe Ruth and in the year when the Bambino hit 60 home runs. Stewart always believed there was magic in these facts, for no bigger fan of the Yankees existed in Chicago than young Art, who came of age during their dynasty of the late 1930s and early 1940s. His father, an engineer for the Radio Corporation of America, died when Art was only eight. A year or so later, curious about his father's life, the youngster climbed into the family attic and discovered a trunk of his father's memorabilia. One treasure was an old baseball glove, "brown and worn and barely held together by leather straps, but in my eyes, it was gorgeous," he remembered in his 2014 memoir, *The Art of Scouting*, written with Sam Mellinger.[1] He used it in neighborhood games for a long time.

Stewart was one of those active young fellows, so familiar throughout the history of scouting, who never could get enough of baseball. He vividly remembered his first Major League game on August 18, 1939. His uncle, a Chicago South Side resident, took him to the second night game ever played at Comiskey Park. The White Sox squared off against Cleveland, which had Bob Feller on the mound. Unheralded Edgar "Eddie" Smith outdueled the future Hall of Famer, as Chicago won on an eleventh-inning home run by future Hall of Fame shortstop Luke Appling. Years later, when Feller was an informal roving ambassador for baseball, Stewart was gifted with an autographed photograph from the Hall of Famer that noted the importance of that game to the baseball lifer. Art cherished another memory from that night, the straw hats tossed into the air by Comiskey Park bleacherites after Appling hit the walk-off homer.[2]

On the playing field, Stewart was a good enough middle infielder that he was the first freshman ever to make the varsity at Schurz High, and later he became team captain. Near the end of his senior season, a neatly dressed man came up to him and introduced himself as George Sisler, a scout for the Brooklyn Dodgers. "Nobody has more holler and hustle than you," exclaimed the recently elected Hall of Fame first baseman now working for his mentor, Branch Rickey. "And you run like a son of a bitch," he added.[3] Speed was, of course, a beloved trait of a Rickey man because it helped on both sides of the ball. Sisler offered Stewart a Minor League contract that would pay him $150 a month.

When Stewart got home, as he was discussing the exciting offer with his mother, the telephone rang. It was a call from George Moriarty, the former Tigers third baseman and manager, now a scout for his former team. He was gauging Art's interest in turning pro and offering the same amount of money as Sisler. Thrilled now at two offers, it dawned on Stewart that since his junior year playing in Chicago city parks, two neatly dressed men standing beyond the outfield foul line had been unobtrusively watching the games. "That must have been Sisler and Moriarty," he thought. Yet, after talking things over with his mother, Stewart politely declined both offers. Before he was even thirteen, he had been chief organizer for local neighborhood teams, picking up cash from team sponsors. He earned more money cleaning up unkempt city fields. Playing semipro games on weekends brought in more cash that could be at least doubled with side bets. He did not feel ready to leave home and his widowed mother.

Too young to serve in the military during World War II, Stewart took another step up the baseball ladder after the war when his local semipro team began attracting notice. Not surprisingly, he called his team the Chicago Yankees. From 1948 through 1952, Stewart estimated that twenty-four of the team's players signed pro contracts.[4] New York Yankee midwestern scouts Tom Greenwade, Fred Hasselman, and Lou Maguolo were impressed by how well the young man organized everything. Just as they had done for scouts

Joe Devine's and Bill Essick's youth teams on the West Coast, the Yankees sent Stewart game-used Major League uniforms and caps. Imagine the thrill experienced by the youngsters when they were outfitted in garb once worn by, among others, Joe DiMaggio, Whitey Ford, Eddie Lopat, Phil Rizzuto, and Gene Woodling. All Stewart had to do was to remove the NY logo and add a CY.[5]

When Fred Hasselman left the Yankees before the 1953 season to scout for the White Sox, Tom Greenwade and Lou Maguolo urged General Manager George Weiss to hire twenty-seven-year-old Stewart as an associate scout. Art felt an immediate bond with Maguolo. They both were small in stature—each barely five feet five—but gifted with boundless passion for teaching the game. Maguolo was glad to share some of the tricks of the trade with his mentee.

The way Maguolo signed outfielder Norm Siebern for the Yankees in 1951 was one memorable example that Stewart never forgot. Raised just outside of St. Louis, Norman Leroy Siebern was a gifted athlete who actually preferred basketball to baseball. When Maguolo first spotted Siebern as a fifteen-year-old on a youth team, he knew he wanted to sign the solid left-handed hitter who exhibited a projectable power stroke. Maguolo came to the Siebern family home with instructions from the Yankees to offer not more than a $30,000 bonus. Siebern and his father, Milton, who later became an official scorer for the Kansas City Athletics, wanted more money. A stalemate loomed when all of a sudden, Siebern's mother, Iva, came out of the kitchen, profusely apologizing for being unable to serve cookies because of a cranky oven. Seizing the opening, Maguolo suggested including a new stove in the final contract, and the deal was sealed.[6]

Siebern was signed after his 1951 high school graduation and began his rise up the crowded Yankees chain. In the off-seasons of 1952 and 1953, he was able to play basketball at Southwest Missouri State Teachers College (today known as Missouri State University). He and future Yankees teammate Jerry Lumpe, another Maguolo signing, led the team to NAIA (National Association of Intercollegiate Athletics) championships in both seasons. Siebern spent 1954 and 1955 in the U.S. Army. His first full season as a New York Yankee was in 1958, when he hit .300 with a .388 on-base percentage and .454 slugging average, as the Yankees won the World Series, avenging the previous year's loss to the Milwaukee Braves. In 1959 Siebern slumped to .271 and after the season he was traded to Kansas City in the deal for Roger Maris. Also going to the Athletics was Jerry Lumpe and outfielder Whitey Herzog, the future Hall of Fame manager who had also been signed by Lou Maguolo.

Maguolo was pleased when in 1958 the Yankees promoted Art Stewart to a full-time position as a midwestern-area scout. Showing his mettle immediately, Stewart signed his first future Major Leaguer, pitcher Jim Bouton, before the end of the year. Bouton was not considered the best prospect on his high school team in Chicago Heights, a suburb south of Chicago. That mantle went to Jerry Colangelo, later to make a big name in professional and Olympic basketball and as the first owner of the expansion Arizona Diamondbacks. One afternoon, when Colangelo was knocked out early, most scouts headed for the exits. Art Stewart remembered that Paul Krichell always advised never leave a game early—you never know what you might see. Sure enough, pitching in relief of Colangelo, Jim Bouton opened the eyes of many scouts with a fourteen-strikeout performance.

According to Bouton's biographer Mitchell Nathanson, Stewart sensed that other scouts were not interested in Bouton. So he instructed William K. Fred, one of his associate scouts, to arrange for Jim to pitch for the Chicago Yankees only in games against prison teams far outside of Chicago. Bouton's potential could not be kept a secret for long. When he starred for the Chicago-area American Legion team in the national tournament in Battle Creek, Michigan, a horde of scouts took notice. George Bouton, Jim's father, decided that his son could improve his prospects in college baseball. After pitching one effective year for Western Michigan University, his father sent a letter to more than a dozen teams, stating that his son wanted to sign before Thanksgiving. Stewart offered a package of more than $30,000, although most of the money would be paid in installments as Bouton climbed up the Minor League ladder. The Yankees flew in recently retired second baseman Jerry Coleman, transitioning to a brief career in management before turning to the broadcast booth, to do his part in convincing the Bouton family about the importance of Yankee pride and excellence.[7]

Jim Bouton arrived in the Majors in 1962 at the age of twenty-three and rocketed to prominence with a 21-7 record in 1963. Though the Dodgers swept the Yankees in the World Series, Bouton pitched brilliantly in Game Three, a 1–0 loss to Don Drysdale. Injuries then took a toll on his career. As the Yankees sunk into the second division two years later, Bouton's fortunes began to fade. By 1969 he was trying to master the knuckleball while pitching for the expansion Seattle Pilots. In 1970 the diary he kept about the previous season brought Bouton national fame when published with the assistance of sportswriter Leonard Shecter as *Ball Four*. Bouton went on to pitch in independent leagues and briefly tried a comeback with the Atlanta Braves before retiring in 1978. His overall career numbers were 62-63 with a 3.57 ERA in ten Major League seasons.

In 1963 Stewart signed another future Major League pitcher, southpaw Fritz Peterson. As Stewart told the story in his memoir, Peterson wrote him a letter after dropping out of Northern Illinois University, which stated that he was a Yankees fan and wanted to pitch for the team of his dreams. Tom Greenwade had taught Stewart to always answer letters from players, so Stewart quickly responded, saying he would be delighted to see Peterson pitch. When he arrived at the ballpark in Genoa, Illinois, not far from Rockford, Stewart gazed upon a baseball field where a cornfield served as an outfield wall. It was almost a foreshadow of the *Field of Dreams* story.[8]

Stewart was impressed by Peterson's performance and wanted to sign the pitcher immediately. However, because it was two years before the start of the amateur draft, the southpaw was being wooed by other teams. Stewart was able to get Peterson to agree to speak to the Yankees before he decided on other offers. When they came to play the White Sox in Chicago, Stewart closed the deal in the visiting clubhouse.[9] Peterson arrived in the Bronx in 1966 and enjoyed an eleven-year career, the first seven with noncontending Yankees teams. He became famous during spring training 1973 when he and fellow southpaw Mike Kekich announced that they were swapping wives and families. (Peterson has stayed with Kekich's former wife, but the relationship between Kekich and the first Mrs. Peterson did not last.)

Stewart received some criticism within the game for the life choices of his signees, but he never criticized them publicly. "When you're a scout, you see the world a little differently," he explained perceptively in his memoir. "To me, Bouton and Peterson each represent scouting successes—talented players off the beaten path who we found, identified, signed, and helped become successful big league pitchers."[10] Peterson finished his career with a record of 133-131 and a 3.30 ERA. His 90 complete games included 20 shutouts, and he retired with an excellent walk-strikeout ratio of 426:1,015.

Art Stewart quickly developed a reputation among his peers for his serious concentration on the game while scouting. At all costs, his colleagues avoided taking or making a phone call until the game was over. Stewart made one momentous exception while scouting an Illinois high school tournament early in the 1960s. He was distracted by the presence in the stands of a very attractive fan who was intently watching the game. She was a friend of Nick Kamzic, one of Stewart's best friends in the scouting fraternity who was working for the expansion California Angels. Knowing that the woman was a Yankees fan, Kamzic introduced Donna Wakely to Stewart; she quickly impressed him with her knowledge of the game. "She could tell when a guy was playing through pain," he wrote in his memoir, "when a guy had a good breaking ball working, . . . and when the batter missed his pitch."[11] If possible, she was more committed to Yankees mystique and aura than he was. It's "the only team to follow," she insisted. With Nick Kamzic as his best man, Art and Donna soon married, and they were an endearing baseball couple until her death in 2008.[12]

Kamzic, who was eight years older, knew Stewart from Chicago. Kamzic starred in both football and baseball at Kelly High School, and some people thought he had the makings of another Phil Rizzuto. But in 1942 he was drafted into the U.S. Army and served in Europe under General George S. Patton, winning two Purple Hearts. Serious war injuries torpedoed his chance of making the Major Leagues, but he fell in love with scouting shortly after retiring as a player in 1948. He worked with the Cincinnati Reds for ten seasons and then joined the Milwaukee Braves. When Roland Hemond, one of the baseball executives most devoted to scouts and player developers, became the scouting director of the expansion California Angels before the start of the 1961 season, he strongly recommended Kamzic to owner Gene Autry, who made the Chicago-born scout his first hire. Kamzic stayed loyal for the rest of his life to the singing cowboy.[13]

Kamzic and Stewart might have been best friends, but the nature of the scouting profession made them fierce competitors. As the college baseball season neared its end in the late spring 1964, the bidding for Rick Reichardt, the University of Wisconsin football and baseball star, intensified. Billed as a right-handed Mickey Mantle, Reichardt was timed in 3.9 seconds to first base and possessed enormous power and a strong arm. He enjoyed two sensational 1963 and 1964 seasons with the baseball Badgers, leading the Big Ten in hitting in each year. In football, he played primarily running back and wide receiver; on the January 1963 Wisconsin Rose Bowl team that lost to USC, 42–37, despite a frantic twenty-three-point comeback in the fourth quarter, he played defensive back. In the fall of 1963 Rick led the Big Ten in receptions, though an ankle injury limited some of his effectiveness.

Stewart believed he might have the inside track on signing Reichardt. He saw him play several times during his high school seasons in Stevens Point, Wisconsin. He developed a good relationship with Rick's father, Dr. Frederick William "Fritz" Reichardt, a local surgeon who worked with the Green Bay Packers when they trained in Stevens Point during the 1950s. Dr. Reichardt was a pillar of the community, giving free medical clinics to local athletes and doing the same on trips to Latin America. He also built cradles for all nine of his children. Stewart was impressed how Dr. Reichardt encouraged Rick, the oldest, to try a different sport each school year. He excelled in them all, one year winning the state broad jump title. Stewart wanted to sign Rick after he graduated from high school, but Dr. Reichardt said firmly that his son was going to follow in his footsteps and attend the University of Wisconsin in Madison.[14]

As Stewart expected, when word got around about Reichardt's Badger baseball exploits, eighteen of the then-twenty Major League teams began following the hot prospect. In one 1964 home game against Illinois, he hit three home runs, one each to left, center, and right field, added two singles, and stole home. Before a game at the University of Minnesota, a photographer coaxed Rick into standing on the dugout holding a bat while dozens of scouts hung their tongues out, salivating at the prospect of signing him. Reichardt said later that he felt uncomfortable about the stunt, but he thought he would have been considered snooty and uncooperative if he had not posed.[15]

After the end of his junior baseball season, Rick's decision on whether to choose pro baseball or pro football became a big national story. NBC television sports broadcaster Bob Wolff narrated a series, "Odyssey of a Bonus Baby—the Courting of Rick Reichardt." *Sports Illustrated* assigned Edwin Shrake to write an in-depth story about his pending choice. Young Reichardt was not used to being in a goldfish bowl. He moved out of his college dormitory and in with his grandfather, who lived not far from the Madison campus. Art Stewart revitalized his hope of landing Reichardt when he heard his father say that although football's quicker pace of play might better fit Rick's active disposition, baseball might be a less risky long-term investment. Dr. Reichardt also said, "You take advantage of the angles, or else the angles will take advantage of you."[16]

As the Yankee scout who knew Reichardt best, Stewart accompanied him on a whirlwind visit to New York. Co-owner Dan Topping pulled out all the stops. He arranged for a private visit to the recently opened World's Fair in Flushing Meadows, Queens. He provided center orchestra tickets for the hottest show on Broadway, *Hello, Dolly!*, and took Rick to a ritzy steakhouse. The next day, at Yankees' offices, Topping laid it on thick about the Yankees' pinstripe tradition. He told Reichardt that he was prepared to offer a team record of $150,000 in bonus money, far more than the reported $100,000 scout Atley Donald gave in 1961 to catcher Jake Gibbs, the former University of Mississippi quarterback (who did not establish himself as a regular until 1967 and then for only two seasons, retiring after a ten-year career with a .233 batting average and .321 slugging average).[17]

During a visit to the Yankees' clubhouse, irrepressible Jim Bouton told Reichardt, "We could use that bat of yours, Rick." Manager Yogi Berra was impressed by the size of the strapping six-foot-four athlete, who weighed well over two hundred pounds. "The kid don't make me feel so tall," Yogi said. But ever worldly wise he added, "Who knows if he's gonna make it?" Ralph Houk, the former manager, now the Yankees general manager, was also guarded in his comments. He is still "an amateur," he reminded the sportswriters who were eager to add to the buildup of the talented but still unproven prospect.[18]

Stewart said goodbye to Reichardt as the prospect headed to Boston to visit the Red Sox. On a tour of Fenway Park, Milt Bolling, former Red Sox infielder turned scout, told Rick that the left-field foul line at the base of the famed Green Monster was just 298 feet and not the listed 315. Some of the Boston press were building Rick up as the "next Ted Williams" even though he was a right-handed hitter. In Chicago, the White Sox gave Reichardt a front row box seat next to Jaye P. Morgan, a popular singer of the day. The team convinced reluctant slugger Dave Nicholson, once a $108,000 bonus boy with the Orioles now desperately trying to hang on to his Major League career, to say hello to a fellow that all experts predicted would far surpass Nicholson's 1962 bonus. Next up was a visit to the St. Louis Cardinals, which enlisted the recently retired Stan Musial in the effort to sign him. Musial, heading into a brief executive role with the team, promised that he would also be available as a batting instructor. Scouting director George Silvey and scout Joe Monahan made the point that the Cardinals were weak in the outfield and Rick could rise quickly in the organization.[19]

Aggressive Charlie Finley of the Kansas City Athletics also tried to get into the bidding, but it was Nick Kamzic and the California Angels who put on the most successful presentation. Kamzic told owner Gene Autry that Reichardt was "the most exciting and most explosive player" he had seen in his eighteen years in the business.[20] Autry was determined to give the Los Angeles Dodgers a run for their money in the Southern California market. In 1962, in only their second year in existence, the Angels had surprised the baseball world by winning eighty-six games and finishing third, ten games behind the Yankees. They fell down to ninth in 1963 with a 70-91 record, making Autry even more determined to bring exciting new blood into the organization. He put on a full court press, inviting entertainment industry friends to meet Reichardt. At a lavish movie party for the opening of Stanley Kramer's *Ship of Fools*, tough-guy actor Lee Marvin advised Reichardt to get all he could out of the high-rolling owners.[21]

As expected, Reichardt's bonus of $205,000 broke all records to date. It surpassed the $175,000 the Pirates had lavished upon high school infielder and outfielder Bob Bailey in 1963. Edwin Shrake gave Reichardt, thoughtful and reflective beyond his years, the last word in his *Sports Illustrated* article. "Now the shoe is on the other foot," the newest Angel said. "Now it's me who has to be nice to them."[22] The hoopla followed Reichardt to his Minor League games in Dubuque, Iowa, where thousands came to cheer him on. He didn't disappoint, with several tape-measure home runs. He made his debut for the Angels in 1964 with 37 at bats, but he didn't become a regular until 1967.

Unfortunately, an injury to his kidney early in his Major League career and subsequent surgery kept Reichardt from fulfilling his promise. In 1971 he started a three-year stint with the White Sox, and after one at bat with the Royals in 1974, he was released. He always thought that being a Players Association representative hastened his retirement at the age of thirty-three. He finished with career numbers of .261 batting average, .414 slugging average, 116 home runs, 445 RBIs, and 391 runs. A few years later, he relocated to Gainesville, Florida, with many members of his family, including Dr. Reichardt. Rick's rooting allegiances shifted from the Wisconsin Badgers to the University of Florida Gators.[23]

The huge amount lavished on Reichardt compelled the majority of baseball owners at their December 1964 Winter Meetings to vote for an amateur free agent draft, effective in June 1965. Very few scouts, including Art Stewart, welcomed the revolutionary switch, but the die had been cast. As midwestern scouting supervisor, Stewart attended the first draft at the Roosevelt Hotel near New York's Grand Central Station. The situation was "chaos. Absolute chaos," he remembered in his memoir. "Clubs didn't know how to prepare for it." Jack Schwarz, longtime scouting director of the Giants since the New York days of Bill Terry and Mel Ott, grew incensed at another team picking "my player" and almost came to blows with the offending scout. In a few years, to avoid similar altercations, Major League Baseball scheduled the next few drafts by phone call, not in person.[24]

The first draft had some moments of levity. A team picked a player in a late round who had been drafted in an earlier round. One Angels official got confused about Glen Burnie, Maryland, in Anne Arundel County, the hometown of number-one draft pick Jim Spencer. The official wanted to know who this Glen Burnie fellow was and what a girl named Anne Arundel had to do with the draft. Despite the chaos, the new world of the draft was here to stay. No longer, in the memorable words of Kevin Kerrane, did a scout have to sell the organization to the player and his family; now he had to sell the player to the organization.

Because the Yankees were slipping in the standings in the late 1960s, they had several high picks in the draft, with decidedly mixed results. In 1965 the Yankees' first-ever first round pick was high school pitcher Bill Burbach from Dickeyville, Wisconsin. He had a short career because of injury, going 6-8 with a 3.65 ERA in 1969, and he never won another Major League game. Their second-round pick, shortstop Danny Thompson from a high school in Oklahoma, did not sign. He eventually enjoyed a seven-year career, six of them with the Twins, before succumbing to cancer at the age of twenty-nine in 1976 while he was still on the active roster of the Texas Rangers.

The most productive Yankees selection in the 1965 draft was pitcher Stan Bahnsen, who was picked in the fourth round from the University of Nebraska. The third of four children born to a Union Pacific brakeman, Bahnsen hailed from Council Bluffs, Iowa, and area scout Joe Thompson advocated for him.[25] Three years later, Bahnsen was voted American League Rookie of the Year after a season in which he went 16-12 with an excellent 2.05 ERA. The earned run average was no doubt influenced by 1968 being the so-called Year of the Pitcher, when batting averages became so depressed throughout baseball that the mound was lowered to aid hitters, starting in 1969. Bahnsen went on to enjoy a sixteen-year career, most of his seasons outside New York. In December 1971 he was traded to the White Sox for infielder Rich McKinney, who never developed into a core piece for the Yankees. Bahnsen's overall career numbers with the Yankees, White Sox, expansion Montreal Expos, Angels, and Phillies were a respectable 146-149 and 3.60 ERA.

The 1966 Yankees draft was not much better. First-round pick Jim Lyttle, an outfielder from Florida State, became a journeyman who played in less than four hundred games over an eight-year career, only the first three with the Yankees. The seventh rounder, pitcher Steve Kline from Washington State University, was one of the favorite picks of Eddie Taylor, the scout who signed Mel Stottlemyre. Kline put up good numbers in 1971 and 1972, winning a combined twenty-eight games with an ERA below 3 runs in each of those seasons. Injury forced an early end to his Major League career after six years. Loving all-around athletes, Stewart had no problem with the pick in the tenth round, Ken Stabler, a left-handed pitcher from the University of

Alabama. He did not sign, but he went on to a football Hall of Fame career as an Oakland Raiders quarterback. The Yankees drafted future slugging third baseman Darrell Evans from California's Pasadena City College in the second round of the January draft, but he did not sign. His twenty-one-year career would start with the Atlanta Braves, and later he was part of the Tigers' 1984 team that started the season 35-5 and wound up winning the World Series.

As a result of falling to the basement in 1966, the Yankees had the first pick in the 1967 draft. Before the season, Ralph Houk returned to the dugout as manager, and veteran baseball man Lee MacPhail became Yankees general manager, but the team improved to only ninth place. In 1968 the Yankees rose to fifth place but only four games over .500; in 1969 they were in fifth, one game under .500.

In 1967 Ron Blomberg from Atlanta's Druid Hills High School became the number-one pick in the nation. Visions of a left-handed-hitting Jewish outfielder and first baseman taking aim at Yankee Stadium's short right-field porch in front of adoring Jewish fans danced in the heads of MacPhail and area scout Atley Donald, but injuries contributed to Blomberg never fulfilling his promise. He is most remembered as being baseball's first designated hitter when the American League introduced the innovation in 1973.

In 1968 the Yankees struck pay dirt, signing the first-round pick, catcher Thurman Munson from Kent State University in Ohio. Former Yankee Gene Woodling, a part-time Midwest-area scout, played an important role in Munson's signing.[26] But no other future Major Leaguer came out of that year's draft for the Yankees. As for the draft in 1969, the first-round selection, outfielder Charlie Spikes from Bogalusa, Louisiana, is mainly remembered for being a key part of the deal in late 1972 that brought over from Cleveland third baseman Graig Nettles, who became a core member of the unit that brought the Yankees back to win three World Series in a row from 1976 to 1978.

As the Yankees fell out of contention, Art Stewart was taking stock of the situation with the team of his dreams. In 1966, the year the team fell to the American League basement, only three products from the farm were on the Yankees' varsity, and only 154 players were in the entire system.[27] Farm director Johnny Johnson argued that the team still had seven farm teams, more than most organizations, but they simply were not producing the talent as in the Paul Krichell days. The lack of success of the draft picks made Stewart doubt the immediate improvement in the Yankee situation. The ownership-management team of the Columbia Broadcasting System and President Michael Burke was obviously spinning its wheels. After landing in the basement, the team improved only to ninth in 1967 and finished fifth in 1968 but only four games above .500. In 1969 the Yankees stayed in fifth at 80-81.

Working for the expansion Kansas City Royals franchise began to intrigue Art Stewart. He remembered the glory days of the Kansas City Blues, the Yankees' American Association franchise that, with its sister Newark Bears of the International League, was so talented that many baseball people thought they could beat the tail-end franchises in the two Major Leagues. He knew that Kansas City was a good baseball town and was finally freed from the mercurial ownership of Charlie Finley, who moved the Athletics to Oakland after the 1967 season. Stewart sensed that the city would likely support a new team building from the ground up. A quick return of Major League Baseball to Kansas City was assured when powerful United States senator Stuart Symington (D-MO) warned of a congressional investigation into baseball's antitrust exemption.

When Art Stewart met the charismatic Royals owner, pharmaceutical magnate Ewing Marion Kauffman, it made the decision easier for Stewart (although he said his wife Donna took more than a year to adjust to a new life without the pinstripes). Kauffman, born on September 21, 1916, on a farm near Garden City, Missouri, fifty miles south of Kansas City, was one of six children of John S. and Effie May Winders Kauffman. A farm accident caused John Kauffman to lose an eye, and he relocated the family to Kansas City, where he became a life insurance adjuster. Effie Kauffman attended a state teacher's college that featured a strong classics program. Ewing himself did not obtain more than a community college degree, yet he had developed a lifelong interest in reading when he was laid up with rheumatic fever for two years during ages ten and eleven.[28]

During his time as a signalman in the United States Navy during World War II, he began to envision the shape of his future success. By his own estimate, he won about $90,000 in poker games, a nest egg for postwar choices. He tried his hand in medical insurance—the field in which Charlie Finley made his fortune—but the work did not truly interest him. He found his niche as a salesman of pharmaceutical products, including oral medications and syringes and remedies for fatigue. He grew so successful that by 1950 he founded his own company, Marion Laboratories. According to Paul Hensler in *The New Boys of Summer: Baseball's Radical Transformation in the Late Sixties*, he motivated his employees "with the vocabulary of trench warfare, where salesmanship [was] equated with patriotism, and malingering with desertion."[29]

Before long, Kauffman entered the ranks of the multimillionaires, and he took advantage of his elite status by becoming an owner of race horses. After the horrible experience with Chicago-born Charlie Finley, Kansas City yearned for a local owner to lead the expansion Royals. Ewing Kauffman was not a baseball fan and didn't know the jargon of the sport—he once quipped to an in-house interviewer that he thought a squeeze play was something mothers urged their daughters to be wary of when going out on a date. But he soon yielded to the pressure from both community leaders and his second wife, Muriel O'Brien Kauffman, and he interviewed with American League officials. Baseball was historically fearful of owners connected to the horse racing business, but Kauffman pledged that he would confine his betting to golf games and card games. Anointed by the owners in early January 1968, Kauffman quickly hired as general manager Cedric Tallis, who had worked his way up from a Class D general manager position in Thomasville, Georgia, to an important assistant general manager's job on both the baseball and business side for the expansion California Angels.[30]

Kauffman hit the ground running, displaying a work ethic that quickly impressed Art Stewart. Always dressed impeccably in powder blue, he encouraged similar fastidiousness and attention to detail in his employees. He was genuinely paternalistic, offering Marion Laboratory workers profit-sharing and stock-sharing programs. He planned to run his baseball business in similar fashion, but he wanted results and swift success. He expected a pennant in Kansas City within five or six years, a prediction that most baseball people felt unrealistic. Undeterred and already impatient with the stand-pat quality of the baseball business, Kauffman kept a copy of Earnshaw Cook's *Percent-*

age Baseball on his desk, a book by a John Hopkins University engineering professor, who twenty years before Bill James, was analyzing the way to win games by understanding statistical probabilities.[31]

Kauffman's new midwestern-area scout, Art Stewart, didn't waste time digging up prospects for his new team. In just his second year on the job, he found his first future Major Leaguer, signing fleet outfielder Tom Poquette from Memorial High School in Eau Claire, Wisconsin, in the fourth round of the 1970 draft. Stewart convinced Poquette, a star in many sports, and his father, a social studies teacher and coach, to turn down a University of Wisconsin athletic scholarship and focus on baseball. Like all great scouts, Stewart had acted on a tip from a reliable source. In this case it was Lois Brandenburg, a reporter for the Appleton, Wisconsin, *Post-Crescent*, who had been following Poquette since his sophomore year in high school. She previously tipped off the White Sox to the merits of left-handed pitcher Ken Frailing, who had a six-year Major League career.[32] (Brandenburg evidently did not stick with baseball scouting in the west-central Wisconsin area because no record exists of any later baseball activities by her.)

Thomas Arthur Poquette broke into the Majors in September 1973 with a hit off Oakland's Vida Blue, but wrist and knee injuries kept him from a regular job until the 1976 season. Never hitting with enough power to become a regular, Poquette was part of the three Royals playoff teams from 1976 through 1978 and enjoyed an eight-year career with three teams. His career stats were modest: 452 games, 1,226 at bats, 329 hits, 10 home runs, 136 RBIs, 81 walks, 82 strikeouts, 13 stolen bases, and 13 caught stealing. Yet among his 329 hits were an impressive 62 doubles and 18 triples. He clearly was one of those players whose value to a team far exceeded the raw numbers.

The 1970 season was the first of Ewing Kauffman's great experiment, the Royals Baseball Academy. It was a great example of the new owner's eagerness to think outside the box, which appealed to Art Stewart. From the moment he bought the team, Kauffman started planning for a new way of scouting and player development that didn't involve expensive acquisition costs of new players or trades for veteran players who had seen better days. He knew that a small-market team like the Royals could not match the size and off-field opportunities of the big cities like New York, Chicago, and Los Angeles.

"There must be a better way to develop players" became Kauffman's mantra. He came up with the idea of building a facility that would be open to athletes under the age of twenty with no professional or college baseball experience. The only qualifications were that players had to run the sixty-yard dash in 6.7 seconds or less (the Major League average was around 7.0 seconds) and to show sufficient arm strength. They would train for a minimum of ten months on land that he purchased five miles outside Sarasota. Kauffman built five immaculate baseball fields, one of them equipped with a grandstand and lights; a swimming pool; a tennis court; and a dormitory to house players. All of the athletes were required to attend speech classes at nearby Manatee Community College to improve their public speaking. English classes for Spanish-speaking players were also scheduled.[33]

Ground-breaking for the Royals Academy in Sarasota started in early February 1970, with Royals outfielder Lou Piniella, the 1969 American League Rookie of the Year, shoveling the first dirt. Piniella was initially signed by the Orioles, but he never could impress Minor League manager Earl Weaver, who reportedly gave him the sarcastic nickname of "Sweet Lou." Not surprisingly, Piniella welcomed getting away from Weaver and coming to an expansion team. As a teenager growing up in the baseball-rich area around Tampa Bay, Lou had taken a year off from baseball to focus on basketball. It has been speculated by some baseball historians that Piniella's success without single-minded devotion to the game reinforced Kauffman's belief that athleticism was more important than traditional methods of creating Major Leaguers.[34]

In early June 1970 Kansas City hosted the first of what would be 128 tryout camps all across the country. Out of the nearly eight thousand applicants, forty-three players from twenty-three states were chosen for the academy's first class. For director of the academy, Ewing Kauffman tapped Syd Thrift, who had been initially hired as a Royals eastern-area scout. (He later became a Pittsburgh general manager.) Thrift hired an impressive group of instructors, including recently retired catcher Charlie Lau. On his way to becoming an acclaimed but controversial hitting guru, Lau was reportedly the first coach to exhaustively film hitters at bat and in practice.

Among the other academy instructors were onetime Red Sox and Senators southpaw Chuck Stobbs; Jim Lemon, Washington Senators outfielder and briefly their manager; and several former Yankees—Joe Gordon, Tommy Henrich, and Johnny Neun, who was a longtime scout, 1946 Yankees interim manager, and later their director of player development. University of Kansas track coach Bill Easton and his star Wes Santee, once the American record holder in the mile, came down to teach base running techniques. Mickey Cobb, soon to become the longtime trainer of the Royals, introduced a mandatory stretching program, probably the first such effort in baseball history.[35]

Art Stewart made his first trip to the academy in the summer of 1970 and was very impressed. He liked that each position player enjoyed thirty minutes of batting practice each day, more than three times as long as the amount at a traditional training camp. Games were scheduled against primarily local junior college teams, with the academy winning the vast majority. June 4, 1971, was noteworthy in the young history of the Royals Academy—the day of the home opener for the Gulf Coast Royals, a new team in the Gulf Coast League, whose opposition would be young players from the Chicago White Sox, Cincinnati, Cleveland, Pittsburgh, and St. Louis organizations. Baseball commissioner Bowie Kuhn and Florida governor Reubin Askew were in attendance for the start of what became a highly successful season. The Royals won the league title handily with a 40-13 record, enjoying, at one point, a twenty-four-game winning streak. They led the league in both hitting and earned run average and succeeded in 103 out of 119 stolen base attempts, an astonishing 48 more than any other team in the Gulf Coast League.[36]

It is commonly agreed that Frank White, who grew up a half mile from Kansas City's Municipal Stadium (where the KC Athletics had played), was the best player to have graduated from the academy. White hadn't been scouted in high school because his school did not field a team and few scouts wanted to go into Black neighborhoods. White did display enough skills playing in local American Legion and Knights of Columbus leagues that he was invited to the academy. His wife was expecting their first child, but she encouraged him to go. She reasoned that his job at a sheet metal factory paying him one hundred dollars a week could wait.[37]

White's progress was swift through the KC system. He arrived in the big leagues at the age of twenty-one in June 1973 and played for seventeen seasons. He won eight gold gloves and played in two World Series (including the Royals' 1985 triumph over the Cardinals). His final career line reads 2,324 games, .255 batting average, .293 on-base percentage, .383 slugging average, 2,006 hits, 178 stolen bases, 412 walks, and 1,035 strikeouts. He later served many seasons as a Royals television broadcaster.

White may have been the most distinguished academy graduate, but thirteen other players reached the Majors, and several others made contributions to baseball at some level. Shortstop U. L. Washington, from the small town of Stringtown, Oklahoma, was White's double play partner for most of the years from Washington's arrival in 1977 through his last year in Kansas City in 1984. U. L. was Washington's given name—it did not stand for anything else. He drew some notoriety for playing with a toothpick in his mouth, reportedly because when playing on the Kansas City artificial turf, he could use no blades of grass instead.[38] He was a swift and solid defensive player who put up respectable career offensive numbers: .251 batting average, .313 on-base percentage, .343 slugging average, and 132 stolen bases.

Another infielder, Ron Washington (no relation), came to the academy from the inner city in New Orleans. During a seventeen-year pro career, Washington was in the Majors for parts of ten seasons, with the Dodgers in 1977 and the next six with the Twins from 1981 through 1986 before finishing with the Orioles, Cleveland, and the Astros. His Major League career numbers reflected that he was not a power hitter: .261 batting average, .292 on-base percentage, and .368 slugging average. He later became renowned as an infield coach and managed the Texas Rangers to two World Series in a row in 2010 and 2011. He returned to coaching and was third base coach for the world champion 2021 Atlanta Braves. First baseman Winston Cole never made the Majors, but he was a 1974 trade piece when the Royals acquired pitcher Nelson Briles from the Pirates. Southpaw Hal Baird spent four years in Triple-A without making the Majors, but he made a big name for himself as baseball coach at Auburn University in Alabama. He tutored future big leaguers Bo Jackson, Hall of Fame slugger Frank Thomas, starting pitcher Tim Hudson, and closer Gregg Olson.

Ewing Kauffman never tired of finding new methods to speed up playing development. He invited European psychologists to work with players at the academy. They might have been somewhat difficult to understand, but future

Royals Doug Bird, primarily a reliever, and Steve Busby, mainly a starter, remembered receiving useful tips from the scientists. During the 1972 season, the Gulf Coast Royals slipped in the standings but still produced a solid record of 41-22; however, the number of students in the academy dropped to twenty-six. The following year, only fourteen students were in the school, and the record of the team fell to one game above .500.[39]

In May 1974 the academy was officially disbanded. Part of the problem was that General Manager Cedric Tallis and farm director Lou Gorman never truly believed in the concept of creating Major Leaguers on the basis of athletic ability alone. Another issue was the expense. With the opening of the new Royals Stadium in Kansas City delayed by construction costs, Kauffman's business advisors argued that shuttering the academy would make up for the cost of spending another season at Municipal Stadium.[40] Not long before he died of bone cancer in August 1993, Kauffman admitted to Art Stewart that pulling the plug on the Sarasota experiment was the biggest mistake he ever made. He felt the Royals could have built a dynasty if he hadn't followed the short-sighted ideas of his business advisors and his less adventurous baseball people.[41]

On the Major League level, there were signs that the Royals were finding some pieces for a future contender. They picked up National Leaguers Fred Patek from the Pirates, a five-foot-five shortstop; Amos Otis, an outfielder from the Mets; Octavio Victor "Cookie" Rojas, a second baseman from the Cardinals, which only had him briefly after his long career with the Phillies; and Hal McRae, an outfielder from the Reds who slipped seamlessly into the role of designated hitter when it started in the American League in 1973.

The Royals were also having good success in the amateur free agent draft. Draft history was made in the second round in 1971 when two future Hall of Famers were selected back-to-back, Kansas City picking George Brett and the Phillies choosing Mike Schmidt. Both were amateur shortstops, Brett at El Segundo High School in Southern California and Schmidt at Ohio University in Athens. Both were converted into renowned Major League third basemen. California area scout Rosey Gilhousen had followed Brett, the youngest of four boys who all played pro baseball, from his earliest days in high school. His oldest brother, Ken, was the fourth overall pick in the 1966 draft, taken by the Red Sox, which projected him as a pitcher despite his offensive potential. Ken became the youngest pitcher to start a World Series game in 1967, but during a six-month stint in the army the following season, he incurred an injury that impacted his career. He did play for parts of fourteen seasons in the Major Leagues, earning 83 wins, but it was youngest brother George who became the Hall of Famer with his talent and enormous passion for the game that Gilhousen and Royals cross-checker Tom Ferrick foresaw.[42]

More riches came in the 1971 draft. Picked ahead of George Brett was the Royals' first round choice, catcher John Wathan from the University of San Diego. He enjoyed a ten-year career, all seasons with the Royals, catching 120 games in one of those seasons. Starting pitcher Steve Busby was selected in the second round of the June secondary draft and would throw two-hitters in a career sadly shortened by injury at the age of thirty-one. Busby's final numbers—a career won-lost record of 70-54 with a 3.72 ERA—suggest a far more prolific career if only he had stayed healthy. He later became an excellent broadcaster for both the Royals and the Texas Rangers.

The bounty in the 1971 draft continued. Future utility player Joe Zdeb, the fourth-round pick in 1971, would play three seasons in Kansas City. Pitcher Mark Littell was a find in the twelfth round out of the University of Tampa. He got his first taste of Major League action in 1973 and then put up identical won-lost numbers of 8-4 in 1976 and 1977, although his ERA was far better in 1976, 2.08, than in 1977, 3.61. His 1976 season ended on a sour note when he gave up the pennant-winning home run to the Yankees' Chris Chambliss in the bottom of the ninth inning. He spent the last years of his career with the St. Louis Cardinals. In the never-ending search for good athletes, in the 1971 January draft the Royals drafted but did not sign Archie Manning, an all-around high school athlete from Drew, Mississippi. It was the fourth time Manning was drafted, but he continued playing football at the University of Mississippi and went on to a Hall of Fame career with the New Orleans Saints.

The prize of the 1972 draft was the second-round pick Dennis Patrick Leonard, who was born in Brooklyn and raised in suburban Nassau County. His father was a New York City policeman, and his mother served as a crossing guard near his home. Leonard played his college baseball at Iona, a small college north of the city in New Rochelle, New York. Royals area scout Al Diez had been following the pitcher's development for a long time and kept cross-checker Tom Ferrick informed about his progress. After Leonard led his summer team in the Atlantic Collegiate Baseball League to a championship, he signed for a $16,000 bonus, a large amount for a player from a cold-weather state where not many games were played. Leonard moved quickly through the Royals' farm system and arrived to stay in the Majors in 1975. He was a big part of the three straight AL Central title winners. From 1975 until the middle of the 1983 season when he ruptured a patellar tendon, Leonard won 136 games, more than any right-handed Major League pitcher in that period. (Hall of Famer southpaw Steve Carlton led all pitchers with 167 wins from 1975 to 1983.)[43]

The name of Tom Ferrick keeps coming up in this chapter; it is time to learn a little more about him. Ferrick turned to scouting in 1967, the last season of the Kansas City Athletics. He joined the Royals shortly after the franchise was established in 1969 and remained an important evaluator until his retirement in 1996. He was born Thomas Jerome Ferrick on January 6, 1915, in the Bronx, not far from Yankee Stadium. His father, also named Thomas, had been a policeman and a good semipro player, but he died when his son was nine. Young Tom attended a preparatory seminary on a path to the priesthood, but the lure of baseball became too great. He didn't immediately turn pro, driving a truck for a living while staying involved with the game in semipro ball and serving as a batting practice pitcher for the New York Giants. In one of Babe Ruth's last years, Ferrick threw to the Babe as he tried to recover from an injury.

In 1936 he signed with the Giants and around this time changed the spelling of his name to the more common Ferrick. He showed great promise in his first two seasons, leading the Cotton States League in innings pitched and earned run average in 1936 and winning twenty games for Richmond in the Class B Piedmont League the following year. But a serious shoulder injury derailed his progress. When the Giants refused to release him, Andrew C. Sharp tells us in a thorough SABR BioProject essay, Ferrick appealed to Commissioner Landis, who decreed him a free agent.[44]

A scout for Connie Mack saw Ferrick pitching semipro baseball with the Bushwicks, a top-notch team in the New York area. Ferrick signed with Mack's

Philadelphia Athletics, and in 1941, he compiled an 8-10 record in 119 innings with a 3.77 ERA. He was a control pitcher, rarely striking out batters but not walking many either. A roster crunch forced Mack to reluctantly release him. (He and Ferrick maintained friendly contact, and when the venerable Mack died in 1956, he was one of his pallbearers.) In 1942 Ferrick statistically enjoyed his best year for Cleveland, throwing eighty-one innings with a sparkling 1.99 earned run average in thirty-one appearances, all but two in relief.

Service in the Navy followed, including pitching on a military team managed by Mickey Cochrane, who would be inducted into Cooperstown in 1947. In January 1946 Ferrick was discharged at the rank of chief petty officer. He started another tour with tail-end teams in the American League—the Browns, the Senators, and the Browns again in 1950. In early June 1950, he earned the enduring praise of beleaguered manager Zack Taylor when he entered a game against the Red Sox with Boston having scored 29 runs. Taylor pleaded with Ferrick not to allow the Bosox to become the first team in baseball history to score 30 runs in a game. Ferrick answered Taylor's prayer by not allowing another run.[45]

One week later, Ferrick might have been thinking of Jimmie Reese's adage "You never know, the best of your life [may be] five minutes ahead in this game," because on June 15, 1950, the Yankees traded for him to add a solid arm to their bullpen. Entitled Yankee fans wanted a bigger name, but Ferrick pitched very well for the rest of 1950, going 8-4 with 10 saves. He won the third game of the World Series by pitching a scoreless ninth inning—the next day the Yanks completed a sweep over the Phillies, with three of the four games closely contested. His grateful teammates voted him a full winner's share. Ferrick's Yankees glory was brief because he was traded to the Senators in June 1951 along with pitcher Bob Porterfield for left-handed reliever Bob Kuzava, who would shine in the 1952 World Series.

Ferrick retired after 1952 and immediately started coaching. He joined manager Birdie Tebbetts at the Reds' Indianapolis farm club as the recently retired catcher started on his new career. Ferrick took to his new job immediately, liking his new role as instructor of pitchers. He insisted that a good reliever is worth as much as a twenty-game winner.[46] Tebbetts brought Ferrick to Cincinnati as his pitching coach in 1954, and he stayed until Birdie resigned before the end of the 1958 season. Tebbetts, who had experienced many things in baseball, told sportswriter Red Smith, "I've never met a fellow so serious about baseball in all my life."[47]

Coaching jobs with the Phillies and the Tigers quickly followed, and in 1964, Kansas City Athletics general manager Hank Peters was so impressed by a report Ferrick filed on the team's Pacific Coast League farm club in Vancouver, Canada, that he offered him a scouting job. Ferrick continued with the A's until their first season in Oakland in 1968 and then joined the expansion Royals. In addition to his advocacy for Dennis Leonard, Ferrick highly recommended southpaw Paul Splittorff, who became the first ace of the expansion franchise.

When Whitey Herzog left the Royals before the end of the 1979 season, new manager Jim Frey, a longtime coach with Earl Weaver's Orioles, wanted Ferrick as his pitching coach. He declined, finding scouting more rewarding. He liked not being confined to a team's rigid schedule for seven months of the year. In 1987 Ferrick became a special assignment scout and remained in that position until his retirement in 1994. He passed away in 1996 at the age of eighty-one. His son Tom Ferrick Jr. never caught the baseball bug during his father's scouting career, instead focusing on his journalism work with the *Philadelphia Inquirer*. In 1980 Ferrick Jr. was part of a team that won a Pulitzer Prize for its coverage of the Three Mile Island nuclear power plant disaster not far from Philadelphia. Late in his father's life, his writer-son grew more fascinated with his dad's baseball life and wished he had taped more of his stories.[48]

Another key member of the staff working with Art Stewart and Tom Ferrick in scouting and player development was William Charles "Bill" Fischer, who was born at the height of the Great Depression in Wausau, Wisconsin, on October 11, 1930. In addition to working at many jobs to support the family, Bill's father grew a garden to feed his wife and Bill, a daughter, and two younger sons who both would pitch Minor League ball. After his high school graduation, Bill Fischer was signed by White Sox scouts John Rigney and Red Ruffing (the former Yankees Hall of Fame pitcher). The Fischer family was proud that they grew up with no frills. The story goes that one day when Bill was playing in a Minor League town, he saw a sign outside a movie theater: "Always Cool Inside." Having grown up without air conditioning, Bill thought it was a strange title for a movie.[49]

Fischer's progress toward the Majors was put on hold during the Korean War, when he served as a Marine drill sergeant supervising seventy-five soldiers. "It was the only two-year contract I have signed," he wryly noted.[50] He ultimately made the White Sox in 1956 and began a nine-year journeyman's career with five teams. He pitched in 281 games to an above-average 4.34 ERA, but he was proudest of a record-breaking streak in 1962 in which he threw 84.1 innings without issuing a walk. In 1963 he achieved notoriety when he gave up a home run to Mickey Mantle that traveled more than five hundred feet. The Yankees commemorated the feat by sending him a framed picture of the event. Like Tom Ferrick, Bill Fischer never struck out too many, finishing with the unappetizing log of 210 walks and 313 strikeouts in 831.1 innings.

Upon retiring, Fischer found his true calling as a coach and instructor. He became expert at teaching pitchers to stay intense without becoming tense. During the first five years of the Royals franchise, he was the team's scouting supervisor in the baseball-rich area of Georgia, Florida, and Alabama. Having learned from his masters, Fischer knew the importance of establishing and maintaining grassroots connections with high school, college, and American Legion coaches. His connection, for instance, with Clint Hurdle and his family proved very important in the Royals' pursuit of the player, one of the country's top prospects in 1975.

Hurdle was born in Big Rapids, Michigan, on July 30, 1957, but when he was three years old his father accepted a job in Florida as a computer data specialist working on a National Aeronautics and Space Administration (NASA) project. Both Clint's father and grandfather were excellent athletes, though neither had played professional sports. As he matured at Merritt Island High School, Clint showed great promise in football and baseball, and both the University of Miami and Harvard were hot on his trail. His academic record was outstanding, with his only B in high school reportedly coming in a driver's education class.[51]

Bill Fischer followed Hurdle from his sophomore year and established a strong relationship with both the prospect and his family. Spurning the college offers, Clint opted to turn pro in 1975 and swiftly rose in the organization. He made his Major League debut in September 1977 and homered in his first game. The ballyhoo about his future reached fever pitch when *Sports Illustrated* put him on the cover of its baseball preview issue on March 20, 1978. Kansas City traded first baseman John Mayberry to Toronto in the off-season, and the rookie opened the season at first base, a position he had never played. Hurdle never got comfortable, and manager Whitey Herzog moved him to the outfield in midseason. His final batting average of .264 with 7 home runs and 56 RBIs might seem mediocre, but Herzog said if there had not been such a buildup, Hurdle's numbers would have comprised a fine rookie season. In ten plate appearances in the playoff loss to the Yankees, Hurdle had two singles, a triple, and two walks.[52]

In the following season, 1979, Hurdle's career went sideways. The swifter, switch-hitting Willie Wilson took over left field, and Hurdle was moved around. The Royals did not repeat as division winner; Jim Frey, longtime first base coach for Earl Weaver's Orioles, replaced Herzog as manager in 1980. Hurdle had his best season in the Majors under Frey—.294, 10 home runs, 60 RBIs, 31 doubles. But after the season he was traded to the Reds for relief pitcher Scott Brown. No longer baseball's best prospect but just another journeyman, Hurdle went to the Mets and then landed with the Cards as a 1985 Rule 5 Draft pick—any player with six or more years of professional experience not on a team's forty-man roster was eligible. Hurdle retired at the age of thirty and started a managing career with the Mets' Port St. Lucie, Florida, lower Minor League team. He found success as manager of both the Colorado Rockies and Pittsburgh Pirates and returned to Major League coaching in the 2022 season.

Bill Fischer wasn't around to see the travails of the onetime top draft pick. He left the Royals organization after the 1978 season to take a job as manager John McNamara's pitching coach for the Cincinnati Reds. When the Reds hit the skids in 1982 and 1983, he returned to work for the Royals farm team in Council Bluffs, Iowa, in 1984. In 1985 Boston Red Sox general manager Lou Gorman, the former Royals farm director who was a longtime admirer, hired him as Boston pitching coach. Fischer had a great influence on Roger Clemens, praising him for issuing no walks in his remarkable 20-strikeout game against the Mariners in 1985. He stayed with the Red Sox until manager Joe Morgan was fired in 1991 and then returned to Minor League work.

In 2001 and 2002 Fischer was pitching coach for the expansion Tampa Bay Devil Rays and then went to the Braves as Minor League pitching coordinator. The Royals called him home in 2007 as senior pitching advisor, where he remained until his death on October 31, 2018. He was praised by General Manager Dayton Moore as someone who didn't just have "opinions" but strongly held and well-reasoned "beliefs." Two examples were the importance of using the four-seam fastball and not walking batters.[53]

As the roots for Kansas City's success in the AL Central were being firmly established, baseball was being engulfed by labor wars. Ewing Kauffman was one of the many owners who were shocked when the Players Association called a strike at the end of 1972 spring training that was not settled until the second week of the regular season. The delay led to an embarrassing outcome in the AL East division where the Tigers beat out the Red Sox by a half game in the standings even though both teams had lost the same number of games. For all of Ewing Kauffman's openness to innovation in player development, he resolutely joined baseball's old guard against the players and their persistent leader Marvin Miller, the former chief economist of the United Steelworkers of America. When arbitrator Peter Seitz ruled two days before Christmas 1975 that veteran pitchers Andy Messersmith and Dave McNally were free to bargain with any team, the floodgates for free agency opened at the end of the 1976 season.

As he saw the sides hardening in baseball's seemingly inevitable labor wars, Art Stewart could well have been thinking of Birdie Tebbetts's observation that in baseball the earth is always shaking beneath the stability of the playing field. Stewart was already living with an imposition after the 1974 season. Kauffman ordered General Manager Joe Burke, who replaced Cedric Tallis before the season, to fire twenty full-time scouts and fifty associate scouts. The number of farm teams was also reduced from seven to four.[54]

Part of the reason for the austerity wave was the creation before the 1975 season of a Major League Baseball Scouting Bureau, designed to streamline the passing of information on prospects to every organization. Kauffman and sixteen other owners were all for the efficiency move, but several organizations, including the Phillies, Cardinals, and Dodgers, were dead set against what they considered another inroad of socialized scouting, something as unwelcome to them as the amateur free agent draft had been ten years earlier.

Fortunately, Art Stewart was one of the seven Royals scouts that escaped the axe, along with Al Diez, Tom Ferrick, Rosey Gilhousen, Art Lilly, and Syd Thrift. Art Lilly, who played infield for sixteen years in the Minors and managed in El Paso, Texas, and Mexicali, Mexico, previously served under General Manager Hank Peters for the Kansas City and Oakland Athletics. He was part of the scouting group that struck pay dirt for the Athletics in the early years of the draft by signing future world champions Sal Bando, Vida Blue, and Reggie Jackson, among others.[55]

Despite all the bitter battles brewing between ownership and the ascendant Players Association, the Royals were slowly beginning to emerge as a contender. Bob Lemon managed them to their first winning record in 1971, but they were still sixteen games behind Oakland, which was at the beginning of a four-year run as AL West champions (and three-time World Series winners from 1972 through 1974). Lemon could not duplicate his success in 1972, as the Royals finished two games under .500. In the next two seasons under manager Jack McKeon, the Royals experienced the same kind of rollercoaster ride, going 88-74 in 1973 and slumping to 77-85 in 1974. Owner Ewing Kauffman, getting impatient, dismissed McKeon in the middle of 1975 despite the team's 50-46 record. Whitey Herzog came in, and the team soared to 91 wins but still seven games behind Oakland.

The 1976 season marked Kansas City's first-ever AL West title with 89 wins. Although the Royals could not beat the Yankees in the next three championship series, the Royals were now a force to be reckoned with in the American League. In 1977 Kauffman reconsidered his scouting cutback, and, to the delight of Art Stewart, the owner added to the staff. Kansas City's new general manager, John Schuerholz, who had started in baseball working for the Orioles' minidynasty, was slowly adding pieces for the coming first pennant winner of 1980. In the American League Championship Series (ACLS), the Royals finally beat the Yankees, a George Brett three-run home run in the top of the ninth inning off formidable closer Goose Gossage silencing the home crowd and leading Kansas City to a three-game sweep. Although they fell to the Phillies in a six-game World Series, the Royals had clearly developed a more consistent winning culture than any other expansion team so far.

Art Stewart loved being an area scout, but in 1984 he accepted the position of scouting director, a worthy honor for a man who epitomized the formidable work ethic and, equally as important, the positivity of the organization. Stewart was always known as someone who looked for what a player can do, not what he cannot do. He was now formally part of a Kansas City front office dream team with General Manager Schuerholz and field manager Richard Dalton "Dick" Howser, who took over for pennant-winning 1980 manager Jim Frey during the next strike-riddled season. Howser came to Kansas City with happy memories. He was the 1961 runner-up for American League Rookie of the Year with the KC Athletics, having been signed from Florida State University by scout Clyde Kluttz, a former Major League catcher who later signed Jim "Catfish" Hunter twice, first for the Athletics and then as a free agent for the Yankees. In one of those twists of baseball fate, Howser managed the 1980 Yankees to the AL East title, but George Steinbrenner replaced him when he wouldn't fire third base coach Mike Ferraro for sending runner Willie Randolph home, where he was thrown out on a perfect relay throw in the third and final game. (The third base coach always enacts the manager's thinking about base running, and Howser had no problem with Ferraro's decision.)[56]

The paternal understanding of owner Kauffman and the calm of Howser, Schuerholz, and Stewart enabled the Royals to stay on an even keel during the cocaine revelations in the offseason of 1983–84 that implicated several players and led to jail sentences for outfielders Jerry Martin and Willie Wilson, first baseman and DH Willie Mays Aikens, and pitcher Vida Blue. By 1985 the Royals were on track to win their first World Series. In the championship series, they beat Toronto, an expansion team in only its ninth season that supplanted Kansas City as the fastest new team to contention. The Royals came from behind to win the World Series against the Cardinals, helped by a blown first base call by umpire Don Denkinger in the sixth game. But they left no doubt of their championship mettle by winning the seventh game in a rout. Closer Dan Quisenberry, signed by Rosey Gilhousen for a few hundred dollars and the offer of Royals memorabilia, played a big role in the triumph.

Quisenberry was not considered a prospect because he didn't throw hard enough. But Ben Hines, his college coach and later batting coach for the 1988 world champion Los Angeles Dodgers, urged him to try side-arming and also encouraged him to take up square dancing to improve his balance. After he signed the contract Rosey Gilhousen offered him, the scout said that Dan almost broke his hand during the congratulatory handshake. From 1980 to 1985, Quisenberry averaged 35 saves. He wound up with 244 saves in his twelve-year career, with nine and a half seasons with the Royals.[57]

Quisenberry was a genuine wit. He credited his pitching success to "thirty ground balls, thirty strikeouts, and thirty great plays." After the Royals won the World Series, he said he couldn't really believe it happened and felt there was another game tomorrow.

He was also a sensitive, published poet, drawing a comparison to Robert Frost from Roger Angell, baseball's most poetic essayist. "The poems in it are like his pitches: modest, smart, dipping across that border [of what is important in life and baseball and what isn't.]"[58] In his last volume, *On Days like This*, Quisenberry reflected on the end of his career in 1989.

It lasted so long
It went so fast
It seems like yesterday
It seems like never.[59]

Beloved by his teammates for his team-first, selfless attitude, he retired to a quiet life as a family man when he was afflicted with a brain tumor. He died on February 7, 1998, at the age of forty-five.

The 1985 World Series would be the high point of the Royals on the Major League level for nearly the next thirty years. In the middle of the 1986 season, Dick Howser was stricken by a brain tumor that led to his death in June 1987 at the age of fifty. It symbolized the decline of the team's fortunes. Yet 1986 was not just a year of decline. In the fourth round of the 1986 draft, what Art Stewart called "the greatest draft pick ever" was selected when Vincent Edward "Bo" Jackson came into the fold. Very few people in baseball thought Jackson, the previous year's Heisman Trophy winner for his football exploits at Auburn

University in Alabama, would forgo the gridiron for baseball even though he had an outstanding junior season, hitting .401 with 17 home runs and 43 RBIs in 42 games. The Royals' area scout Ken Gonzales was one of the few baseball people who thought there was a good chance of making Bo a Royal. Since his high school days, Jackson had been scouted by Gonzales, who developed a friendship with Bo's single mother, Florence Bond. On his trips to Alabama, he always stayed at the hotel in Bessemer where she worked as a maid.[60]

When it was time for the Royals to pick in the fourth round in the draft, the sound of a dropping pin might have been heard when Art Stewart called out the name of Bo Jackson. The press was still skeptical that Bo wanted to play baseball and thought the Royals had wasted a draft pick. Even future teammates were skeptical that he could make the Majors with limited college baseball experience. George Brett was one of those doubters who openly questioned Jackson's baseball abilities and sarcastically wished him good luck in football. "Don't you bet on it!" Jackson angrily responded to Brett when they met in the Royals clubhouse. Stewart marveled at Bo's confidence and the near defiance with which he confronted Brett.[61]

After Bo signed a five-year contract estimated to be worth $1 million, including a $200,000 bonus and placement on the forty-man roster, he did not spend much time in the Minor Leagues, reaching the Majors late in 1985. His best and only All-Star season was in 1989, when he hit 32 home runs with 105 RBIs but walked only 39 times with 172 strikeouts.

But he couldn't stay away from football. In a January 1991 playoff for the Oakland Raiders, Jackson suffered a severe hip injury that ended his football career. When the Royals did not renew his contract for the 1991 season, he finished out his career as a part-time player with the White Sox and the Angels, retiring after the 1994 season. Ewing Kauffman always regretted that he could not talk the proud and stubborn Jackson out of returning to football.[62]

The final numbers of Vincent "Bo" Jackson over eight Major League seasons are .250 batting average, .308 on-base percentage, .480 slugging percentage, 141 home runs, 415 RBIs, 200 walks, 881 strikeouts, 82 stolen bases, and 32 caught stealing. Memories of his spectacular catches, breathtaking speed on the bases, overpowering throws, and tape-measure home runs remain indelible.

Ewing Kauffman succumbed to a long battle against cancer in June 1993. A few years earlier, he had sold the majority of the team to Memphis businessman and memorabilia collector Avrom Fogelman with the promise that the team would never leave Kansas City. The heroes of the first decades of expansion success, George Brett and Frank White, grew old and retired. White hung up his spikes after 1990 and Brett after 1993, both playing their whole careers for one team, a rarity in modern baseball. Art Stewart always loved Brett's description of what his last at bat ideally would be: "I hit a routine grounder to second base, and run like hell to first base and try to beat it out."[63]

In 1988 the Royals Dominican Baseball Academy, patterned after the defunct Sarasota project, was named for Art Stewart. Never seeking personal honors, he was more delighted when Luis Pascual Silverio, a former Royals Minor League infielder, was now playing a prominent role at the Dominican academy. Scouting in Latin America reminded Stewart of the predraft days when he could see a player one time and sign him quickly. Silverio's story was a case in point. He was signed as a seventeen-year-old from Villa González in the Dominican Republic, and his first pro training came at Sarasota in the last weeks of the doomed facility. A shoulder injury hampered his career, but he did reach the Major Leagues briefly in 1978, getting six hits, including two doubles and a triple, in eleven at bats. The speedy infielder was the kind of baseball lifer that Stewart and the Royals made room for. After serving as a Royals coach from 1983 through 1989, Silverio focused on his work in his homeland. In 2008 he completed thirty-five years with the Royals. (As of 2022, he was still working in baseball as field coordinator for the Arizona Diamondbacks.)[64]

Art Stewart was always a person who looked ahead and didn't mope about missed opportunities in the past. He did sigh a little at his near miss in signing Mariano Rivera for the Royals. Yankees Latin American scout Herb Raybourn was a Panamanian native and a friendly scouting rival of Stewart. Raybourn's shared background with Mariano gave him an advantage, but Stewart remembered that he couldn't get the Royals to up the offer $5,000 that would have changed a lot of the recent history of the American League.[65]

After 1997 Stewart left his duties as scouting director to become a special assistant in the general manager's office. It freed him to do more scouting, which was always his first love. He played a part in bringing such major talent into the organization as pitcher Kevin Appier and outfielders Carlos Beltran and Johnny Damon, though the small-market team couldn't keep them from seeking free agent bonanzas. In 2006 Stewart took special pride in the fiftieth-round draft pick, speedy outfielder Jarrod Dyson from Southwest Mississippi Community College. Dyson's stolen base talent played a big role in the 2014 and 2015 pennant winners. In 2010 Stewart was named a special adviser to the Royals new general manager Dayton Moore. Moore had come back to the Midwest after twelve seasons of learning the ropes of traditional scouting and player development with the Atlanta Braves. Starting as an area scout in 1994, Moore moved quickly moved up the ranks to top assistant in the general manager's office. By the time he left for Kansas City after the 2005 season, the Braves had won one World Series in 1995, lost two others, and never missed the playoffs. Moore was thrilled that Stewart was staying active, because when first scouted in a high school tournament, it was the legendary older man who handed Moore his first information card to fill out. "Boy, he was an impressive shortstop," Stewart remembered in an interview for Moore's book written after the Royals' World Series appearances in 2014 and 2015. "He was a pepperpot."[66]

Art suffered a grievous blow in 2008 when Donna Wakely Stewart, his wife of forty-eight years, passed away. A few months later, at a school reunion, he ran into his high school girlfriend. In a remarkable turn of fate, she was a divorcee, and he was widowed, and they soon tied the knot together. As he moved into his nineties, his love of the game was unabated. After the Royals' clinching 2015 World Series victory over the Mets on the road in New York, people around Art were not surprised when he said that he couldn't wait to get to Arizona to see how the Kansas City team was doing in the fall league. As he wrote at the end of *The Art of Scouting*, "I have had a remarkable life. I loved two teams and loved two women."[67] On November 11, 2021, Art Stewart died at the age of ninety-four. At a memorial in Kansas City, among the attendees was Bo Jackson.

The challenges of building expansion teams were always considerable but filled with rewards. I want to turn now in the final section to the stories of scouts who made their careers with the traditional franchises.

1. Charles E. Chapman, one of Branch Rickey's associate scouts in the 1920s who found California talent for the Cardinals' farm system during its heyday. His day job was professor of Spanish and Latin American history at the University of California, Berkeley. Courtesy of the Baseball Hall of Fame.

2. Bill Essick's faith in teenaged Joe DiMaggio's ability to recover from a knee injury led to many more Yankee championships. Paul Krichell (not pictured) endorsed Casey Stengel, seated on Essick's right, for Yankees manager. *Front row, left to right:* Charlie Graham, owner of San Francisco Seals; Lefty O'Doul, former Major Leaguer and S F Seal; Casey Stengel, before he became a genius with the Yankees; Bill Essick, Yankees scout. *Back row, left to right:* Win Clark, Minor League executive; future Hall of Famer Sam "Wahoo" Crawford. Circa 1940. Courtesy of David Eskenazi.

3. Tom Greenwade in a posed photo while working as a Brooklyn Dodger scout in 1942. Courtesy of the Greenwade family.

4. (*opposite top*) Tom Greenwade, who was hired away at a big increase in salary from Branch Rickey's Dodgers by Larry MacPhail and the Yankees, with his prize signing Mickey Mantle at the 1952 World Series. With Joe DiMaggio retired, Mantle was entering his peak years as the latest Yankee hero. Courtesy of Angeline Greenwade McCroskey.

5. (*opposite bottom*) Brooklyn Dodger executives Al Campanis and Fresco Thompson flank bonus boy Sandy Koufax before the start of his first season in 1955. Campanis and Thompson survived Walter O'Malley's purge of Rickey men when Rickey left for Pittsburgh after the 1950 season, but they still believed in his teachings about the importance of pitching, defense, and speed in building champions. Courtesy of the National Baseball Hall of Fame.

6. (*above*) Kansas City Royals scout Art Stewart works on catching fundamentals at a Royals tryout camp. Courtesy of the Kansas City Royals.

7. Stewart in deep baseball conversation with Royals general manager Dayton Moore, who never forgot that Stewart was the first scout who gave him an information card to fill out when he was a teenager at a Kansas City tryout camp. Courtesy of the Kansas City Royals.

8. Mel Didier, versatile scout for many organizations and innovative player developer, pictured with the author at one of the Beverly Hills dinners of the Professional Baseball Scouts Foundation, circa 2011. Elena Arcaro Didier, Mel's wife, is pictured in the background. Photo courtesy of Elena Arcaro Didier.

9. Al LaMacchia, shown as St. Louis Browns pitcher during World War II; he found his niche as outstanding scout for Milwaukee-Atlanta Braves and Toronto Blue Jays. Courtesy of the National Baseball Hall of Fame.

10. Bobby Mattick during tenure as Blue Jays manager, 1980–81; his greatest success came before and after as scout for Cincinnati Reds and Toronto Blue Jays. Courtesy of the National Baseball Hall of Fame.

11. Paul Snyder, who has spent his whole career with the Braves as player, scout, and developer, and Tony DeMacio, who while working for the Braves signed future Hall of Famers Tom Glavine and Chipper Jones, at the induction of Chipper into the Braves Hall of Fame and the retirement of his number 10, June 28, 2013. Courtesy of the Atlanta Braves.

12. Paul Snyder at work evaluating players. Courtesy of the Atlanta Braves.

13. Gene Bennett, a Cincinnati Reds lifer as player, scout, and player developer, prepares to work at a tryout camp. Courtesy of the Cincinnati Reds.

14. Gene Bennett, prior to speaking at a Cincinnati Reds preseason caravan. Courtesy of the Cincinnati Reds.

15. Billy Blitzer (*third from left*) at a retirement ceremony honoring his forty-year career as Chicago Cubs scout, September 19, 2021, at Brooklyn Cyclones Minor League ballpark in Coney Island, near where Blitzer was born and raised. Joe Rigoli (*far right*) is longtime Cardinals scout who competed for players with Blitzer's Cubs, but both men have enjoyed a deep friendship and have worked for decades to foster their profession through the New York Pro Scouts Association. Also pictured (*left to right*): Gary Perone, Cyclones assistant general manager; Nic Jackson, Cyclones hitting coach; Ed Blankmeyer, Cyclones manager; Robert Pertsas, president of the New York Public Schools Athletic League; Dan Palumbo, Phillies area scout. Courtesy of Jesse Manning, Business Lunch Productions.

16. (*opposite top*) Scout Bill Enos at work scouting during a Cape Cod Baseball League summer game, 2001. Over Bill's left shoulder is seated scout Buzz Bowers, one of Bill's successors. Photo was taken the year before Bill was inducted into the first class of the CCBL Hall of Fame. Courtesy of Jeannie Flynn, Bourne MA.

17. (*opposite bottom*) Scout Bill Enos at work during San Diego Padres spring training, 1996, Peoria AZ. Courtesy of Anne Enos.

18. (*above*) The late Yankee scout Kelly Rodman representing the team, along with former Yankee Nick Swisher, at the June 2017 amateur free agent draft at MLB-TV studios in Secaucus, New Jersey. Credit: New York Yankees.

19. *Left to right:* Yankees northeastern area scout Matt Hyde; number one draft pick, shortstop Anthony Volpe; area scout Kelly Rodman; scouting director Damon Oppenheimer, after the drafting of Volpe in 2020. Credit: New York Yankees.

PART 3

TWO VETERAN SCOUTS BOOKEND THREE BASEBALL MONOGAMISTS

5

History has always fascinated Gary Nickels. When talking to author Kevin
Kerrane in the early 1980s for his indispensable book on scouting, *Dollar Sign
on the Muscle*, Nickels asked, "Have you ever thought how much of America
the old scouts have seen?" Looking around at the crowd gathered at a Minor
League game, he added, "I wish we had some Russians here tonight so they
could see how deep the game goes in our society."[1]

Gary Ross Nickels, born on August 20, 1946, in Aurora, Illinois, about
forty miles west of Chicago, grew up on farmland where his English German
ancestors had settled in 1844. The family initially emigrated to Corning in
western New York State and then came west by covered wagon, ultimately
not far from Fort Sheridan, where battles with the local Native American
tribes were still raging. For the first few years of Gary's life, he lived with
his grandparents because Gary's father, Keller Nickels, was just back from
World War II in Europe, where he served as a sergeant in the U.S. Army. One
of Sergeant Keller's assignments had been in General Dwight Eisenhower's
security detail. At the end of the war, he was in the regiment that entered the
concentration camp in Buchenwald after the Germans surrendered. It was a
subject not mentioned at home, but as Gary grew up, he learned about the
horrifying experience.[2]

The year 1951 was special for Gary Nickels. His father was getting ahead
in the concrete mixing business, and the family could finally move into their
own house. Then, in early October, Gary remembered hearing a broadcast of
the National League playoff game that ended with Bobby Thomson's home

run for the New York Giants off the Brooklyn Dodgers' Ralph Branca. The next year, Gary went with his father to a White Sox game with ageless Satchel Paige pitching for the St. Louis Browns. With the Cubs foundering in the 1950s, Gary grew up a big fan of the Go-Go White Sox, which featured a bevy of future Hall of Famers: manager Al López, the double play combination of Luis Aparicio and Nelson Fox, and pitcher Early Wynn. Stylish southpaw Billy Pierce was Gary's favorite because he, too, was a left-handed pitcher.

Gary's high school did not field a baseball team at the time, but he developed his skills in the Aurora Municipal League. One of the opponents Nickels competed against was Gene Lamont, a highly coveted shortstop who in 1965 was the tenth player taken in the first round of the first amateur free agent draft. Lamont was converted into a catcher but never blossomed into a regular Major Leaguer. He did become a coach, often on the staff of manager Jim Leyland. Sliding to the second round in the initial 1965 draft was future Hall of Famer Johnny Bench from tiny Binger, Oklahoma, where the suspect level of competition in the area shied some scouts away. Binger was so small that it did not field a football team and baseball was only played in the fall.[3]

Nickels was not a highly recruited athlete, but he looked forward to playing at Illinois Wesleyan University for highly successful coach Jack Horenberger. After graduating from IWU in 1936, where he starred in baseball and captained an undefeated basketball team, Horenberger played for a season in Branch Rickey's St. Louis Cardinals farm system. He was a speedy outfielder, but he lacked the other tools that would make him a Major League prospect. At the end of the next spring training, Rickey called Horenberger aside and told him the bad news. He added, though, that he liked the way the youngster explained the game to his teammates and suggested a coaching career.

Advice from baseball's renowned Branch Rickey was not to be taken lightly. In 1942 Jack Horenberger was named his alma mater's baseball coach. Except for two years in the wartime U.S. Navy, Horenberger coached at his alma mater through 1981. At times he also held the positions of athletic director, basketball coach, and, for a few years in the 1950s, even dean of students. Horenberger's love for Illinois Wesleyan would come to match Branch Rickey's love for his alma mater, Ohio Wesleyan. Both schools provided a welcoming environment where mind and body could develop together. Horenberger was a great exponent for summer college baseball. He was one of the founders of the Central Illinois Collegiate League (CICL) that, starting in 1963, played a sixty-game schedule, giving hopefuls a chance to develop themselves under the eyes of scouts. It was the first summer baseball program sanctioned by Major League Baseball.[4]

Three years before Horenberger started coaching, Illinois Wesleyan played a part in a little-known event in baseball history. In June 1939, a few days after the opening of the National Baseball Hall of Fame in Cooperstown, the Titans competed on Doubleday Field in a round-robin series against Cornell University from Ithaca, New York, and the University of Virginia in Charlottesville. On the way to the event, the team traveled through Warren, Pennsylvania, where it played against a local town team. At Cooperstown, each team finished with a 1-1 record. The IWU Titans' presence in the historic series was mainly due to the efforts of Fred Young, an indefatigable Bloomington, Illinois, sportswriter who had been a star IWU student-athlete before World War I. He later earned a law degree, but he spent the most joyous years of his life as a pro and college football official and promoter of all sports through his column, Young's Yarns, in the local newspaper, the *Pantagraph*.[5]

In 1948 Jack Horenberger started making more school history by leading the Titans to their first title in the highly competitive College Conference of Illinois (CCI). By the time Gary Nickels arrived on the campus in the fall of 1964, Horenberger's Titans had won nine more league championships, including five in a row from 1956 through 1960, and shared two other titles. One of Horenberger's star players in the class of 1952 was peppery infielder Bobby Winkles, who went on to great success as the Arizona State University baseball coach in the 1960s. He won four College World Series championships in that decade, recruiting nationally such future Major League stars as Sal Bando from Cleveland; southpaw Larry Gura from Joliet, Illinois; Rick Monday from Santa Monica, California; and future Hall of Famer Reggie Jackson from Philadelphia.

Horenberger taught Winkles that players must hustle every moment on the field and never bait umpires. As a result his Sun Devils teams played a lot of fast games, something twenty-first-century teams could learn from. Winkles made sure never to criticize a player publicly, though he was blunt in private conversation. He also sprinkled in a lot of humor, saying that his hometown of Swifton, Arkansas—where he grew up with future Hall of Famer George Kell—was so small that the sign for entering and leaving was on the same telephone pole.[6] Bobby Winkles was less successful as a Major League manager with the Angels and the Athletics in the 1970s, but he left an indelible mark on the growing world of college baseball.

Although Illinois Wesleyan was not a campus roiling with civil rights and anti–Vietnam War protests, sophomore Gary Nickels was part of the large crowd that came on a rainy night in February 1966 to hear the Reverend Martin Luther King Jr. speak. The activist-minister was an hour late because of the bad weather. When he finally arrived, King quipped, "I'd rather be Martin Luther King late than the late Martin Luther King." Near the end of his passionate address, he declared, "It may be true that the law cannot change the heart, but it can restrain the heartless."[7]

Two months later, Nickels and the rest of the Titans baseball team were part of a protest against segregation in southern schools. Jack Horenberger had been one of the first college coaches to take his teams to warm weather sites before the college season started. However, in April 1966, instead of traveling to Louisiana State University and two other still-segregated Mississippi schools, the University of Mississippi and Mississippi State, the Illinois Wesleyan administration scheduled the Titans for a special tournament at the U.S. Keesler Army Base in Biloxi. The team played a round-robin competition against Xavier of Cincinnati; Illinois State, its local rival in Bloomington; and Parsons College of Iowa.

Xavier featured a star shortstop, Rich Donnelly, who became a Minor League catcher and a longtime third base coach for Jim Leyland for both the Pirates and the 1997 world champion Florida Marlins. (In 2019 Donnelly would become the subject of Tom Friend's absorbing book, *The Chicken Runs at Midnight*, a frank, insightful story about how Donnelly succeeded in fulfilling his lifelong ambition of becoming a third base coach—which he did for manager Jim Leyland's Pittsburgh Pirates and Florida Marlins.)[8] Parsons, located in Fairfield, Iowa, featured an overpowering pitching staff led by three future Mets hurlers, Rich Folkers, Jackson Todd, and Charlie Williams (later traded by the Mets to the San Francisco Giants for aging

Willie Mays). Also playing for Parsons was infielder Tony DeMacio, later to become a renowned scout for the Atlanta Braves and prominent in the signing of future Hall of Famers Tom Glavine and Chipper Jones. (More on DeMacio is in the upcoming chapter on Paul Snyder.)

Two seasons later, on April 4, 1968, the tumult of the 1960s swept tragically into the lives of Nickels and his Illinois Wesleyan teammates. Shortly after arriving in Jackson, Tennessee, to play Union University, word came that Martin Luther King Jr. had been assassinated forty miles away in Memphis. Coach Horenberger ordered his team to stay in the hotel, fearing the outbreak of riots that indeed erupted in almost all the major cities of the United States.[9]

When Nickels graduated from IWU a few weeks later, he wasn't drafted by any Major League team. He didn't expect to advance to the professional level, but he knew that he wanted to stay in baseball. He already had made friendships that he knew would last a lifetime, but he wanted more. Pitching during his sophomore year, he could look back at second base and find senior Denny Matthews, who in 1969 would become the radio play-by-play man for the expansion Kansas City Royals, a position he still held as of 2022. Nickels just missed playing with third baseman Doug Rader, who signed with the Astros a term before Gary arrived on campus. He followed Doug's playing career with the Padres and Blue Jays and his journey managing the Rangers, White Sox, and Angels.

Nickels did not limit his pride in Illinois Wesleyan to baseball people. He delighted in the emergence of his Phi Gamma Delta fraternity brother Richard Jenkins, who, after decades of toiling as an actor in obscure roles, would become an overnight sensation in such movies as *The Shape of Water*, *Burn after Reading*, and *The Visitor*. He was pleased when Jack Sikma became a star Illinois Wesleyan basketball player and the eighth pick in the 1978 NBA draft—after a twelve-year career with the Seattle SuperSonics, he was elected in 2020 to the basketball Hall of Fame in Springfield, Massachusetts.

Nickels took his first step toward a nonplaying career in baseball by enrolling in the sports administration graduate program at Ohio University in Athens. He worked as a graduate assistant for the baseball team under coach Bob Wren. Future Major League catcher Steve Swisher—later, the father of another Major Leaguer, outfielder and first baseman Nick Swisher—was on the Ohio Bobcat team. His backup catcher was a future scout James Jackson "Jax" Robertson, who had also played behind Swisher in high school in Cleveland. Robertson never made the Majors as a player but went on to a long career in scouting and coaching with many teams.

He told author Phyllis Dragseth that he was proudest of signing Don Mattingly for the Yankees in the nineteenth round of the 1979 draft. He talked the Evansville, Indiana, native out of a college scholarship offer, and, in an evaluation reminiscent of the glory years of Bronx Bomber scouting, he projected that Mattingly's determination would overcome any issues that were already evident concerning Mattingly's balky back.[10] (The back did ultimately force Mattingly's retirement after a stellar career just short of Hall of Fame recognition.)

During Nickels's year at Ohio University, he watched former Ohio U. star Mike Schmidt, recently signed by the Phillies, working out at the team facilities. Many scouts came by the campus, eager to find more talented players coming through Wren's program. Nickels enjoyed chatting with the diamond detectives, and he began to envision a career in scouting. Through contacts he made in the Ohio program, he landed an assistant administrative position in scouting with the Phillies.

The memory of the 1950 Whiz Kids, just the second pennant-winner in their team's inglorious history, was in the distant past—one wit called the Phillies "the only hundred-year expansion team in history." Recent memories were more painful, including a twenty-three-game losing streak in 1961 and the blowing of the 1964 pennant despite a six-game lead with twelve games to play. Phillies management was seeking energetic new talent evaluators. Robert Ruliph Morgan "Ruly" Carpenter III, son of owner Robert Carpenter Jr., assigned Nickels the task of evaluating the results of the first seven Phillies amateur free agent drafts. They were an organization that opposed the "socialism" of the draft that prevented individual initiative from finding and signing talent, but the Phillies were one of the first teams willing to analyze the results.

Nickels already knew that a draft cannot be fairly judged until several years of development have passed. Exploring the mysteries of the draft would become his career-long fascination and challenge. He saw that there were core pieces of the Phillies' first world championship team in 1980 in the team's first drafts. Among them were left fielder Greg Luzinski in the first round in 1968, catcher Bob Boone in the sixth round in 1969, and future Hall of Famer Mike Schmidt in the second round in 1971. The Phillies also drafted two California high schoolers in 1967, catcher Buck Martinez and corner infielder Darrell Evans from Pasadena. Martinez signed with the Phils, but early in his Minor League career was traded to the expansion Kansas City Royals, where he contributed to their contending teams, among them its first AL West division winner in 1976. Evans did not sign and later was picked by the Atlanta Braves, where he led the National League in walks twice. He lasted twenty-one years in the big leagues, winning a World Series ring with the 1984 Tigers and leading the Major Leagues in home runs with the Tigers in 1985.

Nickels felt blessed that one of his first mentors was the legendary scout Tony Lucadello, who would be immortalized as "Prophet of the Sandlots" in Mark Winegardner's classic biography of the same name.[11] He was thrilled to accompany Lucadello as he set up tryouts throughout the Upper Midwest. Nickels came to know other young scouts in the organization: Casey Lopata, former Phillies catcher Stan Lopata's brother in Detroit; Norm Kramer in Fort Wayne, Indiana; and Dick Hopkins in Columbus, Ohio.

As a history buff, Nickels was fascinated by Lucadello's back story. Born in Thurber, Texas (between Fort Worth and Abilene), on May 5, 1915, in grade school Lucadello moved with his family to Chicago, where his father found a job in the coal mines south of the city. "As a teenager during Prohibition," Winegardner wrote wryly, "Tony got his first job, delivering sealed cases of what he was told was olive oil. His new job was baseball."[12] In 1936 Branch Rickey's Cardinals signed him and assigned him to the Fostoria Redbirds in the Class D Ohio-Indiana League. A five-foot-seven, 145-pound infielder with limited batting tools, Tony spent only two years in the lower Minors. A shoulder injury sustained when he ran into an outfield fence did not help his cause, but he loved being around the ballpark, talking and playing the game.

He was thrilled when the St. Louis Browns signed his younger brother Johnny to a professional contract. Their mother, Maria Lucadello, was concerned that Johnny might get into trouble in their tough Chicago Little Italy neighborhood of Roseland, so she sent him to live with Tony in Fostoria.

As Richard Riis writes in a fascinating SABR BioProject essay, Johnny's performance playing with Fostoria Minor Leaguers in a charity game against inmates from Joliet prison prompted Browns manager Rogers Hornsby to encourage his signing. Johnny displayed a much better bat than his older brother, and in 1941 he played in 107 games as a second baseman for the Browns, putting up good numbers: .279 batting average and .382 slugging average in 351 at bats. Once Pearl Harbor was bombed, Johnny's career was put on hold. After coming out of the U.S. Navy, he returned to the Browns in 1946, but his at bats were reduced almost by half, and his numbers fell to .248 batting average and .305 slugging average. After being released in 1947 spring training, the Yankees signed him, but manager Bucky Harris was not about to replace George Stirnweiss at second base. Johnny Lucadello had only one hit in twelve at bats before being sent to the Minors around the All-Star Game. He never returned to the Majors, but his 1947 Yankee teammates thought enough of him to vote him half a World Series share.[13]

Tony Lucadello would always consider his brother Johnny his first Major League signing. Like so many scouts in this story, after his playing career ended, Tony found work outside of baseball unfulfilling. In 1942 his big break came when Cubs owner Philip K. Wrigley Jr. was convinced that the young man's player evaluations were better than any scout already on his payroll. Among his recommendations were future Major League pitchers Dick Drott and Bob Rush. Tony stayed with the Cubs until the Phillies wooed him away in the late 1950s. When Mark Winegardner was traveling with him throughout the 1987 season, Lucadello was on the hunt for his fiftieth future Major Leaguer. He already had signed two future Cy Young winners, Ferguson Jenkins and reliever Mike Marshall, but they rose to stardom with other organizations, Jenkins with the Cubs and Marshall with the Dodgers.

Tony Lucadello was the living embodiment of the scouting truism that you are only in trouble if you have no opinions. "There are only four kinds of scouts," Lucadello declared. "Poor scouts, pickers, performance scouts, and projection scouts."[14] He said that the majority of scouts fell into the performance group, superficially looking at outcomes instead of the process that led to the outcome. The last group, projection scouts, were the best and the rarest, he proclaimed. They were the people who could forecast how a player would or would not grow, how he would or would not compete at the next level of competition. He believed without hesitation that makeup—mental toughness—was the key to a player's advancement to the Major Leagues.

Nickels listened as the wise scout explained the Lucadello Plan:

Learn to position your feet for ground balls.
Keep your head and glove down.
Grip the ball across the seams.
Throw with a strong, over-the-top delivery.
Take one hundred grounders off the wall every day.
Play with enthusiasm.

The "wall" that Lucadello referenced was his invention, a specially built white cinder-block wall the size of a small shed. Its angles were constructed so aspiring players could develop quick reactions to unexpected bounces.[15]

While with the Cubs, Lucadello signed Wayne Terwilliger, a journeyman player who went on to a coaching career that lasted six decades; reliever Jim Brosnan, future author of the baseball diaries *The Long Season* and *Pennant Race*; and outfielder Lou Johnson, who, after more than ten years in the Minors, contributed vital offense to the 1965 World Series–winning Los Angeles Dodgers. (Brosnan's books were published in the early 1960s a few years before Jim Bouton's *Ball Four*, leading one wit to quip that unlike academia, in baseball one published *and* perished.)

Scouting for the Phillies, Lucadello experienced a similar frustration that he endured with the Cubs when several of his signees went on to star for other organizations. Among them were outfielders Larry Hisle and Alex Johnson, who found success in the American League, and Grant Jackson, a left-handed reliever from Tony's hometown of Fostoria, Ohio, who wound up pitching in two World Series, losing with the 1971 Baltimore Orioles and winning with the 1979 Pittsburgh Pirates.

The biggest feather in Lucadello's cap was signing Mike Schmidt. He had watched Schmidt develop from a middling college shortstop into a power-hitting third baseman. Using the wiles he learned from his fellow old-time scouts, Lucadello got permission from a janitor who worked at a building adjoining the baseball field to climb onto the roof to get an overhead view of Schmidt's mechanics at the plate. When scouting on the ground level, Lucadello firmly believed that you needed eight viewing spots to truly evaluate a player, not just behind the plate but also along both foul lines. But if he could get an extra edge from an overhead view, Lucadello was all for it. From listening to Lucadello, Nickels learned why he knew that Schmidt needed to switch positions. Tony had foreseen that Schmidt's lateral movement was not quick enough for shortstop, but his instincts and strong arm would be fine for the so-called hot corner of third base. To be invited to celebrate Mike Schmidt's five hundredth home run in Philadelphia would become one of Lucadello's greatest thrills.[16]

As Gary Nickels continued his informal apprenticeship with Tony Lucadello in the 1970s, he picked up the lesson of passion for your craft. Nothing could quite match the thrill of finding sleepers—diamonds in the rough—on country fields or in small colleges. City prospects are not hard to find, Lucadello said; they get written up in the newspapers. The thrill of the chase is to find the future star that nobody knows about.

Nickels was grateful for the wisdom of another mentor, veteran scout Eddie Bockman, who was in the middle of a thirty-year career scouting for the Phillies. Signed initially by the Yankees, Bockman's four-year Major League career as an infielder was undistinguished: 190 games, 474 at bats, .230 batting average, .299 on-base percentage, and .350 slugging average. He could lay claim to hitting the first of his 11 career home runs off Allie Reynolds, the pitcher he was traded to Cleveland for, along with second baseman Joe Gordon. It was the rare deal that helped both teams—Gordon helped Cleveland to its 1948 World Series triumph, and Reynolds became part of seven Yankees world champions.

Bockman, a native of Santa Ana in Southern California, made his greatest contributions to baseball as a scout. When the Phillies made the 1980 World Series for only the third time in their history and the first time since 1950, Bockman was proud that he was directly involved in signing seven to their pennant-winning roster, including pitchers Warren Brusstar and Randy Lerch, catcher Bob Boone, and shortstop Larry Bowa. Bockman felt a special affinity for grinders like Bowa who used criticism about his small size as a motivator to prove naysayers wrong. Bockman was only five feet nine, and though Bowa may have been an inch taller, he carried not much more than 150 pounds on his slender frame. You can't measure a player's heart, Bockman often reminded Nickels, but you can see it with your own eyes on the playing field. Bowa wanted to play the game so badly that he "quickly got into the back seat of your car," a vivid scouting phrase that meant he was easy to sign.[17]

Bowa's father was a beer truck driver who also tended bar. He brought up his son to believe in just two things: you never quit, and you never take crap from anybody. Although Bowa's intensity once led to him being ejected in the first inning of each game in a Minor League doubleheader, Bockman remained his steadfast advocate. "If he can keep the bugs out of his head," the scout insisted, "he is a definite major league prospect." Although Bowa's original batting style was once described as "flailing at baseballs with a rolled-up newspaper," his hitting improved when he learned how to switch-hit.[18]

After a decade of noncontention, the Phillies made the National League playoffs three years in a row from 1976 to 1978. But they missed out on the World Series all three times, losing to Cincinnati's eventual world champion Big Red Machine in 1976 and to the LA Dodgers in 1977 and 1978, which went on to lose both times to the Yankees. When the 1979 Phillies slumped, Danny Ozark was replaced in August by Dallas Green, a former Phillies pitcher and currently their farm director. It was a decision made by General Manager Paul Owens, a combat engineer in World War II who, like Green, had worked his way up the Phillies' organizational ladder. Both men were strongly committed to scouting and player development, and in 1980 they led the Phillies to the promised land. In a memorable National League Championship Series, the team defeated the Houston Astros and then eliminated the Kansas City Royals in the World Series in six games. Former New York Met Tug McGraw earned the save in front of an enthusiastic home crowd that was kept from celebrating on the field by heavily armed Philadelphia police and their dogs.

If repeating as champion was the true sign of a dynasty, the Phillies fell short in 1981, the year of Major League Baseball's first long in-season strike from June 12 through August 9. As part of the strike settlement, the season was cut in two. A split-season was created, with the winner of the prestrike first half playing the winner of the poststrike second half in a playoff series before the regular League Championship Series. The Phillies won the first half of the NL East, but they were coasting during the second half, making Dallas Green furious. After one lackadaisical loss, he went off on a memorable clubhouse rant that was secretly taped and shared widely. "Don't you guys have any fucking pride?" he roared. "And don't give me any of this shit about the fucking split fucking season." The Phillies went on to lose the playoff to the Montreal Expos, which had won the second half of the NL East.

Within days of the loss to the Expos, the world of the Phillies was turned upside down. Dallas Green was on his way to Chicago, hired by the Cubs' new owners, the Tribune Company, with the task of reviving the team's fortunes. And the Carpenter family, owners of the team for nearly forty years, announced that they were selling the franchise. The long strike and the rising tide of player salary expenditures were major factors in their decision. More dark years of noncontention were ahead for the Phillies.

Gary Nickels was among the several Phillies scouts and coaches who came to work for the Cubs under the strong-minded, baseball-savvy Green. Nickels was certainly familiar with the area. Although he had been a White Sox fan as a youngster, his professional task was now to find the best players for the Cubs. Dallas Green brought along as his right-hand man Gordon Goldsberry, a baseball lifer who started his pro career in 1944 after his junior year in high school in Southern California. He entered baseball in wartime when, more than twenty years before the amateur free agent draft, there were no enforceable restrictions on signing youngsters still of high school age.

A fancy-fielding, left-handed first baseman, Goldsberry made the Major Leagues with the White Sox in 1950 but was traded to the Browns in late 1951. Because he lacked the power expected of a first baseman, his Major League career was brief. Goldsberry played in only 217 games, never had more than 227 at bats in any one season, and retired with a Major League career line of .241 batting average, .344 on-base percentage, .343 slugging average, 6 home runs, and 56 RBIs, but a good walk-strikeout ratio of 80:66. Dallas Green's career numbers were not much more impressive—in parts of eight seasons, he was 20-22 with a 4.26 ERA, 197 walks, and only 268 strikeouts. In a moment of self-effacement, Green once quipped, "I was a twenty-game winner—it just took me five years to do it."[19] Since both men came up short as consistent Major League players, Green and Goldsberry understood profoundly what it took to become a successful Major Leaguer. They realized that if consistency were an island, it would be lightly populated. Their goal was to find the players who could harness that elusive but vital consistency and not be doomed by their lack of success.

As usually happened in baseball when a new boss came to town, Dallas Green went through a thorough housecleaning, with more than fifty Cubs front office people relieved of their duties. Only a few scouts were retained. One of them was Elvin Tappe, a former backup catcher and a longtime member of the organization. He had served as one of owner Phil Wrigley's "college of coaches" who tried unsuccessfully to bring the Cubs to contention in the early 1960s. The second scout retained was John Thomas Cox Jr., who possessed one of the more fascinating backstories in baseball annals.

John Cox, born on May 5, 1943, in Clinton, Iowa, was the first child of John Sr., who was in U.S. Army basic training in Arcadia, California, during the birth. He flew back to Iowa to see his baby and then returned to California. Soon, John Sr. was off to war to fight with General George Patton's army at the Battle of the Bulge. When he came home from the war, John Jr. remembered bouncing on a chair at the age of three and asking his father, "Do you want to play ball?" His love of baseball grew and grew even though there was no high school baseball in Iowa at the time. His parents supported his passion. Many summers, they sent him to the Art Gaines Baseball Camp in Hunnewell, Missouri, thirty miles west of Hannibal. (Gaines was a former Minor Leaguer who scouted for the Pirates for seventeen years and one for the Phillies before his death in November 1975 at the age of fifty-seven.)[20]

More summer thrills came to the baseball-smitten youth when the family regularly spent two weeks in the Motor City, home to John's maternal grandparents. He became a regular in the right-field bleachers at Tiger Stadium with a great view of future Hall of Famer Al Kaline. "It kept my love of baseball alive," Cox remembered in a March 2022 phone interview.[21] When John Sr.'s bosses at the Swift & Company meat packing firm wanted him to relocate from Iowa to Illinois, he pulled up his roots and headed to Southern California. He liked the area during the time he had been stationed before his wartime service in Europe. When the expansion California Angels took out a full-page ad in the *Los Angeles Times* announcing a tryout camp, young John jumped at the chance. To his pleasant surprise, after three days of working out at shortstop and playing games with other hopefuls, Pep Lee, an area baseball coach working with veteran Angels scouts Rosey Gilhousen and Nick Kamzic, offered Cox a contract to play for the Angels' Idaho Falls team in the Pioneer League. He grabbed his plane ticket and rushed to his first baseball assignment in the organization's first season in 1961. Cox arrived in a rainstorm, dropped his luggage in his hotel room, and walked to the ballpark. It was night and, of course, the field was locked, so he climbed the fence to gaze upon what was truly his field of dreams.

John Cox played four years in the Minors, never hitting over .200, but building a reputation as a fine-fielding shortstop who played the game with passion and proper mechanics. He befriended Angels coach Jimmie Reese and was on the receiving end of many a fungo from Reese's amazing bat. When Cox was traded into the Cubs system, he met John Jordan "Buck" O'Neil Jr. and quickly bonded with another hard-working, upbeat baseball lifer. Baseball's first Major League African American coach was always ready to grab a bat and give him vigorous fielding practice. O'Neil also regaled him with tales of his life as a player and manager of the Kansas City Monarchs in the Negro Leagues. In some spring training games, Cox got to play alongside Major Leaguers Ernie Banks and Don Kessinger.[22]

Cox's last year as a player was in 1967, playing for the Kansas City Athletics farm team in Burlington, Iowa. The following season, the parent club had become the Oakland Athletics, as Charlie Finley had moved the team from Kansas City. Cox was not even twenty-five and looked much younger. He enjoyed Burlington and was named general manager of the team. He almost played for the team in 1968, which certainly would have been a baseball novelty—a player–general manager. When the A's were lukewarm about the idea, Cox decided to retire and served as GM through 1969. His baseball knowledge and his upbeat personality made a good impression on the Cubs organization. In 1970 he became public relations director of the team's Wichita Arrows Triple-A farm club. When the Cubs' Midland, Texas, farm team needed a field manager, Cox, the good company man, accepted the position.

The playing field was kept in exemplary fashion by head groundskeeper Elias "Mali" Velarde Jr., the father of future Major League infielder Randy Velarde. "He made it into a palace," Cox remembered.[23]

Just before the end of the 1975 season, Cox was stunned by a phone call from Cubs general manager John Holland. "I need some reports about players on other National League clubs," Holland said. "We'll pay your way to Chicago."[24] Professional free agency was looming with the Messersmith-McNally arbitration decision due before the end of the calendar year.

Cox had never done any scouting, but Holland and owner Phil Wrigley had confidence in his evaluations. The Cubs needed help, as the contending teams of the late 1960s and early 1970s were long gone.

When Green and Goldsberry arrived, they quickly brought Cox into their inner circle. They all supported area scout Doug Mapson in his advocacy for Las Vegas, Nevada, high schooler Greg Maddux in the second round of the 1984 draft. He did not throw hard, but he was developing a changeup that was quite advanced for a high school pitcher.

After two promising years in the Minors, Maddux was handed a Cubs uniform late in the 1986 season. He soon encountered growing pains common for a young pitcher. After being hit hard by the Mets in a road game in New York, Dallas Green decided that Maddux needed more time in the Minors with the Triple-A Iowa Cubs in Des Moines. The team was playing at Indianapolis, but Green told Maddux to fly to Chicago, take a few days off to relax a little, and then join the team in Iowa. The next day, John Cox was in Indianapolis on a regular scouting assignment. He arrived early and looked out at the bullpen and saw someone in street clothes working with Iowa Cubs pitching coach Dick Pole. It was against the rules for anyone without a contract to work out at a professional baseball park. But as Cox walked closer to the bullpen, he saw it was Greg Maddux working with Pole, who had helped him earlier in his Minor League career.

"I hope you don't mind that I changed my plane ticket from Chicago to Indianapolis," Maddux said. "For some reason I've lost my changeup. It's been driving me nuts."[25] From then on, nothing that Greg Maddux accomplished in a career that wound up in the Hall of Fame after 355 victories would ever surprise John Cox.

In 1984, the third season of the Green-Goldsberry era in Chicago, the Cubs made the postseason for the first time since the 1945 World Series—they had come close in 1969, the year that the Mets roared past them late in the season and won the pennant and the World Series, with Manager Leo Durocher's refusal to rest his regulars not helping the Cubs' cause. In 1984 the Cubs manager was Jim Frey, a longtime Orioles coach under Earl Weaver and manager of the Royals during their first World Series in 1980. Frey could be prickly with the press when asked about pressures that came with the job. "I'll tell you what a challenge is," he said. "A challenge is being too short to play, not being able to see real well and wanting to play in the big leagues. I know what challenges are."[26] Frey's career as a player plateaued at Triple-A, but he did lead Chicago to ninety-six wins and the NL East title by six games over the Mets.

Several former Phillies brought to the Cubs by the Dallas Green group played big roles in the 1984 NL East title. Future Hall of Famer Ryne Sandberg, plucked as a Minor Leaguer from Philadelphia, and shortstop Larry Bowa were the double play combination. Sandberg had been a highly recruited high school quarterback with a firm offer to play football at Washington State University, but he preferred baseball even though his stiff actions in the field soured the Phillies on his potential. The outfield consisted of former Phillies Garry Matthews, Bob Dernier, and Keith Moreland. A huge boost came in a June trade with Cleveland that brought pitcher Rick Sutcliffe to Chicago, and he went 16-1 (though the Cubs did give up future Toronto World Series hero Joe Carter, who was early in his career). Yet more agony lay ahead in the National League Championship Series. The Cubs could not hold on to a lead of two games to none over the Padres and lost three straight games in San Diego and the series. A seventh-inning error at first base by Leon Durham opened the floodgates in the deciding game. The Padres would be no match for the Tigers in the World Series, as the Detroit team that started the regular season 35-5 won in five games.

One of the iron rules of scouting and player development is that you cannot brood too long over a lost pennant. The Cubs' brain trust kept focus on the 1985 draft that brought two accomplished future Major League hitters into the organization. Area scout Earl Winn landed the first-round pick, first baseman and outfielder Rafael Palmeiro, who was signed after an outstanding career playing for coach Ron Polk at Mississippi State University. Palmeiro was a native of Miami, Florida, whose parents came to the United States as exiles from the Castro regime. (On Palmeiro's Mississippi State Bulldog team were two future Major Leaguers, first baseman Will Clark and pitcher Bobby Thigpen, who was also a college outfielder batting fifth behind Palmeiro and Clark.)

In one of the greatest late-round picks in draft history, Mark Grace was selected in the twenty-fourth round from San Diego State University. Area scout John "Spider" Jorgensen, whose playing career included time with the 1947 Brooklyn Dodgers in Jackie Robinson's rookie season, was intrigued with Grace, a fancy-fielding first baseman. During the prior summer of 1984, Gary Nickels was assigned to cover the Alaska Summer League, where Grace was playing for the North Pole Nicks, a team outside of Fairbanks and outfitted in red-and-green uniforms. When they came to Anchorage to play three games each against the Anchorage Glacier Pilots and the Anchorage Bucs, Nickels noticed a change in Grace's swing. He was now pulling the ball and was more than just a flare hitter. "This guy has got the magic wand," an excited Nickels informed Gordon Goldsberry.[27] Nickels credited Grace's coach in Alaska, Mike Gillespie, for playing an important role in getting him to use the whole field instead of mostly slapping the ball to the opposite field. (Gillespie won a College World Series as a player under Rod Dedeaux at USC and later won the CWS as his successor, making him the second man to win the CWS as both player and coach—Jerry Kindall, as a Minnesota player and an Arizona Wildcat coach, was the first.) When the decade of the 1990s ended, Mark Grace and Rafael Palmeiro ranked one-two in most hits amassed by Major Leaguers in that period.

The Cubs' first pick in the 1986 June draft was high school outfielder Derrick May from Newark (Delaware) High School. The son of former Major Leaguer David May, Derrick played for all ten years in the 1990s, the first five with the Cubs before finishing his career with several other teams. (Derrick and his brother David Jr. have since gone into coaching and scouting.) In what would be the last year of the January draft, their first two choices made the Major Leagues, Shawn Boskie, a right-hander from Modesto Junior College, and Jerome Walton, an outfielder from Enterprise State Community College

(Alabama). Walton would be 1989 Rookie of the Year, with teammate Dwight Smith, drafted in 1984, finishing second, but neither would ever duplicate his early success.

In the fifth round of the 1986 draft, Gary Nickels lobbied successfully for the selection of catcher Joe Girardi. He was eligible after his junior year, but Girardi told Nickels that he wanted to honor a pledge to his late mother that he would finish his engineering degree at Northwestern University. Nickels thought Giraldi's commitment showed admirable character and makeup. He reached the Majors in 1989, playing on the playoff team that lost to the San Francisco Giants. He later became a four-time world champion with the Yankees as a player (three times) and as manager (once). He managed the Phillies for two seasons and part of 2022. In a March 2022 phone interview, Nickels said that of all his signings, Girardi brought him "the most satisfaction. . . . He has made a real impact on the game."[28]

As Birdie Tebbetts always warned, the games on the field might seem stable, but underneath, the ground is always shaking. The Tribune Company, owners of the team since the early 1980s, forced out the Dallas Green–Goldsberry tandem before the start of the 1988 season. There had always been tension between the baseball people and the corporate people who purchased the franchise from the Wrigley estate before the 1981 season for $21 million. (When they sold the team to the Ricketts family in 2009, they received a reported $845 million.) Former pro football quarterback Jim Finks, who as an executive built the Minnesota Vikings expansion team into a perennial NFL contender, was Cubs president for barely a year in 1983 and 1984, but he provided firm support for the Green group. When he returned to his first love, football, the conflict intensified. Jim Frey, who had been ousted as field manager during the 1986 season, returned as general manager in 1988, a position for which he had no previous experience, and it showed. Although the Cubs made the playoffs in 1989, they were eliminated by the Giants in the NLCS and would not return to the postseason until 1998.

The inevitable housecleaning began, and most of the hires of the Dallas Green era were soon gone. Gordon Goldsberry became a special assistant to Orioles general manager Roland Hemond, a longtime believer in the importance of scouting. Gary Nickels joined the Orioles as Midwest scouting supervisor under scouting director John Barr. When Barr left to assume the same position in San Diego in 1991 under new general manager Joe McIlvaine, Nickels took on the scouting director's job through 1998.

When Nickels joined the Orioles, they seemed to be righting the ship after losing the first 21 games of the season in 1988 on their way to 107 losses. In the very next year, 1989, they fought the Toronto Blue Jays for the AL East flag until the last weekend of the season. The resurrection earned Frank Robinson the Manager of the Year award. Also in 1989 the Orioles made LSU pitcher Ben McDonald the number one pick in the country. In 1990 the future Hall of Fame pitcher Mike Mussina was picked in the first round out of Stanford University. The Orioles had wanted to sign him after his high school graduation in Montoursville, Pennsylvania, a small town near Williamsport, the home of the Little League World Series. Orioles owner Edward Bennett Williams even offered to send legal business to Mike's father, a lawyer, but the family was determined that their son would attend Stanford. He did and would graduate with a major in economics in three years.

The 1991 Baltimore draft was less successful. Number-one pick Mark Smith, a right-handed-hitting outfielder from USC, never established himself in the big leagues but did play some years in Japan. Seventh-round pick Jimmy Haynes, a right-handed high school pitcher from LaGrange, Georgia, did not last long in the Majors, perhaps, Nickels later observed, because the bright lights of the big time proved too overwhelming. Area scout Jim Howard, who admitted to an appreciation for finesse southpaws, urged the signing of Rich Krivda in the twenty-third round, but he, too, never was a big winner. Krivda did win a gold medal as a member of the 2000 American Olympic baseball team.[29]

In the 1992 draft Jeffrey Hammonds was another right-handed-hitting outfielder picked in the first round from Stanford University. He arrived quickly in the Majors but only once played more than a hundred games a season in his six seasons for Baltimore. (He wound up with a thirteen-year career and only three more seasons of at least a hundred games played.) In the fifteenth round, Ryan Minor, a shortstop from an Oklahoma high school, was drafted; he was also an excellent basketball player, drafted by the Philadelphia 76ers. He became a footnote in baseball history when he replaced Cal Ripken in the lineup after he finally ended his consecutive games streak at 2,630. Minor later managed in the Orioles' Minor League system.

The 1994 Baltimore draft was also not productive, but it is always important to note the selection of players who did not sign but later shined with other teams. In the twenty-fifth round in 1994, the Orioles chose infielder Michael Young from Bishop Amat Memorial High School in La Puente, California, near where the Roenicke brothers, Ron and Gary, had been signed and where their father was a prominent high school coach. Young wound up signing with the Texas Rangers and enjoyed a very productive thirteen-year career. The 1995 draft produced David Dellucci, a left-handed-hitting outfielder from the University of Mississippi, in the tenth round. He enjoyed his greatest success with the expansion Arizona Diamondbacks.

In the forty-second round in 1995, the Orioles chose infielder Jerry Hairston Jr. from a high school in Naperville, Illinois, the town that Gary Nickels had called home since 1984. Hairston was determined to attend Southern Illinois University. Two years later, the Orioles signed him in the eleventh round, and he went on to a sixteen-year career, most of it as a valuable utility infielder and outfielder. Hairston came from baseball royalty. His father, Jerry Sr., and grandfather Sam Hairston played in the Negro Leagues, and both spent some time in the Majors. His mother was an outstanding athlete, and his brother Scott also played in the big leagues.[30]

The first-round pick in 1997 was Jayson Werth from Glenwood High School in Chatham, Illinois. He, too, came from a strong baseball lineage. His grandfather was Dick Schofield, the Cardinals reserve shortstop of the 1950s, and his stepfather was Dennis Werth who was a reserve on the Yankees' World Series champions of 1977 and 1978. Drafted in the twentieth round in 1997 was a Chino, California, high school outfielder, Joe Borchard. He did not sign but attended Stanford and played quarterback. The White Sox ultimately signed him, but he never established himself as a Major League regular.

There was a tragic overtone to Nickels's last draft as Orioles scouting director in 1998. In the third round, the team selected high school right-hander Steve Bechler from Medford, Oregon. Trying extra hard to make the team in spring training in 2003, Bechler died from an overdose of pills he had been taking to get in shape more quickly. Nickels was not around to witness the tragedy. He left after the 1998 season to join the San Diego Padres as pro scouting director.

He joined many friendly faces. Former Orioles executive Larry Lucchino, a protégé of Edward Bennett Williams, was the president of the Padres, and Kevin Towers was the general manager, that rarity in any organization—someone who everyone liked. Also on the staff was administrator Fred Uhlman Jr., the son of the longtime scout Fred Uhlman Sr., who grew up in Charleroi, Pennsylvania, near Pittsburgh. Fred Sr. was an all-around high school athlete who jumped center in basketball at six feet two and frequently competed against another future scout, George Zuraw. Fred Sr. was an only child whose parents allowed him to go to movies alone with his first cousin in the neighborhood, Shirley Jones. In a phone interview with Fred Sr. shortly before he passed away in 2021, he remembered the future musical star of stage and screen: "She was always singing."[31]

Nickels came to the San Diego job a year after the Padres won the National League pennant, only to be swept by the Yankees in the World Series. He was not intimately involved with the draft as a pro scout, but he was pleased that in the fifteenth round, the team selected Jake Peavy, a high school pitcher from Semmes, Alabama, who wound up with a career record of 152-126 with a 3.63 ERA. In 2000 Xavier Nady was selected in the second round from the University of California, Berkeley. He enjoyed a long career as a corner infielder and outfielder. Drafted but unsigned in the twenty-sixth round was Chino, California, high school pitcher Chad Cordero, who in 2001 became the Expos number-one pick and quickly established himself in the big leagues. Kevin Reese, an infielder from the University of San Diego picked in the twenty-seventh round, played only two years in the Majors for the Yankees in 2005 and 2006, but he became a baseball lifer. As of 2022 he was serving as the Yankees director of player development. In his last year in San Diego, Nickels watched the team select, in the first round, shortstop Khalil Greene from Clemson University. He was a highly touted prospect, but somewhere during his development, he lost his love for the game and retired after only a few years of average play in the big leagues.

Gary Nickels really missed amateur scouting, so he was delighted when the Dodgers hired him to become their Midwest scouting supervisor in 2003. He shared duties with Brian Stephenson, a third-generation scout. His grandfather Joe Stephenson scouted California for four decades for the Red Sox; his father, Jerry Stephenson, pitched briefly in the Major Leagues and scouted for both the Red Sox and Dodgers. Nickels was also glad to be working with Logan White, whom he had mentored at the start of White's career. White, the son of a rodeo cowboy, was now the team's scouting director, and, technically, Nickels was working under him. Like most great scouts, titles meant little to them; the adventure of the hunt and finding new talent meant everything. Nickels's territory in his new assignment was huge, ranging from Texas and Oklahoma to the Dakotas and Indiana and Ohio to Kansas and Nebraska.

It brought him tremendous satisfaction to be a part of the Dodgers' perennial years of contention through his retirement after the 2021 season. He played a role in the drafting in 2006 Clayton Kershaw out of high school in Dallas, Texas. In an interesting foreshadowing of mutual success, Kershaw's high school catcher was Matthew Stafford, who quarterbacked the Los Angeles Rams to 2022 Super Bowl title; in high school football, Kershaw was the center who snapped the ball to Stafford. The Dodgers were very successful at drafting college players, but Nickels was glad to be part of the scouting group that picked shortstop Corey Seager as the 2012 number-one draft pick from a high school in Concord, North Carolina. Nickels liked what he saw of Phoenix, Arizona, high schooler Cody Bellinger and was pleased that he looked like he would be a better player than his father, Clay Bellinger, who won two World Series rings with the Yankees and one with the Angels. He saw Ken Griffey Sr., a good player, and his son Ken Griffey Jr., a great player and a Hall of Famer, as an ideal example of each generation improving on the prior one.

Nickels's last day as a baseball employee was October 31, 2021, and his first day had been April 1, 1972. He was honored by the Dodgers before the game with many tributes shown on the scoreboard video. One of them was from his former signee from Naperville, Jerry Hairston Jr. Nickels liked the symmetry of spending fifty seasons in the game, being part of fifty drafts, and winning two World Series rings forty years apart in 1980 with the Phillies and 2020 with the Dodgers. When asked by Naperville sportswriter Matt LeCren for the favorite memory in his career, Nickels did not name anyone in particular.

He simply said, "It was the joy of being the person that saw the player before they became what the public knew them to be."[32]

I want to turn now to the stories of scouts who, unlike most of their brethren, stayed employed with one team for the entirety of their careers. I call them baseball's monogamists and begin with the man who many of his contemporaries have called the Braves' Branch Rickey—Paul Snyder.

6   Paul Snyder, the Braves' Branch Rickey

Paul Luther Snyder has been called the Braves' Branch Rickey because of his knowledge of baseball from A to Z. Born on June 11, 1935, in the small central Pennsylvania town of Dallastown, about eight miles northwest of York, he was making a local name for himself at fifteen by competing against older players in area semipro twilight leagues. The Brooklyn Dodgers were interested in signing the outfielder and first baseman after high school, but Snyder's parents insisted that he become the first in their family to go to college. He bypassed a baseball scholarship to Penn State, accepting instead a football scholarship to Lebanon Valley College in nearby Annville, a school run by the Church of the Brethren, the religion of his mother. Snyder hurt his back while playing football, and his work in the classroom wasn't up to par, so after one school year, he returned home to help his father in the plumbing and heating contracting business. He resumed playing baseball in a top-notch twilight league in nearby Red Lion.[1]

Sterling Arnold, a bird-dog scout for the Washington Senators, expressed interest in signing him, but the amateur free agent draft was still eight years away, so Snyder could entertain other offers. Milwaukee Braves scout John Ogden, who had made a prominent name for himself as a scout for Connie Mack's Philadelphia Athletics and later as an executive with the Minor League Baltimore Orioles, convinced Snyder that the Braves were a more stable and prosperous organization than the penny-pinching Senators. The Braves had just won the World Series over the Yankees (and would lose a rematch in 1958 and a National League tie-breaker playoff to Los Angeles in 1959). Ogden didn't need a hard sell to sign Snyder to a Braves Minor League contract that would pay him $2,500 if he made the roster of a Minor League team in his first season.[2]

In 1958 Snyder enjoyed an outstanding rookie year for Midland, Texas, in the Class D Sophomore League—.350 batting average, .574 slugging average, 15 home runs, and 106 RBIs. (The new, short-lived league soon folded.) He felt that playing semipro ball back home with older men had prepared him very well for the pros. In 1959 Snyder was promoted to Cedar Rapids in the Class B Three-I League (Illinois, Indiana, Iowa), but a roster crunch forced him down to the Eau Claire Braves in the Class C Northern League. He wound up hitting over .300 in both stops, but his back flared up while traveling on the rickety team bus to a road game in Winnipeg, Canada. He garnered only 326 at bats, 120 fewer than in his rookie season. His balky back would require spinal surgery, and it became a chronic problem.

The 1960 season found Snyder demoted to the Class D Wellsville Braves of the New York–Penn League. Still plagued by the bad back, he hit .241 in only 101 at bats for the franchise in western New York State. But Snyder always found a silver lining whatever his circumstances. He developed a lifelong friendship with Wellsville player-manager Harry Minor. A native of Long Beach, California, Minor was at the end of a twelve-year Minor League playing career. In 1961 Minor started scouting for the Braves, and in 1968 he joined the Mets, where he enjoyed a forty-four-year career and was instrumental in signing such future stars on the 1986 world champions as Darryl Strawberry, Lenny Dykstra, Kevin Elster, and Kevin Mitchell. In 2013 Harry Minor became the first and still the only scout elected to the Mets Hall of Fame.

Minor took an immediate liking to Snyder, who was seven years his junior. It wasn't just Snyder's batting tools, his line-drive stroke, and his ability to wait on the pitch. He liked even more Snyder's aptitude for the mental side of game, noticing that he was an attentive listener and observer and was looked up to by younger teammates. Minor shared with Snyder a lot of his accumulated baseball knowledge, some of it delivered while driving the team bus. Among the lessons Snyder learned was never to criticize any individual in front of the team. After a game, whether a win or a loss, Minor just asked the players to sit in silence for about fifteen minutes thinking about the day's events. He then told them to flush the experience and prepare for tomorrow.

In 1961 Snyder's back issues abated, and he enjoyed a stellar season. Assigned again to Class B Cedar Rapids, he led the Three-I League in hits and compiled the impressive line of .310 batting average, 14 home runs, 76 RBIs, and .450 slugging average. In 1962 the strapping six-foot-two, 200-pound Snyder enjoyed his best year as a player, hitting .312 and slugging .495 with 19 home runs and 113 RBIs for the Austin Senators in the Double-A Texas League. In 1963 he was promoted to the Denver Bears, the Braves' Triple-A Pacific Coast League franchise. His elation at arriving one step from the Majors was quickly doused when his back flared up again.

After one game early in the season, Denver manager Jack Tighe called him in for a heart-to-heart discussion. The former skipper of the Detroit Tigers noted Snyder's declining mobility. "You have only one tool now, line-drive power," Tighe frankly told him, adding that at nearly the age of twenty-eight he wasn't getting any younger.[3] Yet like others in the Braves organization, Tighe didn't want to lose Snyder's services. He told him that a player-manager job was open at Greenville, South Carolina, in the Class A Western Carolinas League, and he knew that farm director John Mullen wanted to hire him.

The death of a dream is never easy for any player, but after letting the bad news sink in, Snyder thought about his future. His wife was due with their first child, and he knew he had to make a living to support his family. He didn't want to leave baseball, so he quickly accepted the offer and headed to his first assignment as player-manager. As the years passed, Snyder never failed to credit Jack Tighe for his honesty and for kick-starting him toward his new career. "Never lie to a player" is the lesson from Tighe that Snyder always kept in mind.

At Greenville, Snyder took over for Jim Fanning, who was a rising star in the Braves' player-development system, and, as discussed, would become a key member of the Montreal Expos expansion franchise. "He was like a big brother to me," Snyder remembered in an October 2019 phone interview. "You could take any problem to Fanning, and he would always suggest a sensible solution." In the same interview Snyder also lavished praise on Roland Hemond, another vital early influence before he left to join the expansion

California Angels. "Roland taught me to always call players by their first names," Snyder recalled.[4]

Snyder's managerial career started auspiciously, as the Greenville Braves won the 1963 Western Carolina League playoffs. He was at the plate for over 260 at bats in his last semiregular year as a player, hitting .316, just a little below his career average of .318. The year 1964 started with Snyder working as a co-manager with Andy Pafko for the Binghamton Triplets in the Class A New York–Penn League. On the staff with Pafko, the former slugger with the Cubs, Brooklyn Dodgers, and Milwaukee Braves, was Walter "Boom Boom" Beck, the pre–World War II Phillies hurler who had gotten his nickname for giving up line drives that loudly caromed off the tin wall at cozy Baker Bowl.

During the 1964 season, the future "Braves' Branch Rickey" had his first and only encounter with Branch Rickey himself, who was in his last season as a consultant with the Cardinals. (He died late the next year a few days before his eighty-fourth birthday.) Snyder was part of a Braves contingent that traveled to a meeting in Sarasota where the Braves, Cardinals, White Sox, and Yankees were finalizing plans for a new cooperative league to be called the Sarasota Rookie League. Snyder vividly remembered Rickey arriving in a Chrysler limousine and holding forth for most of the day on the fundamentals of running, throwing, sliding, and base running. He recalled that Rickey stressed the importance of using games in this cooperative league as lessons in player development.[5]

Snyder managed the Sarasota Braves to a 1964 pennant with a 36-23 record. In 1965 he returned to Florida to manage again, this time in West Palm Beach, where the Braves had moved their franchise in what was then called the Florida Rookie League. (In 1966 the name was changed again to the Florida Gulf Coast League.) Snyder led the team to a strong second-place finish; one of his young players was Wayne Garrett, who four years later was a platoon third baseman on the World Series champion New York Mets.

Meanwhile, the parent franchise was facing a serious problem as it prepared to set up shop in Atlanta for the 1966 season. Nobody in the organization knew anything about stadium operations. Already seen as a good company man, Snyder was asked by Braves president John McHale to fill the void, although he knew nothing about hiring and organizing grounds crews, arranging stadium cleaning contracts, and other business issues. The workload was so heavy that at times, Snyder told author Bill Shanks, "I slept in the first aid room."[6] The stadium operations job became the only job in Snyder's baseball career that he did not enjoy because he was far removed from working with players.

After the season, he was rescued from the administrative side when he learned that Jack Tighe, who had turned from managing to scouting, was leaving the organization. Snyder asked Braves general manager Paul Richards for Tighe's job, and his wish was granted. Always a sponge for picking up lessons from his elders, Snyder learned a lot about baseball strategy and techniques from Richards, who encouraged talking the game with players—in practices and before and after games. Snyder picked up many durable insights from Richards' fertile baseball brain without developing the oversized ego of the well-traveled manager.

Snyder started his career as a Braves scout in 1967 and immediately fell in love with the profession. He loved being out in the field doing hands-on development work with aspiring players. The good company man did return to manage in the lower Minors four more times in the early 1970s, and led each team to a winning record: in 1970, the Magic Valley Cowboys in Twin Falls, Idaho, in the Pioneer League; in 1971 and 1973, Wytheville, North Carolina, in the Appalachian League; and in 1972, Greenwood, South Carolina, in the Western Carolinas League. But his commitment to building lasting organizational success through scouting and player development became permanent when the Braves named Snyder's former Austin Senators teammate Bill Lucas scouting director in 1972. That the two men belonged to a mutual admiration society was made clear when Lucas immediately named Snyder his assistant scouting director.

William DeVaughn Lucas was a rarity in the baseball business, an African American who worked his way up the ladder to a prominent front-office position. Born January 25, 1936, in Jacksonville, Florida, Bill Lucas, like Paul Snyder, got the baseball bug early on. He broke in as a peanut vendor for the local Braves affiliate in the Class A South Atlantic League, rose to team batboy, and, in high school, developed into a star shortstop. At the historically Black Florida A & M University in Tallahassee, he earned All-American honors from the NAIA. A six-year Minor League career ensued, interrupted at times by military service. Paul Snyder is convinced that Lucas would have made the Majors had he not suffered a knee injury when they were teammates in 1962. Lucas retired two years later with a career .273 batting average. He briefly tried teaching school, but as you have seen throughout this saga, the siren call of baseball was too strong.[7]

In 1965, the last year of the Minor League Triple-A Atlanta Crackers' existence, Lucas served as the team's public relations director. The 1966 season began with Lucas working in the mailroom of the newly minted Atlanta Braves, but he quickly was tapped to start a community relations department aimed at building interest in the Braves in the Black community. In 1967 Lucas became assistant to farm director Eddie Robinson, the former Indians and Yankees first baseman. When Robinson was promoted in 1972 to vice president in charge of baseball operations, Lucas was named his successor as farm director. It did not hurt Lucas's rise in the organization that his sister, Barbara, was married at the time to the Braves' reigning superstar, Hank Aaron. But there was no doubt that the Braves had found a man blessed with the rare combination of passion, compassion, and dispassion. As Eddie Robinson later wrote in his memoir *Lucky Me*, Lucas was "a talented fellow" and a "forward thinker."[8]

Paul Snyder found in Bill Lucas a soul baseball brother. He once described him as a rare teammate who read books on the team bus "that had no pictures."[9] For his part, Lucas never forgot that during their season as teammates in Austin, Paul had been heartsick at the segregated second-class living conditions Lucas endured. "A lot of nights he'd sleep in a boarded-up hotel downtown," Snyder remembered to writer Lee Walburn, who worked for the Braves in their first few years in Atlanta. "He just buttoned his lip, went out and played his heart out."[10] He realized that for Paul Snyder color did not exist. What only mattered were the answers to two basic questions: Could the farmhands play the game? And how could we make them better players?

Lucas took special pains to ease the transition to pro baseball for the many players of color the Braves were bringing into the organization. One of those players was Johnnie B. "Dusty" Baker Jr., who was drafted in the twenty-fifth round in 1967 from a high school in Carmichael, California, near Sacramento.

Baker still glows with the memory of how Lucas cushioned him from the worst aspects of racism in the South that Baker had never experienced so directly in California. He warned him of the dangers while teaching him about "maintaining your honor and dignity as a man."[11] Lucas took such an interest in Baker's advancement as a person as well as a player that when Dusty graduated with honors from the Dress Blue program in his Marine Reserve training camp a few years later, Lucas attended the ceremony. The idea that the Braves organization was a family that took care of each other was not lost on Baker, who made it a point to pick up his African American teammate Ralph Garr in Louisiana on his annual cross-country automobile trip to Florida for spring training. Garr, who was signed out of Grambling College by Mel Didier, himself felt the warm vibes from Lucas. He was thrilled when the Braves hired him as a scout in 1984, a position he still held as of 2022. In 2021 Garr won a Midwest Scout of the Year award from MLB for his work with the Braves.[12]

As the Braves scouting and philosophy program took hold under Lucas and Snyder, certain principles became obvious. There was a strong belief that high school players with high ceilings were the preferred athletes to draft and develop under the care of veteran coaches. The organization especially encouraged the scouting of high school pitchers, or at most community college pitchers who hadn't been ruined by overuse and could be trained by pro coaches to throw correctly. They might take two or three extra years to develop, but Lucas and Snyder firmly believed that the patience was worth the end result. Hiring good pitching coaches and hitting coaches and instructors for the Minor Leagues became paramount. Soon, former Major League hurlers Bruce Dal Canton, Bill Fischer, and Eddie Watt would be hired by the system for their teaching abilities.

As Snyder's career blossomed, he was especially grateful to Lucas for introducing him to one of the Braves' most respected area scouts, Bill Wight. "What a gift Bill Lucas gave me by assigning me to two weeks on the road with Bill Wight," Snyder told me in our phone interview. Although the southpaw's career record of 77-99 didn't look impressive, Wight lasted twelve years in the Majors after being traded in 1948 from the Yankees in the deal for fellow southpaw (and future scout) Eddie Lopat. Wight earned industrywide respect from his peers for the intensity and guile in which he approached his craft. As discussed, pitchers were particularly awed at the pickoff move to first base that Wight developed. Shortly after retiring, Wight turned to scouting. He first joined the expansion Houston Colt .45s and then, from 1967 through 1994, he served the Braves as a California-area scout who played a very influential role in meetings before the amateur draft. He would be central to the signing of such future Braves stars as Dale Murphy, Bob Horner, Ron Gant, Brian Hunter, and David Justice.

What fascinated Paul Snyder about Bill Wight's scouting acumen was that he was more expert at appraising hitters than pitchers. He guessed that Wight's keen evaluation of hitters arose from an awareness that he didn't have overpowering stuff as a pitcher so he had to understand hitters' weaknesses to survive. "At times I'd scout with him, and he'd ask about my radar gun: 'Whatdya get? Whatdya get?'" Snyder remembered with a chuckle.[13]

Before the arrival of Bill Lucas at the helm of the farm system in 1972, the Braves did not have great success with the amateur free agent draft. However, on the horizon in Portland, Oregon, was Dale Murphy, a gifted athlete who as early as the ninth grade was attracting the attention of legendary Ohio State football coach Woody Hayes. The strong consensus of the Braves scouting staff was that Murphy should be a first-round draft pick, and he was indeed taken at that level in 1974. He did not excel immediately in the Minors, and a knee injury would ultimately force his switch from catcher to the outfield. Yet compassionate understanding, the watchword under Lucas and Snyder, worked wonders with Murphy. He never forgot the generosity of the Braves for insisting that he accept a bonus for his production in his mediocre Minor League season of 1976 even though he didn't reach the requisite numbers.[14]

Paul Snyder always liked to cite the old adage that you needed to draft ten pitchers to find one who would have a significant career. In addition to signing Dale Murphy in the first round of the June 1974 draft, the Braves selected southpaw Larry McWilliams in the first round of the January draft. McWilliams, a Paris, Texas, junior college hurler, went on to a thirteen-year Major League career. Picked in June out of small colleges were two future longtime Braves hurlers, Rick Camp in the seventh round and lefty Mickey

Mahler in the tenth round. With the trade of Hank Aaron back to Milwaukee at the end of the 1974 season, the organization's youth movement seemed to be accelerating.

On the Major League level, however, ownership was in flux. The whirlwind known as Ted Turner arrived on the scene in 1973 as a part owner eager to use Braves' games as programming for his WCTG-TV station in Atlanta. The station was still showing mostly old movies, with his emphasis on news still a ways off. "I hate the news. News is evil. It makes people feel bad," he said at the time.[15] When rumors were flying that the Braves might be sold and moved to another city, Turner bought full ownership in the team after the 1975 season.

The Braves were competing in the tough NL West Division dominated by the Cincinnati Reds and the Los Angeles Dodgers. Yet in 1976, the first season with Turner as full owner, attendance picked up by 53 percent. Braves games became carnivals, with pregame ostrich races, contests in pushing a baseball with one's nose between first base and home plate in which Turner occasionally took part, and scantily clad damsels cavorting around the field. He relished the publicity of being of an owner. He even managed one game after he sent incumbent skipper Dave Bristol on a "scouting vacation" during a long losing streak. The Braves lost in Turner's one-game turn at the helm, and afterward the baseball establishment came down hard on him for making a "mockery of the game." National League President Chub Feeney dug up an obscure rule that prevented an owner from managing a game without special permission from the commissioner, and Bowie Kuhn refused to grant a waiver.[16]

Paul Snyder admired Ted Turner's energy and showmanship, but he sensed early on that Turner did not understand how to develop baseball players. Out in the field evaluating amateur talent and Minor Leaguers, Snyder stayed out of Turner's way, feeling confident that Bill Lucas had earned the respect of the owner. Indeed, Lucas was promoted in 1976 to vice president of player development, becoming the first Black general manager. (He was not given the GM title, something Turner kept for himself.) Lucas displayed such charisma and fierce honesty that he could tell Turner to his face that he did not know baseball and to leave the big decisions to him.

Unfortunately, the indefatigable Paul Snyder was allowing danger warnings about his health go unheeded. In the fall of 1975, he went on a hunting trip with two of his favorite players, pitchers Joe and Phil Niekro. Snyder's doctor warned him that a serious heart condition must be monitored, but when he returned from the trip, he thrust himself back into work. There were drafts to prepare for—the January draft of players not eligible in June and then the big June one.[17] The 1976 draft would be a fruitful one—in the fifth round the Braves picked University of Nebraska Omaha catcher Bruce Benedict, who would play twelve years in the Majors and later become a coach.

Then, the night after the June draft, while watching the Johnny Carson *Tonight Show* and planning to stay awake for the rebroadcast of a Braves game on TBS, Paul Snyder felt all the lights go out. He had suffered a major stroke. He was rushed to a hospital in Atlanta where he stayed for two weeks. Only forty years old, Snyder lost almost all feeling in his right side. Once back at home, his wife, Marguerite (called Petie by everyone), who usually doubled as his radar gun assistant, took on an even more crucial role as his main physical therapist. He slowly began to feel better, but he told author Bill Shanks that he may have lost two years of memory during his ordeal. Bill Lucas stood firmly beside his ailing friend, insisting that Snyder must be kept on the payroll and everything must be done to nurse him back to health. When some in the organization thought about cutting ties with Paul, Lucas responded, "I could do that, but you'd have to replace me, too."[18]

When Snyder went back to full-time work in 1977, the baseball world had gone through revolutionary changes. As a result of impartial arbitrator Peter Seitz's decision just before Christmas in 1975, veteran pitchers Andy Messermith and Dave McNally were freed from the constraints of the perpetual reserve system. The Players Association worked out a compromise with the owners that created a professional free agent draft after the 1976 season, in which all players with six or more years of Major League service could be free to sell themselves to the highest bidder. Not surprisingly, Ted Turner immediately barged into the free agent market by signing Andy Messersmith. He was not allowed, however, to give Andy the number 17 and the word *Channel* above it on the back. Commissioner Bowie Kuhn nixed that blatant advertising ploy for Turner's TV station. Turner also incurred the wrath of Kuhn for declaring publicly that he wanted to sign Giants outfielder Gary Matthews before the professional free agent draft even started. He was slapped with a year's suspension, although it wasn't fully enforced.[19]

Messersmith never regained his twenty-game-winning form with the Braves and was gone after two seasons. Matthews did become a Brave for four seasons, but his defensive liabilities took away from his relatively adequate offense. The 1977 and 1978 Braves plummeted to the NL West basement, but organizationally some promising signs were in scouting and player development. After a fallow 1977 draft, the Braves were far more productive in 1978. Three future Major Leaguers were signed from the first three rounds. Slugging third baseman Bob Horner was the first-round pick. He was rushed to the Majors from Arizona State University without any Minor League seasoning, as Ted Turner salivated at the prospect of a big bopper to pair with the emerging Dale Murphy as a potent one-two punch. Horner was voted National League Rookie of the Year.

Catcher Matt Sinatro came aboard in the second round from a West Hartford, Connecticut, high school, and he would enjoy a ten-year Major League career. Steve Bedrosian was nabbed in the third round, another player from a cold-weather area, the University of New Haven in Connecticut. Paul Snyder felt a special affinity for players from the Northeast who learned to play in chilly if not frigid conditions. Bedrosian went on to enjoy greater success with other teams, winning the 1987 Cy Young Award as a Phillies reliever and later pitching for the Giants and Twins.

Then on May 1, 1979, tragedy hit the Braves organization. After some stressful days of dealing with Bucky Woy, Bob Horner's aggressive agent, the hard-working Bill Lucas had just finished watching Phil Niekro's 200th victory in Pittsburgh on TV when he suffered a brain aneurysm. He died four days later at the unconscionably young age of forty-three. At the funeral at the Cross Catholic Church in west Atlanta, an overflow crowd of mourners extolled the baseball pioneer. Renowned Florida A&M football coach Jake Gaither said that he had never met a finer leader than Bill Lucas and called him "one of God's great men." (Bob Lucas, Bill's younger brother, would later coach baseball at Florida A&M and also scout for the Braves.) Flamboyant Ted Turner said that Lucas was now the general manager on a team in heaven with Ty Cobb, Babe Ruth, and Lou Gehrig. Dale Murphy struck a more subdued and genuine note when he spoke of how Lucas greeted him warmly at the airport after he arrived in Atlanta on his first-ever flight. "Bill's dream was for this organization to be a success," Murphy said. "It is our sacred honor to fulfill his dream."[20]

When the Braves moved to Sun Trust Park in Cobb County in 2018, they continued to remember Bill Lucas as they had done at their prior locations, Fulton County Stadium and Turner Field. The main street was named Bill Lucas Way, a Bill Lucas Conference Room was created, and a Bill Lucas Diversity Apprenticeship was established. It was a fitting honor for the gifted man, who, when he started out in the community relations department, made it a point to try to hire an African American for every white person he brought into the organization. Longtime Braves publicist Bob Hope never forgot how Lucas had demonstrated his belief in gender equality when he escorted Hope's wife Susan to a sports dinner where no women had ever been invited. "Come on, someone's got to be the first woman to integrate baseball," he told her.[21] When Lucas was elected to the Braves Hall of Fame in 2006, Paul Snyder said simply, "He planted a seed, and we just carried through with it."[22]

John Mullen, who started his front-office career with the Boston Braves and offered Snyder his first managing job, returned from the Houston Astros to become Lucas's replacement with the title of general manager. Yet the Braves continued to be also-rans and often basement dwellers in the tough AL West division dominated by the Dodgers and the Reds, with the Giants also becoming contenders. Though the Braves finished one game over .500 in 1980 during Bobby Cox's first tenure as Braves manager, a 1981 slip to fifth place in the division led Ted Turner to replace him with Joe Torre.

Titles never meant anything to Paul Snyder, but with the loss of Bill Lucas, he was now named the Braves scouting director and poised to start the most brilliant decade of his service to the Braves. He kept most of Lucas's talented scouts like Bill Wight and added some key ones of his own. Rod Gilbreath, a third-round 1970 middle-infield draft choice from a Laurel, Mississippi, high school, was named a West Coast scout. In 1970 Snyder managed Gilbreath at Magic Valley in the Pioneer League, and a paternal relationship quickly developed. Gilbreath was amazed at the depth of Snyder's evaluating skills and his ability to be frank without being insensitive. He knew how "to recognize players who could play, and what to do with players who couldn't play," Gilbreath told Bill Shanks.[23]

In 1980 Snyder hired Harold "Hep" Cronin as a full-time midwestern-area scout who later became a national cross-checker. Hep had been in the organization as an associate scout since 1969, selected after coaching high school baseball in Cincinnati. Coaching and scouting were obviously different activities—coaching focused on immediate wins, and scouting emphasized long-range development. Yet the Braves Way that Bill Lucas started and Paul Snyder continued looked at the whole player, his mental makeup and not just his tools or his statistics. Cronin, the father of UCLA basketball coach Mick Cronin, loved working for a boss who always listened intently to his area scouts' opinions. Paul never pulled rank, Cronin told Bill Shanks, because "he'd rather migrate to talk to the area scout from Tennessee or something."[24]

One of the older scouts whom Snyder brought into the fold was indeed from Tennessee—Lou Fitzgerald, from Cleveland, Tennessee, near Chattanooga. He had been one of Paul Richards's right-hand men when Richards was with the White Sox, Orioles, Colt .45s and then Astros, and Braves. From the White Sox, Snyder picked up another savvy evaluator, Fred Schaffer, who specialized in pitching. Back in the mid-1950s Schaffer signed future American League All-Star southpaw Gary Peters, and in 1988, as I will soon discuss, Fitzgerald would be one of the biggest advocates for signing Michigan high school southpaw Steve Avery.

Though Bill Lucas did not live to see the June 1979 draft, he was pleased with the January 1979 results when Milt Thompson became a Brave. He was signed out of a Gaithersburg, Maryland, high school in the second round and would enjoy a thirteen-year Major League career, mainly as a utility outfielder. Ventura, California, high school outfielder Brook Jacoby was picked in the seventh round in January. The June 1979 draft brought into the fold first-rounder Brad Komminsk from a Lima, Ohio, high school; Jacksonville University shortstop Paul Runge in the ninth round (who would have an eight-year Major League career); and a steal in the twenty-third round, Southeastern Oklahoma State outfielder Brett Butler. Of course, neither Paul Snyder nor any of the scouting and player-development staff had much input when Ted Turner okayed the 1983 trade of Butler and Jacoby to the Indians for Len "No Hit" Barker that turned out disastrously for the Braves—Barker went 10-20 for Atlanta and was out of baseball by 1987. As for Komminsk's failure to live up to his billing as a can't-miss prospect, Snyder remained baffled. Except for average running speed, Komminsk seemed to possess all the tools, Snyder reflected in our phone interview. He probably lost confidence and listened to too many suggestions.

In 1980 the Braves hit pay dirt in the first round of both drafts. Right-hander Craig McMurtry from McLennan Community College in Texas was picked in January, and southpaw Ken Dayley from the University of Portland was the June first-rounder. Another serviceable future utility fielder came in the fifteenth round, when Stanford University's Paul Zuvella was selected. Though Dayley wound up enjoying a fruitful career as a relief pitcher, mainly for the Cardinals, Snyder regretted that Dayley never became a core Braves starter. "He should have lasted a long time with us," Snyder told Bill Shanks. "His psyche was beaten down."[25]

That the draft can be very unpredictable was proven when the 1981 and 1982 drafts produced no future Major League Braves. They did select Livermore, California, high school southpaw Randy Johnson in the fourth round, but he chose college at UCLA and later was signed by the Expos before starting to show his Hall of Fame form with the Mariners. The 1983 draft was much more fruitful. Two gems were found, one relatively high and one far lower in the draft. Shortstop Ron Gant from a Victoria, Texas, high school wasn't even in the registry of the Major League Baseball Scouting Bureau. Gant was known more for his football and basketball skills, but when tipped off by a local source, influential Bill Wight made a trip to Texas. When he filed a glowing report on the Texan's promising athletic tools, Gant shot up the Braves' draft lists, and they nabbed him in the fourth round.

The lower-round find in the 1983 draft was unheralded future starting second baseman Mark Lemke, picked in the twenty-seventh round out of Notre Dame High School in Whitesboro, New York, in the central part of the state. He epitomized the Lucas-Snyder belief that a team cannot win without grinders who may lack glamour but care only about winning. Listed at five feet ten and 167 pounds, Lemke played in the spirit of his predecessor Glenn

Hubbard, who had been drafted in the twentieth round in 1975 and played ten seasons for the Braves. Lemke's offensive stats were not gaudy, but they would increase noticeably in the postseason. He was a peerless defender, the kind of fielder fans wanted the ball hit to. When Lemke tried a comeback as a knuckleballer in an independent league in 1999, he told *New York Times* feature writer Dan Barry, "To be honest with you, I enjoy playing the game of baseball."[26]

The Braves also selected, in 1983's ninth round, outfielder Jay Buhner from McLennan Community College in Texas, but he did not sign. The Pirates drafted Buhner later, the Yankees picked him up in a trade, and he became a star when traded to the Mariners for Ken Phelps—a transaction that drew the scorn of George Costanza in a memorable *Seinfeld* episode.

The 1984 draft turned out to be crucial to the Braves' future success. Future Hall of Famer Tom Glavine came aboard in the second round, and Lemke's future double-play partner Jeff Blauser was picked in the first round of the January secondary draft. Blauser's signing was relatively easy, but the wooing of Glavine away from a professional hockey career was more complicated. It provided a prime example of how the Braves Way, started under Bill Lucas and continued under Paul Snyder, was beginning to function smoothly and successfully.

Newly appointed Braves northeastern-area scout Tony DeMacio knew what kind of athletic talent Glavine possessed. He was the star of both his hockey and baseball teams at Billerica High School, a few miles northwest of Boston, where his father, Thomas, had been a star football player. The Braves knew that the senior Glavine had discouraged Tom from playing football because of the chance of permanent injury. Yet they weren't sure how deep Glavine's love of hockey was. He had been offered a four-year hockey scholarship to the University of Massachusetts Lowell and was also drafted in the fourth round by the Los Angeles Kings of the National Hockey League. With the Red Sox the only team in town since 1953, DeMacio wanted to downplay his interest in Glavine lest the Boston newspapers were to get wind of it and pressure the Red Sox to get in on the bidding.[27]

Like all good scouts, DeMacio held firm to his opinions. The thirty-nine-year-old native of McKees Rocks, Pennsylvania, near Pittsburgh, grew up an ardent Pirates fan. As mentioned, he attended Parsons College in Fairfield, Iowa, and played infield on a dominant team that featured three future New York Mets pitchers, Rich Folkers, Jackson Todd, and Charlie Williams. DeMacio was not good enough to consider a pro career, so he turned to coaching and teaching at the Staunton Military Academy (pronounced "STAN-ton") in Virginia. In the summers he coached in college leagues in the Shenandoah Valley and built a solid reputation among veteran baseball scouts for the way he taught fundamentals while letting his players enjoy playing the game. DeMacio was eternally grateful for what he learned early in the mornings and after games from veteran scouts Ralph DiLullo of the Scouting Bureau; Tom Giordano, then with the Orioles; Herb Stein of the Twins; and Paul Snyder, who gave him his big break by offering him the important job as northeastern-area scout.[28]

By the time of Tom Glavine's senior year, DeMacio succeeded in allaying any internal doubts among the Braves' brass about the young southpaw's baseball abilities. He had a sensational season both on the mound and playing center field on days he wasn't pitching. Billerica High made the Eastern Massachusetts high school state finals against Brockton with Glavine pitching nine scoreless innings and then throwing out from center field a potential winning run in the bottom of the tenth. (The victim happened to be a nephew of late heavyweight champion Rocky Marciano.) To cap off his great day, Glavine started the winning rally in the thirteenth inning.

When it was time for Snyder, DeMacio, and Bob Turzilli, the Braves' northeastern scouting supervisor, to meet with Glavine and his father shortly before the draft, they were all impressed by the youngster's maturity. It was Tom, not his father, who took charge of the meeting, asking good questions about what Minor League life would be like and how fast he could expect promotion. The Braves contingent left the room, convinced that Glavine wanted to play baseball and would turn down the hockey scholarship offer. When draft day came, the Braves breathed a sigh of relief when he was still available in the second round. According to *Baseball America's Ultimate Draft Book*, the Blue Jays would have picked him next.[29] Bill Wight summed up Glavine's learning curve by saying, "He knew he had to acquire what he didn't have. He knew his shortcomings and his strengths."[30]

In 1985 the Braves made an out-of-the-box selection by choosing in the fourth round David Justice from tiny Thomas More College in Crestview Hills, Kentucky. Justice was another player whom scouting's conventional wisdom branded as too raw and undisciplined to develop in baseball; after all, he started college on a basketball scholarship before he became bored with all the running. Scout Lou Fitzgerald loved Justice's athleticism and felt confident that the Braves' growing stable of coaches and instructors would bring out the baseball player in him. He saw Justice as a genuine diamond in the rough who had finished high school at the age of fifteen and was only eighteen when he left Thomas More after his junior year because of its weak noncompetitive baseball program.[31]

Other future Major Leaguers were selected in the 1985 draft. The first-rounder was right-hander Tommy Greene from Whiteville (North Carolina) High School, who wound up having an eight-year Major League career, though injuries curtailed what might have led to greater success. The eighth-round pick in 1985 was West Covina, California, high school outfielder and first baseman Al Martin, who stayed in the Majors for most of eleven seasons.

Atlanta's 1986 first-round June pick turned out to be southpaw Kent Mercker, who entered the organization out of Dublin Coffman High School in Ohio. He never emerged as a star with the Braves but did contribute during the Braves' remarkable string of playoff teams, including the 1995 world champions; Mercker had a 74-67 record and 4.25 ERA in an eighteen-year career, the last ten with other teams. The 1986 Braves draft has a what-if quality because they selected three high schoolers who did not sign until later with other teams. Southern Illinois University outfielder Steve Finley in the eleventh round and Louisiana high school pitcher Ben McDonald in the twenty-seventh round were both later signed by the Orioles with McDonald as 1990's number one pick in the country. In 1987's eighteenth round, drafted but unsigned by the Braves was Phoenix, Arizona, high school outfielder Tim Salmon, the future Angels star right fielder.

If 1986's draft was not very productive, the year still goes down as a vital one in Braves history because it marked the return of Bobby Cox as field manager (in that capacity he had led the expansion Blue Jays to the playoffs) and the hiring of Stan Kasten as general manager. At the age of twenty-seven in 1977, Kasten had become the youthful general manager of Turner's Atlanta Hawks in the National Basketball Association. He previously turned down Turner's offer to take on the top position in both sports, but by 1986 he felt ready and willing. Kasten, Cox, and Paul Snyder were all on the same page about the importance of investing in scouting and player development. When Kasten expressed the hope that tryout camps could be established in every state where TBS was already airing, Snyder and Cox positively beamed. At the time, the Dodgers had more than four times as many scouts on their payroll as the Braves, but Kasten, with Ted Turner's blessing, rapidly closed the gap, raising the number of full-time scouts from five to eighteen and hiring many more Minor League coaches and instructors.[32]

Starting in 1987, only one amateur free agent draft took place, in June, and the Braves picked two important contributors to the future 1995 champions. Infielder and outfielder Brian Hunter was selected in the eighth round out of Cerritos College in California—he went on to a nine-year Major League career. Lefty short reliever Mike Stanton came in the thirteenth round out of Alvin (Texas) Community College, and he went on to enjoy a nineteen-year Major League career. Number-one draft pick southpaw Derek Lilliquist was signed out of the University of Georgia and would enjoy an eight-year Major League career and later a long tenure as Major League pitching coach for various teams.

In 1988, Taylor, Michigan, high school southpaw Steve Avery was the Braves' number-one selection. On the scholastic level, Avery had been virtually unhittable. Scout Fred Schaffer, Paul Snyder's top pitching adviser, drooled over Avery's arsenal of velocity and movement that was rare in someone so young. Snyder loved to tell the story that in one game the plate umpire gave Steve Avery a gift strike call. "Mr. Ump, this guy don't need no help," the overmatched batter wailed to the plate umpire.[33] The 1988 draft also brought to the Braves, in the eighth round, future closer Mark Wohlers, signed after high school in Holyoke, Massachusetts. Enjoying his first full season in the Braves organization in 1988 was youthful future Hall of Famer John Smoltz, whom the Braves had pilfered from the Detroit Tigers for veteran pitcher Doyle Alexander during the 1987 pennant race. Alexander did help the Bengals win the AL East, but he retired two years later. In picking Glavine earlier, and now Wohlers and Smoltz, another pitcher hardened by a cold-weather upbringing in Michigan, the Braves were beginning to see the fruits of their strong commitment to youthful pitching.

The Braves were not so fortunate in the first round of the 1989 draft when they selected catcher Tyler Houston from a Las Vegas high school. Houston did not reach the Majors until 1996 and spent most of his short three-year career as a backup with the Cubs. Far more successful was fifth-round selection Ryan Klesko, from high school in Westminster, California, drafted as both an outfielder and left-handed pitcher. A nagging elbow injury curtailed his development as a pitcher. Although his potent bat soon brought him soon to the Majors, the arm ailment led to his ultimate switch from the outfield to first base. Klesko would be a key contributor to the 1995 champions and last for sixteen seasons in the Majors, the last few in San Diego.

The last great coup of Snyder's fruitful decade as Braves director of amateur scouting came with the selection of Larry Wayne "Chipper" Jones Jr. in the 1990 draft. The Braves hierarchy was split between choosing the switch-hitting Jacksonville, Florida, prep school shortstop and the Arlington, Texas, high school right-hander Todd Van Poppel. Scout Red Murff, who nurtured and signed Nolan Ryan for the Mets out of an Alvin, Texas, high school, was very high on Van Poppel. In fact, he had already developed a friendship with the prospect's father and publicly compared the youngster to Ryan. Murff admitted in his memoir, *The Scout*, that he probably had driven up the price the Braves would have to pay.[34]

Young Todd Van Poppel possessed several bargaining chips: a baseball scholarship offer from the University of Texas, a reported desire to pitch for the 1992 USA Olympic team, and representation by rising player agent Scott Boras. Manager Bobby Cox and Paul Snyder flew to Texas shortly before the draft to meet with the prospective draft pick. "There were no negotiations at all with the young man," Snyder later told *Baseball America*. "We talked to his mother and father, but never to him."[35] He even spurned meeting with Red Murff, his biggest advocate among the scouts. It led Murff and other people to believe that Van Poppel and Boras had already made a deal with the reigning World Series champion Oakland Athletics, who picked him sixth in the draft and signed him to a contract reportedly worth $1.2 million with an immediate placement on the forty-man roster.[36] Van Poppel never became a Major League star, finishing with a 40-52 record and an unsightly 5.58 ERA.

The Braves quickly turned to gauge the interest of Chipper Jones in becoming a Brave. Paul Snyder sent scouts DeMacio and Dean Jongewaard, the latter an expert on the contractual side of baseball, to meet with Jones and his family at their home in Pierson, Florida. The Joneses greeted the Braves emissaries far more warmly than the Van Poppels had. They had seen DeMacio, Snyder, Hep Cronin, and Bill Wight at many of Chipper's high school games. In a lovely example of scouts being interested in developing great young talent, when Chipper was still in the eighth grade, veteran Reds scout George Zuraw had gifted him with a bunch of wooden bats that he would need to get used to after high school. By the age of fourteen, Chipper was already playing in American Legion tournaments. He was also a top-notch wide receiver in football, leading all Florida high schools in catches.[37]

As much as Jones's physical talents tantalized the Braves hierarchy, his background and makeup attracted them even more. Chipper's mother was an expert in equestrian arts, specializing in dressage, which Chipper described in his autobiography, *Ballplayer*, as "ballet for horses." Larry Sr. was a schoolteacher and his only child's longtime baseball coach. After the ninth grade, Chipper's parents sent him to the Bolles School in Jacksonville for better schooling, good athletic competition, and more discipline. Chipper tells the story in *Ballplayer* that his parents told Boller coach Charles Edwards, "If he steps out of line, you jerk a knot in his tail." It turned out that Edwards, an African American and former star wide receiver at Vanderbilt, became one of Chipper's biggest boosters and friends.[38]

It did not take long for an agreement to be reached. DeMacio and Jongewaard saw immediately that Chipper wanted to turn pro and turn down a baseball scholarship offer from the University of Miami. He had interviewed Scott Boras as a possible representative but was turned off by the agent's aggressiveness and his willingness to threaten enrollment at Miami as a bargaining ploy to raise the ante. Jones wound up accepting less than a $300,000 bonus, approximately one-quarter of Van Poppel's haul. But Jones wanted to be a Brave and enjoyed a far longer career than Van Poppel, and all years with one team.[39]

The remainder of the 1990 draft did not produce any future regulars for the Braves, and the organization was still having trouble winning at the Major League level. A 1990 dip into the free agent market to sign first baseman Nick Esasky backfired when Nick developed vertigo early in the season and had to abruptly retire. With the team struggling in midseason, manager Russ Nixon was fired and Bobby Cox, who had been general manager, returned to the dugout. After the season, John Schuerholz was lured from Kansas City to become general manager. Wanting to bring in his own people, Schuerholz replaced Snyder as scouting director with Chuck LaMar, and Snyder was given the title of special assistant to the general manager.

Paul Snyder lived by the adage that the success of an organization comes when people are not concerned about who gets the credit. If he was miffed at having his scouting directorship taken away, he kept quiet, good company man that he always was. He still saw the Braves' future as bright. "Oh my God, we had so much talent coming," Snyder remembered during my phone interview. So Snyder continued to work in the field with scouts and player developers as the Braves startled the baseball world by rising from the 1990 basement to the 1991 NL East title, their first in what would be a remarkable run of fourteen consecutive postseason appearances, excluding 1994, when the World Series was canceled in a labor dispute. The signing of free agent third baseman Terry Pendleton gave the Braves a good run producer, defender, and, maybe most of all, leader.

John Schuerholz also believed in scouting and player development as the key to any successful organization, but he was willing if necessary to sign a key free agent—especially if his trusted scouts told him that Pendleton would recover from injuries that had hampered his production in St. Louis. Paul Snyder reflected later on Schuerholz's tenure with the Braves: "He taught us how to win. . . . He'll talk at our organizational meetings in January, and those scouts can't wait to get out of that room, and get their radar guns and get to work."[40] Meanwhile, the organization was continuing to hire new scouting blood, with Snyder's input always valued. In 1994 Dayton Moore was hired as a mid-Atlantic scout. He said of Snyder, "You go away from your interaction with Paul knowing that he had listened to everything you said."[41] In 2008, as discussed, Moore became general manager of the Kansas City Royals and led the team to back-to-back World Series appearances, a dramatic seven-game loss to the Giants in 2014 and a five-game Series victory over the Mets in 2015.

In the summer of 1995 Chuck LaMar left the Braves to become general manager of the expansion Tampa Bay Devil Rays. Snyder was asked to take over the duties of director of player development starting the next season. Always willing to help the company in any way, he gladly accepted the new assignment. In the meantime, he started to advance-scout the possible opponents for the Braves in the 1995 playoffs. When the Braves at last won the World Series in 1995, he rejoiced quietly with the rest of the staff, who voiced their appreciation for his steady work over the decades. Snyder found it especially satisfying that Tom Glavine won the clinching game. He thought back with pleasure to eleven years earlier when he first brought into the organization the gifted hard-working teenager who, like the scout himself in his younger days, did not mind working in construction to keep himself fit and active during the offseason.

Snyder served as player development director through 1998 and then answered the call in 1999 to resume his job as scouting director. In 2001 he was again given the title of assistant to the general manager, where he remained until his retirement in 2006. Yet he never really left the organization and never will. When enshrined in June 2013 into the Professional Scouts Hall of Fame at the home of the Charleston River Dogs of the South Atlantic League, Snyder explained, "You have to step away from the game before you realize how great it is. . . . Guys you work with every day for thirty or thirty-five years are what matter to me."[42]

Next, I tell the story of a second baseball monogamist, Gene Bennett, who spent his whole career, first as a Minor League player and then as scout, for the dream team of his youth, the Cincinnati Reds.

7

As Paul Snyder was called the Atlanta Braves' Branch Rickey, Gene Bennett proudly wore that mantle with the Cincinnati Reds. I found that out in the late summer of 2011 when I journeyed to Portsmouth, Ohio, to attend the rededication of a Portsmouth Flood Wall mural depicting the first meeting of Branch Rickey and Jackie Robinson. Another ceremony that afternoon was the renaming of Front Street to Branch Rickey Way. When Gene Bennett found out that I had written a sympathetic Rickey biography, he said that we must talk. The next day, we met at Portsmouth's Welcome Center, a block from the Ohio River and across the street from the murals. As I entered the building, I saw a huge blowup of a photograph of youthful Gene Bennett escorting a proud if aged Rickey into some meeting.

I discovered that the connection between the two men went back into Gene's early days. He was born in Wheelersburg, Ohio, on July 29, 1928, not far from Rickey's birthplace on Duck Run, also in Scioto County. When Gene was nine years old in 1937, Branch Rickey's Cardinals brought Minor League Baseball back to Portsmouth after a long absence. This was years before Little League baseball and even consistent high school ball came to the county, so Gene and his friends became big fans of the Class D Redbirds in the Middle Atlantic League. At first, they viewed the action from a hole in the outfield fence, but before long, they were daring enough to squeeze through the hole and rush in and find seats.[1]

The Redbirds franchise lasted only four seasons before being transferred to Springfield, Ohio, but it contributed to baseball history. Its first manager,

Bennie Borgmann, a longtime Cardinals Minor League infielder, in 1961 became the first former baseball player elected to the Basketball Hall of Fame in Springfield, Massachusetts, in recognition of his outstanding offensive skills during the 1910s and 1920s. (John "Honey" Russell, a longtime Braves scout and outstanding Seton Hall University basketball coach, was the second, elected in 1962.)[2] The team's last manager was future Hall of Famer Walter Alston. Passing through in 1938 was third baseman Whitey Kurowski, who hit a sensational .387 and slugged .587 on his way to a nine-year career with the St. Louis Cardinals.

Gene Bennett grew up to become a great all-around athlete in high school. During his career, Wheelersburg amassed an astounding 90-4 record. As a guard on the basketball team, he once scored 47 points in a game. At Portsmouth Business College, he continued to shine in both sports while playing on area teams in the summertime. Although Bennett dreamed of playing baseball professionally, he did not feel ready to leave home. He had met his future wife, Lorraine Maxine Jones, in high school, and she was two years behind him. When she graduated, they married. "She was the absolute best first round draft choice someone like me could have made," Bennett told writer-broadcaster Steve Hayes.[3] Gene's dad, Roscoe, a retired railway worker, was ill, and Gene helped support the family by selling insurance and mobile homes. In March 1951 Connie Mack's Philadelphia Athletics offered him a Minor League contract, but he didn't sign because of the worsening condition of his father, who passed away at the end of the year.

In the fall of 1952 Gene finally felt ready to take the leap into pro ball. Reds scout Buzz Boyle, who two years later signed Pete Rose to his first contract, long admired Bennett's trademark speed, quick bat, outfield play, and determination. After a tournament in nearby Huntington, West Virginia, Boyle offered him a contract to play for the Reds' Single-A Burlington, Iowa, team in the Three-I League (Illinois, Indiana, Iowa). In spring training 1953 Bennett met his first manager, Johnny Vander Meer, the former Cincinnati southpaw who pitched back-to-back no-hitters in 1938 (a feat likely never to be duplicated). The rookie never forgot Vander Meer's advice: "The harder you work, the luckier you get."[4]

Unfortunately, in his last season before turning pro, Bennett damaged his shoulder diving for a ball. He was not in playing shape at Burlington and was demoted to the Reds' Class D affiliate in Jackson, Tennessee. His recuperation was slow, and the injury cost him all of the 1954 season, but in a sign of the great regard the Cincinnati organization already held him, Bennett was paid his full salary. At Daytona Beach the next two seasons, Bennett responded with banner years. He amassed double-digit numbers in doubles and triples, and in 1956 displayed new power with 16 home runs and 117 RBIs. When the shoulder flared up again in 1957, he saw limited playing time. The Major League dream of Gene Bennett, nearly thirty years old, was fading to darkness.[5]

Reds management did not want to lose someone with his work ethic and teaching ability. They offered him a choice of either managing in Class D or starting a scouting career in southern Ohio. The pivotal moment in Gene Bennett's life came in October 1957 when he encountered Branch Rickey at a shopping mall in Portsmouth. "He was not the kind of person you could just call up on the phone," Bennett recalled. But Gene was not going to miss his chance to ask his idol for advice face-to-face. The avuncular executive, always eager to encourage ambitious young people, gladly took time to break down Bennett's two choices. If he doesn't have the talent, even a good manager could be fired, Rickey said. However, by being a scout, "if you work hard and make the right decisions, you just might keep the job for the rest of your life."[6]

Bennett saw the wisdom in Rickey's advice and he started on his new career in 1958. General Manager Gabe Paul had convinced Reds owner Powel Crosley Jr. that the scouting and player development departments must be increased, but when Bennett came on board there were only six or seven full-time scouts in the organization. He was determined to be one of those people who would never be outworked. Before long, Bennett was looking for talent in Kentucky and Indiana and Michigan, in addition to southern Ohio.[7]

He became a firm advocate of the Rickey method of organizing tryout camps in every region under his control. It cannot be emphasized enough that although Rickey became best known for his great work in creating the farm system, he always insisted that the tryout camps were the horse before the cart of Minor League affiliates. Of course, Rickey's greatest success happened between 1920 and 1950, when baseball was indisputably the national pastime and clearly the most popular team sport in America. By the late 1950s football was making inroads and soon so would basketball, but for energetic new scouts like Gene Bennett, baseball remained number one. He left no stone unturned in his search for young talent.

He hired bird dogs from as far north as Battle Creek, Michigan, and as south as Louisville, Kentucky. They all spread the word among the coming tryout camps. Bennett organized them meticulously with at least five people on hand, including himself, one to hit fungoes to infielders and outfielders, two to handle pitching tryouts, and one person in charge of publicity. Bennett made a point that the tryout camps were to be located so that no hopeful had to travel more than seventy-five miles from his home. A player could arrive early in the morning, take part in the first intensive workouts, eat a lunch provided by the team, and play in the afternoon practice games. He could then return home and be ready for the next day. At the end of the final day's session, if a player was one of the lucky ones chosen, a contract would be offered. Every player received a number when he arrived for a tryout and got a chance to show off his arm strength and his foot speed. If he was below average in either category, it was a likely death knell, but at least he had an opportunity he could talk about for the rest of his life.

Bennett's first years as a scout coincided with the last years of unbridled amateur free agency, and he did not immediately sign any future Major Leaguers. It wasn't for a lack of knowledge of talent in his area. In 1964 and 1965, Scioto County (pronounced "see-OH-ta") produced three of the hottest prospects in the country, outfielders Larry Hisle and Al Oliver and shortstop Gene Tenace, all stars on a local American Legion team, and each of them became outstanding Major Leaguers. In the initial amateur draft in 1965, Larry Eugene Hisle was drafted by the Phillies in the second round. He reached the Majors in 1968, but the best years of his twelve full seasons came with the Twins and the Brewers. In 1978 he was a key part of Milwaukee's first season of 90-plus wins since the departed Braves' pennant winners in 1957 and 1958. Unfortunately, injuries cut short what likely would have been a truly outstanding career. Gene Tenace, born Fiori Gino Tennaci in Russelton, Pennsylvania, was picked by the Kansas City Athletics in 1965's twentieth round. Converted to a catcher and first baseman, he became a contributor to the Oakland Athletics' three consecutive World Series winners from 1972 through 1974. He won the MVP of the 1972 World Series, as the A's beat Cincinnati in seven games.

The vagaries of the draft, where nineteen other teams were vying for the same talent, prevented Bennett from signing Hisle or Tenace. He did not land Albert "Al" Oliver, either, in the last year before the draft, but he would come to know him well. A rival scout, Joe Consoli of the Pirates, landed Oliver after he performed well at a tryout camp at a junior college in Delaware. In one of the more serendipitous stories in scouting annals, Consoli had been given a tip about Oliver from a player who competed against him in American Legion ball. The gesture was made because at an earlier tryout camp Consoli had cut the player who came back to a later camp using an assumed name. Consoli threatened to report the player to authorities, but he relented when he received the tip on Oliver.[8] Al performed so well at his tryout that Consoli offered a $5,000 bonus and convinced him to turn down a basketball scholarship to Kent State University. The senior Albert Oliver wanted his son to play in college because he played the sport as a pro before he became a bricklayer. In one of baseball's bittersweet stories, the senior Oliver died on the day that his son was first called up to the Major Leagues late in the 1968 season.[9]

Another poignant moment in Al Oliver's formative years occurred in 1958 when his mother died at the age of thirty-three. So did Larry Hisle's around the same time. As Rory Costello has written in one of his excellent SABR BioProject essays, Oliver and Hisle developed a lifelong bond working through their wrenching personal losses. Oliver wound up his career with the Pirates, Expos, Rangers, and other teams with 2,743 hits, .303 batting average, .344 on-base percentage, .451 slugging average, 535 walks, 756 strikeouts, 84 stolen bases, and 64 caught stealing, making him at the very least worthy of discussion for the Hall of Fame. In the 1990s he became an ordained Baptist minister and has remained active in the life of his hometown. He regularly delivers a moving invocation at the annual Portsmouth Murals fund-raising banquet.[10]

Scout Joe Consoli lived a colorful, peripatetic life. A tireless organizer of tryout camps all over the Eastern Seaboard, he spent his winters working as a conductor for the Baltimore and Ohio Railroad. Although he never worked for the Orioles, he lived near Memorial Stadium, the team's home before Oriole Park at Camden Yards was opened in 1992. In his later scouting years, Consoli worked for the Major League Baseball Scouting Bureau and put in a glowing report on high school prospect Cal Ripken Jr., who he said had the best mental approach to the game that he had ever seen. On the edge of retirement in 1989, Consoli won a lottery, and while waiting on line to cash his ticket, he suffered a fatal heart attack. He was seventy years old.[11]

Although Gene Bennett missed out on signing the three local future stars, he was part of the Reds evaluation team that laid the roots for the Big Red Machine in the following decade. In the first free agent draft in June 1965, Cincinnati's first pick was outfielder Bernardo "Bernie" Carbo from Livonia High School in Garden City, Michigan, outside of Detroit. He arrived in Cincinnati in 1969, but his big moments occurred in other uniforms. His game-tying, three-run pinch-hit home run for the Red Sox in the bottom of the eighth inning in the sixth game of the 1975 World Series set up the famous Carlton Fisk twelfth-inning walk-off homer as the national T V cameras captured the Boston catcher willing the ball fair over Fenway Park's fabled Green Monster. Carbo's original team would win the seventh game and the first of two consecutive World Series.

Future Hall of Famer Johnny Bench, selected in the second round, made a huge difference in the team's fortunes. In retrospect, the slot seemed amazingly low, but, Bench was coming from a small high school in Binger, Oklahoma, that only played a limited schedule in the fall. By 1968 Bench was a regular in Cincinnati and on his way to a Hall of Fame career. The 1965 draft also netted, in the sixth round, outfielder Hal McRae from the historically Black Florida A & M University. Arriving in Cincinnati in 1968, the bulk of his career would be spent with the Kansas City Royals, where he served primarily as a designated hitter until his retirement in 1987. He later managed the Royals.

In 1966 both of the Reds' first two picks would make the Majors. First-rounder Gary Nolan from a high school in Oroville, California, was what Branch Rickey would have called a "quickie," meaning he needed very little time in the Minor Leagues. He was 14-8 in his rookie 1967 season and pitched his whole ten-year career for the Reds. His final numbers of 110-70 and 3.06 E R A were excellent, but he had trouble staying healthy. Second-round pick

Darrel Chaney carved out an eleven-year career as a good-field, no-hit short-stop and utility infielder for the Reds and the Braves. His career ended with a .212 batting average and .288 slugging average.

In 1967 Gene Bennett signed his first future Major Leaguer, Dave Tomlin, a left-handed high school pitcher from West Union, Ohio, about fifty-five miles southeast of Cincinnati in Adams County. Tomlin would pitch in the Majors from 1972 through 1986, a remarkable accomplishment for both the scout and the player who was drafted in the twenty-ninth round.

In the thirtieth round, the Reds selected John Thomas Young, a left-handed-hitting first baseman from a Los Angeles high school, but he did not sign. In 1969 the Tigers selected him from Compton Junior College in the first round of the January secondary draft. He sipped his cup of coffee in the Majors late in the 1971 season, getting two hits in four at bats. He turned to scouting, and in 1981 he became the Tigers scouting director, making him baseball's first African American in that role. Young became more well known for founding the RBI program, Restore Baseball in the Inner City, in 1986. Several future Major Leaguers attended RBI programs, including pitcher C. C. Sabathia, shortstop Jimmy Rollins, outfielder Coco Crisp, and the Upton brothers, Justin and Melvin Jr. Unfortunately, Young passed away on May 8, 2016, at the age of sixty-seven.[12]

In 1967 the Reds' first-round pick was pitcher Wayne Simpson from a Los Angeles high school who went on to an injury-shortened seven-year career. Advocating for Simpson was new Reds scout Bob Thurman, a veteran of the Negro Leagues and a former productive pinch-hitter for the power-hitting Reds of the late 1950s. Working earlier for the Twins, Thurman signed the versatile southpaw Rudy May. He spent his latter scouting years at the Major League Baseball Scouting Bureau while working for a marketing firm in his adopted hometown of Wichita, Kansas.[13]

In 1968 second-rounder Milt Wilcox enjoyed a fifteen-year-career for both Cincinnati and Detroit. His career record was 119-113 with a 4.07 ERA, but he won a game in the World Series for each team. The Reds also had success in the January 1969 draft that was open to community college players, college dropouts, and any player over twenty-one years old. Their first rounder was Ross Grimsley III, a left-handed starter who compiled a career record of 124-99 with a 3.81 ERA, only the first thirty-seven wins coming in Cincinnati.

Gene Bennett always believed in trusting his bird dogs or associate scouts because they were the first people to contact the player and the player's family. He never went into a player's house without the bird dog. It was a tip from such a loyal associate that brought Gene Bennett's his greatest thrill yet as a scout. He was told that there was a seventh-grader in South Shore, Kentucky, near Lynn, just across the Ohio River from Cincinnati, with amazing talent. Donald Edward Gullett was a left-handed pitcher as well as a great basketball and football player. In the summer before Gullett was to enter McKell High, Bennett invited his supervisor Cliff Alexander to see the prospect in a tryout camp across the river in Ironton, Ohio. In a couple of innings of work against high school seniors and good college players, Gullett struck out the first six batters. "Don't ever come back to a tryout camp," Bennett advised the youngster, hoping that somehow his talent could be hidden until the Reds had a chance to draft him after his high school graduation.[14]

Bennett must have felt like Branch Rickey did when he saw freshman George Sisler mowing down the Michigan Wolverine varsity, but unlike Sisler, Gullett was still years away from college. The scout kept in touch with Gullett's high school and American Legion coaches to make sure he was maturing at a smooth and healthy pace. "His changeup was better than anyone's fastball," Bennett marveled. He kept crossing fingers that no other scouts were on Gullett's trail. Having started in scouting in the last years before the draft, he knew some of the tricks of the trade to scare away rivals. He occasionally traveled with X-rays that indicated the pitcher was a risk. Bennett confided his interest in Gullett only to Reds' scouting colleagues that now included two longtime Rickey men, the Bowen brothers Rex and Joe, who left the Pirates after the 1968 season to join the Reds. Rex Bowen, who had played in Rickey's St. Louis farm system and scouted for him in Brooklyn and Pittsburgh, became General Manager Bob Howsam's special assistant, and his brother Joe became scouting director.[15]

As the 1969 draft neared, all eyes were on the Washington Senators, the second and most ill-fated edition of a franchise that was soon to relocate to

Texas after only eleven years in existence. Senators manager Ted Williams was pushing for a hitter and convinced the brass to use the team's first pick on high schooler Jeff Burroughs from Long Beach, California. Bennett watched nervously as division-rival Houston took the hard-throwing, high school right-hander J. R. Richard from Ruston, Louisiana, next. The Angels made infielder Alan Bannister the fifth pick in the first round from a high school in Buena Vista, California. In the eighth slot, the Reds' archrival Los Angeles Dodgers took Terry McDermott, a catcher from West Hempstead, Long Island, who played only nine games in the Majors three years later. For the eleventh pick, the Yankees chose Louisiana high schooler Charlie Spikes, whose greatest contribution to the Yankees' cause would be his trade to Cleveland for third baseman Graig Nettles after the 1972 season. The suspense finally ended for Gene Bennett when, as the fourteenth pick in the first round, Don Gullett was announced as Cincinnati's pick.

Bennett had developed a good relationship with Don's father, Buford Gullett, a hard-working farmer who had a wife and eight children to support. Don's younger brother William would play a year in the Tigers organization, but the fans and neighbors of Greenup County had never seen an all-around talent like Don, the sixth child in the Gullett family. During his McKell High School sports career, Gullett posted a 30-4 baseball record, once scored eleven touchdowns and kicked six extra points in a football game, and scored forty-seven points in a basketball game. Baseball remained Gullett's first love, a passion that, of course, delighted Gene Bennett.

Bennett and Buford Gullett ultimately settled on a $25,000 bonus for Don, whose family certainly needed the money. The Reds' original plan was to send him to the Florida Gulf Coast League, but management decided he could handle playing for Sioux Falls, South Dakota, in the tougher Northern League (where just a few years earlier at Aberdeen, South Dakota, future Orioles star hurlers Dave McNally and Jim Palmer had entered pro ball). Bennett drove Don and his father to the airport in Huntington, West Virginia, for Don's flight to South Dakota. The Gulletts were a close-knit family, though there wasn't much talking in the car. After the plane took off, Buford asked Gene, "How long do you think it will be before I see my son pitching for the Cincinnati Reds?"

"Quicker than quick," Bennett replied.[16]

Bennett was as good as his word because Gullett impressed manager Sparky Anderson so much in spring training 1970 that he broke camp with the team. He was mainly used out of the bullpen as the Reds won the National League pennant. In the World Series, though, they fell in five games to the Orioles, who were still smarting from their shocking World Series loss to the Mets in 1969. In 1971 Gullett became a fixture in the Reds' starting rotation for the next six seasons, but injuries and ailments were a constant issue. He was limited by hepatitis in 1972, although the Reds won the pennant, dethroning the 1971 world champion Pirates. Gullett pitched well against the Athletics in the World Series, but Oakland won in seven games. He was a key part of the Reds' rotation as they won back-to-back World Series in 1975, the seven-game nail-biter over the Red Sox, and the 1976 sweep of the Yankees, winning the last two games in the newly renovated Yankee Stadium.

General Manager Bob Howsam should have been happy at the Big Red Machine's most recent accomplishment, but he was wistful at best. He told the press, "This may be the last time you see a club win that has been built this way."[17] He meant with home-grown players like Johnny Bench, Pete Rose, Tony Perez, Gullett, and Ken Griffey Sr., drafted in the same year as Gullettt. He went as late as the twenty-ninth round because he was considered more of a football, basketball, and track prospect, but scout Elmer Gray was convinced that Griffey's lightning speed would be needed as the Reds moved to the Astroturf field at Riverfront Stadium in 1970. Griffey's hitting and fielding tools developed later. The Big Red Machine was augmented by brilliant trade acquisitions, like future Hall of Famer Joe Morgan and Cesar Geromino, the underrated center fielder. But Howsam realized that when the first off-season of free agency began shortly after the World Series, veteran players with more than six years of Major League service would be free to go to the highest bidder.

Don Gullett was one of those eligible players, and he signed a seven-year deal with the Yankees for a package reportedly over $1 million. He would be part of two more World Series winners in 1977 and 1978, making him the first player in baseball history to win four consecutive World Series with two different teams. He compiled an overall record of 18-6 in his two seasons with the Yankees, but he only pitched a total of 202 innings before he retired because of serious injuries to both his shoulders. His overall winning percentage of .686 (109-50 win-loss record) puts him in the top five of all pitchers with over 100 wins. Without the injuries, Gullett may well have lived up to his billing as the next Sandy Koufax.

Gullett stayed in Greenup County after he retired at the tender age of twenty-seven. He remained close to Gene Bennett, who had become a family friend. Sadly, Gullett was victimized by ailments even in retirement. At thirty-five, he suffered a heart attack and needed a triple bypass operation. Smoking three packs of cigarettes a day and drinking lots of coffee didn't help his overall condition.[18] He recovered to return to baseball as a coach, serving as Reds Major League pitching coach from 1993 through the middle of the 2005 season. He helped Don Gullett Jr.'s development as an everyday college first baseman. Gullett Jr. later became a respected high school coach, drawing on his father's advice that he should "instruct, guide, but don't push" players.[19] When I met Gene Bennett in Portsmouth, Ohio, during his later years when his declining mobility required assistance, I was touched by the sight of Gullett driving his friend and mentor around to events in a cart with a big Reds *C* on the top.

Since the small-market Reds were not going to be players for big-ticket free agents, the scouts would have to find overlooked players and make them into Major Leaguers. How Gene Bennett in 1971 signed undrafted Doug Flynn from Lexington, Kentucky, is a shining example of how his network of friends served him well. Bennett always kept in shape during the off-season by refereeing basketball games. Just as he did in baseball, he worked his way up from the bottom, starting as a high school referee and graduating to college games. He worked NCAA games from 1970 through 1991, refereeing in eleven NCAA regional tournaments. He still kept close to the high school game and was voted into the Ohio High School Athletic Association Hall of Fame in 1993.[20]

One of Bennett's refereeing partners was Bobby Flynn, father of Doug Flynn. Both father and son were Lexington, Kentucky, natives and fiercely loyal to their hometown, a sense of pride that appealed to Bennett who was

Mr. Wheelersburg, Ohio. Doug Flynn owned impressive athletic genes. Bobby Flynn played Class D baseball for the Brooklyn Dodgers, and his wife had competed in fast-pitch softball before she started raising a family. Though only five feet eleven and barely 160 pounds, Doug Flynn played point guard for coach Joe B. Hall's freshman team at the University of Kentucky. He also made the baseball team but didn't get much playing time. When the university didn't renew Flynn's scholarship for his sophomore year, he dropped out and enrolled at Somerset Community College, a school that didn't even have a baseball team. Flynn kept sharp by playing semipro ball in the area around Lexington. He loved to play any infield position, especially short or second, but he was frustrated that no Major League team wanted him.

Bobby Flynn maintained his faith in his son's abilities. He told Gene Bennett many times that his son was a player. He made up for his lack of size with great hands, a strong arm, and unbridled enthusiasm. Gene alerted the Reds' Lexington-area scouts, and Doug Flynn got his chance. It took appearances at four tryout camps, but in August 1971 Flynn was signed to a Reds contract and received a $2,500 bonus. He started off slowly as a pro player and even wondered if he had a chance to make the Majors after a tough year in the lowest rungs of the Reds system. The tools were still there, the hands and arm, along with enthusiasm, and slowly he found the keys to unlock them. By 1975 he was an important utility infielder on the first of the Reds back-to-back World Series–winning Big Red Machines.

At the June 15, 1977, trading deadline, Flynn was traded to the Mets along with outfielders Steve Henderson and Dan Norman and pitcher Pat Zachry for Tom Seaver.

When first told of the trade, Flynn quipped, "Was it even-up? Me for Seaver?"[21] When the Reds fell out of pennant contention in the early 1980s, Flynn marketed mock T-shirts that read, "Doug Flynn: The Glue." It was his joke that the Big Red Machine never won again after he left, although he hardly ever played behind second baseman Joe Morgan and shortstop Dave Concepcion. Flynn did become a regular with the Expos in the early 1980s and enjoyed an eleven-year Major League career. It would not have happened without his father's refereeing partner Gene Bennett acting on a tip to check out Bobby Flynn's son.

Bennett still understood that the best way to build a regularly contending team was through the draft, an opinion deeply shared by General Manager Bob Howsam and the Bowen brothers. "Joe Bowen was the kind of person you'd go to battle for," West Coast–area scout Larry D'Amato remembered in an April 2022 phone interview.[22] In the 1970 draft, George Zuraw, a veteran southeastern-area scout, signed Charles Ray Knight, a tenth-rounder from high school in Albany, Georgia. A pitcher as well as an infielder in high school—and at times an amateur boxer—Ray Knight made the conversion to full-time third baseman in the Minors. Starting in 1977 he became the regular third baseman for the Reds. He played on the 1979 team that reached the championship series. He became best known for his leadership role on the 1986 World Series–winning Mets.

George Zuraw, born in Charleroi, Pennsylvania, near Pittsburgh, played baseball and basketball in high school against Fred Uhlman Sr., another future baseball scout. He was an outfielder in the Cleveland organization with service in the Korean War in between his four-year Minor League career. When he retired in 1954, he started to work selling advertising for a hometown newspaper when Rex Bowen offered him a chance in 1956 to scout for the Pirates. He won a World Series ring thanks to Bill Mazeroski's home run in 1960, and after 1968 followed the Bowen brothers to Cincinnati, where he picked up two more rings via the Big Red Machine's triumphs. He took the most pleasure from finding future Major Leaguers in the lowest rounds of the draft, a list that included players like utilityman Lenny Harris, who wound up as the National League's record-breaking pinch-hitter; backup catcher Steve Broadway; and infielder Jeff Treadway.[23]

In 1975 Bennett was given the title of regional scouting director, but he remained an area scout at heart. Like most of the great scouts, he wasn't interested in titles but just assuring a steady flow of talent to the organization. He always had his eyes and ears open for the game-changing star, but not at the expense of overlooking the hustling player who, through hard work, might turn his limited tools into successful production at the Major League level. As it turned out, the 1975 draft was not very productive. Area scout Larry Barton Jr. signed two pitchers from Southern California, Frank Pastore in the second round from high school in Upland, California, and Paul Moskau in the third round from Azusa Pacific Junior College. Neither emerged as a mainstay in Cincinnati, pointing out again that there are no sure things in any draft. But Barton Jr. was widely respected among his peers, his baseball lineage dating back to Larry Barton Sr., who played in the Minors for twenty-four seasons, later umpired, and served as extra scouting eyes for his son and the Reds organization as a whole.[24]

The 1976 draft was again rather fallow. One of Gene Bennett's picks, out-fielder Eddie Milner from Central State College in Columbus, Ohio, was chosen in the twenty-first round, but he never developed into a core piece of a contender in his seven full Major League seasons. He showed good plate discipline with a now-rare positive walk-strikeout ratio of 286:280, but his overall offensive numbers were pedestrian: .253 batting average, .335 on-base percentage, and .376 slugging average. Pat Sheridan was a thirty-sixth-round draft pick that made the Majors, but his career as a utility outfielder flowered in the 1980s in the uniform of first the Tigers and then the Royals.

In the January 1977 draft, the Reds picked two future Major Leaguers: center fielder Bob Dernier from Longview Community College in Missouri, who played in the Majors for the Phillies and the Cubs, and southpaw Bill Scherrer from the University of Nevada, Las Vegas (UNLV). Scherrer pitched for seven years from 1982 through 1988 and then became a scout.

The June 1977 draft brought in southpaw Joe Price from the University of Oklahoma in the fourth round and infielder Tom Foley from Pinecrest's Miami Palmetto High School in the seventh round. Price had a journeyman's eleven-year career, mainly in the bullpen, finishing with a 45-49 record and 3.65 ERA. Foley enjoyed thirteen seasons in the big leagues, the first two and a half with the Reds and the key ones with Montreal from 1987 to 1992. He later became a coach with Tampa Bay. He was with the team when it was the struggling expansion Devil Rays and was still around to enjoy their emergence as the Rays in the World Series year of 2008 and beyond.

Gene Bennett shared Zuraw's interest in finding grinders who did everything to help a team win even if their tools suggested they weren't of the highest caliber. In a very successful 1978 draft, Gene Bennett took pride in drafting middle infielder Ron Oester in the ninth round. The Cincinnati native played sixteen seasons in the big leagues, all with the Reds. He later served for many years as a Reds coach. Outfielder Lynn Jones from Thiel College in western Pennsylvania was drafted in the tenth round but never played in Cincinnati. He was picked by the Tigers in the 1978 Rule 5 Draft of Minor Leaguers and played eight years, first with the Tigers and then with the Royals on the 1985 World Series champions.

In the thirty-sixth round, the Reds picked pitcher Andy McGaffigan from a West Palm Beach, Florida, high school. He wound up having a ten-year Major League career, arriving first with the Yankees in 1981 and pitching only briefly for the 1984–85 Reds. His final numbers were quite respectable: 38-33 win-loss record, 3.38 ERA, 833 innings pitched, 733 hits, 294 walks, 810 strikeouts, and 24 saves. McGaffigan's stats probably exceed any thirty-sixth-round draft pick in draft history. The 1978 draft produced two more future Major Leaguers, even though they played more in other uniforms. Left-hander Charlie Leibrandt was picked in the ninth round from Miami University (Ohio). The Chicago native wound up with a career record of 140-119 and 3.71 ERA, only the first four seasons with the Reds. He pitched in hard luck in the World Series for Kansas City and Atlanta. He might be best remembered for giving up the Game Six home run to Kirby Puckett that brought the Twins to a seventh game they won against Atlanta in the 1991 World Series, but his overall postseason record was outstanding. William Henry "Skeeter" Barnes was drafted in the sixteenth round in 1978; he carved out a seven-year career as a utility infielder. In recent years he has been a roving infield instructor for the Tampa Bay Rays.

In 1978 Bob Howsam handed over the general manager's reins to Dick Wagner, a former U.S. Navy officer who had worked closely with Howsam ever since he came to Cincinnati. Wagner was not a people person like Howsam, and by 1983 Howsam returned to his former job. During the 1984–85 postseason, an ownership change led to frugal, racially insensitive Marge Schott taking over as chief owner. Pete Rose had been brought back in 1984 to become player-manager and break Ty Cobb's career-hit record in a Cincinnati uniform. His suspension for incessant gambling lay only five years ahead. More than ever, Birdie Tebbetts's warning about the earth trembling beneath the ground seemed prophetic for anyone working in the Reds organization.

As always, scouts and good company men like Gene Bennett had to keep their focus on finding and developing new talent year by year. Bennett's courting of future Hall of Fame shortstop Barry Larkin was a great case in point. A multisport star at fabled Moeller High School in Cincinnati, he was determined to go to the University of Michigan to try to play both baseball and football. Eligible after graduation in 1982, his mother, Shirley, told Bennett to not bother to draft him because he wanted to go to Michigan. Gene was enough of an old school scout to know that the mother's wishes were top priority. "I'll be back when he is eligible again after his junior year," Gene promised Shirley.[25] Michigan football coach Bo Schembechler allowed Larkin to play freshman baseball, and after Lankin enjoyed a stellar season on the diamond, he told the stunned coach that he was giving up the gridiron.

As the 1985 draft neared, Gene Bennett argued in Larkin's behalf. Other scouts did not think the shortstop merited first-round status. Bob Howsam, who had returned after Dick Wagner's ouster, asked Bennett how soon he thought Larkin could reach the Major Leagues. Bennett looked at the clock on the wall of the meeting room. It read 9:00 p.m. "At 9:10, Mr. Howsam," he replied.[26] Bennett's opinion prevailed, and by 1987 Larkin was the starting Reds shortstop and continued to be into the early twenty-first century. He was a rarity in modern baseball, someone who played his entire career for one team and, even rarer, in his hometown. He retired with a very impressive stat line: 2,340 hits, .295 batting average, .371 on-base percentage, .444 slugging average, 198 home runs, 960 RBIs, 379 stolen bases, and 77 caught stealing. He also won three gold gloves and nine silver sluggers, appeared in twelve All-Star Games, and was the 1995 National League MVP. He was elected into the Hall of Fame in 2012.

Bennett's scouting and signing of Paul O'Neill in 1981 was another study in good evaluation and wise family contact. O'Neill, an all-around athlete from the state capital of Columbus, was an outstanding pitcher in high school when he wasn't playing outfield and first base. Gene developed a good relationship with Paul's father, and they both agreed that Paul's future would best be served with his bat and outfield glove and arm and not on the mound.[27] He was drafted in the fourth round and began the long climb to the Majors. He gave up pitching early on and arrived in Cincinnati at the end of the

1985 season. In 1988, the year he played in Tom Browning's perfect game, he became the full-time right fielder. In the Reds' surprise run to the 1990 world championship, sweeping Oakland in the World Series, he starred in the playoffs against Pittsburgh, but only went 1-12 against Oakland.

After the 1993 season, O'Neill was traded to the Yankees for center fielder Roberto Kelly. Gene Bennett did not approve of the trade, but, of course, it wasn't his decision to make. Kelly was gone from the Major Leagues within three years, while O'Neill became a core piece of the Yankees' last twentieth-century dynasty from 1996 through 2001. He drove in 100 runs or more from 1997 through 2000 and participated in David Wells's and David Cone's perfect games, making him the only player in Major League Baseball history to have played in three perfect games.

In 1991 Bennett, age sixty-four, was named senior special assistant to the young Reds general manager, Jim Bowden, who was thirty-one. Age didn't matter to either one of them—passion for the game and baseball intelligence were the only things that did. However, Bennett experienced another disappointment when high school shortstop Derek Jeter slipped through the Reds' fingers in the 1992 draft. Freddie Hayes, Bennett's long-time bird dog in Michigan, had been raving about Jeter since he was a high school freshman in Kalamazoo. He hit over .500 in his final three seasons and showed baseball smarts far beyond his years. But Cincinnati with the fifth pick in the draft chose University of Central Florida outfielder Chad Mottola. Jeter went to the Yankees in the next pick. Mottola only had 125 at bats in a five-year Major League career spread over eleven seasons with four teams (Toronto twice). Injuries and lost confidence plagued him, but he has since become a respected and compassionate hitting coach with the Tampa Bay Rays. Like all good coaches and scouts, he has tried to help players stay positive and not beat up themselves, as he did too often during his aborted career.

Four other teams passed on Jeter, too. The Astros used the first overall pick on Cal State Fullerton first baseman Phil Nevin, the Indians chose University of North Carolina pitcher Paul Shuey, the Expos selected Mississippi State pitcher B. J. Wallace, the Orioles picked Stanford outfielder Jeffrey Hammonds, and then it was Mottola and Jeter. All of them spent time in the Majors except for Wallace, but none of them, of course, had the impact of the future Hall of Fame and multiple World Series winner Jeter.

The disappointments never got Gene Bennett down for long. He understood that defeat was part of the game in every aspect and that how he overcame the setbacks was the key to his success. "He never saw obstacles, only solutions" is how longtime Cincinnati broadcaster George Grande explained Bennett's philosophy.[28] Hal McCoy, the veteran sportswriter from Dayton, Ohio, met Bennett when Gene was refereeing a basketball game in the mid-1960s of the University of Dayton Flyers. McCoy did not like a call Bennett had made, but his patient explanation made an immediate impression on the sportswriter. They became lifelong friends. "He didn't have an ego bone in his body," McCoy marveled.[29]

McCoy was delighted when in 2010 Bennett's likeness was added to the Portsmouth Flood Wall mural collection. Internationally renowned artist Robert Dafford, who has been responsible for every one of the more than one hundred works there since its inception in 1993, has kept adding baseball portraits in the twenty-first century. Larry Hisle, Al Oliver, and Gene Tenace are now represented on the wall. So have more recent players, like Blue Jays catcher Pat Borders and Giants shortstop Johnnie LeMaster from across the river in Paintsville, Kentucky.

The mural was just one of the many deserved honors he received late in his career. In 1996 the Little League in Wheelersburg was named after him, and a Gene Bennett Classic was started in 2010, pitting the best high school players in southern Ohio and northern Kentucky against each other. A Gene Bennett Scholarship Fund is another ongoing effort to help deserving high school students further their dreams in college. Gene Bennett died on August 16, 2017, at the age of ninety-one. His spirit lives on in all his good works.

Now it is time to visit the third baseball monogamist in the pantheon of scouts who served baseball through only one organization.

8

Billy Blitzer Finally Wins His
Chicago Cubs' Ring

On the eve of spring training in 2012, newly appointed Chicago Cubs president Theo Epstein gathered his front office staff for a meeting at the club's base in Mesa, Arizona. Hired by new owner Tom Ricketts to end the team's World Series–winning drought of over a century, Epstein invited longtime New York–based scout Billy Blitzer to speak. "I wanted someone to testify about what the organization means to people, how deep that connection runs, how it can be," Epstein said.[1] Blitzer was a Cubs lifer, having worked for no other team in his thirty years as a full-time scout. By his own calculation, he lived through six general managers, eight scouting directors, and eleven East Coast scouting supervisors and still was not wearing any championship jewelry.[2] He spoke earnestly about his search for talent and how it had not yet been rewarded. "Look, no ring," he dramatically ended his talk, holding up his bare fingers. "I don't have another thirty years to give."[3]

Three years later, the Cubs made the 2015 National League playoffs for the first time since 2003. Before the first postseason game, Epstein rewarded the scouting staff with a parade around the warning track at Wrigley Field. Blitzer was moved to tears by being asked to lead the parade. One year later, the Cubs finally won a World Series for the first time since 1908. Even when down 3-1 in games to the Cleveland Indians, Blitzer never lost faith. "Our starting pitching was set up to win," he remembered, flashing his impressive World Series ring during a 2018 interview. The Cubs did give their supporters a scare when the Indians' Rajai Davis homered off closer Aroldis Chapman to tie the seventh game in the bottom of the eighth inning. After a scoreless ninth inning, a short rain delay helped the Cubs refocus. They took the lead in the top of the tenth on Ben Zobrist's double, and journeyman southpaw Mike Montgomery secured the last out in the bottom half of the inning. On Billy Blitzer's ring was engraved not only his name but also the words *We Never Quit.*[4]

How Billy Blitzer stayed the course with one organization and at last won his World Series ring is another instructive story in scouting annals about perseverance and loyalty. Born on August 14, 1953, in Brighton Beach, Brooklyn, not far from Coney Island, he was the oldest of two sons of Herman, the owner of a local trucking and messenger company, and Lillian Gruskin Blitzer, who worked as a hair dresser. When he was eight years old, he was taken by a neighbor to see his first Major League game, at the original "House That Ruth Built." The Yankees faced the expansion California Angels in that team's initial 1961 season. He still marvels at "how green the grass was!" He holds dear another vivid memory of the day his father took him to register for his first Little League team. The office was directly opposite from Nathan's Famous hot dog stand near the boardwalk. An active youngster, Blitzer played all sports in season and usually ran the few miles back and forth to the playground to stay in shape.[5]

He made the baseball team at Abraham Lincoln High School, but he harbored no illusions about becoming a Major League player. He evaluated himself as a "good-hit, no-run outfielder." When he was a senior, a sophomore switch-hitting outfielder joined the team. "I didn't have to be a scout to see that Lee Mazzilli would be in the big leagues one day," Blitzer remembered about a player who showed an obvious feel for the game and made a hard game look easy.[6] In 1973 Mazzilli became the Mets number one draft choice.

Blitzer went on to play his college baseball at Hunter College, a Manhattan constituent college of the City University of New York. Not exactly a baseball powerhouse, Hunter didn't even have a home field. It played in Central Park on a permit granted by the city; sometimes Billy sent his players out early to make sure that the diamond would not be seized by others wanting to play. Inconvenience did not matter to Billy Blitzer because the coaching bug had bitten him. When he heard that a new team, Youth Service, was starting play at Brooklyn's Parade Grounds and it might be looking for instructors, he introduced himself to Herb Zitter and his son Mel. Blitzer struck up an immediate friendship with the Zitters, two stern but devoted teachers of the game. Billy became part of the Youth Service group and a regular presence at the legendary group of fields in the heart of New York's largest borough. Many future Major Leaguers had improved their games at the Parade Grounds, including National League batting champion Tommy Davis, second baseman Willie Randolph, catcher Joe Torre, and southpaw John Candelaria.

One summer afternoon in 1975 before Blitzer's senior year at Hunter, he was sitting on a bench at the Parade Grounds waiting for Youth Service to play the second game of a doubleheader. The first game was a matchup between two local amateur teams, one of them, the Raiders, consisting mainly of Hispanic and other minorities. The Raiders coach was Luis Rosa, a native of Puerto Rico who soon moved on to an advisory role with the Texas Rangers, for whom he signed future American League home run leader Juan González and future Hall of Fame catcher Iván "Pudge" Rodríguez. Later, working for the San Diego Padres, Rosa recruited the Alomar brothers, catcher Sandy Alomar Jr. and his younger sibling, future Hall of Fame second baseman Roberto Alomar.[7]

As Blitzer was watching the first game, a well-dressed older man wearing a floppy fisherman's hat sat down next to him. They started engaging in one of the joys of the sport, friendly baseball chatter. When speedy outfielder Dallas Williams, another Lincoln High graduate, legged out a triple, Blitzer and the friendly stranger agreed that he was a Major Leaguer in the making. On the advice of Orioles northeastern-area scout John Stokoe (pronounced "STO-kee"), Baltimore made Williams its number one pick in the June 1976 draft. Williams would have only 3 hits in 38 at bats in the Major Leagues, but Stokoe went on to sign future Cy Young Award–winning southpaw Mike Flanagan. He also delivered the advance scouting report that helped the Orioles win the 1983 World Series over the Philadelphia Phillies.[8]

As he was packing up the equipment after the doubleheader, Blitzer saw the mysterious man walking over. He thought he would be asking him about Youth Service shortstop Willie Lozado, a Brooklyn high school player who would be drafted by the Milwaukee Brewers and hit .271 in 107 at bats in his one Major League season in 1984. "No, I want to talk to you," the man said.

"I've been watching you, and I like how you relate to your players." The man in the floppy fisherman's hat gave him his card: "Ralph DiLullo—Major League Baseball Scouting Bureau."

DiLullo was impressed that the players were responding well to his instruction even though Blitzer seemed only a year or two older. "I want to sit down and watch a game with you next week," he said. Blitzer didn't know what to make of the offer. All sorts of characters came to watch games at the park, and most of them didn't know what they were talking about. After conferring with his parents, the Blitzer family decided there was nothing to lose by another encounter with the scout. When they met again the following weekend, the rapport grew stronger between the older man and the younger player-coach. DiLullo told Blitzer that he was organizing tryout camps in the New York metropolitan area. He wanted him to use his knowledge of the local prospects and invite them to the tryouts. The offer was made appealing when DiLullo promised that the Scouting Bureau would take care of Billy's expenses. At the age of twenty, if Billy Blitzer wasn't the youngest associate scout in the country, he was close to it, and he still had his senior season at Hunter to play in the spring of 1976.

Low-budget Hunter did not give Blitzer the title of player-coach, but he was the de facto assistant coach. One day during Blitzer's senior year, Hunter was preparing to play Pace University at its Pleasantville campus north of the city. Billy was leading the players in crisp infield drills when Pete Smith, an associate scout for the Mets, came by and looked on favorably. After the pregame work was over, Smith asked Billy for his lineup card. He looked it over and saw Blitzer's name on it.

"You can't play," Smith said. "A coach can't play."

"I'm playing; I'm a senior," Billy replied.

The following year, Blitzer was named Hunter's head coach, once again breaking a barrier as likely the youngest coach in the nation. During the season, with Hunter playing at Pace again, Billy gave Pete Smith the lineup card when he came by to scout. "This year, I'm not playing—I am the coach," Blitzer told Smith, and they shared a good laugh.[9]

When Blitzer wasn't coaching, he was beating the bushes for talent in the largely untapped New York region. It was a time of social unrest in the area.

"The Bronx is burning!" Howard Cosell shouted during an ABC network World Series broadcast, describing the smoke and fire from social disturbances he saw not far from the ballpark. Fear of the inner city kept most baseball teams from scouting players, but Blitzer knew that great baseball talent was to be found in the New York metropolitan area.

Ralph DiLullo was impressed by Blitzer's work and, by the end of the 1979 season, arranged for Billy to become a full-time employee of the Scouting Bureau with a three-year contract. He became a great mentor to Blitzer. He stressed in his quiet but firm way that baseball was a very difficult game to master, and a scout must maintain a positive outlook. A scout can always find something wrong with a player, but the scout should try to find something right about him and build up his confidence. DiLullo was always dressed neatly in coat and tie, but he moved so fast from game to game on his scouting rounds that Blitzer dubbed him "the Jet."[10]

As Billy learned more about his new friend's background, he discovered the scout had another nickname: "Corp." Ralph DiLullo was born on March 31, 1911, in the small village of Caprasotta, Italy, about fifty miles east of Rome. His father had been a corporal in the Italian Army during World War I, but he was gassed and killed in action. Around the age of six, Ralph emigrated with his family to the United States, settling in Paterson, New Jersey. His mother married an Italian widower with children, and the couple merged into one large family with Ralph the oldest of eleven. The nickname "Corp" was bestowed in honor of his late father, the corporal.

Like so many future scouts who grew up in the boisterous Jazz Age of the 1920s, baseball became Ralph DiLullo's passion. A born leader, his position was catcher, and he played on many local teams in the north Jersey area. His Paterson Emblems won the New Jersey American Legion championship in 1930.[11] On the eve of his twentieth birthday in 1931, with the Great Depression raging, DiLullo signed with the Pittsburgh Pirates organization. He toiled for fifteen years in the Minor Leagues with the Browns, Pirates, and Tigers without getting a taste of Major League action. However, he was making an impression on front office people with his leadership skills.

In 1947 he ran the Pittsburgh Pirates spring training camp for General Manager Ray Kennedy, who had been George Weiss's longtime Yankees assistant.

In January 1948 DiLullo worked with Ralph Houk at George Stirnweiss's baseball school in Bartow, Florida, that provided instruction for prospective Major Leaguers. Paul Post tells the story in his wonderful portrait of DiLullo, *Foresight 20/20*, that Ray Kennedy took the blame for the forthcoming disastrous 1948 trade of Billy Cox and Preacher Roe to the Dodgers for an over-the-hill Dixie Walker, resulting in his firing after the season. In 1949 Kennedy joined the Tigers front office and brought DiLullo with him.[12]

In 1950 DiLullo served as player-manager for Detroit's Richmond (Indiana) Tigers in the Class C Ohio-Indiana League. One of his rookie pitchers was an eighteen-year-old fresh out of high school in Fort Thomas, Kentucky, a suburb of Cincinnati. Blitzer heard DiLullo tell a few stories about this pitcher. The connection really came alive at a hot stove league dinner in the late 1970s when future Hall of Famer and future United States senator Jim Bunning dropped everything during a cocktail hour to embrace his first pro manager. "Hey, Skip, how are you doing?" Bunning exclaimed.[13]

In 1953 Ralph DiLullo joined the Cubs as a full-time northeastern-area scout and stayed with them until he joined the Major League Scouting Bureau in its initial year in 1975. Blitzer never got enough of DiLullo's stories about players he signed and how their development was sometimes slow and arduous. Two stories in particular stood out. In the summer of 1971, Ralph worked out a reliever before an independent league game of the York (Pennsylvania) White Roses. The previous spring, the pitcher had been a late-round draft choice of the second edition of the Washington Senators, but he had not yet graduated from high school at the time of the draft. So he started college at Old Dominion University in Richmond, Virginia, but dropped out after a term. When DiLullo saw the movement on the youngster's pitches in the workout, he brought into the Cubs' fold future Hall of Famer Bruce Sutter for a bonus of $500.[14]

An elbow injury, perhaps caused by the stress of painting cigar boxes in an off-season job, delayed Sutter's development. He didn't pitch a full season in the Minors until 1973, and his rookie-season coach Gene Dixon was unimpressed. "When Sutter makes the Major Leagues, the communists will be ready to take over," he groused.[15] Cubs Minor League pitching coach Fred Martin was more encouraging. He noticed that Sutter's fingers were unusually long, and he encouraged him to develop the split-finger pitch that enabled him to become baseball's most consistent reliever from 1977 to 1984. He joined the Cardinals in the last years of his streak, closing for their 1982 World Series–winning team.

DiLullo also told Blitzer about Joe Niekro, another one of his under-the-radar signings. The younger brother of future Hall of Famer Phil Niekro, Joe grew up with his brother in Lansing, Ohio, near the West Virginia border. It was a small town where one of their friends and playmates was John Havlicek, the future basketball Hall of Famer. Phil Niekro Sr. could reportedly throw the ball nearly one hundred miles an hour—faster than his two sons combined, someone cracked—but he went to work in the coal mines. Yet he never was too tired to have a catch with his sons.[16]

After a stellar career at the small West Liberty College in West Virginia, Niekro was drafted in the third round of a June 1966 secondary draft, and DiLullo signed him for another $500 bonus. He reached the big leagues the following season, and he won a total of 24 games in 1967 and 1968. His career then stalled, and he bounced around to the Padres, Tigers, and Braves, which put him on waivers in 1975. The Astros signed him, and from 1977 through 1985 Joe Niekro won 136 of his career total of 221 victories for Houston. The lesson Billy Blitzer absorbed from DiLullo is that you can't control what happens when players get into your system. They may get confused by too many suggestions and lose confidence in themselves. You just have to do your job of finding and appraising the talent and hope that the baseball gods and the player's hard work ultimately produce positive results. Joe Niekro's mastery of the knuckleball to go with other adequate pitches proved the secret to his success.

Lenny Merullo, another mentor Billy met at the Scouting Bureau, was a baseball lifer with an even deeper connection to the Cubs than Ralph DiLullo. Born in 1917, Merullo was the eighth child among twelve siblings raised in a multiethnic neighborhood in East Boston, Massachusetts. His skills as a shortstop became quickly recognized by Ralph Wheeler, who ran the amateur Suburban League and also was a bird dog for the Cubs. As Merullo remembered to Paul Motyka in a fascinating 2000 SABR oral history interview, Wheeler encouraged Lenny to switch from a commercial high school program to an academic one so he could become eligible for a college athletic scholarship. After prep school, Lenny enrolled at Villanova and played summer ball on Cape Cod and in Nova Scotia. When word came that Cubs owner Philip Wrigley Jr. wanted to meet him, he was flown out to Chicago and met the owner at his office in the ornate and impressive Wrigley Building. Wrigley flattered Merullo, telling him about the good things he had heard about his play. Before the awed youngster left the mogul's office, he was given more than a thousand dollars to outfit himself in clothes befitting a future Major Leaguer. When Lenny returned east, Yankees scout Paul Krichell expressed interest in signing him, but when Krichell found out about the gifts from Wrigley, he backed away, considering Merullo already Cubs property.[17]

Merullo debuted in Chicago late in the 1941 season. In the second game of a doubleheader the following season, he committed four errors on a day when he learned that his first child, Len Jr., was born. The nickname "Boots" was immediately given to Junior, who wound up having a brief Minor League career. Boots's son Matt went on to a six-year career as a Major League catcher, mainly with the White Sox in the early 1990s. Matt's son also played in the Minors. Lenny Merullo wound up playing in the Majors for parts of seven seasons, retiring at the end of 1947 with career numbers of .240 batting average, .291 on-base percentage, .301 slugging average, 6 home runs, 152 RBIs, 191 runs, 38 stolen bases, and 17 caught stealing. He did put the ball in play, with 136 career walks and only 174 strikeouts.

Merullo almost immediately started a scouting career with the Cubs. After the 1974 season, he was one of the scouts drafted for the new Major League Baseball Scouting Bureau that opened the following year. After the 1979 season, Billy Blitzer's first official function as a newly minted MLBSB member came at a meeting in Arizona where Lenny Merullo was assigned as his roommate. When Billy entered, the veteran scout gave him the silent treatment as if to say, "Who are you?" The ice soon broke, and Merullo became another valued mentor for Billy Blitzer.[18] Longtime New England scout George Biron never forgot the encouragement that Merullo gave him after Biron's dream of advancing to the Majors died. He also helped break Biron in to his new profession by stressing how important attention to detail was to success in the game.[19]

Like most scouts who developed their craft before the amateur draft, Merullo kept the press at arm's length. Chicago columnist Mike Royko liked to poke fun at Lenny's mediocre career and his role as a survivor of the Cubs' 1945 World Series loss (he only took two at bats in the Series without a hit). Royko's derision prompted Merullo to write a public letter, saying that he was sixty-six years old, was still married to his high school sweetheart, and was the father of four grown children and several grandchildren. He concluded, "I've spent my entire years in baseball, a very much respected scout here in the New England area and on special assignments throughout the country."[20] The letter put an end to Royko's barbs. Unfortunately, Merullo did not live to see the Cubs win the 2016 World Series, but he came close, dying in June 2015 at the age of ninety-seven.

Minnesota Twins area scout Herb Stein was another man Blitzer met at the Scouting Bureau. As they began to share opinions, it dawned on Blitzer that Stein used to come to watch some of his high school and Youth Service games, along with two other veteran New York–area scouts, Joe DiCarlo of the Yankees, who later signed southpaw Al Leiter, and Al Harper of the Mets, who signed Lee Mazzilli. Stein stressed to Blitzer that scouts have to watch games closely and make their own judgments. "Hearing about a player is not scouting a player," Stein emphasized. Another watchword from the avuncular scout was "Once you like a player, don't give up on him." Like DiLullo and virtually every great scout I discuss, Stein believed in positivity once a scout has decided that the player's raw tools can be developed into Major League tools. He insisted that "the moment you sign a player, he is automatically better because the monkey is off his back." He did caution, "Don't go overboard in your evaluations of a player. Just be firm and strong about your opinions."[21]

Herb Stein was born on March 8, 1917, in the Washington Heights section of northern Manhattan, not far from Yankee Stadium. One of his neighbors was John "Buddy" Kerr, who became a New York Giants and Boston Braves shortstop in the late 1940s and early 1950s and later a longtime scout for the Mets. (Another neighbor was a recent emigrant from Germany, Henry Kissinger.) After graduating from George Washington High School, Stein played in the Minor League system of the Twins' predecessor, the Washington

Senators. A versatile middle infielder, Stein reached Chattanooga in the Class A Southern Association, before World War II intervened. Stein rose to the rank of sergeant in the European theater of the war, where one of his duties was supervising prisoners of war.

When he returned after the war, he brought home a wife of Belgian descent, Marie-Josee Goffin, known as Josee, who became mother to Herb's two sons and daughter. Like many players who served in the war and could not play baseball, Stein lost his chance of advancing, but the Griffith family, the team owners, had not forgotten him and his expertise in pitching and fielding. He continued to play, advancing as high as Binghamton in 1948 in the Class A Eastern League. In 1950, while serving as player-manager for the Jesup (Georgia) Bees in the Class D Georgia-Florida League, he experienced the shock of the segregated Deep South. A Jesup ballpark groundskeeper told him that he was the only Black person in town who had an indoor bathtub. While getting a haircut, Stein remembered the barber pausing and calling the shoeshine boy over to shake out Stein's apron and then ordering him back to his stand. Stein endured his own run-ins with anti-Semitic opponents and hostile crowds. He still succeeded in leading Jesup to a .500 record.[22]

Shortly after his retirement as a player in 1952, he started scouting for the Senators while maintaining his day job as a New York City transit policeman. Stein's revered mentor became Joe Cambria, who since 1932 had been sending legions of inexpensive Cuban ballplayers to the Griffith family's franchise. Born in Messina, Italy in 1890 or 1889, Joseph Carlo Cambria came to Boston with his father and two older brothers when he was three years old. His mother did not make the trip and died young. After service in World War I, Cambria became an entrepreneur, running a laundry business outside Baltimore while owning and operating many Minor League and Negro League teams. Cambria knew very little Spanish, but he spent a lot of time in Havana, enjoying his celebrity, handing out "Papa Joe Cambria" cigars and tending to an invalided wife.[23] Herb Stein revered Cambria and picked his mind about player evaluation and the importance of mental makeup. Describing his mentor's peripatetic lifestyle, Stein marveled, "He wore his luggage!" traveling with only two suits, the one that he was wearing stuffed with information in the pockets and the other in a bag.[24]

Cambria did not live to see Minnesota's first pennant in 1965, dying in Minneapolis in late September 1962. But Stein vowed to apply his many insights about player evaluation. In 1964, with the help of Associate Scout Monroe Berger, he zeroed in on Rod Carew, who at the age of fifteen recently emigrated from Panama. He was playing for a local sandlot team, the Bronx Cavaliers. Although Carew was attending Stein's alma mater George Washington High School, he never played high school baseball. He had difficulties learning English and was so embarrassed by his torn shoes, he later told biographer Ira Berkow, that he walked the halls in high school close to the walls so his fellow students would not see them.[25]

It was a year before the amateur free agent draft, so Stein tried to keep Carew's whereabouts away from his scouting rivals. Drawing on the long history of subterfuge, Stein deliberately gave wrong directions to imaginary fields when asked where Carew might be playing. The scout was aghast when before a tryout at Yankee Stadium, eager Twins owner Calvin Griffith presented Carew with a Minnesota cap. So much for hiding the raw yet obvious talent of the prospect's quick bat from which the ball jumped. Stein marveled that Carew possessed a "grown man's wrists at the age of eighteen."[26]

Shortly after the workout at Yankee Stadium, Herb Stein got very nervous when many of his rivals turned out to see Carew's Bronx Cavaliers play a doubleheader. The scout was not aware that there was another left-handed hitting prospect on Carew's team. When the other player did not start the second game, the horde of scouts exited. One of those who stayed, Hal Keller, told Stein he could now relax.[27] (Keller, the younger brother of the Yankees outfielder Charlie Keller, had a noteworthy career scouting for the second edition of the Senators that became the Texas Rangers. He was one of the first scouts to utilize the radar gun to measure throwing velocity, and later he scouted for, and was general manager of, the Seattle Mariners.) Fortunately, Stein had built up a good relationship with Carew's mother and prevailed in signing the future Hall of Famer. At his Hall of Fame induction in 1991, Carew thanked Stein for scouting him all over the New York metropolitan area and his mother for always seeing to it that he had a baseball glove.

Two years earlier in 1962, Stein reached into the inner city by signing infielder Joe Foy from Evander Childs High School in the Bronx. Foy starred in the annual New York versus the World All-Star Game at the Polo Grounds, sponsored by the *New York Journal-American*. Stein was aware that Foy might ultimately develop a weight problem, but he liked his "good body control" and described him as "flexible for his size."[28] After one year in the Minors, the Twins did not protect Foy, and the Red Sox signed him. For the pennant-winning 1967 Bostonians, he performed solidly in 446 at bats, with a .251 batting average, .426 slugging average, 16 home runs, 49 RBIs, and 70 runs. He was left exposed to the expansion draft after the 1968 season, and the Kansas City Royals picked him up. After one season, he was traded to the Mets for third baseman and outfielder Amos Otis. Foy faded from the scene after 1971, even faster than Jim Fregosi. Sadly, Joe Foy died at the age of forty-nine.

Herb Stein knew the truth that even harder than making the Major Leagues was staying there. He often reminded Billy Blitzer of that hard fact of life. He was saddened at the quick demise of Joe Foy, but he was overjoyed at the success of Rod Carew (even if free agency drew him to the Angels after the 1978 season). Stein later signed a future Cy Young Award winner Frank Viola from St. John's University in Queens and first baseman Gene Larkin from Columbia University, who delivered the 1987 World Series–winning extra-inning single against the Atlanta Braves. Herb Stein desperately wanted the Twins to sign Manny Ramírez from his high school alma mater, George Washington, but they passed on the Dominican-born slugger. It was Cleveland's New York–area scout Joe DeLucca who delivered the impressive slugger to General Manager Hank Peters and scouting director Tom "T-Bone" Giordano; Ramírez was the thirteenth choice in the first round of the 1991 draft.[29]

Billy Blitzer's work at the Scouting Bureau was beginning to attract notice throughout the baseball community. He wrote a good report on southpaw John Franco, a graduate of Brooklyn's Lafayette High School (Sandy Koufax's alma mater). He was pitching for St. John's University in Queens when the Dodgers area scout Steve Lembo drafted him in the fifth round in 1985. He was later traded to the Reds and again to the Mets, where he later became a star closer for his hometown team.

Blitzer filed good reports on two players from Westchester County who went on to stellar careers. Shortstop Walt Weiss from Suffern, New York, starred for the Oakland Athletics' pennant winners from 1988 through 1990 and played for twelve seasons, finishing up with the Colorado Rockies. He later became Rockies manager and in 2021 was the bench coach for the World Series–winning Atlanta Braves. His career numbers—.258 batting average, .351 on-base percentage, .326 slugging average, 25 home runs, 386 RBIs, 96 stolen bases, and 35 caught stealing—don't jump off the page, but his walk-strikeout ratio of 1:1 (exactly 658 in each category) suggest that he was a hard out. After an outstanding career at the University of North Carolina, B. J. Surhoff, raised in Rye, New York, and whose father, Richard, briefly played basketball for the New York Knicks, was selected by the Milwaukee Brewers as the first overall pick in the 1984 draft. He went on to an eighteen-year Major League career with Milwaukee, Baltimore, and Atlanta. After playing his first few seasons as a catcher, he was shifted primarily to the infield and outfield corners. His career numbers were solid: .282 batting average, .332 on-base percentage, .413 slugging average, 188 home runs, 1,153 RBIs, 1,102 runs, 640 walks, and 839 strikeouts. He stole 141 bases but was caught 84 times, which suggests that he was more aggressive on the bases than he should have been.

Blitzer was learning his lessons well from his mentors about how to dig deeply into the circumstances of a prospect's situation to obtain a fuller picture. Because he was impressed with the throwing arm of shortstop Devon White at Manhattan's Park West High School, Blitzer urged his Scouting Bureau supervisor, Randy Gumpert, a former Major League pitcher, to drive into New York from his home in Reading, Pennsylvania, to scout White. Gumpert agreed reluctantly because he was one of the many scouts not eager to come into the big city.

It turned out to be a game that scouts have nightmares about. White's first at bat resulted in a strikeout when Devon fanned on a pitch far out of the strike zone. He popped out on the second at bat. In the field, he lobbed his first chance at shortstop far wide of first base. Blitzer came over to White after the half inning was over. "Is there something wrong with your arm, Devon?" he asked urgently. White explained that the first baseman could not handle his throws so he eased up. "I don't care about the first baseman," Blitzer pleaded. "When you're being scouted, you can't ease up." On the next grounder to short, White threw a bullet that sailed over the poor first baseman's head. The throw might have killed him if it had been more accurate.[30]

Though the day was cold and rainy, both scouts followed one of scouting's adages: "Never leave until the last out because you never know who and what you might see." The adage didn't apply this day, however, as the first pitch to White during his third at bat hit him on his rear end. He was hitless for the day, and Randy Gumpert gave him a zero on his Scouting Bureau report. Blitzer still believed in White's talents, following another precept he had learned: "Don't give up on a player, and don't be talked out of your opinion." A few weeks later, playing in a summer league on Manhattan's Lower East Side, White hit two home runs into the East River in a game that the Angels' Al Goldis was scouting. The following spring of 1981, California drafted White in the fifth round and five years later shifted him to center field, and he became a Major League regular. After being traded to the Blue Jays, he became a key component of the Toronto world champions in 1992 and 1993. White also played for the 1997 world champion Florida Marlins. Though he struck out almost three times as much as he walked, he played for seventeen seasons and ended with a .262 batting average, .319 on-base percentage, .418 slugging average, 208 home runs, 846 RBIs, 346 stolen bases, and 98 caught stealing. Baseball Reference shows that he has used the original spelling of his last name, Whyte, since 2003. (Later in the 1980s, Al Goldis became scouting director for the White Sox; among his signees that made the Major Leagues was future Hall of Fame slugger Frank Thomas.)

Blitzer discovered that another future Major League star, the Bronx's Roberto Martin Antonio "Bobby" Bonilla, was dealing with a personality conflict with a high school coach who played him all over the field. Without a definite position, Bonilla was not drafted because he had not established a consistent body of work. Blitzer saw the promise in Bonilla and wrote up a positive report for the Scouting Bureau. Other scouts were unconvinced when seeing Bonilla play. Al Goldis told Blitzer, "This guy can't pitch." Yankees scout Al Cuccinello, brother of longtime Major League coach Tony Cuccinello, said, "This guy can't catch." Blitzer held his ground, saying that Bonilla could play first and third base. Bonilla's outstanding performance in an early summer international tournament in the Netherlands put him back on the scouting radar. His coach, Jim Thrift, son of Syd Thrift, who was serving as Pittsburgh general manager, put in a good word about him. So did the Pirates area scout in the New York area, Pete Gebrian, a former Mets scouting director.

When Bonilla returned home, he started playing in the top-notch summer Atlantic Coast Baseball League (ACBL). Pete Gebrian visited Bonilla at home and offered him a contract. He was attending New York Technological University and developing an interest in computers but was not fully invested in academics. The formerly undrafted player now had a choice to make, and he immediately called Billy Blitzer for advice. The scout advised, "Lock the door and don't let Mr. Gebrian out of your house until he shows you a contract." Bonilla went on a sixteen-year career and put up impressive numbers: .279 batting average, .358 slugging average, .472 on-base percentage, 287 home runs, 1,173 RBIs, 1,084 runs, 912 walks, and 1,204 strikeouts. He may be most remembered for the huge contract that his agent Dennis Gilbert negotiated for him when the Mets bought him out in 2000—it guaranteed him over a million dollars a year from 2011 through 2035.[31]

At the end of the 1981 season, the Cubs' Gary Nickels visited Billy Blitzer's household. If you'll recall, Nickels had been one of the Phillies scouts that built Philadelphia's 1980 world champions and a year later joined the Chicagoans with the Dallas Green group. Nickels convinced the Blitzer family that Billy's move to the Cubs would be a financially secure one and a promotion from the Bureau. Ralph DiLullo and others at the Bureau wished Blitzer well. DiLullo and Lenny Merullo were particularly glad that their mentee was going to the Cubs, their former employer. They assured him that the long-suffering fan base would be delirious once a winner came to the Second City. (Billy's mother Lillian was not so enthusiastic. She didn't fully give up rooting for the Mets until they won the World Series in 1986, and now satisfied, she turned to backing her son's team.)

Technically, the Scouting Bureau did not finalize Blitzer's departure until later in 1982, but for all intents and purposes, Billy was working for Chicago as the June 1982 draft loomed. The Cubs wanted to tap into his knowledge of Brooklyn high school shortstop Shawon Dunston, who was widely predicted to be the number one draft pick in the nation. Billy first spotted Shawon as a budding athletic talent when he was just eleven years old. He became batboy for Youth Service and soon began shining on the field. As he grew into his body, he became a sensation at Thomas Jefferson High School. In his senior year, Dunston hit an astonishing .790, a remarkable number even given the lack of tough competition offered by most public school pitchers.

A problem did arise during Shawon's last high school season because too often he was playing third base, not shortstop. His inexperienced coach thought he had a better shortstop on the roster. Blitzer worried that the coach might also use Dunston as a pitcher, and sure enough, one night Shawon came home with an aching arm. When Billy found out, he sat down with Shawon and his father. He sternly told them that never again should they allow such an abuse of his precious arm to happen. As the June draft neared, New York City tabloids started building up the possibility that a kid from the sandlots might become the first pick in the nation. Influential New York *Daily News* columnist Dick Young wrote that veteran scout Dutch Deutsch, who had signed John Candelaria and Willie Randolph for the Pirates, thought that Dunston was the greatest talent in the New York City area since Carl Yastrzemski came out of Long Island's Suffolk County.[32] Young opined that whatever the Cubs were offering to Shawon would not be enough. Jack Dunston, Shawon's father, liked Blitzer, who obviously cared about his son, but he began to doubt the wisdom of accepting the $100,000 offer.

As expected, the Cubs made Dunston the number one pick in the country. Blitzer and Nickels attended the ceremony at Major League Baseball's offices on Park Avenue, along with Dunston's parents, Jack and Brenda, and Brenda's mother. (This was long before the televised drafts of the early twenty-first century.) Monte Irvin, the great former Negro Leaguer and New York Giants outfielder, was serving as a special assistant to commissioner Bowie Kuhn. When he came in to greet the honored guests, Shawon's grandmother was overwhelmed with joy. As her grandson looked on in bewilderment, she grew deliriously happy at meeting one of the heroes of her youth.[33]

For the ceremony and the signing, the Dunstons had come into Manhattan from Brooklyn and were staying at a Sheraton Hotel north of Times Square. Blitzer and Nickels went over to the hotel and found no Dunston registered. The scouts wondered whether it was going to be a far more protracted negotiation than they expected. Then Billy remembered that two Sheratons were in the area and then met the family at the other hotel. Jack Dunston, a taxi driver who delivered furniture, and his wife, Brenda, who worked in a woman's clothing store, still were skeptical that Shawon was getting the best deal. Blitzer stressed it was better to be number one overall in the nation than number two or three for some other team. Billy added that there would be plenty of money at the end of Dunston's career, and Shawon did sign.

Blitzer was not exaggerating. By the end of the Brooklyn native's eighteen-year Major League career, it was estimated that Shawon Dunston earned over $25 million. He became a regular in 1986, but after hitting .250 and amassing an unsightly walk-strikeout ratio of 16:114, he spent the next season in Triple-A. Starting in 1988 Dunston became the Cubs' regular shortstop before being traded to the Giants in 1996 and winding up his career as a utility player for the Mets. His final stats were .269 batting average, .296 on-base percentage, .416 slugging average, 150 home runs, 668 RBIs, and 736 runs, but plate discipline remained a problem, as his 203 career walks and exactly 1,000 strikeouts attest.

The 1983 draft for the Cubs did not turn out notably for either Blitzer or the rest of the team, with the exception of outfielder Dave Martinez being picked in the third round of the January secondary draft. Though he was born in New York City, Martinez and his family had moved to Florida when he was in grade school. The future manager of the 2019 world champion Washington Nationals was signed out of Valencia Junior College and went on to a solid thirteen-year career as a utility outfielder for several teams.

The 1984 season turned out to be special for the Cubs and Billy Blitzer. In June's second round, Greg Maddux was signed after graduating from high school in Las Vegas, Nevada. At five feet ten and only 155 pounds, Maddux did not fit the profile of the husky six-foot-three, 225-pound power pitcher that most organizations craved. But area scout Doug Mapson had followed Maddux's development since junior high school. He loved Greg's competitiveness and ability to repeat his motion time and again. As noted, scouting director Gordon Goldsberry, a man beloved by his scouts because he listened to them, read their reports carefully, and trusted their evaluations.

In the sixth round of the 1984 draft, Billy Blitzer signed southpaw Jamie Moyer from Souderton, Pennsylvania, located about thirty-miles north of Philadelphia. He first saw Moyer pitch at the then-prestigious Labor Day weekend tournament in York, Pennsylvania, 1983. He realized that the slender six-foot-one, 170-pound southpaw was not a hard thrower, but he liked the way he changed speeds and exuded confidence on the mound. The following spring, Blitzer followed up on Moyer as he entered his junior season with the St. Joseph's Hawks of the Atlantic Ten conference. Moyer was on his way to setting school records for most wins, best earned run average, and most strikeouts.[34]

When it came time to seal the deal with Moyer, the Cubs front office instructed Blitzer, negotiating the contract on his own, not to offer more than a $12,000 signing bonus. Jamie's parents were satisfied with the deal, but Jamie wanted $3,000 more. An impasse was possible, but the tension eased when Jamie's mother came out of the kitchen with a freshly made batch of cookies. Unlike the malfunctioning oven in Norm Siebern's household, the appliance in the kitchen of Jamie's mother, who worked in a bakery, was in fine shape. Blitzer did not have to offer a new appliance because Moyer relented and accepted Blitzer's initial offer. Years later, Moyer always wondered what might have happened if he had turned down the offer.[35]

By 1986 Moyer was pitching for the Cubs. It was a special moment for the southpaw to be on the same field as Keith Moreland and future Hall of Famer Ryne Sandberg because, after his summer league games, Jamie and his father, Jim, often saw them play for the Double-A Eastern League Reading Phillies.[36] Moyer pitched to a 28-30 record in his first three seasons in Chicago. Although he went 9-15 in 1988, his ERA dropped by more than a run and a half to a creditable 3.51. Nonetheless, he was traded to Texas after the season along with Rafael Palmeiro, who was to hit more than 500 home runs, in a nine-player deal that brought closer Mitch Williams to the Cubs.

In two seasons with the Rangers, Moyer went 6-15 in forty-eight games, some of the appearances out of the bullpen. His earned run average in each year was just a little under the unsightly 5.00. He didn't win a game for the Cardinals in 1991 in only eight appearances. The Cubs invited Moyer back for a second chance in 1992 spring training, but he was cut and offered a pitching coach job in the Minor Leagues. Still only twenty-nine years old, he wasn't ready to retire.[37]

Good scouts always felt paternal toward their signees, and Billy Blitzer followed the ups and downs of Moyer's career in the newspapers. But he had been taught that you didn't offer advice unless the player asks. One day, though, after seeing Jamie pitch on television, he phoned him. "You're not the pitcher I signed," he said frankly. "Your motion and your mechanics are all out of whack."[38] Moyer appreciated the appraisal and was determined to regain his form. He continued working with sports psychologist Harvey Dorfman, who had built a stellar reputation among many Major League players for understanding the difficulty of their craft. His first book, *The Mental Game of Baseball*, which he coauthored in 1989 with baseball scout Karl Kuehl, had built a loyal following. One of Dorfman's insights that particularly opened Moyer's eyes was "No one can make you feel like a failure without your consent."[39]

Moyer's career began to trend upward when he signed with the Orioles in 1993. His work with Orioles pitching coach Dick Bosman helped him to regain the feel for his changeup, the pitch that was vital to his success.[40] Despite the signs of improvement, the Orioles still released Moyer after the 1995 season, the third pink slip of his career. He signed as a free agent with the Red Sox in 1996. When traded to Seattle in the middle of the season for an outfielder Darren Bragg, who was destined to be a journeyman, Moyer was ready to start on a remarkable late-career resurgence. He would win 149 games for the Mariners and lose only 75 through 2005. He became a twenty-game winner twice, and in 2000 he became at age thirty-eight the oldest pitcher in baseball history to throw a shutout. He joined the Phillies in 2006, and at the age of forty-six in 2008 became the oldest pitcher to start a World Series game, helping the Philadelphia Phillies claim only their second world championship, beating the Tampa Bay Rays in five games. Before he retired at the age of forty-nine at the end of the 2012 season, Moyer, pitching for the Colorado Rockies, became the oldest pitcher ever to win a Major League game.

In 2008 St. Joseph's College awarded Jamie Moyer an honorary doctorate. Billy Blitzer happened to be scouting the Mets in Philadelphia that weekend, and he stopped by the ceremony, sitting in the back of the hall. When Moyer and his wife, Karen Phelps Moyer, daughter of basketball coach turned TV broadcaster Digger Phelps, spotted Billy in the audience, they insisted he come down to the VIP section. "You're family, you know," Karen and Jamie told him. It was a special moment of appreciation in the life of a scout used to working alone in the shadows.

When Billy was at another ceremony at Villanova University near Philadelphia, he happened to make eye contact with Gary Scott, whom he had signed in the third round of the 1989 draft. A third baseman ballyhooed as "the next Ron Santo," Scott did not live up to his promise and played in only parts of three seasons in the big leagues before retiring to start a successful career in the finance industry. He tried to avoid Blitzer's gaze, but the scout insisted on greeting him. When Scott said he felt embarrassed that he never fulfilled his promise, Blitzer cut him off. "You didn't fail," he declared. "You made the Major Leagues, and that's quite an accomplishment."

A happier story about one of Blitzer's signings involved center fielder Doug Glanville, who was a student-athlete at the University of Pennsylvania school of engineering and the Cubs' 1992 number one draft pick. Billy was assigned the job of meeting the Glanvilles at their home in Teaneck, New Jersey. He had not met Doug beforehand, so when Glanville walked down the spiral staircase at the family home, Blitzer's heart sank. He saw a slender young man clad in a T-shirt and shorts without noticeable athletic definition. Pointing to the piano, his mother said, "Douglas, play something for Mr. Blitzer." Billy's eyes widened a little more. He thought, "Have we drafted a Liberace instead of a ballplayer?"[41]

It turned out that Glanville was an excellent athlete and a deeply concerned human being who possessed a wide variety of interests. Blitzer saw that immediately when they were at a newsstand together; Billy bought the *Sporting News*, and Doug bought the *Wall Street Journal*. Glanville made the Major League roster in Chicago in 1996 and hit .300 in his second season but was traded to the Phillies, where he spent most of his nine-year career. He retired with career numbers of .277 batting average, .315 on-base percentage, .380 slugging average, 59 home runs, 333 RBIs, 553 runs, 168 stolen bases, and 36 caught stealing. He walked 205 times and struck out 502 times.

Growing up in Teaneck in the 1970s in a town that tried to enforce racial integration, Glanville became very forthright in his opposition to racism. Living in a comfortable suburb did not free him from being targeted by police. Nor did it when starting a family after his retirement, as he moved into another tony suburb, Bloomfield, Connecticut. Glanville has become a leading participant in the Baseball Alliance, a group of past and present African American Major Leaguers that was created in the wake of the George Floyd riots in 2020. In addition to his work as a television broadcaster, he has authored a memoir *The Game from Where I Stand* and is an adjunct professor in sport and society at the University of Connecticut.

Billy Blitzer retired from the Cubs after the 2021 season, but he has kept alive his love and interest in the game, its people, and their stories. Although he spent the last twenty years of his career as a professional scout, he cherishes memories of starting out in the baseball business as an amateur scout, the most challenging and rewarding job because the talent is still in its formative stage. He has compared the selections on draft day to Christmas morning when someone opens presents. He always finds something new to analyze and to entertain himself at a ball park because he never knows whom he might meet.

One day at Yankee Stadium late last century when Roger Clemens was pitching for the Toronto Blue Jays, Billy Blitzer was scouting with a radar gun on his lap. After Clemens finished the fifth inning, singer Paul Simon came down the aisle and asked, "What's he throwing?"

"About ninety-three to ninety-six," Billy replied.

"And the slider?"

"Around eighty-six to eighty-nine."

"Who are you with?"

"The Chicago Cubs."

"Do you live in Chicago?"

"No, I live near Julio, down by the schoolyard," came Blitzer's spontaneous reply that he had no idea where it came from. "I'm from Brooklyn."

Simon laughed uproariously and, walking away, said, "Yeah, you're from Brooklyn."

A few years later, Blitzer was scouting on the Fourth of July in Des Moines, Iowa, where the Mets' New Orleans farm team was playing the Iowa Cubs. The voice singing the National Anthem sounded very familiar. It belonged to opera singer Allan Glassman from Billy's old neighborhood of Brighton Beach in Brooklyn. When they were eight or nine years old, Billy used to accompany Allan on the subway to Manhattan, where he was taking voice lessons. Glassman has since become a world-famous tenor, performing at the Metropolitan Opera and other houses all over the world while teaching at Roosevelt University in Chicago.

Billy Blitzer once described the essence of his craft as "getting paid for your opinions." After nearly forty years with the Cubs, he may no longer be on their payroll, but he retains a love of the game and a hope that young people can be taught to appreciate it the way he did. A lifelong passion does not fade easily. You don't forget the lush green grass at your first game and bicycling to Little League games and opening a batting cage where hopefuls can keep their swings primed by off-season practice.

To conclude this journey with some of baseball's engendered species, I turn to the saga of Bill Enos, born and bred in Red Sox country, who traveled an adventurous route to return to serving the region of his birth.

9

Bill Enos's Roundabout Journey to Massachusetts Scouting Immortality

William Donovan Enos, born in Cohasset, Massachusetts, on August 5, 1920, was the oldest of two children born to Abraham Soito Enos and Helena Donovan Enos. Bill grew up in an antique Cape Cod house built by an ancestor in the late eighteenth century that was home for the Enos family for generations, including Bill's grandfather, a sea captain, and his father, a master plumber. Cohasset is located between Boston and Cape Cod and the whole region of New England was baseball mad. Bill's passion for the game came naturally because his father, Abe, was a talented semipro second baseman who also pitched many a Sunday doubleheader in area amateur leagues, sometimes in tandem with Everett Gammons, the great-uncle of Hall of Fame sportswriter Peter Gammons. Big Ed Flanagan, grandfather of Cy Young Award–winning southpaw Mike Flanagan, was often the opposition.[1]

No Little League was available for Bill Enos to play in growing up between the world wars (as was true for others outlined in this book), but there was plenty of local action, and he was in the middle of it. He developed such a reputation as a fancy-fielding left-handed first baseman that when he was only twelve years old, first baseman Joe Judge, recently acquired by the Red Sox, gifted him a glove Judge used during his long career with the Washington Senators that was capped by victory in the 1924 World Series. Enos treasured that gift and, though it showed many signs of wear, he used it for a long time. He brought it to a Braves Field tryout camp in 1935; he had to sneak in because, at fourteen, he was ineligible to try out. He performed so well that his ruse wasn't discovered for four days.[2]

Like most baseball-smitten youths in his day, young Bill devoured the *Sporting News*, the weekly newspaper published in St. Louis known to millions of baseball lovers as "the bible of baseball." Fans passionately read the paper from cover to cover, including the box scores of every game in pro baseball from the Majors down to Class D. One day in early autumn 1936, sixteen-year-old Bill Enos noticed an ad stating that the weekly was sponsoring a contest for the best subscription salesmen. Ten winners would receive a six-week all-expenses-paid spring training trip to Ray L. Doan's All-Star Baseball School in Hot Springs, Arkansas. Bill arose mornings at 5:00 a.m. to gather a bundle of free copies of the newspaper. Not old enough for a driver's license, he made his rounds on foot, trudging through snow from town to town, drumming up customers for the St. Louis sports weekly. Imagine the thrill when Bill received a telegram in early February 1937 informing him that he was one of the ten lucky winners. In fact, he was second in the nation in amassing the most points for subscriptions.[3]

The invitation told Enos to report to Hot Springs by Valentine's Day. As he hurriedly got ready, the Boston *Evening Traveller* headlined, "Cohasset Boy Peddles His Way to Spring Training." Abe Enos proudly drove his son to the Boston train station, where Bill met three other winners from New England. One fellow had been driven from Maine by his father in a truck with a coop of chickens in the back. The youngster carried a few homemade bats built by his father, but none survived its first use at Doan's school.[4]

When the excited teenagers arrived in Hot Springs shortly before Valentine's Day, they were eager to meet the colorful operator of the baseball school. Born in Muscatine, Iowa, in 1897, Ray Doan was once a promising right-handed pitcher, but he injured his arm from overuse. He did the next best thing, turning to coaching at varied places, including local teams in Springfield, Massachusetts, and at U.S. Army installations. He was a born salesman who counted among his clients the Negro League Kansas City Monarchs and the House of David traveling team. Sporting a Clark Gable mustache that added to his mystique, Doan marketed Donkey Baseball, up there in novelty with Great Depression events like marathon dancing and six-day bicycle racing. Every player except the pitcher and the catcher started the action astride a donkey. Doan also created goat softball, in which women infielders and outfielders played the game while riding goats. Never at a loss for new promotional ideas, Doan marketed a woman's basketball team, the Babe Didrikson All-Stars, led by the remarkable all-around athlete best known in later years as a championship golfer.[5]

The Ray L. Doan All-Star Baseball School was a natural fit for Hot Springs because, early in the twentieth century, the spa town hosted several Major League teams in spring training, with the Pittsburgh Pirates and Boston Red Sox the most frequent visitors. Future Hall of Fame outfielder Al Simmons of the A's and pitcher Mel Harder of the Indians—a 223-game winner, all with Cleveland—made frequent visits on their own dime.[6] So, not surprisingly, did Babe Ruth. Drawing on the model of previous baseball schools—one had been run by Pop Kelchner, one of Branch Rickey's top scouts—Ray Doan hired several past and present top-notch Major Leaguers as instructors. Bill Enos and his fellow students listened raptly to the words of future Hall of Famers Dizzy Dean, George Sisler, and Rogers Hornsby, who reportedly owned a piece of the academy. Another future immortal, young Bob Feller, came by to deliver a day's worth of instruction. The finer points of defense were taught by Cardinals scout Wid Matthews. Lon Warneke, three-time 20-game winner for the Cubs, was one of the pitching instructors—his home was so close to the Hot Springs ballfields that he could walk to work. After his retirement, Warneke became a National League umpire before being elected a judge in Garland County where Hot Springs was located.[7] In 1946 in the neighboring town of Hope, Arkansas, William Jefferson Clinton, the forty-second president of the United States, was born.

Doan charged sixty dollars for tuition and fifty dollars if payment was received before the end of January. Bill Enos won a scholarship, so he didn't have to worry about tuition. As for housing, students lived either in respectable hotels—Hot Springs was known for its bawdy side—or with families in the area, with no rent of more than seven dollars a week. Doan's curriculum consisted of conditioning drills and lectures in the morning and games in the afternoon. Bill tried to absorb every pearl of wisdom from the famous instructors. Although the perfectionism and bluntness of Rogers Hornsby proved a constant irritant to his Major League teammates, the fledgling students at Doan's school held him in awe. He made friends with students by running laps with them at the beginning of the day, encouraging them to keep up the pace. Soon, they felt comfortable calling him by his popular nickname, "Rajah."

One memorable moment for Bill Enos came when Dizzy Dean and Lon Warneke were showing students films of themselves throwing effortlessly. You will have days like this, they said, when every pitch is thrown perfectly. But the day could be spoiled when the umpire wouldn't call a strike. Dizzy held up a picture of George Barr just as the umpire happened to walk into the classroom. Barr, who ran an umpiring school affiliated with Doan's school, laughed along with the joke, but in the regular season Barr and Dizzy were hardly friends. Once Dean got so upset with a missed strike call by Barr that he started lobbing pitches to the plate, forcing his manager Frankie Frisch to yank him from the game.[8] (Another time, he reacted to what he thought was a bad balk call by throwing pitches at the players' heads of the archrival New York Giants, except at his former teammate, second baseman Burgess Whitehead.)

The unfiltered Dean was, of course, a big favorite of the Doan students, even as he warned them about the dangers of alcohol and tobacco. Always dissatisfied with his contract, Dean was publicly demanding a $50,000 salary in 1937, though he ultimately settled for much less. He told the youngsters that if they made the Major Leagues, the "tight-fisted owners will try to cut you down."[9] Don't let it happen to you, he advised the campers. Bill Enos listened to Dizzy's primer on the business side of baseball, and in the years ahead he would learn to fight for what was due him.

At the moment, though, he was having the time of his life, absorbing the instruction from his renowned teachers and enjoying the perks and the camaraderie of fellow students. He loved wearing the flannel uniform with "*The Sporting News*" emblazoned on the front. His first pair of Lefty O'Doul–endorsed spikes were three sizes too large, but he found a pair that fit. Barely two weeks into his adventure, he was thrilled when Jack Ryan, a scout for Branch Rickey's Cardinals, offered him a contract for $137 a month if he accepted an assignment to the lower Minor Leagues. When Bill wired his parents the good news, they were not enthusiastic. They wanted him to return to high school at Thayer Academy, which had given him a leave of absence so he could travel to Hot Springs.[10]

In addition to Bill, approximately one-third of the 373 Doan Academy students received contracts for the upcoming season. Catcher Benny Huffman, whom Bill befriended at Hot Springs, was one of the older students at twenty-two—he was signed by the St. Louis Browns and went directly to the Major Leagues (where he performed well, hitting .273 and slugging .348 in 154 at bats that season, but he never returned to the big leagues). Bill was dreaming of the day when he would follow in the footsteps of Huffman and other recent graduates who made the Majors: Browns pitcher John Grodzicki, Indians outfielder Thurman Tucker, and Dodgers catcher Sam Narron, the first of eight North Carolina Narrons to enter pro baseball.[11]

When Bill returned to Cohasset, his parents began to relent on their opposition to their son turning pro before graduation. They saw that the Cardinals really wanted to develop Bill. Branch Rickey sent him a telegram inviting him to work out with the team when they made an eastern swing. In Boston, Cardinals player-manager Frank Frisch greeted him, and the *Evening Traveller* took a picture of Bill with the skipper. A few weeks later, Enos traveled to New York to meet the Cards at the Polo Grounds for their big series against the archrival New York Giants. It turned out that both St. Louis first basemen, future Hall of Famer Johnny Mize and Dick Siebert, a future College World Series–winning University of Minnesota coach, were injured. "We might have to put you in, kid," Frisch told Enos.[12] Fortunately, Mize felt good enough to play, and Enos could relax. Before Bill left the field, a photo was taken with Frisch and Enos, the teenager wearing a Cardinals uniform below his high school cap.

Bill then went into the stands to watch with a capacity crowd one of the classic duels between future Hall of Famers Dizzy Dean and Carl Hubbell. Hubbell was the southpaw whom the Tigers released, thinking he didn't throw hard enough to stick in the Major Leagues. But when picked up by John McGraw on the advice of his top scout Dick Kinsella, he mastered a screwball, and his ticket to immortality was cast. (After finishing his career with a 253-154 record and a 1947 induction into the Hall of Fame, Hubbell enjoyed a long and successful career as a Giants farm director.)[13] Bill Enos's amazing teenage experience was not yet over. He stayed with the Cardinals for two more weeks on their road trip to the East. Rookie catcher Mickey Owen treated him warmly and drove him to the ballpark every day.[14] (Owen wound up having two big moments in baseball history, one on the field and one off. In Game Four of the 1941 World Series, he committed a passed ball with two outs in the ninth inning that enabled the Yankees to come from behind and win. In 1946 he left for the "outlaw" Mexican League, and when he returned shortly thereafter, he was placed on a five-year ineligible list. The suspension was eventually reduced.)

When Bill Enos returned to Cohasset, he was expecting to hear any day that the Cardinals planned to put him on the roster of their top affiliate in Rochester, New York, for probable assignment to a lower classification. When the wire came, however, it was not good news. He learned that the Cardinals had released him. He never found out why, but Rickey's Cardinals system was loaded with more than seven hundred players at this time. In fact, a few months later on March 23, 1938, baseball commissioner Kenesaw Mountain Landis issued his so-called Cedar Rapids Decision freeing seventy-four Cardinal farmhands from Rickey's dominion. If Enos had been eligible to play in the Cardinals' system in 1937, he might have been one of those freed from Rickey's control. (Significantly, most of the players returned to the Cardinals' system, and one of them, George Silvey, went on to a long career as an instructor and administrator in the St. Louis Minor Leagues.)

No longer attached to a pro baseball organization, Enos spent part of the 1937 summer playing for Orleans in the amateur Cape Cod Baseball League. It would be his only season as a Cape Cod player, but it began a long association with an organization that in 2000 inducted him into the initial class of the CCBL Hall of Fame. After the 1937 Cape Cod season ended, Enos finished the summer playing for the Cambridge, Massachusetts, Frisoli team in the semipro Suburban Twilight League. In coming to Cambridge, he switched places with future Major Leaguer Eddie Waitkus, a first baseman and left fielder, who moved on to a team in northern Maine. They both were named All-Stars in their respective leagues. Twelve years later, Enos shuddered when learning the news of Waitkus's shooting by an obsessed woman fan. The incident became one of the inspirations for Bernard Malamud's novel *The Natural*.

Although Waitkus enjoyed an eleven-year Major League career and won a pennant with the 1950 Phillies, the injuries from the shooting undoubtedly hampered his career.[15]

Despite his release by the Cardinals, Bill Enos was still on the radar of many pro baseball people. Early in 1938 Enos was one of two hundred players to receive an invitation from Giants player-manager Bill Terry to attend his monthlong baseball school before spring training, in Baton Rouge, Louisiana. Terry's only caveat to the youngsters was to heed jaywalking regulations in the state capital because two-dollar fines would be enforced. The prominent coaches on Terry's staff included former Major Leaguers Heinie Groh, Hank DeBerry, and Mel Ott (a future Hall of Famer and Terry's teammate), and infield coaches Fred "Dutch" Dorman, Dickie Kerr, and Johnny Mostil. At the end of the session, however, Bill Enos was not offered a contract. He returned to Cohasset and played summer ball for a couple of teams, including one sponsored by the Sons of Italy (though Bill's lineage was mainly Irish with some Portuguese).[16]

February 1939 found Bill back at Ray Doan's school, which had moved to Jackson, Mississippi. George Barr had also transferred his umpire school to the state capital. (Future Pirates, Reds, and Braves scout Bill Clark, one of the pioneers in international baseball scouting, would get his start in baseball at George Barr's school.)[17] Ray Doan and Bill Enos got along swimmingly. Bill learned a lot from the staff that again included Rogers Hornsby and Dizzy Dean, plus two important members of Branch Rickey's Cardinals player development staff, former White Sox pitcher Dickie Kerr, who won two games in the 1919 World Series, despite the presence of several "Black Sox" who weren't trying their best, and longtime scout Joe Mathes. Other instructors included Gabby Street, who had managed the Cardinals to a 1931 World Series title, and future Hall of Fame pitcher Burleigh Grimes, the last of the grandfathered spitball pitchers, who recently managed the Brooklyn Dodgers and now worked in their Minor League organization.[18]

The 1939 Doan School had 250 students; they attended classes in the morning at a local hotel and scrimmaged on the school grounds in the afternoon. On rainy days they gathered to watch baseball instructional movies. At the end of the session in late March, Enos was delighted to entertain two offers from

Major League organizations. Johnny Mostil tried to sign him for the White Sox, but Ray Doan suggested that Bill accept Burleigh Grimes's offer to join a Class D Brooklyn Dodgers farm club, the Gloversville-Johnstown Glovers in the Canadian-American League.[19] The Glovers were finishing spring training with the parent Double-A Montreal Royals in Lake Wales, Florida. Without delay, Enos jumped on the next bus to the central Florida town and reported to his first pro team on April Fools' Day 1939. He had crossed the Rubicon. There would be no senior year for him at Thayer Academy, as he made the choice to follow his baseball dream.

Bill saw action in only the final exhibition game of the Royals against their International League rival Buffalo Bisons. He didn't get into regular season action until early May, but he quickly became a favorite of both sportswriters and fans. The scribes compared his defense at first base to another Massachusetts-bred first baseman, John "Stuffy" McInnis, who had played for Connie Mack's pre–World War I championship teams. He was dubbed "the stretch kid," an homage to his agility in catching throws at first base. One of the highlights of his year was before a game on May 18 in Ottawa, Ontario, he stood close to Queen Elizabeth I and King George VI, who were traveling by train through all the Canadian provinces.

Enos was invited to the Glovers' 1940 spring training in Kingston, New York, but he couldn't reach agreement on a contract and was released before the start of the season. Dizzy Dean's warning of three years earlier had borne fruit. Enos tried independent ball in Cornwall, Ontario, but the franchise folded in early July. He spent the rest of the season playing for a summer college team against semipro and Negro League teams, including the Baltimore Elite Giants with future Hall of Famer Roy Campanella.[20]

Ray Doan had not forgotten about Bill Enos—in February 1941 he was invited to the school to serve as a full-time instructor. It meant hitting fungoes to fielders, giving infield instruction, and playing in games. Doan had moved to the school to Palatka in northeast Florida near the St. John's River. Burleigh Grimes was again supervising pitching. Another notable on the 1941 staff was Babe Ruth, who had been unable to land a permanent position in baseball since his 1935 midseason retirement as a player. Doan had brought Ruth down the previous year.

As he watched him giving tips and encouragement to the aspiring players, Bob Considine, a nationally prominent writer and radio personality and future Ruth biographer, penned a column saying that the Bambino was getting paid very little to work with the youngsters because he loved the game. Ruth was effusive in his praise of Enos, comparing him to the Dodgers star first baseman Dolph Camilli. When Abe Enos found out that Babe Ruth was with his son in Florida, he dropped everything in Cohasset to come down and sit in on the sessions. One evening, Bill Enos went bowling with Babe Ruth.[21]

At the end of the Doan school session, Bill was delighted to accept a job with the Lafayette (Louisiana) White Sox, a St. Louis Browns affiliate in the Class D Evangeline League. The Browns were one of the most economically impoverished teams in Major League Baseball—if not for Pearl Harbor a few months in the future, new owner Donald Barnes might have moved them to Los Angeles—but young Bill Enos was thrilled to be part again of any big league organization. It was an association that lasted for the next fifteen years, including the franchise's first years as the Baltimore Orioles.

As a member of the Lafayette White Sox, Enos made the All-Star team and, as always, played solid defense, although he hit only .215. He again became a fan favorite. The Black fans in the segregated sections of the ballpark loved his colorful play and enthusiasm. He lived with another player in the back apartment of a supportive local family. Like future colleague Herb Stein, Bill Enos saw up close for the first time the indignities of Deep South racial segregation. He finished the season on loan to a Philadelphia Athletics farm team in Fredericksburg, Maryland, in the Class D Eastern Shore League.

On December 7, 1941, all lives in America changed dramatically after the bombing of Pearl Harbor. Before "the date which will live in infamy," as President Roosevelt called it, Bill thought he might be headed for a higher classification for the 1942 season. As it turned out, he was assigned to the Double-A Toledo roster, whereas he had hoped that the team would assign him to at least Class C. Now that America had gone to war, it was only a matter of time before Uncle Sam called. Having grown up near Cape Cod, he didn't want to go into the Army. He looked into the Navy's Gene Tunney Athletic Program, sponsored by the former undefeated heavyweight champion. On May 1, 1942, Bill Enos was sworn in as an associate seaman and soon advanced to physical training specialist. He was assigned to the Newport, Rhode Island, naval base, where he lived on the USS *Constellation Baltimore*. For a brief time, one of his bunk mates was jazz bandleader Artie Shaw.

Bill was able to keep in baseball shape by playing on the *Constellation* team at Newport. He was happy to reunite with Benny Huffman, his friend from Doan's Hot Springs camp who played briefly with the Browns before starting the Minor League grind. The team played against other military squads and local Ivy League colleges Brown and Harvard. Early in 1945 Bill Enos and his unit were ordered to the Pacific. As they were waiting at the dock in San Francisco for their trip to the South Pacific, Bill heard tales of another sailor named Bill Enos who was also a pro baseball player; he was a better hitter than Cohasset Bill and had reached Triple-A. The two Bill Enoses never met each other.

When Bill's ship arrived in Hawaii, the unit was assigned to Tinian Island in the Northern Mariannas, which had been captured by American armed forces in July 1944. His unit was charged with guarding Japanese prisoners; there, Bill became the director of athletics. In November, Vic Wertz, the first baseman whose World Series smash to deep center nine years later landed in Willie Mays's glove, selected Enos to play on an Army Air Force All-Star team that traveled to Guam, Saipan, and Iwo Jima. At the end of January 1946, Bill Enos was mustered out of the U.S. Navy at the final rank petty officer first class, physical education. He was sworn into the Naval Reserves and headed back home with fellow New Englander Connie Ryan, a Boston Braves utility infielder.

After a happy reunion with his family in Cohasset, Bill Enos was eager to resume his professional baseball career. He knew nearing the age of twenty-six he was in for tough competition against a horde of other returning veterans and the wave of younger players eager to get their start in what was still by far America's most popular sport. He continued to love everything about the game and was ready to do anything to stay in it. He remained on the Browns' Toledo roster and went to spring training with them. After being shuttled from teams in Spartansburg, South Carolina, and Asheville, North Carolina, he arrived in Miami in late June 1946 to play for the Sun Sox in the Class C Florida International League.

After being in the Pacific in wartime, he loved being near the Atlantic in peacetime. Paul Waner, one of scout Joe Devine's great discoveries, was player-manager of the Sun Sox. Bill listened carefully to every word from the future Hall of Famer, a member of the select 3,000-hit club, who possessed a rich storehouse of hitting and inside baseball knowledge. Enos also said a silent prayer of thanks when he learned of the bus accident near Spokane, Washington, that cost the lives of several Minor Leaguers; fortunately, his former Newport teammate Gus Hallbourg survived.

In 1947 Enos was again in Florida, playing for the West Palm Beach Indians in the same Florida International League. He enjoyed a respectable offensive year, playing in 124 games with a .271 batting average and .349 slugging average. In 1948 he was promoted to the Port Chester Clippers, a franchise north of New York City in the Class B Connecticut League. Enos enjoyed another solid offensive year: 113 games, .269 batting average, .322 slugging average, 1 home run, and 40 RBIs. Of course, these were still not the power numbers expected of a first baseman, but he almost always put the ball in play, striking out only 18 times in the regular season. He was voted the most popular player on the Clippers and given a special day when he was presented with many gifts, including a television set. When he returned home after the season, the TV became one of the first sets in Cohasset, making Bill even more of a local celebrity.

He never had as much fun playing the game than during his season as a Port Chester Clipper. Owner Lester Osterman Jr. was a former University of Virginia player who had become successful on Wall Street (and later a prominent Broadway theater producer). He was lavish in his generosity. His father owned Bond Clothes, and Lester Jr. gifted leather coats to players who performed well. He promised to give a car to any pitcher who threw a no-hitter but gave one to someone who threw only a one-hitter. On the last day of the regular season, with the Colonial League pennant already clinched by the Clippers with an 86-53 record, Osterman went out to the mound and completed a shutout with one inning of work. Bill Enos always thought it was the only time an active Wall Street trader played in a professional game. The season was capped when the Clippers won the playoffs against the Waterbury Connecticut Eagles.

After the season, Bill Enos took stock of his career. He was turning twenty-nine by the start of the 1949 season and obviously was not getting any younger. The dream of playing in the Majors, first hatched in Ray Doan's Hot Springs school, was fading. He was working in the off-season as a salesman back in Cohasset, but he knew that the Browns liked him and wanted him to stay in their system. When player development director Jim McLaughlin offered Enos a choice of two player-manager positions for 1949—Ada, Oklahoma, or Mayfield, Kentucky—he chose Mayfield, the one closer to home.

Unfortunately, he endured a difficult 1949 season for the Mayfield Clothiers in the Class D Kitty League (Kentucky-Illinois-Tennessee). They finished in the cellar with a 38-86 record, but Bill as always flashed great leather and finished second in the league in fielding average. He was a fan favorite again and was given a day during which he was named an honorary Kentucky Colonel, an award presented by current MLB commissioner A. B. "Happy" Chandler, the former Kentucky governor and United States senator.

From 1950 through 1952, Enos was player-manager in other Class D cities in the Browns' farm system—Baxley, Georgia; Ada, Oklahoma; and Pittsburg, Kansas. He was also gaining valuable experience as the baseball director of the Browns' Minor League spring training facility that in 1952 moved from Pine Bluff, Arkansas, to Thomasville, Georgia. He learned the nuts and bolts of housing and feeding dozens of Minor Leaguers. He got to meet and know all the players and encourage them as he had been encouraged. After the 1952 season Jim McLaughlin offered Bill a full-time scouting job. It was a timely offer because Bill was shortly to marry Grace Helen Jones, a head nurse he met when visiting a friend at a hospital near Cohasset. When he arrived at 1953 spring training, he was one of the youngest scouts in baseball. He was eager to use his varied experiences in the game to perform one of the hardest and least-recognized jobs in baseball—finding, signing, and projecting the next generation of Major League players.

It turned out that 1953 would be the final year for the St. Louis Browns franchise. Once the Cardinals won its first World Series in 1926 and established itself as a regular contender and nine-time champion over the next twenty years, the Browns had become an afterthought in St. Louis. They did meet the

Cardinals in the fall—the St. Louis 1944 World Series—and lost in six games, but their days were numbered. By 1953 the Browns treasury was so depleted that it couldn't afford fresh supplies of new baseballs and clean uniforms. Bill Enos happened to be in the office on the last day of the season when it became official that starting in 1954, the team would move to Maryland and become the Baltimore Orioles. After nobody in the office could remove the elegant embroidered "Browns" stitching on the front of the uniforms, Jim McLaughlin ordered Enos to "get rid" of them. They were given to kids in the street, Bill remembered in an interview with his older daughter Anne.[22]

When the Orioles set up in shop in Baltimore in 1954, Bill Enos was promoted to national scout under McLaughlin and his assistant Henry J. "Hank" Peters. Every now and then, Bill was still needed as an emergency Minor League manager. In one dramatic instance, Bill was called upon to replace player-manager Frank Lucchesi, a future skipper of the Texas Rangers. Lucchesi had been hit by a pitch and needed immediate brain surgery. Bill rushed in to take his place, but in less than two weeks Lucchesi was back on the job. Happily back in street clothes, Enos returned to evaluating amateur talent while picking up valuable lessons from his mentors, McLaughlin and Peters.

Jim McLaughlin, who came to baseball from the world of insurance, was not a baseball fan. He was more interested in understanding the psychology that made teams and players tick. He devised a circle called "The Whole Ball Player" that became famous within the game and would be a key component of the Orioles' coming success as a perennial contender from 1960 through 1983. The top half of the circle consisted of qualities that "can be seen with the eye," such basic traits as arm strength, running speed, body control, stamina, durability, poise, and instincts. For pitchers, McLaughlin stressed the importance of velocity, location, and movement. The bottom and darker half of the circle, labeled "cannot be seen with the eye," consisted of such vital traits as attitude, personality, competitiveness, and family background.[23]

Jim McLaughlin moved to Baltimore with the franchise in 1954, but Hank Peters stayed in the Midwest. Peters joined the team shortly after World War II when he answered a want ad for a job in the farm system. He was a hard-working, unassuming young man who rose quickly in the organization. A sportswriter once wrote that Peters possessed as much charisma "as a rubber plant in an insurance office," but beneath the surface there lived a very perceptive and caring baseball mind.[24] Bill Enos kept alive his connection with Peters when in 1955 he took the position of farm director of the Kansas City Athletics, the historic franchise that had just moved from Philadelphia.

Enos's connection to Peters proved very handy early in the next season when Bill resigned from his job with the Orioles. He had endured enough of the unfortunate crossfire between farm director McLaughlin and the new Orioles manager and general manager Paul Richards. No one ever doubted the baseball knowledge of Richards, a former Major League catcher who never maximized his talent as a player—a .227 batting average in parts of eight seasons with 15 home runs and 155 RBIs. No doubt, he had knowledge of every aspect of the game, but it was his way or the highway. The last straw for Bill Enos was Richards's interference in Bill's 1956 spring training program. Before the regular season started, Bill sent in his resignation letter. His last contribution to the Orioles was signing Western Michigan University infielder Bill Lajoie after the College World Series the previous June. Lajoie never made the Majors as a player, but he became a superior scout.[25] Lajoie was scouting director for the Tigers in the 1970s when they signed the core of their 1984 world champions that were never behind after a 35-5 start to the regular season. He had become general manager and could bask in the achievements of the core he had drafted, among Hall of Famers Jack Morris and Alan Trammell, in addition to Lance Parrish and Dan Petry.

Bill Enos was not unemployed for long. Hank Peters quickly hired him as a northeastern scouting supervisor for the Kansas City Athletics. The team was determined to build up a farm system that had grown fallow in Philadelphia. Like all the great scouts, Bill Enos loved being a hunter, going into the backwoods where no rival had ever trod to find that elusive diamond in the rough. "Postage stamps don't go to some of these places, but I do," he once said.[26] He grew to love the camaraderie on the A's staff.

Another Hank Peters mentee was Tom "T-Bone" Giordano, son of Grace and Paolo "Patsy" Giordano, an Italian immigrant butcher and grocery-deli owner who had settled in Newark, New Jersey. The elder Giordano was not thrilled that his oldest son, born Carmine, was hooked on playing baseball. He even once cut up Tom's cleats and glove with his butcher knife until he realized how much the game meant to his son. He started feeding him steaks at lunch before games, and thus the nickname "T-Bone" developed. Because of severe flat feet, young Giordano was not drafted during World War II and started a pro baseball career in the Red Sox organization. A severe beaning in a game at Hartford, Connecticut, on the next-to-last day of the 1945 season led to his release and an absence from competition for a few years.[27]

He enrolled at Panzer College, now part of Montclair University in northern New Jersey. An empathetic coach and athletic director eased him back into competition by throwing tennis balls at his head to allay his fear of the ball, and he was encouraged to become a soccer goalie to revive his competitive juices. Giordano returned to pro baseball in 1948, now adopting the more American first name of Thomas. The highlight of T-Bone's Minor League career came in 1953 while playing in Savannah for Manager Les Bell, the Pop Kelchner signee who starred for the 1926 world champion Cardinals. T-Bone deprived Hank Aaron of the triple crown in the South Atlantic League (Sally League) by outhomering the future home run king by one long ball. (The short left-field fence at T-Bone's home field in Savannah, Georgia, probably abetted his 24–home run season.)[28]

His power outburst led to a September callup with Philadelphia. He hit his first Major League home run off the Detroit Tigers standout right-hander Virgil Trucks and also homered off the onetime Yankee Frank "Spec" Shea, but T-Bone hit only .157 in 35 Major League at bats. He never returned to the Majors, but Hank Peters nurtured him through careers as a coach, Minor League manager, scout, and scouting director for the Orioles and later the then-Indians. For the 1978 draft, the Orioles possessed four of the first forty-eight draft picks, and Giordano held his breath while waiting to name Cal Ripken Jr. as their fourth pick.[29]

The joy of working for such solid baseball people as Hank Peters and T-Bone Giordano enabled Bill Enos to survive the arrival of medical insurance innovator Charles O. Finley as Kansas City A's owner in 1961. A survivor of a long bout with tuberculosis after World War II, "Charlie O" was colorful to say the least. If you accepted telephone calls at late hours from an excitable boss, you could accept Charlie, and he was generous with his employees. Bill's daughter Anne Enos recalled that Finley sent every Major League player and full-time scout a fancy Bulova Accutron Astronaut watch for Christmas in 1961. It was a state-of-the-art timepiece, although no one could figure out how to repair it. Finley was also lavish with a bonus budget that helped Enos on the scouting trail.

You had to put up, of course, with his eccentricities. For instance, during the Christmas season before the introduction of the free agent draft in 1965, Finley invited four recent signees, including Enos's top northeastern pick, Holy Cross's Dick Joyce, to a ceremony in which Pat Friday, Finley's beleaguered assistant, dressed up as Santa Claus. Hank Bauer, arriving in Kansas City after the Roger Maris trade, found out he was managing the team when Finley put a congratulatory note on the scoreboard saying that Bauer had retired as a player and was now the manager.[30]

It was still rewarding for Bill Enos to be part of an A's scouting team that was laying the foundation for the threepeat champions from 1972 to 1974. Though Enos had mixed feelings about the draft itself, the A's found core players of the future in the first three drafts: Sal Bando in the sixth round and Gene Tenace in twentieth round in 1965, and Rick Monday, the number one overall pick in the first draft in 1965. In 1972 Monday was traded for southpaw Ken Holtzman, who would be part of three World Series–winning starting rotations. In 1966, future Hall of Famer Reggie Jackson was the A's number one pick, and future Cy Young Award winner and MVP Vida Blue was picked in the second round in 1967.

Charlie Finley was restless, however. He didn't like the old stadium in Kansas City and threatened to move if a new one wasn't built. Given his tempestuous nature, he made few influential local friends who could help his quest. After the 1967 season, he moved the franchise to Oakland despite warnings from the baseball hierarchy that a second franchise in the Bay Area would hurt the attendance of the National League's San Francisco Giants. There was an immediate uproar in Kansas City about abandoning a city that possessed a deep baseball heritage. Powerful United States senator Stuart Symington (D-MO) raised the specter of Congress reexamining baseball's antitrust exemption. The American League quickly voted to replace the Athletics with a new team in 1969, the Royals. The Seattle Pilots would also join the AL, with Montreal and San Diego joining the National League.

When Ray Swallow, former scouting director of the Athletics now with the Pilots, offered Bill a similar job in northeastern-area scouting, he decided to change organizations. One of his very first signings for the Pilots was Joseph M. Jabar, whom Bill inked after Jabar pitched two impressive summers for Chatham in the Cape Cod League. Jabar did not have a long pro career, but after going to law school, he rose to become associate justice on Maine's Supreme Judicial Court. Bill was pleased when a player from the Northeast, six-foot-eight southpaw Ray Peters from Buffalo, New York, and Harvard University, was Seattle's number one draft pick in the January 1969 draft, which was for players not eligible for the main June draft. (After 1986 the January draft was abandoned.) The son of two postal workers, Ray Peters was drafted four previous times, but he insisted on graduating before turning pro. After leading Harvard to the 1968 College World Series, Peters's future looked promising. As it turned out, he peaked in college. He was rushed to the big leagues in 1970 and started only two games, the first one lasting only two innings, and he never recorded an out in the second one. He was soon traded to the Phillies, and after being hit hard in the Minors, he retired.

Happily, Ray Peters did not let his baseball failure define his life. He enjoyed a happy and successful postplaying career in the real estate lending business near Dallas. During his first visit to Cooperstown in 2015, he looked back without bitterness about his career. He only wished he could have performed better, but nerves did him in. His advice to youngsters was "Get as good an education as you can," and don't expect to become a Major Leaguer. If it does happen, that is wonderful, he said.[31]

Looking back on his life, Ray Peters felt proud that he was the first player to wear number 41 in Milwaukee since Hall of Famer Eddie Mathews and the Braves left for Atlanta. He mentioned Milwaukee because the Seattle Pilots lasted only a year in the state of Washington. During spring training in 1970, Major League Baseball announced the transfer of the franchise to Milwaukee with a new nickname, the Brewers, in honor of the longtime local Minor League team. Pilots ownership always needed money in Seattle, and the local owners, the Soriano brothers, Dewey and Max, could not attract enough financing to guarantee a domed stadium. It was comical the conditions the Pilots endured in their one year in Seattle. Jim Bouton's *Ball Four* about the season was almost tame. Renovations of Minor League Sicks Stadium were never completed. The front office was so understaffed that the farm director was giving out bats on Bat Night. On those rare nights when there were over ten thousand fans, the plumbing was so inadequate that writers in the press box dared not use the toilets until late in the game—"the seventh inning flush." It was fitting that the formal announcement of the move to Milwaukee was made on April Fools' Day.[32]

The ownership group of the Brewers was headed by used automobile dealer Allan H. "Bud" Selig, who had never given up on finding a replacement for the Braves after they departed in 1966 to Atlanta and its far larger TV market. Continuing as the northeastern regional scout, Bill Enos still felt the excitement of being part of a new franchise with nowhere to go but up.

One of his first signings, pitcher Claude Edward "Skip" Lockwood, was a case study in how a good scout never forgets the tools of a talent. In 1964, the last year before the amateur draft, Enos was still working for the Athletics. A lot of scouts were on the trail of Lockwood, who went 22-2 in his last year of high school and hit over .400. Enos thought Skip was blessed with the best arm he had ever seen.

Enos bonded well with Lockwood's parents. The mother had been a former Radio City Music Hall Rockette in New York, and the father had worked his way up from lathe operator to the purchasing department of a Boston-area clothing supply corporation. According to Skip, who later wrote a book, *Insight Pitch: My Life as a Major League Closer*, Enos earned the right to have the last visit with the family before he signed. Bill came in the company of Pat Friday, a former insurance man, who may have gifted Mr. Lockwood with a box of cigars.[33]

Enos and Friday won the bidding, and Lockwood signed a contract providing for at least a $35,000 bonus. But the regulations at the time forced the teenager onto the Major League roster for all of 1965, and he saw little action. He did learn a lot about the game from two future Hall of Famers, Catfish Hunter and Satchel Paige, whom Finley, in an act of kindness, signed to enable the ageless pitcher to qualify for a Major League pension. In 1966 Lockwood started his apprenticeship in the Minors but never mastered the art of hitting. When he started pitching, injuries plagued him. The A's gave up on him, and the Astros looked at him briefly in spring training 1968 but farmed him out. When Lockwood was made eligible for the expansion draft, Enos lobbied successfully for him, and he made his debut with the Pilots in their only year of existence.[34]

After one decision with the Pilots, Lockwood pitched four seasons in Milwaukee before going to the Mets, where in three of his five seasons there he collected double-digit saves. His overall career record of 57-97 was unsightly, but his ERA was somewhat respectable at 3.55, as was his walk-strikeout ratio of 480:829. Looking back on his career in 2018, Lockwood conceded that he was too intense on the mound. He admitted to making the mistake "that my role in the game was to be better than the last pitcher that they just took out."[35]

By a similarly labyrinthine process, Bill Enos was part of the scouting team that brought into the Brewers fold catcher Eliseo "Ellie" Rodríguez. Born in Fajardo, Puerto Rico, on May 24, 1946, Rodríguez moved with his family in 1953 to the Bronx, only a half mile from Yankee Stadium. He was a tough competitor who engaged in Golden Glove boxing until he broke a finger in a fight and concentrated on baseball. Tom Giordano signed him for the Athletics in 1964, but the Yankees picked him out of the Minor League draft the following season. It was a dream come true for Rodríguez, who grew up an ardent Yankees fan. He made his debut in the Bronx on May 26, 1968, but, unprotected in the expansion draft, he was picked up by the Royals. He was their only All-Star in 1969, but the power-hitting Darrell Porter ultimately won the job. Bill Enos recommended the trade that brought Ellie to the Brewers before the 1971 season. In one of those twists that make baseball transactions fascinating, he was traded to the Angels after the 1973 season along with Skip Lockwood and three others for southpaw Clyde Wright and catcher Art Kusnyer. After his eight-year career ended, Rodríguez turned to coaching and teaching. His Roosevelt Baseball School in San Juan, Puerto Rico, is still functioning, and among the players it developed was outfielder Angel Pagan.[36]

There was no convoluted story in Bill Enos's signing of William Edward "Bill" Travers, a Norwood High graduate picked in the sixth round of the draft in 1970. The son of a Norwood police officer, Travers was a tall, stylish southpaw, the epitome of the finesse pitcher who needed pinpoint control and command to be successful. He arrived in Milwaukee in 1974, winning a bet with Enos, who promised he'd buy him dinner if he made the Majors within four years. Travers was the Brewers' opening day starter in 1977, a breakthrough year for the expansion franchise. But injuries plagued him, and he never was a big winner. He finished his career with the Angels but all his victories came with the Brewers. His final log read 65-71, 4.10 ERA, 1,120 innings pitched, 1,139 hits, 410 walks, and 488 strikeouts. In his postplaying career he excelled at duckpin bowling and was part of the 1998 USA world championship team.[37]

At the end of the 1973 season, Bill Enos's dream job opened up when Haywood Sullivan, the Red Sox scouting director, offered him the position of amateur area scout for Massachusetts, Maine, New Hampshire, and Vermont. He joined Wilfrid Henry "Lefty" Lefevbre, the former Major League pitcher, who was responsible for Connecticut and Rhode Island. So began Enos's longest association in baseball that would cement his place in scouting annals. One of his first future Major League signees was southpaw John Thomas Tudor from Schenectady, New York. The oldest son of a General Electric engineer, Tudor was raised primarily in Peabody, Massachusetts, where Enos scouted him starting in high school. He didn't throw hard enough to attract much Major League interest. Eligible for the 1975 draft after two years at a local community college and one year at Georgia Southern College, Tudor turned down the Mets after they picked him in the twenty-first round. Tudor's good showing for Falmouth in the Cape Cod League during the summer of 1975 stimulated Enos's interest, and the Red Sox signed him after his selection in the third round of the January 1976 draft. Tudor wound up his twelve-year Major League with an excellent won-lost record of 117-72 and a 3.12 ERA. He pitched in two World Series for the Cardinals.[38]

Enos was fast becoming a legend in Cape Cod baseball circles. When he arrived to see a summer league game, fans and young admirers that yearned to become scouts gravitated to him. Players knew when he was there and tried not to feel extra pressure. Ken Ryan, whom Enos signed late in his career and would become a Boston bullpen stalwart in the 1990s, remembered being puzzled when he noticed the scout sitting on his folding chair facing away from the field. He found out later that Enos felt Ryan didn't know how to warm up correctly and didn't show his good stuff on the mound until the third or fourth inning.[39]

Enos's experience in the Cape league was not lost on Commissioner Bowie Kuhn. Kuhn always had his hands full squaring off against Marvin Miller and the ascendant Major League Baseball Players Association, but he delighted in watching amateur baseball and wanted to develop improved relationships between the pros and the colleges. In one of his last acts before he was not reelected by the owners as commissioner in 1984, Kuhn named Enos, along with Cleveland scout Bobby Malkmus and Twins scout Bob Oldis, a former Major League second baseman and catcher, respectively, as official (unpaid) liaisons between the Major Leagues and summer amateur baseball. Enos took the job very seriously, making sure that scheduling was consistently followed, umpiring was professional, lineups were posted for scouts, and playing fields were maintained well. He kept in mind how a field on the Cape might compare to the quirky dimensions of Fenway Park. Enos knew that the history of scouting was replete with evaluators coming to games to look at a hot prospect and discovering that someone unknown was making a good showing.

Like all the great scouts who came of age before the introduction of the draft, Enos loved signing and helping to develop undrafted players. The saga of Rich Gedman was one of his favorite stories about a player overlooked in high school who demonstrated enough tools and desire to become a Major Leaguer. Enos had always been impressed by the raw power of the Worcester, Massachusetts, native. He once saw him belt a mammoth home run over a basketball game being played beyond the outfield fence.[40] Yet in the June 1977 draft Gedman was passed over by all twenty-six teams. After a strong showing on the Cape, Enos signed Gedman and strongly urged him to lose weight, put away his first baseman's glove, and take up catching. When future Hall of Famer Carlton Fisk left the Red Sox for the White Sox after the 1980 season, the road to a starting position in Boston opened for Gedman.

Gedman started the 1981 season at the Red Sox's Triple-A farm team in Pawtucket, Rhode Island. He played in the late April game against the Rochester Red Wings that, when completed in June, became at thirty-three innings the longest game in professional baseball history. He wasn't around when the game was finished several weeks later because in early May he reported to the Red Sox. Gedman enjoyed a thirteen-year Major League career, mostly with Boston. He starred in the 1986 American League Championship Series against the California Angels but had the misfortune of not being able to corral Bob Stanley's wild pitch in sixth game of the World Series that preceded the game-ending error by Bill Buckner. An AL All-Star in 1985 and 1986, Gedman ended his career with a .252 batting average, .307 on-base percentage, .399 slugging average, 795 hits, 88 home runs, 382 RBIs, 236 walks, and 509 strikeouts. In the absorbing article that sportswriter Mike Hauser wrote about Bill Enos, Gedman was lavish in his praise. "He looked at my body shape and saw something that no one else saw," he marveled. "He saw something in me that I did not ever see in myself."[41]

Bill Enos's status in New England baseball circles continued to grow. *Cape Cod Times* writer Bill Higgins penned a vivid description of Enos, wearing "a shirt and shoes stained by tobacco juice. He moved slowly and wisely, seeing everything and hearing all."[42] As shown, Enos was one of those scouts who believed in the importance of family dynamics. Whenever he could, without becoming a pest, he wanted to assess a player's home life. He knew how to flatter a mother's meat loaf or her tasty cookies. There is a legend that he was so determined to sign a Williams College player that during the graduation ceremonies he put on a cap and gown and joined the procession just behind his target. Once the player received his diploma, he pulled him out of the line and got his signature on a contract. It seems more likely that he waited until after the ceremony and inked the player to his first professional contract when the magic hour of signing allowable in the days before the free agent draft arrived.[43]

Aspiring scouts were in awe of Bill Enos. If necessary, they would wait for hours after a Cape Cod game, eager for his advice and counsel. Ray Fagnant, a native of Chicopee in western Massachusetts, was a star catcher at Holyoke Catholic High School and played college ball at Assumption in Worcester. He went undrafted after his junior year in 1988, but the Pirates signed him to a Minor League contract. After two years in the Pittsburgh organization, the Red Sox signed him. He played two seasons in the Boston organization, reaching Double-A New Britain, Connecticut, in the Eastern League. His career batting average of .153 did not look promising. His age clock was ticking, and he began to wonder if he needed to give up his baseball dream. Backed by his math major from Assumption, he was already working off-seasons for the Cigna health insurance company.[44]

Bill Enos spotted Ray Fagnant as a comer he didn't want to lose. He saw his obvious passion for the game, intelligence, and work ethic. When Enos recommended that Fagnant read Mark Winegardner's classic biography of legendary Phillies scout Tony Lucadello, *Prophet of the Sandlots*, he read it and reread it and visited Lucadello's hometown of Fostoria, Ohio. He wanted to gaze upon the famous wall the size of a small shed that the scout had devised to test the reflexes and fielding agility of infielders. He took home a brick from Lucadello's invention as a memento. Fagnant's wife took a brick, too, and uses a facsimile of the wall in her softball coaching. As his career started, he created his own portable wall to travel with. As Bill Enos neared retirement age in 1992, the Red Sox gave the scout the rare privilege of naming his successors. When Fagnant learned that his mentor had tapped him, he considered it a "one hundred per cent honor."[45]

Enos's other choice as a replacement was a more veteran scout, Charles "Buzz" Bowers, another Massachusetts native. Born in Waltham and raised in Wayland, Bowers was an all-around athlete who starred in high school as a pitcher, football quarterback, and basketball forward—at six feet two he often jumped center. Bowers's skills impressed Newton High School coach Jeff Jones, an associate scout with the Red Sox, and he recommended him to a short summer league in Montpelier, Vermont. Future Hall of Famer Robin Roberts was one of Bowers's teammates, and he, too, was impressed. Roberts urged his alma mater Michigan State University to offer Bowers a scholarship. After two years in college, Bowers signed with the Phillies for a reported $5,000 bonus. His progress was interrupted by two years of service in the Korean War. By 1955 he had only reached Double-A in the Phillies organization, so after the season he retired. Pitching in 239 Minor League games, he compiled a record of 54-44 and a 3.38 ERA.[46]

Bowers returned to his home area where he served as Wayland High School's baseball, basketball, and ski coach. He also scouted for the Phillies and then the Dodgers for thirty years. Like Fagnant, he was thrilled when Enos chose him as a replacement. Bowers and Ray Fagnant became an effective duo; they signed such future Major League Red Sox players as infielder (now broadcaster) Lou Merloni and pitchers Manny Delcarmen, Craig Hansen, Carl Pavano, and Brian Rose. In 1997 Pavano was traded to the Montreal Expos in the deal that brought future Hall of Famer Pedro Martinez to Boston.

Following the example of his mentor, Bowers took great satisfaction in bringing in baseball players who might not reach the highest levels of the game but wound up as scouts or coaches or just ardent fans. As Joe Porrell, one of his former Wayland players who wound up coaching state title teams in 1988 and 1991, put it, Bowers "helped you in anything in life."[47] Afflicted with Parkinson's disease in his later years, Bowers still attended many games, often behind home plate, intently taking notes on the players. Buzz Bowers died in 2015 and in 2020 was elected to the Cape Cod Baseball Hall of Fame, where he joins two other scouts, Bill Enos and Lenny Merullo.

After Bill Enos handed the reins of his area over Ray Fagnant and Buzz Bowers in 1992, he received a monthly stipend as a consultant for the next ten years.[48] He saw the players that his successors signed and offered his opinions, but they made the decisions. He lost his desire to see much baseball after his wife died in 2000. He moved to Arizona after the 2002 season, so he was not around to see the Red Sox break the so-called curse of the Bambino in 2004—and in the most dramatic way, beating the Yankees in the playoffs after losing the first three games of the ALCS and then sweeping the Cardinals in the World Series. He was gratified when the Red Sox invited him to be their guest for Games One and Two of the Series. He also was the team's guest at the opening games of the 2007 World Series.

Bill Enos died in Scottsdale, Arizona, on December 10, 2014, at the age of ninety-three, not long after seeing one of his favorite players, second baseman Dustin Pedroia, inducted into the Arizona Fall League Hall of Fame.

Ray Fagnant has kept up Bill Enos's mission of giving back to the game, and somewhere in the great beyond Enos is smoking his big cigar and signaling his approval. For over ten years, Fagnant and Yankees northeastern scout Matt Hyde have organized a summer program for high school and younger college players. Prospects come from all over the country to improve their baseball techniques by learning from experienced pro coaches and scouts. The sessions end with a game, often at Fenway Park but sometimes at Yankee Stadium, and in 2022 it was played at the Double-A Eastern League park in Hartford, Connecticut. For the climactic game of the summer program, one team is outfitted in Red Sox home uniforms and the other in Yankees road uniforms. Talk about a lifetime memory for older high schoolers and younger collegians! "Though Matt Hyde is obviously a rival of mine on the larger scale, we have both enjoyed the spirit of cooperation in teaching the game on the lower levels," Fagnant said—competitors and colleagues in the best sense.[49]

Since August 2020, the concluding game has been called the Kelly Rodman Memorial Classic. At a time when Major League Baseball is making a concerted effort to bring women into the game on every level, Kelly Anne Rodman was one of the recent pioneers. She displayed a passion for diamond sports from an early age by playing softball in middle school. She became a four-year starter, a left-handed-hitting outfielder at Eastern Connecticut State University, not far from her home in Wallingford. Afterward, she spent twelve years playing for the Lynn (Massachusetts) Lady Spirits in the National Women's Baseball League. She traveled the world, playing in the Dominican Republic, Japan, the Netherlands, and other countries to satisfy her passion. When she retired as a player, working for a sports apparel company enabled her to make connections with American baseball organizations. She expanded her horizons by volunteering for such charities as sportscaster Ed Randall's Fans for the Cure, which raises prostate cancer awareness, and White Sox scout John Tumminia's Baseball Miracles, which, until its cessation in 2022, put on baseball clinics and brought baseball equipment to underserviced regions both nationally and internationally.[50]

In the fall of 2013, she was invited to enroll in Major League Baseball's intensive three-week Scout School, unfortunately no longer extant. She excelled in the program and received offers from several teams, but the Yankees won the services of a onetime Mets fan who was now all in for her new employer. She started as an associate scout in 2014, and in 2017 she had become a full-time Yankees scout, only one of three women scouts in baseball at the time. She always liked working with younger players, and she taught them two simple mantras: "Go for it!" and "Be great today!"

I will never forget her leading a Baseball Miracles clinic for players of pre–junior high school age in Newburgh, New York, on a wintry Sunday in 2016. The event was held in an old armory that had been restored by the philanthropy of a local manufacturer. The kids were assigned different stations to learn the tools of running and hitting and fielding. As in clinics for older students and possible pro prospects, the participants had to run to each post. There was Kelly leading the kids joyously through their paces, extorting them to keep up with her and get ready for the new adventures awaiting them. I thought of Rogers Hornsby leading Bill Enos and other youngsters through their paces at Ray Doan's All-American Baseball School nearly a century earlier.

About a year or so later, Kelly received the diagnosis of a malignant brain tumor. She fought the disease with her customary passion and work ethic. Her flowing strawberry-blonde hair disappeared and then grew back, but remission was only temporary. She was only forty-four when she died on March 4, 2020. It is fitting that she will be remembered not only on the Fenway Park scoreboard during the annual late-August Kelly Rodman Memorial Classic but wherever players are gathering to test themselves on a level playing field with determination and passion and joy—indeed "going for it!" Kelly Rodman certainly answered in a positive way the questions that scout Julian Mock posed and listed in this book's introduction. She surely loved the game of baseball, worked harder than she ever had before, was willing to learn new things, was able to laugh every day, and never forgot where she came from.

NOTES

Introduction

1. Fabian Ardaya, "How Mike Trout Became the Centerpiece of the Angels' Epic 2009 Draft Class," The Athletic, March 26, 2019, https://theathletic.com/888430/2019 /03/26.
2. Roland Hemond, "Interview: Roland Hemond on 63 Years of Baseball," interview by Rob Neyer, SBNation, June 20, 2013, https://www.sbnation.com/2013/6/20/4447638 /roland-hemond-interview-buck-oneil-award-winner-diamondbacks.
3. Lindbergh and Sawchik, *MVP Machine*, 19.
4. Phillips, *Scouting and Scoring*, 140.
5. Kerrane, *Dollar Sign on the Muscle*, 107.
6. Dragseth, *Eye for Talent*, 221.

Prologue

1. Robert Creamer, "The Three Worlds of Birdie Tebbetts: Portrait of a Manager in a Setting of Snowdrifts and Kitchen Tables," *Sports Illustrated*, February 25, 1957, https://vault.si .com/vault/1957/02/25/the-three-worlds-of-birdie-tebbetts.
2. Tebbetts and Morrison, *Birdie*, 169.
3. Cleon Walpoort, "Tebbetts Tries to Be Ahead of the Game," *Milwaukee Journal*, June 19, 1961.
4. Tom Simon, "Birdie Tebbetts," SABR BioProject, n.d., https://sabr.org/bioproj/person /birdie-tebbetts.
5. Jay Feldman, "Make Scouts Eligible for Cooperstown," *Sports Illustrated*, February 5, 1990, https://vault.si.com/vault/1990/02/05/make-scouts-eligible-for-cooperstown.
6. Frank Litsky, obituary of Birdie Tebbetts, "Birdie Tebbetts: Plain Speaker with 53-Year Baseball Career," *New York Times*, March 26, 1999.

7. Karen E. Bush, "Aloysius 'Wish' Egan Remembered," July 18, 2009, https://www
.vintagedetroit.com/legendary-detroit-tigers-scout-aloysius-wish-egan-remembered/;
Red Smith, "The World of George Robert (Birdie) Tebbetts," *New York Times*, Sunday
April 6, 1980.

8. Michael Globetti, "Tebbetts Back at the Ballyard with New Cause," *Boston Herald*, 1988,
Anne Enos private collection. I thank Anne Enos, Bill's daughter, for providing the
clipping from her archive. It has no date besides the year but was probably from early
summer.

9. Tebbetts and Morrison, *Birdie*, 151.

10. Tebbetts and Morrison, *Birdie*, 169.

11. "A Game of Inches," *Time*, July 8, 1957, quoted in Tebbetts and Morrison, *Birdie*, xv.

12. Globetti, "Tebbetts Back at the Ballyard."

13. Globetti, "Tebbetts Back at the Ballyard."

1. Charley Barrett and Branch Rickey

1. Mitchell, *Mr. Rickey's Redbirds*, 111.

2. Sandoval, "Charley Barrett," 10.

3. Polner, *Branch Rickey*, 62.

4. Mitchell, *Mr. Rickey's Redbirds*, 58; Steve Steinberg, "Robert Hedges," SABR BioProject,
n.d., https://sabr.org/bioproj/person/robert-hedges.

5. Sandoval, "Charley Barrett," 10.

6. Steinberg, "Robert Hedges."

7. Steinberg, "Robert Hedges."

8. Lowenfish, *Branch Rickey*, 71.

9. Sandoval, "Charley Barrett." 10.

10. Lowenfish, *Branch Rickey*, 65.

11. Huhn, *Sizzler*, 78–80.

12. Steinberg, "Robert Hedges."

13. Dwayne Isgrig, "Muddy Ruel," SABR BioProject, n.d., https://sabr.org/bioproj/person
/muddy-ruel. He probably got his nickname from coming home so often with mud on
his clothes after all his activity behind the plate.

14. Mark Pelesh, "Away Flies the Boy," Hardball Times, October 15, 2015, https://tht
.fangraphs.com/away-flies-the-boy/.

15. Isrig, "Muddy Ruel."

16. Pelish, "Away Flies the Boy."

17. Bill Johnson, "Hank Severeid," SABR BioProject, n.d., https://sabr.org/bioproj/person
/hank-severeid.

18. Mitchell, *Mr. Rickey's Redbirds*, 80.

19. Mitchell, *Mr. Rickey's Redbirds*, 99.

20. Steve Steinberg, "Bill Doak," SABR BioProject, n.d., https://sabr.org/bioproject/person/bill-doak; Gomez and Goldstone, *Lefty*, 40.

21. Mitchell, *Mr. Rickey's Redbirds*, 71; Steve Steinberg, "Bob Connery," SABR BioProject, n.d., https://sabr.org/bioproject/person/bob-connery.

22. Rickey, *American Diamond*, 56.

23. Mitchell, *Mr. Rickey's Redbirds*, 86.

24. A. Mann, *Branch Rickey: American in Action*, 74.

25. Mark Armour, "Sam Breadon," SABR BioProject, n.d., https://sabr.org/bioproject/person/sam-breadon.

26. Mitchell, *Mr. Rickey's Redbirds*, 86.

27. Lowenfish, *Branch Rickey*, 118.

28. Lowenfish, *Branch Rickey*, 124.

29. Mitchell, *Mr. Rickey's Redbirds*, 195.

30. Mitchell, *Mr. Rickey's Redbirds*, 183.

31. Nancy Snell Griffith, "Flint Rhem," SABR BioProject, n.d., https://sabr.org/bioproject/person/flint-rhem.

32. Warren Corbett, "Tommy Thevenow," SABR BioProject, n.d., https://sabr.org/bioproject/person/tommy-thevenow.

33. Smiley and Sandoval, "Charles 'Pop' Kelchner," 8.

34. Smiley and Sandoval, "Charles 'Pop' Kelchner," 8.

35. Smiley and Sandoval, "Charles 'Pop' Kelchner," 8.

36. Chapman, "Second Rate Scout," 6.

37. Chapman, "Adventures of Professorial Scout," 3.

38. Sandoval, "Charles Edward Chapman," 16–17.

39. Chapman, "Adventures of a Professorial Scout," 9.

40. *New York Times*, "St. Louis in Frenzy as Cardinals Win," October 11, 1926.

41. "Barrett, Cardinal Scout, Is Honored," *St. Louis Post-Dispatch*, October 13, 1926.

42. Runyon, "Chain Store Baseball," 406–7.

43. W. J. McGoogan, "Barrett Played a Strong Role in Building Great Cardinal System," *St. Louis Post-Dispatch*, July 6, 1939.

44. Lowenfish, *Branch Rickey*, 173.

45. A. Mann, *Branch Rickey: American in Action*, 89.

46. *Fireman, Save My Child*, directed by Lloyd Bacon.

47. Norm King, "Pepper Martin," SABR BioProject, n.d., https://sabr.org/bioproj/person/pepper-martin.

48. Harry Grayson, "Martin on the Basepath," *Santa Ana (CA) Register*, March 16, 1932.

49. Heinz, "Happiest Hooligan," in *Top of His Game*, 264.

50. King, "Pepper Martin."

51. Karst and Jones, *Who's Who in Professional Baseball*, 257.

52. John J. Watkins, "Taylor Douthit," SABR BioProject, n.d., https://sabr.org/bioproj/person/taylor-douthit/.

53. Matthew Carter, "Shortstops: A Dash of Pepper," National Baseball Hall of Fame, n.d., https://baseballhall.org/discover/shortstops/a-dash-of-pepper.

54. Heinz, "Happiest Hooligan," 257.

55. Boxerman and Boxerman, *Bill DeWitt, Sr.*, 20.

56. Hood, *Gashouse Gang*, 67.

57. Harry Grayson, "50 Games for $50," *Santa Ana (CA) Register*, August 13, 1934.

58. Fred Stein, "Carl Hubbell," SABR BioProject, n.d., https://sabr.org/biorpoject/person/carl-hubbell.

59. Charles F. Faber, "Joe Medwick," SABR BioProject, n.d., https://sabr.org/bioproj/person/joe-medwick/.

60. Lowenfish, *Branch Rickey*, 260–63.

61. King, "Pepper Martin."

62. Heinz, "Happiest Hooligan," 273.

63. McGoogan, "Barrett Played a Strong Role."

64. Lowenfish, *Branch Rickey*, 596.

65. Lowenfish, *Branch Rickey*, 596.

66. Lowenfish, *Branch Rickey*, 292–93.

67. Gene Karst, in discussion with author, St. Louis MO, August 4, 2001.

68. Karst and Jones, *Who's Who in Professional Baseball*, 52.

69. Sandoval, "Charley Barrett," 10.

70. Anna McDonald, "Pruitt Heir Remembers Ruthian Legacy," ESPN, March 2, 2014, https://www.espn.com/blog/sweetspot/post/_/id/44743/pruitt-heir-remembers-ruthian-legacy.

71. Chapman, "Second Rate Scout," 6.

72. Chapman and Severeid, *Play Ball!*, xi.

73. Chapman and Severeid, *Play Ball!*, 4.

74. Chapman and Severeid, *Play Ball!*, 224.

75. Spink, *Judge Landis*, 199–203.

76. Evelyn Smith, "Angels Scout Gives Dodgers Nod for '63," *Palos Verdes Peninsula News*, April 11, 1963.

77. Warren Corbett, "George Kissell," SABR BioProject, n.d., https://sabr.org/bioproject/person/george-kissell.

78. Corbett, "George Kissell."

79. Rory Costello, "Al McBean," SABR BioProject, n.d., https://https://sabr.org/bioproj/person/al-mcbean/. Thanks go to retired scout Larry D'Amato for first telling me the story of McBean's signing.

80. Lowenfish, "Eyeball to Eyeball," 99.

2. Paul Krichell

1. Dave Camerer, "Secret Weapon of the Yankees," *Esquire*, May 1957, 155.
2. Frederick C. Lieb, "Criss-Crossing Talent Trails with Krichell," *Sporting News*, April 20, 1939, 3.
3. "Collision with Ty Cobb Left Lasting Impression on Paul," *Sporting News*, June 14, 1957, 28.
4. Frederick C. Lieb, "Cutting the Plate with Fred Lieb," March 4, 1932, 3.
5. Dave Camerer, "Secret Weapon of the Yankees," *Esquire*, May 1957, 154.
6. Heinz, *Top of His Game*, 192.
7. Camerer, "Secret Weapon," 155.
8. R. Robinson and Jennison, *Pennants and Pinstripes*, 29.
9. Tara Krieger, "Andy Coakley," SABR BioProject, n.d., https://sabr.org/bioproject/person/andy-coakley.
10. R. Robinson, *Iron Horse*, 47.
11. Krieger, "Andy Coakley."
12. Dom Amore, "From Gehrig to Bagwell, a Proud History of Baseball in Connecticut," *Hartford Courant*, March 2, 2014, https://www.courant.com/courant-250/moments-in-history/hc-from-gehrig-to-bagwell-a-proud-history-of-baseball-in-connecticut-20140301-htmlstory.html.
13. Heinz, *Top of His Game*, 192.
14. Heinz, *Top of His Game*, 194.
15. Daniel R. Levitt, "Paul Krichell," SABR BioProject, n.d., https://sabr.org/bioproject/person/paul-krichell.
16. Baldassaro, *Tony Lazzeri*, 2.
17. Levitt, *Ed Barrow*, 133; Baldassaro, *Tony Lazzeri*, 34.
18. J. G. Taylor Spink, "He Digs Up Diamonds for the Yanks," *Sporting News*, February 17, 1954, 3.
19. Red Smith, "Players of the Year," *Baseball Digest*, February 1949, 42.
20. Gomez and Goldstone, *Lefty*, 141.
21. Kyle Crichton, "A Yankee Scout," *Colliers*, March 12, 1938, 18.
22. Jesse Temple, "Bill Essick," *Alumni Review (Knox College)*, Summer 2009, 97.
23. Daniel R. Levitt, "Bill Essick," SABR BioProject, n.d., https://sabr.org/bioproject/person/bill-essick.
24. Ralph Berger, "Jimmie Reese," SABR BioProject, n.d., https://sabr.org/bioproj/person/jimmie-reese/. Reese Ryan has become a prominent baseball business executive.
25. Vernona Gomez, email to author, March 10, 2021.

26. Levitt, "Bill Essick."

27. Tara Krieger, "Frankie Crosetti," SABR BioProject, n.d., https://sabr.org/bioproj/person/frankie-crosetti/, reprinted in Spatz, *Bridging Two Dynasties*, 82.

28. Levy, *Joe McCarthy*, 147–48.

29. Dwayne Kling, "Joe Devine," SABR BioProject, n.d., https://sabr.org/bioproj/person/joe-devine.

30. Ritter, *Glory of Their Times*, 332–33.

31. Ritter, *Glory of Their Times*, 338.

32. Parker, *Big Poison and Little Poison*, 48.

33. Joseph Wancho, "Paul Waner," SABR BioProject, n.d., https://sabr.org/bioproject/person/paul-waner.

34. Armour, *Joe Cronin*, 15, 19.

35. Armour, *Joe Cronin*, 37.

36. Joseph Wancho, "Joe Gordon," SABR BioProject, n.d., https://sabr.org/bioproject/person/joe-gordon.

37. "Bill Essick Is Still on Talent Hunt," *St. Joseph News-Press Gazette*, July 5, 1942.

38. Chapman, "Second Rate Scout," 9; Bobby Brown, phone discussion with author, September 8, 2020.

39. Bill Nowlin, "Bill Wight," SABR BioProject, n.d., https://sabr.org/bioproject/person/bill-wight, reprinted in Spatz, *Bridging Two Dynasties*, 250.

40. Nowlin, "Bill Wight"; Spatz, *Bridging Two Dynasties*, 251.

41. Walter Judge, Judge's Bench, *San Francisco Examiner*, January 26, 1951.

42. Obituary of Joe Devine, *Sporting News*, October 15, 1951.

43. Joseph Wancho, "Bill Dickey," SABR BioProject, n.d., https://sabr.org/bioproject/person/bill-dickey.

44. Wancho, "Bill Dickey."

45. Mark Stewart, "Spud Chandler," SABR BioProject, n.d., https://sabr.org/bioproject/person/spud-chandler.

46. Stewart, "Spud Chandler."

47. Kerrane, *Dollar Sign on the Muscle*, 223. John Coleman "Johnny" Nee died on April 22, 1957, in St. Petersburg, Florida.

48. Kerrane, *Dollar Sign on the Muscle*, 243.

49. Obituary of Richard Goldstein, *New York Times*, November 12, 2000.

50. Stewart, "Spud Chandler."

51. Thomas Van Hyning, "Atley Donald," SABR BioProject, n.d., https://sabr.org/bioproject/person/atley-donald.

52. Rory Costello, "Clint Courtney," SABR BioProject, n.d., https://sabr.org/bioproject/person/clint-courtney.

53. Dave Anderson, "Atley Donald Not Rehired by Yankees," *New York Times*, March 20, 1978.

54. John Vorperian, "Johnny Murphy," SABR BioProject, n.d., https://sabr.org/biopreject /person/johnny-murphy.

55. Vorperian. "Johnny Murphy."

56. Rolfe, *View from the Dugout*, 7.

57. Cort Vitty, "Red Rolfe," SABR BioProject, n.d., https://sabr.org/bioproj/person/red -rolfe/.

58. Nelson "Chip" Greene, "Charlie Keller," SABR BioProject, n.d., https://sabr.org/bioproj /person/red-rolfe, reprinted in Spatz, *Bridging Two Dynasties*, 116.

59. Spink, "He Digs Up Diamonds," 3.

60. Lawrence Baldassaro, "Vic Raschi," SABR BioProject, n.d., https://sabr.org/bioproject /person/vic-raschi, reprinted in Spatz, *Bridging Two Dynasties*, 139.

61. Camerer, "Secret Weapon," 153.

62. Camerer, "Secret Weapon," 157.

63. Don Harrison, "Spec Shea," SABR BioProject, n.d., https://sabr.org/bioproj/person /spec-shea, reprinted in Spatz, *Between Two Dynasties*, 127.

64. Harrison, "Spec Shea," 130.

65. Durocher and Linn, *Nice Guys Finish Last*, 124.

66. Lowenfish and Marshall, "Branch Rickey versus Larry MacPhail," 230.

67. Kreuz, "Tom Greenwade," 47.

68. Kreuz, "Tom Greenwade," 44.

69. Warren Corbett, "Hank Bauer," SABR BioProject, n.d., https://sabr.org/bioproj/person /hank-bauer.

70. Corbett, "Hank Bauer."

71. Robert Pearson, obituary of Tom Greenwade, *Washington Post*, August 14, 1986.

72. James McDonald, "Lou Maguolo," SABR BioProject, n.d., https://sabr.org/bioproj/person /lou-maguolo.

73. Mitchell, *Mr. Rickey's Redbirds*, 211.

74. McDonald, "Lou Maguolo."

75. Richard Goldstein, "Bill Skowron, Slugger in Yankee Golden Era, Dies at 81," *New York Times*, April 27, 2012.

76. Tony Kubek, phone discussion with author, January 21, 2021.

77. Kubek, discussion.

78. McDonald, "Lou Maguolo."

79. Jerry Krause, discussion with author, Los Angeles, California, January 10, 2010.

80. Bobby Richardsdon, phone discussion with author, October 21, 2020.

81. Boxerman and Boxerman, *George Weiss*, 40.

82. Camerer, "Secret Weapon," 157.

83. Heinz, *Top of His Game*, 195–96.

84. Camerer, "Secret Weapon," 152.

85. Snelling, *Glimpse of Fame*, 234.

86. Gregory H. Wolf, "Tom Carroll," SABR BioProject, n.d., https://sabr.org/bioproj/person/tom-carroll.

87. Kelley, *Baseball's Biggest Blunder*, 89.

88. Dan Cichalski, "Youngest Yankee to Appear in World Series Dies at 85," MLB.com, October 2, 2021, https://www.mlb.com/news/tom-carroll-youngest-yankee-to-appear-in-world-series-dies-at-85.

89. Obituary of Paul Krichell, *New York Times*, June 6, 1957.

90. Rick Swaine, "Bob Thurman," SABR BioProject, n.d., https://sabr.org/bioproj/person/bob-thurman.

91. Gregory H. Wolf, "Mel Stottlemyre," SABR BioProject, n.d., https://sabr.org/bioproject/person/bob-thurman; David Eskenazi and Steve Rudman, "Wayback Machine: Pint-Sized Eddie Taylor," SportspressNW.com, September 11, 2012, https://www.sportspressnw.com/2137536/2012/wayback-machine-pint-sized-eddie-taylor.

92. Warren Corbett, "Michael Burke," SABR BioProject, n.d., https://sabr.org/bioproj/person/michael-burke.

93. J. Mann, *Decline and Fall*, 184.

94. Russo and Hammel, *Super Scout*, 33.

95. Frank Cashen, phone discussion with author, February 27, 2013.

96. Kelley, *Pastime in Turbulence*, 121.

97. Dan Holmes, "Willie Horton," SABR BioProject, n.d., https://sabr.org/bioproj/person/willie-horton.

98. Jerry Nechai, "Mickey Stanley," SABR BioProject, n.d., https://sabr.org/bioproj/person/mickey-stanley.

3. Red Murff

1. Joe Healing, "Murff Dealing for Talent at Camp Gary Job Corps," *Sporting News*, November 6, 1965.

2. Phil Hicks, "Murff's Career Forever Linked with Ryan's," *Tyler Tribune*, January 6, 2002.

3. Murff and Capps, *Scout*, 290.

4. Michael J. Bielawa, "Red Murff," SABR BioProject, n.d., https://sabr.org/bioproj/person/red-murff.

5. Bill White, phone conversation with author, November 11, 2020.

6. Bielawa, "Red Murff."

7. Hicks, "Murff's Career."

8. Buzzie Bavasi, "The Real Secret of Trading," *Sports Illustrated*, June 5, 1967, https://www
.si.com/vault/1967/06/05610053.the-real-secret-of-trading.

9. Murff and Capps, *Scout*, 90.

10. Joseph Wancho, "Jerry Grote," SABR BioProject, n.d., https://sabr.org/bioproj/person
/jerry-grote.

11. Murff and Capps, *Scout*, 71.

12. Murff and Capps, *Scout*, 77–78.

13. Irv Goldfarb, "Jerry Koosman," SABR BioProject, n.d., https://sabr.org/bioproject/person
/jerry-koosman; Jack Lang, "Mets Uncover a Sleeper in Mound Whiz Koosman," *Sporting
News*, April 27, 1968, 27.

14. Lang, "Mets Uncover Sleeper."

15. Maxwell Kates, "Tom Seaver," SABR BioProject, n.d., https://sabr.org/bioproj/person
/tom-seaver.

16. Murff and Capps, *Scout*, 123–26.

17. Mike Bender, "Ken Boswell," SABR BioProject, n.d., https://sabr.org/bioproj/person
/ken-boswell.

18. Douglas McDaniel, "A Scout with Honor: The Man Who Discovered Nolan Ryan,"
Bleacher Report, July 11, 2009, https://bleacherreport.com/articles/216158-a-scout-with
-honor-the-man-who-discovered-nolan-ryan.

19. Simpson, *Baseball America's Ultimate Draft Book*, 301.

20. McDaniel, "Scout with Honor."

21. Hicks, "Murff's Career."

22. Talmage Boston, "Nolan Ryan," SABR BioProject, n.d., https://sabr.org/bioproj/person
/nolan-ryan.

23. Boston, "Nolan Ryan."

24. Hicks, "Murff's Career."

25. Boston, "Nolan Ryan."

26. Because the Mets had more farm teams than some other clubs, Ryan was actually their
twelfth overall pick in the inaugural free agent draft. Simpson, *Baseball America's Ultimate
Draft Book*, 33.

27. Murff and Capps, *Scout*, 21.

28. Jim Bretz Sr., Lexington Giants general manager, phone conversation with author, March
26, 2021.

29. "Brine for Nolan Ryan," *Life*, May 31, 1968, 29–30.

30. Boston, "Nolan Ryan."

31. Boston, "Nolan Ryan."

32. Bob Trostler, "Burt Hooton," SABR BioProject, n.d., https://sabr.org/bioproj/person
/burt-hooton.

33. Emil Tagliabue, "Red Murff: Better Late Than Never," *Corpus Christi Times*, January 17, 1977.

34. Bronfman and Green, *Distilled*, 75–85.

35. Bronfman and Green, *Distilled*, 85.

36. Rory Costello, "John McHale," SABR BioProject, n.d., https://sabr.org/bioproj/person /john-mchale.

37. Didier and Sullivan, *Podnuh*, 24; Rory Costello, "Mel Didier," SABR BioProject, n.d., https://sabr.org/bioproj/person/mel-didier.

38. Elena Arcaro Didier, email message to author, November 20, 2021.

39. Costello, "Mel Didier."

40. Didier and Sullivan, *Podnuh*, 40–42.

41. Norm King, "Bill Stoneman," SABR BioProject, n.d., https://sabr.org/bioproj/person /bill-stoneman.

42. Murff and Capps, *Scout*, 242.

43. David Skelton, "John Bateman," SABR BioProject, n.d., https://sabr.org/bioproj/person /john-bateman.

44. Skelton, "John Bateman."

45. Kevin Glew, "Ex-Expos and Ex–Blue Jays: Whatever Happened To? . . . Balor Moore," *Cooperstowners in Canada* (blog), February 25, 2016, https://cooperstownersincanada .com/2016/02/25/ex-expos-and-ex-blue-jays-whatever-happened-to-balor-moore/.

46. Didier and Sullivan, *Podnuh*, 75.

47. Norm King, "Steve Rogers," SABR BioProject, n.d., https://sabr.org/bioproj/person /steve-rogers.

48. Stargell and Bird, *Willie Stargell*, 53–55.

49. Norm King, "Ellis Valentine," SABR BioProject, n.d., https://sabr.org/bioproj/person /ellis-valentine.

50. Didier and Sullivan, *Podnuh*, 15–22.

51. Didier and Sullivan, *Podnuh*, 66.

52. Didier and Sullivan, *Podnuh*, 69.

53. Murff and Capps, *Scout*, 181.

54. Didier and Sullivan, *Podnuh*, 87.

55. Kevin T. Czerwinski, "Kuehl Combined Smarts, Strong Resolve," MLB.com, April 9, 2008, https://www.milb.com/news/kuehl-combined-smarts-strong-resolve-312696274.

56. Didier and Sullivan, *Podnuh*, 92.

57. Didier and Sullivan, *Podnuh*, 84.

58. Damberger, *Scout's Honor*; Didier and Arbic, *Power Baseball*, 4, 114.

59. Nick Waddell, "Mike Stanton," SABR BioProject, n.d., https://sabr.org/bioproj/person /mike-stanton.

60. Murff and Capps, *Scout*, 244.

61. Brunt, *Diamond Dreams*, 87.

62. King, "Al LaMacchia," 76–77.

63. Sandoval, "Epy Guerrero," 103–4.

64. Don Scott, "With Eye for Talent, Bob Engle Enjoyed Amazing Professional Baseball Scouting Career," Lebanon Sports Buzz, November 2, 2020, https://lebanonsportsbuzz .com/with-eye-for-talent-bob-engle-enjoyed-amazing-professional-baseball-scouting -career/.

65. Dragseth, *Major League Baseball Scouts*, s.v. "Welke, Don," 294.

4. Art Stewart

1. Stewart and Mellinger, *Art of Scouting*, 65.

2. Stewart and Mellinger, *Art of Scouting*, 68.

3. Stewart and Mellinger, *Art of Scouting*, 70, 74–75.

4. Kary Booher, "Art Stewart: Royals Scout Since '69 and the Man Who Drafted Bo," Missouri Sports Hall of Fame, January 21, 2016, http://mosportshalloffame.com/4804-2/.

5. Stewart and Mellinger, *Art of Scouting*, 73.

6. Stewart and Mellinger, *Art of Scouting*, 109–10.

7. Nathanson, *Bouton*, 29; Mark Armour, "Jim Bouton," SABR BioProject, n.d., https:// sabr.org/bioproj/person/jim-bouton.

8. Stewart and Mellinger, *Art of Scouting*, 182.

9. Stewart and Mellinger, *Art of Scouting*, 183.

10. Stewart and Mellinger, *Art of Scouting*, 190.

11. Stewart and Mellinger, *Art of Scouting*, 20.

12. Stewart and Mellinger, *Art of Scouting*, 18.

13. Dragseth, *Major League Baseball Scouts*, s.v. "Kamzic, Nick," 158.

14. Stewart and Mellinger, *Art of Scouting*, 118; Schmitt, *History of Badger Baseball*, 119.

15. Edwin Shrake, "The Richest Bonus Baby Ever," *Sports Illustrated*, July 6, 1964, https:// vault.si.com/vault/1964/07/06/the-richest-bonus-baby-ever.

16. Shrake, "Richest Bonus Baby."

17. Stewart and Mellinger, *Art of Scouting*, 120.

18. Shrake, "Richest Bonus Baby."

19. Shrake, "Richest Bonus Baby."

20. Shrake, "Richest Bonus Baby."

21. *Courtship of Rick Reichardt*, directed by John J. Sughrue Jr.

22. Shrake, "Richest Bonus Baby."

23. Lee Lowenfish, "Reichardt Headed to College Hall of Fame," MLB.com, June 23, 2015, https://www.mlb.com/news/rick-reichardt-headed-to-college-hall-of-fame/c-132378494.

24. Stewart and Mellinger, *Art of Scouting*, 122. After the early reluctance to publicize the draft, Major League Baseball started to televise it in 2002.
25. John Gabcik, "Stan Bahnsen," SABR BioProject, n.d., https://sabr.org/bioproj/person/stan-bahnsen.
26. Appel, *Munson*, 43–44.
27. J. Mann, *Decline and Fall*, 184.
28. Morgan, *Prescription for Success*, 242.
29. Hensler, *New Boys of Summer*, 20.
30. Armour and Levitt, *In Pursuit of Pennants*, 251–53.
31. Daniel R. Levitt, "Ewing Kauffman," SABR BioProject, n.d., https://sabr.org/bioproj/person/ewing-kauffman.
32. Len Pasculli, "Tom Poquette," SABR BioProject, updated March 7, 2021, https://sabr.org/bioproj/person/tom-poquette; Lois Brandenburg, "Ken Frailing: A Worthy Talent," *Appleton Press-Crescent*, March 17, 1968; Rob Neyer, "In the Major Leagues, Female Scouts Are Few. Their Skills Aren't," *New York Times*, March 28, 2016, https://www.nytimes.com/2016/03/29/sports/baseball/a-harder-look-at-female-scouts-shows-more-in-the-job-than-thought.html?searchResultPosition=1.
33. Puerzer, "Kansas City Royals' Baseball Academy," 5; Morgan, *Prescription for Success*, 246; Stewart and Mellinger, *Art of Scouting*, 201–14.
34. Puerzer, "Kansas City Royals' Baseball Academy," 6.
35. Puerzer, "Kansas City Royals' Baseball Academy," 10.
36. Puerzer, "Kansas City Royals' Baseball Academy," 7; Morgan, *Prescription for Success*, 255.
37. Morgan, *Prescription for Success*, 259.
38. Malcolm Allen, "U. L. Washington," SABR BioProject, n.d., https://sabr.org/bioproj/person/u-l-washington/.
39. Puerzer, "Kansas City Royals Baseball Academy," 7.
40. Morgan, *Prescription for Success*, 256.
41. Stewart and Mellinger, *Art of Scouting*, 214.
42. Stewart and Mellinger, *Art of Scouting*, 41, 45–47.
43. Gregory H. Wolf, "Dennis Leonard," SABR BioProject, n.d., https://sabr.org/bioproj/person/dennis-leonard. The article is also available in Nowlin, *Kansas City Royals*.
44. Andrew Sharp, "Tom Ferrick," SABR BioProject, n.d., https://sabr.org/bioproj/person/tom-ferrick.
45. Sharp, "Tom Ferrick."
46. Harold Rosenthal, "Ferrick to Join Tebbetts in Cincinnati," *Sporting News*, November 25, 1953, 5.
47. Sharp, "Tom Ferrick."
48. Sharp, "Tom Ferrick."

49. Rustin Dodd, "'A Giant as a Baseball Person': Fischer Was the Epitome of a Lifer," The Athletic, November 1, 2018, https://theathletic.com/627085/2018/11/01; Bob LeMoine, "Bill Fischer," SABR BioProject, n.d., https://sabr.org/bioproj/person/bill-fischer.

50. LeMoine, "Bill Fischer."

51. Brian Engelhardt, "Clint Hurdle," SABR BioProject, updated April 1, 2018, https://sabr.org/bioproject/person/clint-hurdle.

52. Engelhardt, "Clint Hurdle."

53. Dodd, "'Giant as a Baseball Person.'"

54. Morgan, *Prescription for Success*, 264; Joe McGuff, "Royals Cut Scouting Staff," *Sporting News*, November 23, 1974, 4.

55. Hank Peters, discussion with author, Baltimore, Maryland, July 20, 2002.

56. Alan Cohen, "Dick Howser," SABR BioProject, n.d., https://sabr.org/bioproj/person/dick-howser.

57. Steve Wulf, "Dan Quisenberry," SABR BioProject, updated February 21, 2021, https://sabr.org/bioproj/person/dan-quisenberry.

58. Roger Angell, "The Lives They Lived: Dan Quisenberry, the Sinkerball Poet," *New York Times Magazine*, January 3, 1999, https://www.nytimes.com/1999/01/03/magazine/the-lives-they-lived-dan-quisenberry-the-sinkerball-poet.html?searchResultPosition=1.

59. Wulf, "Dan Quisenberry."

60. Stewart and Mellinger, *Art of Scouting*, 25.

61. Stewart and Mellinger, *Art of Scouting*, 31.

62. Morgan, *Prescription for Success*, 286.

63. Stewart and Mellinger, *Art of Scouting*, 52.

64. Stewart and Mellinger, *Art of Scouting*, 77–82.

65. Stewart and Mellinger, *Art of Scouting*, 88–89.

66. Moore and Fulks, *More Than a Season*, 14.

67. Stewart and Mellinger, *Art of Scouting*, 260.

5. Gary Nickels

1. Kerrane, *Dollar Sign on the Muscle*, 223.

2. Gary Nickels, phone discussion with author, March 23, 2022.

3. Nickels, discussion, March 23, 2002.

4. Bob Verdi, "The Coach Proves a Champion Even as Time Runs Out," *Chicago Tribune*, November 26, 2000, https://www.chicagotribune.com/news/ct-xpm-2000-11-26-0011260337-story.html; Oscar Kahan, "College Summer League Saluted as Success," *Sporting News*, August 31, 1963, 5.

5. "Titans Invited to Play Cornell," *The Argus*, April 18, 1939, https://collections.carli.illinois.edu/digital/collection/iwu_argus/id/19017/rec/1; Obituary of Fred Young, *Pantagraph*, November 30, 1980, folder 1, item 2, Fred Young Collection, McLean County Museum

of History, Bloomington IL, https://mchistory.org/perch/resources/Finding/young -fred-collection.pdf.

6. Norm King, "Bobby Winkles," SABR BioProject, n.d., https://sabr.org/bioproj/person /bobby-winkles.

7. Sarah Zeller, "One Senator's Inspired Idea Led to a Great Moment in IWU History," *Ohio Wesleyan University Magazine*, Spring 2007, https://digitalcommons.iwu.edu/cgi /viewcontent.cgi?article=1155&context=iwumag.

8. Friend, *Chicken Runs at Midnight*.

9. Gary Nickels, discussion with author, January 10, 2011.

10. Dragseth, *Major League Baseball Scouts*, s.v. "Robertson, James Jackson 'Jax,'" 242.

11. Published in 1990, *Prophet of the Sandlots* became a posthumous tribute after the scout shocked the baseball world by committing suicide the previous May at the age of seventy-seven. Winegardner, *Prophet of the Sandlots*.

12. Winegardner, *Prophet of the Sandlots*, 5.

13. Richard Riis, "Johnny Lucadello," SABR BioProject, n.d., https://sabr.org/bioproj/person /johnny-lucadello/.

14. Winegardner, *Prophet of the Sandlots*, 97. "Pickers" refers to nitpickers who are always looking for something wrong in a player.

15. Winegardner, *Prophet of the Sandlots*, 3.

16. Winegardner, *Prophet of the Sandlots*, 258.

17. Kashatus, *Almost a Dynasty*, 93.

18. Kashatus, *Almost a Dynasty*, 36–37.

19. Frank Fitzpatrick, "Dallas Green, First Phillies Manager to Win World Series, Dies at 82," *Philadelphia Inquirer*, March 22, 2017.

20. John T. Cox Jr., phone discussion with author, March 20, 2022; Associated Press, obituary of Art Gaines, *New York Times*, November 15, 1975.

21. Cox, discussion, March 20, 2022.

22. Nickels, discussion, March 23, 2022.

23. Cox, discussion, March 20, 2022.

24. Cox, discussion, March 20, 2022.

25. John T. Cox Jr., phone discussion with author, March 25, 2022.

26. Colletti, *You Gotta Have Heart*, 57.

27. Nickels, discussion, March 23, 2022.

28. Nickels, discussion, March 23, 2022.

29. Jim Howard, discussion with author, January 20, 2012.

30. George Castle, "A Major Deal: Naperville North Graduate Jerry Hairston Jr. Develops as TV Baseball Analyst for Los Angeles Dodgers," *Naperville Sun*, September 27, 2020.

31. Fred Uhlman Sr., phone discussion with author, November 20, 2020.

32. Matt LeCren, "Fifty Years as an Amateur Scout," *Naperville Sun*, October 19, 2021.

6. Paul Snyder

1. Paul Snyder, phone discussion with author, September 22, 2019.
2. Andrew Sharp, "Jack Ogden," SABR BioProject, n.d., https://sabr.org/bioproj/person/jack-ogden/; Snyder, discussion.
3. Snyder, discussion.
4. Snyder, discussion.
5. Snyder, discussion.
6. Shanks, *Scout's Honor*, 43.
7. Alex Putterman, "The Forgotten Legacy of Bill Lucas," *The Atlantic*, June 4, 2017, https://www.theatlantic.com/entertainment/archive/2017/06/the-forgotten-legacy-of-bill-lucas/528828/.
8. E. Robinson and Rogers, *Lucky Me*, 164.
9. Putterman, "Forgotten Legacy."
10. Lee Walburn, "Bill Lucas," *Atlanta Magazine*, May 1, 2011, https://www.atlantamagazine.com/great-reads/bill-lucas/.
11. Putterman, "Forgotten Legacy."
12. Dusty Baker, in phone discussion with author, September 26, 2019; Ralph Garr, in discussion with author, New York City, November 9, 2019.
13. Snyder, discussion; Baker, discussion; Tony DeMacio, email message to author, December 16, 2019.
14. Hope, *We Could've Finished Last*, 188.
15. Hope, *We Could've Finished Last*, 156.
16. O'Connor, *Ted Turner*, 72–75.
17. Shanks, *Scout's Honor*, 45.
18. Shanks, *Scout's Honor*, 46.
19. O'Connor, *Ted Turner*, 74.
20. Walburn, "Bill Lucas."
21. Walburn, "Bill Lucas."
22. Hope, *We Could've Finished Last*; Putterman, "Forgotten Legacy."
23. Shanks, *Scout's Honor*, 48.
24. Shanks, *Scout's Honor*, 43; Paul Daugherty, "Jim Leyritz, Chipper Jones and Cal Ripken. Hep Cronin's Seen It All," Cincinnati.com, June 5, 2018, https://www.cincinnati.com/story/sports/columnists/paul-daugherty/2018/06/05/mlb-draft-insight-conversation-longtime-atlanta-braves-scout-hep-cronin-mick-cincinnati/673802002/.
25. Shanks, *Scout's Honor*, 87.
26. Dan Barry, "Loose Grip on a Ball, Tight Grip on Dream," *New York Times*, August 8, 1999.
27. Glavine and Cafardo, *None but the Braves*, 22–34; Tony DeMacio, email message to author, December 30, 2019.

28. Tony DeMacio, in phone discussion with author, November 1, 2019; Dragseth, *Major League Baseball Scouts*, s.v. "DeMacio, Tony," 75.

29. Simpson, *Baseball America's Ultimate Draft Book*, 294.

30. Shanks, *Scout's Honor*, 119.

31. John Ed Bradley, "Justice Prevails," *Sports Illustrated*, June 6, 1994.

32. Shanks, *Scout's Honor*, 111; Paul Snyder, phone discussion with author, January 8, 2020.

33. Shanks, *Scout's Honor*, 134.

34. Murff and Capps, *Scout*, 283.

35. Simpson, *Baseball America's Ultimate Draft Book*, 377.

36. Murff and Capps, *Scout*, 284–85.

37. DeMacio, email message to author, December 30, 2019; Jones and Walton, *Ballplayer*, 25–26.

38. Jones and Walton, *Ballplayer*, 13, 25–26, 30.

39. Jones and Walton, *Ballplayer*, 49–61; DeMacio, message, December 16, 2019. Dean Jongewaard, brother of Roger Jongewaard, the renowned scout who insisted the Mariners draft Ken Griffey Jr. as number-one pick in nation, was an expert Braves negotiator. He informed the Jones family that Chipper could have access to a full four-year college scholarship later in his career.

40. Fountain, *Under the March Sun*, 152.

41. Shanks, *Scout's Honor*, 49.

42. Charleston River Dogs, "Braves' Paul Snyder Inducted into Professional Baseball Scouts Hall of Fame," news release, June 16, 2013.

7. Gene Bennett

1. Robert Sawyer, "Gene Bennett," SABR BioProject, n.d., https://sabr.org/bioproj/person/gene-bennett/.

2. Gerry Brown, "Basketball Hall of Fame Has Come a Long Way," *Springfield (MA) Republican*, June 22, 2018.

3. Bennett, Hayes, and Brennaman, *Gene Bennett*, 21.

4. Sawyer, "Gene Bennett."

5. Sawyer, "Gene Bennett."

6. Sawyer, "Gene Bennett."

7. Sawyer, "Gene Bennett"; Dragseth, *Major League Baseball Scouts*, s.v. "Bennett, Walter Eugene 'Gene,'" 28.

8. Dragseth, *Major League Baseball Scouts*, s.v. "Consoli, Joe," 64.

9. Rory Costello, "Al Oliver," SABR BioProject, last updated July 10, 2019, https://sabr.org/bioproj/person/al-oliver/.

10. Costello, "Al Oliver."

11. Dragseth, *Major League Baseball Scouts*, s.v. "Consoli, Joe," 63–64.

12. Daniel E. Slotnik, "John Young, Promoter of Baseball for the Underprivileged, Dies at 67," *New York Times*, May 11, 2016.

13. Rick Swaine, "Bob Thurman," SABR BioProject, n.d., https://sabr.org/bioproj/person/bob-thurman/.

14. Gene Bennett, in discussion with author, Portsmouth, Ohio, August 30, 2011.

15. Larry D'Amato, phone discussion with author, March 29, 2022.

16. Gene Bennett, discussion.

17. Howsam and Jones, *My Life in Sports*, prologue.

18. Charles F. Faber, "Don Gullett," SABR BioProject, last updated May 1, 2014, https://sabr.org/bioproj/person/don-gullett/.

19. Hirsh, "Lessons from a Reds Legend."

20. Hirsh, "Lessons from a Reds Legend."

21. Bennett, Hayes, and Brennaman, *Gene Bennett*, 53.

22. Larry D'Amato, phone discussion with author, April 4, 2022.

23. Dragseth, *Major League Baseball Scouts*, s.v. "Zuraw, George," 310.

24. Dragseth, *Major League Baseball Scouts*, s.v. "Barton, Larry," 23.

25. Bennett, Hayes, and Brennaman, *Gene Bennett*, 75.

26. Bennett, Hayes, and Brennaman, *Gene Bennett*, 58.

27. Bennett, Hayes, and Brennaman, *Gene Bennett*, 134.

28. Bennett, Hayes, and Brennaman, *Gene Bennett*, 61.

29. Kevin Colley, "Bennett's Life Celebrated in Grand Fashion," *Portsmouth Daily Times*, January 11, 2018, https://www.portsmouth-dailytimes.com/news/23183/bennetts-life-celebrated-in-grand-fashion.

8. Billy Blitzer

1. Carrie Muskat, "Full Circle: Rings Mean World to Cubs Scouts," April 20, 2017, https://www.mlb.com/news/longtime-cubs-scouts-thrilled-to-receive-rings-c225462742.

2. Lowenfish, "29 Years," 47.

3. Muskat, "Full Circle."

4. Muskat, "Full Circle."

5. Billy Blitzer, "Billy Blitzer: Longtime Baseball Scout for the Chicago Cubs and Sea Gate Resident," interview by Kaara Baptiste, Coney Island History Project, January 31, 2018, audio, 32:43, https://www.coneyislandhistory.org/oral-history-archive/billy-blitzer.

6. Blitzer, interview.

7. Edwin Fernandez Cruz, "Juan Gonzalez," SABR BioProject, last updated August 1, 2018, https://sabr.org/bioproject/person/Juan-Gonzalez.

8. John Stokoe, discussion with author, January 25, 2012.

9. Billy Blitzer, phone discussion with author, March 23, 2022.

10. Lowenfish, "29 Years," 48.

11. Post, *Foresight 20/20*, 66.

12. Post, *Foresight 20/20*, 78.

13. Blitzer, discussion, March 23, 2022.

14. Norm King, "Bruce Sutter," SABR BioProject, last updated May 12, 2015, https://sabr
    .org/bioproject/person/bruce-sutter.

15. King, "Bruce Sutter."

16. Richard Goldstein, "Joe Niekro, a Master of the Knuckleball, Dies," *New York Times*,
    October 29, 2006.

17. Lenny Merullo, "Lenny Merullo (2000)," interview by Paul Motyka, SABR Oral History Collection, December 28, 2000, audio, 2:06:32, https://sabr.org/interview/lennie
    -merullo-2000/.

18. Blitzer, discussion, March 23, 2022.

19. George Biron, discussion with author, March 13, 2020.

20. Richard Goldstein, "Lennie Merullo, the Last Cub to Play in a World Series, Dies at 98,"
    New York Times, May 31, 2015.

21. Lowenfish, "Don't Get Too Domestic," 145.

22. Lowenfish, "Don't Get Too Domestic," 143.

23. McKenna, "Joe Cambria," 93.

24. Lowenfish, "Don't Get Too Domestic," 143.

25. Ira Berkow, "A Rumble in Valhalla," *New York Times*, July 22, 1991.

26. Lowenfish, "Don't Get Too Domestic," 143.

27. Ted Leavengood, "Hal Keller Remembered," SeamHeads.com, June 8, 2012, https://
    seamheads.com/2012/06/08/hal-keller-remembered/; Fox Sports, "Keller Remembered as Top-Notch Scout," June 5, 2012, https://www.foxsports.com/stories/mlb/keller
    -remembered-as-top-notch-scout.

28. Ray Birch, "Joe Foy," SABR BioProject, n.d., https://sabr.org/bioproject/person/joe-foy.

29. Sara Rimer, "From Washington Heights to Pros," *New York Times*, June 4, 1991.

30. Blitzer, discussion, March 23, 2022.

31. Neil Paine, "Bobby Bonilla Was More Than the Patron Saint of Bad Contracts,"
    Fivethirtyeight.com, September 30, 2010, https://fivethirtyeight.com/videos/bobby
    -bonilla-was-more-than-the-patron-saint-of-bad-contracts/.

32. Blitzer, discussion, March 23, 2022.

33. Gary Nickels, phone discussion with author, March 26, 2022.

34. Frederick C. Bush, "Jamie Moyer," SABR BioProject, last updated September 14, 2017,
    https://sabr.org/bioproj/person/jamie-moyer/.

35. Blitzer, discussion, March 23, 2022.

36. Brian Smith, "Former Phillies Pitcher Jamie Moyer Remembers Trips to Reading, 2008
    World Series Championship," *Reading Eagle*, last updated January 23, 2022, https://www
    .readingeagle.com/2022/01/22/moyerrememberstripstoreading/.

37. Bush, "Jamie Moyer."

38. Lowenfish, "29 Years," 52.

39. Moyer and Platt, *Just Tell Me I Can't*, 47.

40. Bush, "Jamie Moyer."

41. Billy Blitzer, discussion with author, July 17, 2015.

9. Bill Enos

1. Anne Enos, email message to author, September 20, 2019.

2. Mike Hauser, "Bill Enos Made a Career out of Creating Baseball Opportunities," *Leader-Herald* (Gloversville NY), October 17, 2020.

3. Anne Enos, email message to author, December 11, 2019.

4. Anne Enos, phone discussion with author, May 20, 2020.

5. Gay, *Satch, Dizzy & Rapid Robert*, 77–78.

6. Mark Blaeuer, "Reaching for the Brass Ring: A Portrait of Doan's Baseball's School," Hot Springs, Arkansas, Historic Baseball Trail, January 13, 2014, https://hotspringsbaseballtrail.com/untold-stories/reaching-brass-ring-portrait-doans-1937-baseball-school/; Jack Schnedler, "Play Ball! Historic Baseball Trail a Hit in Hot Springs," *Arkansas Living Magazine*, June 30, 2020, https://arkansaslivingmagazine.com/article/play-ball-historic-baseball-trail-a-hit-in-hot-springs/; Foley, *First Boys of Spring*.

7. Don Duren, "Lon Warkeke," SABR BioProject, n.d., https://sabr.org/bioproj/person/lon-warneke/.

8. Lowenfish, *Branch Rickey*, 265.

9. *Sporting News*, "Dean Offered $22,500, Ready to Bolt Cards," February 25, 1937, 1.

10. Anne Enos, email message to author, December 3, 2021.

11. Blaeuer, "Reaching for the Brass Ring."

12. Hauser, "Bill Enos Made Career."

13. Fred Stein, "Carl Hubbell," SABR BioProject, n.d., https://sabr.org/bioproj/person/carl-hubbell.

14. Anne Enos, email message to author, January 6, 2022.

15. C. Paul Rogers III, "Eddie Waitkus," SABR BioProject, n.d., https://sabr.org/bioproj/person/eddie-waitkus.

16. Anne Enos, email message, January 6, 2022.

17. Nowlin, "Bill Clark," 105; Bill Clark, phone discussion with author, November 16, 2021.

18. Anne Enos, email message, January 6, 2022.

19. Burleigh Grimes to Anne Enos, May 24, 1939, Anne Enos private collection.

20. Hauser, "Bill Enos Made Career."

21. Anne Enos, email message, January 6, 2022.

22. Anne Enos, email message, January 6, 2022.

23. Kerrane, *Dollar Sign on the Muscle*, 114.

24. Mike Klingaman, "Hank Peters, Former Oriole GM, Dies at 90," *Baltimore Sun*, January 4, 2015.

25. Sinha and Lajoie, *Character Is Not a Statistic*, 24.

26. Barry Stavro, "Red Sox Scout Stalks 'Prey' Tenaciously," *New York Times*, June 11, 1979.

27. Andrew Sharp, "Tommy Giordano," SABR BioProject, n.d., https://sabr.org/bioproj/person/tommy-giordano/.

28. Pete Caldera, "New Jersey's Tom Giordano, at 92 Years Old, Sharp as Ever as Major League Baseball Scout," Northjersey.com, July 7, 2018, https://www.northjersey.com/story/sports/mlb/yankees/2018/07/07/tom-giordano-92-years-old-mlb-scout-stays-sharp/762305002/.

29. Sharp, "Tommy Giordano."

30. Warren Corbett, "Hank Bauer," SABR BioProject, n.d., https://sabr.org/bioproj/person/hank-bauer.

31. Ryan Turnquist, "Former Seattle Pilot Ray Peters Visits the Hall of Fame," National Baseball Hall of Fame, June 12, 2015, https://baseballhall.org/discover-more/news/ray-peters-visits-hall-of-fame.

32. Larry Stone, "'An Unstable Roller Coaster': 50 Years Later, the Pilots Remain Seattle's Fun Fascination," *Seattle Times*, June 21, 2019, https://www.seattletimes.com/sports/mariners/it-was-a-one-season-roller-coaster-ride-at-sicks-stadium-50-years-later-the-pilots-remain-seattles-fun-fascination/.

33. Bill Nowlin, "Skip Lockwood," SABR BioProject, n.d., https://sabr.org/bioproj/person/skip-lockwood.

34. Nowlin, "Skip Lockwood."

35. Nowlin, "Skip Lockwood."

36. Steven Schmitt, "Ellie Rodriguez," SABR BioProject, last updated December 1, 2018, https://sabr.org/bioproj/person/ellie-rodriguez.

37. Robert Carroll, "His Fastball Is Gone, but His Quips Still Have Zing," *Boston Globe*, July 25, 2004.

38. Rory Costello, "John Tudor," SABR BioProject, last updated August 11, 2011, https://sabr.org/bioproj/person/john-tudor.

39. Bill Higgins, "'The Old Bull' Was One of a Kind," *Cape Cod Times*, December 21, 2014.

40. Mel Allen, "A Scout for All Seasons," *Yankee Magazine*, June 1980, clipping courtesy of Anne Enos. The writer Mel Allen is not the same person as the legendary New York Yankees broadcaster.

41. Hauser, "Bill Enos Made Career."

42. Higgins, "'Old Bull.'"

43. Anne Enos, email message to author, January 4, 2022.

44. Troy Watkins, "Dream Maker," *Assumption College Magazine*, Summer 1988, 20.

45. Ray Fagnant, phone discussion with author, August 20, 2019.

46. Higgins, "'Old Bull.'"
47. Higgins, "'Old Bull.'"
48. Anne Enos, email message, January 6, 2022.
49. Ray Fagnant, phone discussion with author, August 19, 2019.
50. Lori Riley, "Female MLB Scout from Wallingford Was a Trailblazer," *Hartford Courant*, March 15, 2020, https://www.courant.com/sports/hc-sp-riley-column-kelly-rodman -0315-20200315-w2arjlxwvrb37ehgqqp6imdr54-story.html.

BIBLIOGRAPHY

Amore, Dom. *A Franchise on the Rise: The First Twenty Years of the New York Yankees*. New York: Sports Publishing, 2018.

Appel, Marty. *Casey Stengel: Baseball's Greatest Character*. New York: Doubleday, 2017.

——. *Munson: The Life and Death of a Yankee Captain*. New York: Simon and Schuster, 2017.

Armour, Mark. *Joe Cronin: A Baseball Life*. Lincoln: University of Nebraska Press, 2014.

Armour, Mark, and Daniel R. Levitt. *In Pursuit of Pennants: From Deadball to Moneyball*. Lincoln: University of Nebraska Press, 2005.

Bacon, Lloyd, dir. *Fireman, Save My Child*. 1932; Burbank CA: Warner Brothers.

Baldassaro, Lawrence. *Tony Lazzeri: Yankees Legend and Baseball Pioneer*. Lincoln: University of Nebraska Press, 2021.

Bennett, Gene, Steven Hayes, and Marty Brennaman. *Gene Bennett: My 58 Years with the Cincinnati Reds*. Wheelersburg OH: self-published, 2016.

Boxerman, A. Burton, and Benita W. Boxerman. *George Weiss: Architect of the Golden Age Yankees*. Jefferson NC: McFarland, 2016.

——. *Bill DeWitt, Sr.: Patriarch of a Baseball Family*. Jefferson NC: McFarland, 2021.

Bronfman, Charles, and Howard Green. *Distilled: A Memoir of Family, Seagram, Baseball and Philanthropy*. Toronto: Harper Collins, 2016.

Brunt, Stephen. *Diamond Dreams: 20 Years of Blue Jays Baseball*. Toronto: Viking-Penguin, 1996.

Chapman, Charles. "Adventures of a Professional Scout." Unpublished manuscript, n.d. Box 1, SMSC 83/153c. Bancroft Library, University of California, Berkeley.

——. "A Second Rate Scout." Unpublished manuscript, n.d. Box 1, SMSC 83/153c. Bancroft Library, University of California, Berkeley.

Chapman, Charles E., and Henry L. Severeid. *Play Ball! Advice for Young Ballplayers*. New York: Harper & Brothers, 1941.

Coffey, Wayne. *They Said It Couldn't Be Done: The '69 Mets, New York City, and the Most Astounding Season in Baseball History*. New York: Crown Archetype, 2019.

Colletti, Ned. *You Gotta Have Heart: Dallas Green's Rebuilding of the Cubs*. South Bend IN: Diamond Communications, 1984.

Colletti, Ned, and Joseph A. Reaves. *The Big Chair: The Smooth Hops and Bad Bounces from the Inside World of the Acclaimed Los Angeles Dodgers General Manager*. New York: G. P. Putnam's Sons, 2017.

Couch, J. Hudson. *The Braves First Fifteen Years in Atlanta*. Atlanta: The Other Alligator Creek, 1984.

Creamer, Robert W. *Stengel: His Life and Times*. New York: Simon and Schuster, 1984.

Damberger, Francis, dir. *Scout's Honor: The Mel Didier Story*. Edmonton AB: SHMD Productions, 2014. DVD.

Day, Frederick J., and Raymond J. McKenna. *Feeling a Draft: Baseball Scouting and the First 50 Years of the Amateur Player Draft*. Bloomington IN: I-Universe, 2021.

Devine, Bing, and Tom Wheatley. *The Memoirs of Bing Devine: Stealing Lou Brock and Other Winning Moves by a Master GM*. New York: Sports Publishing, 2004.

Didier, Mel, and Gerry Arbic. *Power Baseball: Dynamic Techniques of Winning*. Toronto ON: Prentice-Hall Canada, 1972.

Didier, Mel, and T. R. Sullivan. *Podnuh Let Me Tell You a Story: A Baseball Life*. Baton Rouge LA: Gulf South Books, 2007.

Dragseth, P. J. *Baseball and the House of David: The Legendary Barnstorming Teams, 1915–1956*. Jefferson NC: McFarland, 2021.

———. *Major League Baseball Scouts: A Biographical Dictionary*. Jefferson NC: McFarland, 2012.

Durocher, Leo, and Edward Linn. *Nice Guys Finish Last*. New York: Simon and Schuster, 1975.

Eig, Jonathan. *Luckiest Man: The Life and Death of Lou Gehrig*. New York: Simon and Schuster, 2005.

Foley, Larry, dir. *The First Boys of Spring*. Hot Springs AR: Walter Lemke Department of Journalism, University of Arkansas Press, 2015. DVD.

Fountain, Charles. *Under the March Sun: The Story of Spring Training*. New York: Oxford University Press, 2009.

Friend, Tom. *The Chicken Runs at Midnight: A Daughter's Message from Heaven That Changed a Father's Heart and Won a World Series*. Grand Rapids MI: Zondervan, 2018.

Gay, Timothy M. *Satch, Dizzy & Rapid Robert: The Wild Saga of Interracial Baseball before Jackie Robinson*. New York: Simon and Schuster, 2010.

Genovese, George, and Dan Taylor. *Fate's Take-Out Slide: A Baseball Scout Recalls Can't-Miss Prospects Who Did Miss*. Jefferson NC: 2017.

———. *A Scout's Report: My 70 Years in Baseball*. Jefferson NC: McFarland, 2015.

Glavine, Tom, and Nick Cafardo. *None but the Braves: A Pitcher, a Team, a Champion*. New York: Harper Collins, 1996.

Goldis, Al, and John Wolff. *How to Make Pro Baseball Scouts Notice You: An Insider's Guide to Big League Scouting*. New York: Skyhorse, 2009.

Gomez, Vernona, and Lawrence Goldstone. *Lefty: An American Odyssey*. New York: Ballantine Books, 2012.

Heinz, W. C. *The Top of His Game: The Best Sportswriting of W. C. Heinz*. Edited by Bill Littlefield. New York: Library of America, 2015.

Hensler, Paul. *The New Boys of Summer: Baseball's Radical Transformation in the Late Sixties*. Lanham MD: Rowman and Littlefield, 2017.

Hirsh, Jeff, reporter. "Lessons from a Reds Legend: Famous Name in the Coaching Box." *Local 12 News*. Aired April 20, 2016, on WKRC-TV. Transcript and video, 3:02. https://local12.com/news/local/lessons-from-a-reds-legend-famous-name-in-the-coaching-box.

Holmes, Tommy. *Dodger Daze and Knights: Enough of a Ball Club's History to Explain Its Reputation*. New York: D. McKay, 1953.

Hood, Robert E. *The Gashouse Gang: The Incredible Madcap St. Louis Cardinals of 1934*. New York: William Morrow, 1976.

Hope, Bob. *We Could've Finished Last without You*. Atlanta: Longstreet Press, 1991.

Howsam, Robert Lee, and Bob Jones. *My Life in Sports*. Cincinnati OH: self-published, 1999.

Hufford, Tom, and Bill Nowlin, eds. *Braves Win! Braves Win! Braves Win! The 1995 World Champion Atlanta Braves*. Phoenix AZ: Society for American Baseball Research, 2020.

Huhn, Rick. *The Sizzler: George Sisler, Baseball's Forgotten Great*. Columbia: University of Missouri Press, 2004.

Jamail, Milton H. *Venezuelan Bust, Baseball Boom: Andres Reiner and Scouting on the New Frontier*. Lincoln: University of Nebraska Press, 2007.

Jones, Chipper, and Carroll Rogers Walton. *Ballplayer*. New York: Dutton, 2017.

Karst, Gene, and Martin J. Jones Jr. *Who's Who in Professional Baseball*. New Rochelle NY: Arlington House, 1973.

Kashatus, William. *Almost a Dynasty: The Rise and Fall of the Philadelphia Phillies*. Philadelphia: University of Pennsylvania Press, 2008.

Kelley, Brent P. *Baseball's Biggest Blunder: The Bonus Rule of 1953–1957*. Lanham MD: Scarecrow Press, 1997.

——. *The Pastime in Turbulence: Interviews with Baseball Players of the 1940s*. Jefferson NC: McFarland, 2001.

Kerrane, Kevin. *Dollar Sign on the Muscle: The World of Baseball Scouting*. New York: Beaufort Books, 1984. Reprinted with new introduction and new concluding chapter. New York: Baseball Prospectus, 2013. Page references are to the 2013 edition.

King, Dave. "Al LaMacchia." In Sandoval and Nowlin, *Can He Play?*, 76–77.

Kreuz, Jim. "Tom Greenwade: Destined for the Hall of Fame." In Sandoval and Nowlin, *Can He Play?*, 44–48.

Levitt, Daniel R. *Ed Barrow: The Bulldog Who Built the Yankees First Dynasty*. Lincoln: University of Nebraska Press, 2008.

Levy, Alan H. *Joe McCarthy: Architect of the Yankee Dynasty*. Jefferson NC: McFarland, 2005.

Lindbergh, Ben, and Travis Sawchik. *The MVP Machine: How Baseball's New Nonconformists Are Using Data to Build Better Players*. New York: Basic Books, 2019.

Littlefield, Bill. *Prospect: A Novel*. Boston: Houghton Mifflin, 1989.

Lowenfish, Lee. *Branch Rickey: Baseball's Ferocious Gentleman*. Lincoln: University of Nebraska Press, 2007.

———. "'Don't Get Too Domestic Out There': The Baseball Life and Insights of Herb Stein." In Sandoval and Nowlin, *Can He Play?*, 143–45.

———. "Eyeball to Eyeball, Belly-Button to Belly-Button: Inside the Dodger Way of Scouting." *National Pastime* (2011): 97–100.

———. "29 Years and Counting: A Visit with Longtime Cubs Scout Billy Blitzer," *Baseball Research Journal* (Spring 2011): 47–52.

Lowenfish, Lee, and William Marshall. "Branch Rickey versus Larry MacPhail: How a Rivalry Turned Feud Impacted Major League Baseball on the Eve of Racial Integration." In *The Cooperstown Symposium on Baseball and American Culture, 2009–2010*, edited by William M. Simons, 229–38. Jefferson NC: McFarland, 2011.

Mann, Arthur. *Branch Rickey: American in Action*. Boston: Houghton Mifflin, 1957.

Mann, Jack. *The Decline and Fall of the New York Yankees*. New York: Simon and Schuster, 1967.

McKenna, Brian. "Joe Cambria." In Sandoval and Nowlin, *Can He Play?*, 90–95.

Mitchell, Mike. *Mr. Rickey's Redbirds: Baseball, Beer, Scandals and Celebrations in St. Louis*. Self-published, 2020.

Moore, Dayton, and Matt Fulks. *More Than a Season: Building a Championship Culture*. Chicago: Triumph Books, 2016.

Morgan, Anne. *Prescription for Success: The Life and Values of Ewing Marion Kauffman*. Kansas City MO: Andrews McMeel, 1995.

Moyer, Jamie, and Larry Platt. *Just Tell Me I Can't: How Jamie Moyer Defied the Radar Gun and Defeated Time*. New York: Anchor Books, 2010.

Murff, Red, and Mike Capps. *The Scout: Searching for the Best in Baseball*. Dallas TX: Word Publishers, 1996.

Nathanson, Mitchell. *Bouton: The Life of a Baseball Original*. Lincoln: University of Nebraska Press, 2020.

Nowlin, Bill. "Bill Clark: Baseball's Leonardo Da Vinci." In Sandoval and Nowlin, *Can He Play?*, 105–10.

————, ed. *The Kansas City Royals: A Royal Tradition*. Phoenix AZ: Society for American Baseball Research, 2019.

O'Connor, Michael. *Ted Turner: A Biography*. Santa Barbara CA: Greenwood Press, 2010.

Parker, Clifton Blue. *Big Poison and Little Poison: Paul and Lloyd Waner, Baseball Brothers*. Jefferson NC: McFarland, 2003.

Phillips, Christopher J. *Scouting and Scoring: How We Know What We Know about Baseball*. Princeton NJ: Princeton University Press, 2019.

Polner, Murray. *Branch Rickey: A Biography*. New York: Atheneum Books, 1982.

Post, Paul. *Foresight 20/20: The Life of Baseball Scout Ralph DiLullo*. Self-published, 1995.

Puerzer, Richard. "The Kansas City Royals' Baseball Academy." *National Pastime* (2004): 3–14.

Rickey, Branch. *The American Diamond: A Documentary of the Game of Baseball*. With illustrations by Robert Riger. New York: Simon and Schuster, 1965.

Ritter, Lawrence. *The Glory of Their Times*. New York: William Morrow and Company, 1966. Reprinted enlarged edition. New York: William Morrow and Company, 1984. Page references are to the 1984 edition.

Robinson, Eddie, and C. Paul Rogers III. *Lucky Me: My Sixty-Five Years in Baseball*. Dallas TX: Southern Methodist University Press, 2011.

Robinson, Ray. *Iron Horse: Lou Gehrig in His Time*. New York: W. W. Norton, 1990.

Robinson, Ray, and Christopher Jennison. *Pennants and Pinstripes: The New York Yankees, 1903–2002*. New York: Viking Studio, 2002.

Rolfe, Red. *The View from the Dugout: The Journals of Red Rolfe*. Edited by William M. Anderson. Ann Arbor: University of Michigan Press, 2006.

Runyon, Damon. "Chain Store Baseball. That's St. Louis Idea. Cards Own Five Clubs. And 200 Players." In *Guys, Dolls, and Curveballs*, edited by Jim Reisler, 407–8. New York: Carroll and Graf, 2005.

Russell, John. *Honey Russell between Games between Halves*. Washington DC: Dryad Press, 1986.

Russo, Jim, and Bob Hammel. *Super Scout: Thirty-Five Years of Major League Scouting*. Chicago: Bonus Books, 1992.

Sandoval, Jim. "Charles Edward Chapman, Ph. D., Baseball's Renaissance Man." In Sandoval and Nowlin, *Can He Play?*, 16–18.

————. "Charley Barrett, King of Weeds." In Sandoval and Nowlin, *Can He Play?*, 10–11.

————. "Epy Guerrero, Super Scout." In Sandoval and Nowlin, *Can He Play?*, 103–4.

Sandoval, Jim, and Bill Nowlin, eds. *Can He Play? A Look at Baseball Scouts and Their Profession*. Phoenix AZ: Society for American Baseball Research, 2011.

Schmitt, Steven D. *A History of Badger Baseball: The Rise and Fall of America's Pastime at the University of Wisconsin*. Madison: University of Wisconsin Press, 2017.

Shanks, Bill. *Scout's Honor: The Bravest Way to Build a Winning Team*. New York: Sterling and Ross, 2005.

Simpson, Allan, ed. *Baseball America's Ultimate Draft Book, 1965–2016*. Durham NC: Baseball America, 2016.

Sinha, Anup, and Bill Lajoie. *Character Is Not a Statistic: The Legacy and Wisdom of Baseball's Godfather Scout Bill Lajoie*. Self-published, Xlibris, 2010.

Smiley, Ron, and Jim Sandoval. "Charles 'Pop' Smiley." In Sandoval and Nowlin, *Can He Play?*, 8–9.

Snelling, Dennis. *A Glimpse of Fame: Brilliant but Fleeting Major League Careers*. Jefferson NC: McFarland, 1993.

Spatz, Lyle, ed. *Bridging Two Dynasties: The 1947 New York Yankees*. Lincoln: University of Nebraska Press, 2013.

Spink, J. G. Taylor. *Judge Landis and 25 Years of Baseball*. St. Louis: Sporting News Publishing, 1974. First published 1947 by Thomas Y. Crowell (New York).

Stargell, Willie, and Tom Bird. *Willie Stargell: An Autobiography*. New York: Harper & Row, 1984.

Steinberg, Steve, and Lyle Spatz. *The Colonel and Hug: The Partnership That Transformed the New York Yankees*. Lincoln: University of Nebraska Press, 2015.

Stewart, Art, and Sam Mellinger. *The Art of Scouting: Seven Decades Chasing Hopes and Dreams in Major League Baseball*. Olathe KS: Ascend Books, 2014.

Sughrue, John J., Jr., dir. *The Courtship of Rick Reichardt*. Aired July 4, 1964, on NBC. https://www.paleycenter.org/collection/item/?q=john&p=352&item=T77:0192.

Taylor, Dan. *Lights, Camera, Fastball: How the Hollywood Stars Changed Baseball*. Lanham MD: Rowman & Littlefield, 2021.

Tebbetts, Birdie, and James Morrison. *Birdie: Confessions of a Baseball Nomad*. Chicago: Triumph Books, 2002.

Winegardner, Mark. *Prophet of the Sandlots: Journeys with a Major League Scout*. New York: Atlantic Monthly Press, 1990.

League Baseball, 258; Minor League
career of, 247–49; and Pilots/Brewers,
254–57; and Ray Fagnant, 260–61; and
Ray L. Doan's All-Star Baseball School,
239–42, 244–46; and Red Sox, 257–62;
and World War II, 246–47
Enos, Grace, 249
Enos, Helena Donovan, 238
Epstein, Theo, 216
Esasky, Nick, 196
Essick, Bill, 51–52, 58, 79, 82, 100, 121
Essick, Eula Bennett, 52
Evans, Darrell, 130, 159
Evers, Hoot, 4, 85

Fagnant, Ray, 259–62
Fanning, Jim, 178
Farrell, Dick "Turk," 97
Feeney, Chub, 184
Feller, Bob, 65, 119, 240
Fernandez, Tony, 117
Ferraro, Mike, 146
Ferrick, Tom, 138–41, 145
Finley, Charlie, 127, 131–32, 166, 252–53, 255
Finley, Steve, 192
Fireman, Save My Child, 30
Fischer, Bill, 141–42, 182
Fisk, Carlton, 203
Fitzgerald, Lou, 188, 192
Flanagan, Ed, 238
Flanagan, Mike, 218, 238
Fletcher, Art, 11
Flood, Curt, 116
Florence, Paul, 63
Flynn, Bobby, 208–9
Flynn, Doug, 208–9
Fogelman, Avrom, 149
Foley, Tom, 211
Folkers, Rich, 154

Foote, Barry, 107
Ford, Whitey, 70
Fox, Charlie, 111
Fox, Nelson, 154
Foxx, Jimmie, 79
Foy, Joe, 226–27
Frailing, Ken, 133
Franco, John, 227
Frazee, Harry, 45
Fred, William K., 122
Freehan, Bill, 86
Fregosi, Jim, 100
Frey, Jim, 143, 168, 170
Friend, Tom, 154
Frisch, Frank, 29, 241, 242
Fryman, Woodie, 107

Gaither, Jake, 186
Gammons, Everett, 238
Gammons, Peter, 238
Gant, Ron, 183, 189
Garcia, Damaso, 117
Garcia, Silvio, 73
Garner, Phil, 107
Garr, Ralph, 182
Garrett, Wayne, 179
Gashouse Gang, 32
Gaskill, Red, 96
Gebrian, Pete, 230
Gedman, Rich, 258–59
Gehrig, Lou, 37, 46–49, 57, 64, 82, 186; as
   Lou Lewis, 47
Gehringer, Charlie, 60
Gene Bennett Scholarship Fund, 215
Gene Tunney Athletic Program, 246
Geromino, Cesar, 207
Gibbs, Jake, 65
Gibson, Bob, 83–84
Gilbert, Dennis, 230